The Brazilian State

Bildner Western Hemisphere Studies

Series Editor: Mauricio A. Font
The Graduate Center and Queens College
City University of New York

This series represents a joint publication initiative of the Bildner Center for Western Hemisphere Studies at the City University of New York Graduate Center and Lexington Books. The books published in this series endeavor to support the Center's mission of generating greater comprehension of contemporary issues in the Americas, creating an international dialogue on policy issues, and producing research on a range of topics that are both country and theme specific.

TITLES IN SERIES

Reforming Brazil, edited by Mauricio A. Font with the assistance of Anthony Peter Spanakos and Cristina Bordin

Cuban Counterpoints: The Legacy of Fernando Ortiz, edited by Mauricio A. Font and Alfonso W. Quiroz

The Cuban Republic and José Martí: Reception and Use of a National Symbol, edited by Mauricio A. Font and Alfonso W. Quiroz.

The Brazilian State: Debate and Agenda, edited by Mauricio A. Font and Laura Randall

The Brazilian State

Debate and Agenda

Edited by Mauricio A. Font and Laura Randall

with the assistance of Janaina Saad

LEXINGTON BOOKS
Lanham • Boulder • New York • Toronto • Plymouth, UK

Published by Lexington Books
A wholly owned subsidiary of The Rowman & Littlefield Publishing Group, Inc.
4501 Forbes Boulevard, Suite 200, Lanham, Maryland 20706
www.rowman.com

10 Thornbury Road, Plymouth PL6 7PP, United Kingdom

First paperback edition 2013

British Library Cataloguing in Publication Information Available

Library of Congress Cataloging-in-Publication Data

The hardback edition of this book was previously cataloged by the Library of Congress as follows:

The Brazilian State: debate and agenda/ edited by Mauricio A. Font and Laura Randall
p. cm.
Includes bibliographical references and index.
ISBN 978-0-7391-6731-1 (hardback) — ISBN 978-0-7391-6889-9 (electronic)
1. Brazil—Politics and government—1985–2002—Congresses. 2. Brazil—Politics and government—2003—Congresses. 3. Brazil—Economic policy—Congresses. 4. Brazil—Economic conditions—1985—Congresses. 5. Brazil—Social conditions—1985—Congresses. I. Font, Mauricio A. (Mauricio Augusto) II. Randall, Laura.
F2538.3.B7524 2011
981.06'4—dc23 2011021149

ISBN 978-0-7391-6731-1 (cloth : alk. paper)
ISBN 978-0-7391-8626-8 (pbk. : alk. paper)
ISBN 978-0-7391-6889-9 (electronic)

Contents

Tables

Figures

Acknowledgments

The Bildner Center for Western Hemisphere Studies is grateful to the many individuals who were involved with this book and with the International Symposium "The Brazilian State: Paths and Prospects of Dirigisme and Liberalization" held at The Graduate Center, City University of New York, on November 9-10, 2009. We thank all contributors and participants for their papers and comments, as well as for their patience throughout the process of publishing this book. As co-editor, Laura Randall provided essential guidance on the papers as well as in the overall organization of the book. The Bildner Center staff played a significant role in the entire production process of this book. Janaina Saad helped edit the papers, arrange texts and graphics, and organize the conference. We also thank Carlos Ruiz and Ben Guttmann for their assistance with formatting and structuring the book. We greatly appreciate the efforts of professors Desmond Arias, Amy Chazkel, John Collins, and Kenneth Erickson in providing continued guidance to participants. Jackie Slater, John Arias, and Jacqueline Ha provided greatly helped in the preparation and logistics of the conference. Dr. Brian Schwartz and The Graduate Center must be thanked for their support of the Bildner Center.

As part of the *Bildner Western Hemisphere Studies* series, this volume advances the Bildner Center's mission of generating greater comprehension, dialogue, and debate about contemporary issues in the Americas. In particular, the Center's Brazil Project focuses on issues of state and society in Brazil. Naturally, authors are responsible for their own views and their positions do not necessarily represent those of the Bildner Center. Our hope is that by exposing different approaches and ideas, this series will shed light on contemporary issues in the Americas.We salute Justin Race and Lexington Books as we expand the list of exciting titles in this series.

Mauricio A. Font
Director, Bildner Center for Western Hemisphere Studies

Part I
Approaches, Actors, and Dynamics

1

INTRODUCTION

Mauricio A. Font

In the late 1990s and then again in 2005, Brazil faced economic and political adversities that seemed to confirm chronic institutional and political blocks to development. Very shortly after, however, news about the country focused on its achievements in economic performance, social development, and enhanced international standing. Increasingly after 2005, perceptions and realities stood old Brazilian clichés on their heads—the "sleeping giant" had awakened, the "country of the future" had arrived (e.g., Nóbrega 2005).

Success has many fathers. The reforms of the 1990s, the policies of the Lula presidency, the commodities boom driven by Asian demand, and yet other factors have been singled out as providing the main impetus for change. The role of the state in the new phase of Brazilian development is the main concern of this volume. On a practical level, it addresses the question of the extent to which state actions have reduced bottlenecks to the country's sustained development and global standing.

Reform, Recovery, and Development

The disastrous stagnation and hyperinflation in the 1980s and early 1990s provides the background to understanding the Brazilian economy and polity since the mid-1990s. The debt crisis of the 1980s and the increasing public deficit had undermined the government's traditional role in promoting development and indicated the exhaustion of the statist economic model that had been in place for decades. Several emergency economic plans attempted to control hyperinflation but failed miserably. Pessimism grew about the ability of policy makers to manage fiscal affairs and stabilize the economy.[1] In 1993-94, the Real Plan (*Plano Real*) and the related reforms that followed ended high inflation, made public administration more fiscally responsible, ushered in a new era in the organization of the state and its development roles, and began to reposition Brazil in the world scene. As Brazilian prices stabilized so did politics. The economy began to grow. Optimism and faith in democracy gradually returned. Still, vulnerability remained. The hard-achieved results were endangered by the global financial meltdown related to the Asian crisis of 1997–1998 and the disruption it brought to ongoing reform processes in emergent countries, including neighboring Chile and Argentina. Argentina's catastrophic meltdown in 2001 had a major impact on the region. To prevent a comparable financial collapse, Brazilian authorities adopted a floating exchange rate. The Brazilian *real*—introduced in 1994—lost value, but inflation did not return. Confidence gradually returned and so did economic growth. The new fiscal approach had obviously made a major difference.

Policymakers were relieved. Still, the lingering effects of the crisis contributed to the 2002 electoral defeat of the original reformist coalition that had been put together by outgoing president Fernando Henrique Cardoso. Luiz Inácio Lula da Silva's election as president of Brazil fueled fears of a return to past populist practices. Many observers braced for the rejection of policies that leftist Lula and his associates in the Workers' Party had attacked as part of neoliberal "damned legacy,"[2] but the new authorities largely maintained the previous government's policies of economic stabilization and fiscal responsibility after taking office in early 2003.

1. My own account of this period is found in Font (2002), from which I draw my discussion of conditions from the 1990s through 2002. For the earlier collapse of public finances, see Baer (2008), Galle and Bertolli (2004).

2. The "damned legacy" ("*herança maldita*") became a political cliché of the Brazilian left, implying the excise of the fiscal adjustment and much of the reform effort of the 1990s.

Brazil seemed to have entered a new era of stabilization, fiscal responsibility, and related liberalization policies—even as many voices within the Workers' Party and aligned intellectuals continued to press hard for a return to and a larger development role for the state and policies associated with "developmentalism" of past decades.

As growth gathered speed after 2006, it did so in the framework of continuity as well as new initiatives in economic policy. Economic momentum and continuity strengthened Brazil's defenses against international shocks. A test of this ability came sooner than expected. When the global financial crisis of 2008 wreaked havoc to the world economy, its local impact was relatively mild.[3] Together with the impact of social policies, the optimistic economic scenario decisively contributed to the election of Dilma Rousseff as President in 2010. Like Lula da Silva's, her campaign had sent reassuring signs that the economic model would not change.

Current Brazilian policymakers are the first to argue that monetary and fiscal policies have been and remain pillars of sustained recovery. But other factors stand out. The seemingly insatiable Asian demand for soy, minerals, and other commodities remains very important. Together with the opening of the soy frontier in the central plateau, Brazil's energy sector had a bonanza with the expanded prospects for biofuels and then the discovery of huge new oil fields. In fact, the economy found itself in a veritable boom. In addition to natural resource endowment and private entrepreneurship, other socio-economic factors would also need to be taken into account in a full understanding of the new dynamism.

Debate continues about institutional modernization and the precise role of the state in the economy. Some actors and analysts still view the reforms and related state policies since the 1990s in the context of the arrival of a new liberal order either imposed by international agencies or brought about by the diffusion of ideas and practices.[4] Others emphasize endogenous factors centering on coalitional shifts or the impact of institutions. Sallum (1996) provides a careful analysis of the role of social classes and interest groups. Font (2002: chapter 9) presents a structural realignment perspective linking political actors to the rise of a new paradigm. Some authors

---

3. In 2009, the Brazilian economy contracted by only 0.18 percent in 2009, while the US economy shrank by 2.4 percent. Meanwhile, Brazil's unemployment rate continued to decline—from 9.6 percent in 2007 to 7.9 percent in 2009 (see Appendix and World Bank, 2009).

4. Various works by Bresser-Pereira illustrate this view. A full discussion of the broader intellectual debate is beyond the reach of this introduction.

focus on single dimensions of the shift. For example, João Paulo Peixoto notes the rise of pragmatism.

Either catastrophic or highly optimistic scenarios are often found in the debate about consequences. The focus in this volume is on empirically grounded attempts to isolate the impact of policies, while acknowledging that politicization adds to the challenge of assessing the impact of policies.

Arguments about continuity between recent governments can place rather different emphases. For instance, Renato Boschi's chapter emphasizes the survival of the statist tradition and the emergence of a new developmental economic model. Various other works view the Cardoso and Lula governments as part of the same era of reform (Font 2002).

A significant number of Brazilian intellectuals support the idea of a new developmentalist economic model. For instance, several essays in *São Paulo em Perspectiva (*20 [3], 2006) argue for a new statism or developmentalism while addressing the debate about continuity or convergence between liberalization and development policy. These articles generally tend to share a critical reading of the liberalizing reforms as well as an equally emphatic defense of developmentalism, both old and new. The older version of developmentalism is seen as responsible for much of Brazilian development from 1930 through 1980, while the second is put forth as alternative to the liberalization model of the 1990s. The opening essay by Bresser-Pereira (2006) argues that conventional economic orthodoxy—"neoliberal policies and reforms"—have failed in Brazil as well as throughout Latin America, creating conditions for the rise of national development strategies sharing a "new developmentalism." Like its older version, the new developmentalism is nationalist and rejects "pressures from the North," but accepts such basic principles as export-orientation, rejection of protectionism, and support for fiscal discipline and public saving. The new Brazilian developmentalism rejects FDI-directed growth strategies, open capital accounts, unregulated exchange rates, and monetarism.[5]

This Volume

The chapters in this volume present historical, theoretical-interpretive, and substantive perspectives on the above set of issues. Part I dwells on actors, con-

5. Besides Bresser-Pereira, this issue contains essays by economists Luiz Fernando de Paula, Ricardo Carneiro, José Eli da Veiga, and others. The article by Armando Castelar Pinheiro and Fabio Giambiagi ("Sem clima para crescer") deviates from the main emphasis of this publication and presents arguments critical of the state and the dysfunctions of the development state.

texts, institutions, and ideas. João Paulo Peixoto reviews the changing role of the state in the trajectory from the Vargas years (including his return as president in 1950) to the Cardoso years, discussing implications for modernization of the state and development strategies. Over time, he argues, the debate between different ideologies and institution-building efforts converged on the rise of pragmatism as well as a reaffirmation of the need for administrative modernization.

Renato Boschi explores what he sees as the revival of state developmentalism in the wake of the market-oriented reforms from 1990 to 2002. He emphasizes continuity in regard to the role of the state. The expansion of state capabilities from the 1930s to the 1970s, together with the social priorities of the Lula government, opened up the internal market as a major way of promoting growth and employment. In this view, economic stabilization and the regulation of the banking and financial industries achieved in the 1990s did not represent a sharp break from the previous state-sponsored model. Brazil preserved strategic bureaucratic nuclei and patterns of business-state relations facilitating the country's search for a new model in the era of globalization.

Glauco Arbix and Scott Martin cover the same ground and reach only partly similar conclusions. Their review of the Brazilian debate about developmentalism focuses on the rise of new state capacities in fiscal and competitiveness policies (including trade, industry, science and technology, and social policy) since the mid-1990s. These capabilities are leading to a new model of economic expansion based on pro-market intervention with an emphasis on social policy. Brazil has thus defined and brought into existence the tools for a new development model, even if this experience with the neo-activist state has yet to be fully conceptualized and understood.

Political scientist Eiiti Sato shares an optimistic assessment of the short-term prospects for economic expansion and vitality, and goes on to highlight the structural investments still needed for sustained long-term growth, arguing that the federal government has in fact performed poorly in the area of competitiveness. Economic policy has been too cautious in relation to international capital flows, limiting the country's ability to benefit from the cycle of growth in the world economy but also has helped to insulate the nation against shocks. Sato is hence more skeptical than the authors of the previous two chapters.

Other authors in this volume illuminate policy-making processes and further highlight the need for a sustained reform process. Maria Rita Loureiro et al. shed light on the role of the bureaucracy relative to political parties and interest groups, providing a deeper understanding of Brazilian political dynamics. They identify important political actors and review major studies of the Brazilian polity. David Fleischer reviews the successful and unsuccessful attempts at political reform during the Cardoso and Lula presidencies, showing that much of the reform agenda has yet to be accomplished: from the 1997 constitutional amendment allowing reelection, to aspects of the system of proportional representation (PR) lists, the adoption of electronic voting machines, and the disposition of blank ballots. Probing the failure of proposals to change election rules (in 2003, 2007 and 2009), he thus provides a full map of the country's political reform agenda.

The chapter by J. Ricardo Tranjan discusses different participatory budgeting programs in Porto Alegre and concludes that the coexistence of such programs has had a positive impact on local democratic practices. He advances the term "constructive confluence" as challenge to other views of a "perverse confluence" detrimental to democratization. Tranjan argues that despite their different views of the scale and scope of civil society engagement, both the *participatory budgeting* practices and the *local solidarity governance* initiatives attempt to surmount traditional statist and free-market models. In Porto Alegre, the confluence of civil society discourses and participatory practices is augmenting democratization and creating new spaces for citizens' participation.

Part II of this volume deepens the focus on social and cultural policy. The first two chapters discuss how the changing Brazilian state responds to demands from different social groups. José Roberto Savoia's study of pensions identifies significant imbalances in Brazil's social security system. Distortions include the disparity between contributions and disbursements as well as unequal benefits or rights and a large informal sector. Savoia discusses the effects of reform efforts by the Lula government and argues for further reform to improve the nation's pension laws and system.

Lia Zanotta Machado concentrates on the Brazilian feminist movement and its interactions with the federal government. Growing out of the confrontation against the military regime in the seventies, the feminist movement shifted to a strategy of negotiation beginning in the twenty-first century. Throughout this change, the logic of addressing the state has always been present. During the Lula years, government-supported initiatives such as the National Council of Women's Rights and the proposal of National Conferences for Women's Policies showed a proactive state response not only to the demands of feminist movements but also efforts at coalition formation. Divergence within the government in how to respond to political pressures and key proposals on women's rights has resulted in cleavages between political positions of the government and feminist groups. In the context of increased public space for dialogue and institutionalization of the feminist movement, Lia Zanotta Machado concludes that the women's movement must build on its momentum and engage in new alliances.

Anthropologist John Collins sheds light on the also proactive presence of the state in the cultural sphere. Cultural policy has not received adequate attention in the past. Collins links policies of cultural patrimony to efforts at state consolidation, placing the state at the center of the analysis of culture and federal institutions on cultural heritage, analyzing two distinct approaches to heritage planning in different historical periods. The concern with monuments and buildings overlaps with that of people's everyday habits. His position is that understanding the role of cultural heritage in Brazilian citizenship and political economy depends on tracking this relationship between buildings and quotidian habits.

Part III shifts the focus to Brazil's financial sector, responses to the global financial crisis of 2008, and shifts in capital market dynamics. Fernando Sotelino, Monica Arruda de Almeida, and Elaine da Silveira Leite comment on the trends and performance of economic and financial policies. Sotelino's analysis of the structure of Brazil's financial industry underlines its particularities. He highlights the balance between private and public sector banks as well as between domestic and foreign banks. Brazil's financial market remains one of the world's best capitalized and supervised. Sotelino reviews the prospects for the consolidation of a sustainable credit market in Brazil, noting that public sector banks finance much of new investments.

Monica Arruda de Almeida studies Brazil's adherence to the main international efforts to combat money laundering and financial terrorism in order to improve the reputation of its financial institutions and their capacity to attract foreign capital. Though these measures have resulted in enhanced international credibility, the improvement in Brazil's international reputation is largely due to the country's more effective management of its debt portfolio and the stability of its monetary and fiscal policies.

The last chapter in this section on finances is Elaine Leite's examination of how the Brazilian financial system encourages savings and investment by constituents previously unfamiliar with, or even marginalized by, the financial system. Although the new process of "financialization" involves traditional state and non-state actors, she brings out the role of emergent financial intermediaries popularly known as "gurus" in promoting ideas of self-help that legitimate personal finance and directly contribute to this recent trend in Brazilian society. The new "moral entrepreneurs" of finance educate the broad public on ways to invest to achieve economic security. While pointing to state incentives and efforts at establishing a conducive legal and institutional framework, she argues that a new culture of investment blending notions of success, happiness, and wealth is emerging in Brazil.

Part IV gives attention to Brazil's shifting global relations, particularly its strategic economic and political relations with the transatlantic community and its regional energy policy agenda. Thomas Trebat's discussion of Brazil's evolving global economic and political role highlights areas of cooperation and conflict with the transatlantic community. Though Brazil's economic and political development policies have been broadly in tune with the American and European agenda, noteworthy areas of conflict and disagreements are also present. Brazil's aspirations of becoming a regional and global power-broker have resulted in divergences with members of the transatlantic community. Trebat makes the case for an agenda for future cooperation between Brazil and the United States that aims at greater global and economic stability while respecting Brazil's autonomy in global affairs.

Christine Gustafson and Leslie Elliott Armijo discuss the Brazilian state's approach to regional energy policy from 1990 to 2009. Comparing its vision of energy cooperation in the Americas with those of the United States and Venezuela, all of which represent different patterns of regional integration, the authors argue that the Brazilian approach may be the most likely to be implemented.

Together, the papers in this volume illuminate the lineaments of state action and critical details of the debates on the role of the state in Brazil. They shed light on the impact of political institutional processes on social change in this large and dynamic country. Together with the increasingly rich studies of other large emerging countries, the focus on newly dynamic Brazil enriches the comparative discussion of development processes and the role that political actors and institutions play in them. Brazilian society, the Brazilian polity, and internal debate are still in flux. The essays in this volume serve as invitation to an exciting, diverse, and dynamic field of inquiry.

2

The Brazilian State since Vargas

João Paulo M. Peixoto

Abstract: This paper discusses the scope and profile of the state in Brazil since the Vargas Era (1930-1945 and 1951-1954) through the Cardoso (1995-2002) and Lula (2003-2010) administrations. It addresses issues about the changing role of the state and its implications for economic development and political modernization. This period of time encompasses the diverse ideologies and institution-building efforts implemented during these years.

Structural reforms, as changes in the political and economic roles of the state, must be analyzed in light of simultaneous changes in the political and economic spheres. This is regardless of which happens first—whether economic reform, as in Chile, or political change, as in Brazil, or both at the same time, as was the case in Russia.

From this perspective, the state reform process is yet another variation of timeless ideological dispute between liberals and statists; between liberalism and socialism; between market economy and state economy; between capitalism and socialism; and in the end, a new version of the classic "battle" between right and left. Still, regardless of political regime or ideology, the search for an efficient state has been among the top priorities of politicians in almost every country in the world.

State reform in Brazil has been a goal pursued by dictators, authoritarians, and liberals alike. Since at least the 1930s, the country has experienced a continuous process of state modernization. This process characterized the 1930s, 1960s, and 1990s, regardless of the type of political regime.

In Latin America in the 1990s, a set of liberal economic policy prescriptions known as the "Washington Consensus" constituted a new "light" for state reform and economic restructuring. Brazil was not an exception (Williamson, 1990; Evans, 1992 and1995; Haggard and Kaufman, 1992). State sponsorship of economic development in Latin America had been present prior to the advent of neo-liberalism and was most heavily entrenched during the 20th century. In Brazil, State existed until the breakdown of its economic policy of Import Substitution Industrialization during the debt crisis of the 1980s. These experiences lead to a greater role for the state in policy and decision-making and a far smaller one for civil society.

The shift towards a less interventionist or "neoliberal" state occurred most significantly under the Fernando Henrique Cardoso administration (1995-2002). The administration accomplished this transformation without losing sight of the proper role of government as prioritizing basic "public goods" such as education and health. Under Luis Inácio Lula da Silva (2003-2010), however, the pendulum seems to have returned to the previous model, in which the state is viewed as a paramount for economic development. This shift is very reminiscent of the ideological perspective in place under Getúlio Dornelles Vargas (1930-1945) and the authoritarian regime (1964-1985).

TABLE 2-1. The Brazilian State Since 1822

	Type of State	Political Regime	Constitution	Form of Government
1822-1889	Unitary	Limited Democracy	Pre-Constitutional 1822 to 1824 and Constitutional 1824 to 1889	Monarchy
1889-1937	Federal	Limited Democracy	Provisory Government 1889-1891; Constitutional 1891-1930; Provisory Government 1930-1934; Constitutional 1934-1937	Republic
1937- 1945	Unitary in practice, federal in theory	Dictatorship	Dictatorship	Republic
1946-1964	Federal	Democracy	Constitutional	Republic
1964-1985	Federal	Authoritarian	Constitutional	Republic
1985- Present	Federal	Democracy	Constitutional	Republic

Source: Peixoto, 2009.

This article addresses the phases of the Brazilian state mainly concerning its political, economic, and administrative functions over contrasting administrations since 1930.

Historical Context

Since its founding, the Brazilian state has gone through multiple political structures (see Table 2-1) and has been tied to ever-changing economic priorities (see Table 2-2). Its functions are seen as the maintenance of internal peace; the conquest, unity, and expansion of territory; and sovereignty. Since political survival and internal peace are more easily defined in economic terms, states have shifted responsibility to economic transformation. The Liberal, the Socialist, and the Welfare State were the three predominant forms of the state throughout the 20th century. The crises of the state during the 1990s impacted all three political ideologies. Soviet Communism disappeared; liberalism became more embedded in social matters; and social democracy embraced an open market economy under the "third wave" of revisionism.

The changing role of the state continues to be affected by mutations of the international political system. As a result of this process, the interventionist state has emerged as a distinct and modernized institution that is able to impose its priorities upon society. A strictly non-interventionist state has never existed and probably never will, the recurring dilemma is not whether the state should intervene in economic sectors. Rather its the limits and scope of such actions. As the twentieth century progressed in Brazil, reform became a basic theme for public administrations.

The first initial attempt to modernize the public sector occurred during the first Vargas presidency with the creation of the nation's first civil service apparatus DASP Departamento Administrativo do Serviço Público (The Public Service Management Department) in 1936. This reformation also included the implementation of administrative reforms designed to eliminate nepotism and clientelism.

The standardization of civil service employment through merit-based exams was a cornerstone for the modernization of Brazil's public sector. This merit system was introduced aiming at establishing a new era of government efficiency in the tropics, replacing a system based on spoils, clientelism, and nepotism. Unfortunately, even today merit-based requirements have not been fully implemented in Brazil. This is despite a new wave of professionalization that came along with the military regime's administrative provisions for the public sector. Entrance by examination, promotion by merit, and the unification of administrative functions formed the foundation for this initial phase of Brazil's modernization in the spirit of the Northcote-Trevelyan Report (1854) in the United Kingdom.[1] From the developmental state of the 1960s to the contemporary regulatory state, the role of government and the proper model for a public administration were at the center of this field of literature, especially after the passage of the 1988 Constitution. During the 1960s and 1980s, the actions of government and public administrations alternately were acclaimed and denigrated.

Due to globalization and the subsequent change the international system, state reform, and public sector modernization has once again captured the attention of governments. It is viewed not only as a mechanism to encourage changes in government but also as a way to improve public sector efficiency and to adapt to the cultural, economic, and political forces of modernization.

Cycles of the Brazilian Government

The reformist agenda that Brazil adopted in recent years is only one of the various models that has defined the role of government since the founding of the First Republic. In total there are five distinct phases of Brazil's political evolution.

The first phase occurred soon after the proclamation of the Republic in 1889, when the country established its first Republican Constitution (1891) and ended with the Revolution of October 1930. During this period, Brazil was a predominantly rural and oligarchic society.

The second phase, often seen as the rise of *modern Brazil*, came about during the Getúlio Vargas era (1930 to 1945).[2] Vargas incorporated into the government's agenda the imperative for change and the quest for modernity, drawing from the ideals espoused by the revolutionary movement that brought him to power. When looking at these early years of Vargas' rule, it is important to focus upon the period 1937-1945. During this phase of his dictatorship, also known as the "New State" (*Estado Novo*) political parties were

---

1. *Report on the Organization of the Permanent Civil Service*, 1853. London, House of Commons.
2. The Vargas Era means a specific political and economic model used in the two different periods that President Getúlio Vargas governed Brazil (1930-1945 and 1951-1954). The first was essentially characterized by authoritarianism and modernization, and the second was characterized by nationalism and populism. Both profoundly marked the Brazilian political and economic development, and levied long after President Vargas' death in 1954.

TABLE 2-2. Cycles of the Brazilian Government, 1930-2011

Period	President	Features
Nov. 1930–Oct. 1945	Getúlio Vargas	Industrialization, Modernization of the Public Sector, State Intervention in the Economy
Jan. 1946–Jan. 1951	General Eurico Gaspar Dutra	Economic Liberalization Redemocratization, Exchange Rate Crises
Jan. 1951–Aug. 1954	Getúlio Vargas	Nationalism, Populism, State Intervention in the Economy
Jan. 1956–Jan. 1961	Juscelino Kubitschek	Developmentalism, New Capital of Brasilia, Inflation, Industrialization
Jan. 1961–Aug. 1961 and Sep. 1961–Mar. 1964, respectively	Jânio Quadros and João Goulart	Right and Left Wing Populism, Parliamentary
Mar. 1964–Mar. 1985	Humberto de Alencar Castelo Branco, Artur da Costa e Silva, Emílio Garrastazu Médici, Ernesto Geisel, João Batista de Oliveira Figueiredo	Nationalism; State Modernization; Economic Reforms; National Security and Development Doctrine; Debt Crisis
Mar. 1985–Mar. 1990	José Sarney	New Republic, Constitution of 1988, Economic Nationalism, High Inflation, and Cruzado Plan
Mar. 1990–Dec. 1992	Fernando Collor	Economic Reforms, Neoliberalism, Administrative Reform, Impeachment, Privatization
Dec. 1992–Jan. 1995	Itamar Franco	Real Plan, Statism, Economic Nationalism
Jan. 1995–Jan. 2002	Fernando Henrique Cardoso	Real Plan, Economic Stabilization, State Reform, Privatization, Reelection, Pragmatism
Jan. 2003–Jan. 2011	Luis Inácio Lula da Silva	Pragmatism, Economic Stability, Populism, Statism, Democratic Left, Extensive Social Policies

Source: Own elaboration, Peixoto (2009).

abolished, the Congress was closed, interventors (federally appointed Governors also vested with legislative powers) were nominated in the states, and a rigorous censorship of the press was established. Vargas seized the opportunity to introduce substantial changes to public administration in Brazil. He institutionalized the centralization of power at the federal level of government, making the president and the state omnipresent figures in Brazilian politics. During the *Estado Novo*, Vargas practically abolished the Federation, ruling Brazil as if it were a unitary state rather than a federal one.

The third phase of Brazil's political evolution immediately followed Vargas' first period in office (1930-1945). Eurico Gaspar Dutra (1946-1951) worked to return Brazil to normal conditions and democracy. He called a Constituent Assembly, which wrote a new constitution on September 18,

1946. Politically, it was characterized by a new liberal constitution that attempted to re-democratize Brazil and its political institutions. Investment focused on infrastructure, per capita income grew a little more than 3.5%, and inflation was roughly 12% (Goldsmith, 1986: 221). Juscelino Kubitschek's administration (1956-1960) emphasized economic development despite its very high inflationary cost and the sharp rise of the public sector deficit. After Jânio Quadros' brief presidential rule (December 1960 to August 1961), João Goulart adopted a populist, leftist style of government that ended in a political and economic collapse of the administration, opening the political arena for the military intervention in 1964.

The fourth phase began with the 1964 military regime and lasted up to its end in 1985. During these twenty-one years, successive military presidents ruled Brazil, motivated basically by a two-fold ideology: national security and development. Modernization, development, and economic and political stability were the signposts of the regime. But the use of a bureaucratic authoritarian to achieve these goals led to unavoidably elevated political and social costs.

The fifth and final stage of Brazil's political evolution began with the so-called "New Republic" (1985-1989) which ushered in the first civilian president (Tancredo Neves) after two decades of military rule. However, Neves never took office after falling victim to a fatal illness. His vice-president José Sarney was installed instead and governed the country from 1985 to 1989. Sarney's administration was marked by an open, full-fledged democracy. The 1988 Constitution incorporated the return of economic nationalism and a pro-state orientation for policies. During his administration, Brazil experienced high inflation (80 percent a month in his final days) and worsening levels of public service, despite achieving social progress. However, the circumstances in which President Sarney's administration ended (high inflation, political erosion due to weak presidential leadership, and society's despising of an entire generation of old politicians), gave birth to a new style of leadership. The inauguration of President Fernando Collor de Mello on 15 March 1990 represented a turning point. He introduced a vigorous program of structural reforms based on center-right, neo-liberal economic policies to cope with the crisis caused by Brazil's Vargas-era economic and political institutions. His first act was to implant a form of market-oriented liberalism that was to be politically tempered by social democrat precepts.

The sharpest contrast between Collor and his predecessors was his determination to push ahead with the privatization of state-owned enterprises and to attack inflation. Collor assumed power with a radical and vigorous economic plan (Provisional Measure 155, 15 March 1990) to fight the legacy of economic disorder left by the Sarney administration. President Collor had to confront inflation rates of over 70 percent per month, plummeting exports, an overvalued currency, an unsustainable budget deficit, low investment levels, and an inefficient and oversized bureaucracy. Most bank deposits were frozen, as were wages and prices, and economic activity was immediately and adversely affected. Evasions of these economic restrictions soon occurred and additional reforms stalled. As a result, price restrictions were released, and inflation returned but this time at a much higher annual rate because of the government's loose monetary policy. The Collor administration responded with Collor Plan II, a feeble attempt to regain control of spiraling inflation. Its primary contribution was to recognize that if a tight fiscal policy would be sustained, prices of public goods that had been held constant would have to be raised.

In the months following Collor's impeachment under accusations of corruption in 1992, the economy continued on its path of extreme turbulence. His successor, Itamar Franco (Collor's vice president) had four finance ministers in a period of 8 months until he finally appointed Fernando Henrique Cardoso, often referred to as FHC (June 1993). Cardoso was the creator of the Real (Brazilian monetary unit) Plan—*Plano Real* which officially took effect on July 1st, 1994. Although some of its measures had been gradually introduced after he first became finance minister (1993-1994), the Real Plan changed both the political and economic future of the country.

Following his success as finance minister, Cardoso won a landslide victory in his bid for the presidency of Brazil. His party, the PSDB (Partido da Social Democracia Brasileira), formed a pragmatic political alliance with the PFL (Partido da Frente Liberal, now Democratas) to garner broader support in the elections. Upon his inauguration (1 January 1995), he pledged to continue the fight against inflation and upheld the Real Plan as his main political objective.

It is also important to point out that the 1990s saw the inauguration of the first directly-elected president of the Republic after more than two decades of military rule, as well as the first impeachment of a president (Fernando Collor de Mello) in Brazilian history. Additionally significant a constitutional change in 1997 allowed the nation to re-elect a president for the first time in its history as a Republic. These years of structural reforms and upheavals produced a politically and economically transformed Brazil.

Political modernization and economic stabilization are probably the lasting legacy of FHC's administration to Brazilian democracy and capitalism. President Cardoso eliminated several state monopolies, as discussed below, followed by a vigorous program of privatization. Along with these measures he tried to introduce a program of reforms (tax, social security, and labor) in the economic sphere, but his efforts were unsuccessful in Congress.

When President Lula took over the presidency of the Republic in January 2003, he wanted to complete the unfinished reform agenda and also to implement a program of microeconomic reforms intended to sustain growth in the long run. This was elaborated by economist Marcos Lisboa as Under Secretary for Economic Policy at the Ministry of Finance. Micro reform measures included improving the quality of the taxation system; policies for social inclusion anchored in widening credit opportunities for public servants and the retired population as a whole; and bureaucratic simplification in order to attract private investments.

There also was an incomplete Social Security reform. Despite Lula's union experience, labor reforms were abandoned. This was due to the large number of union leaders holding governmental positions, political obstacles in Congress, and pressure exercised by the PT. Another Cardoso policy Lula discontinued was the privatization of state owned companies because of the PT's ideological views about the role of the state.

State and Development in Brazil

Throughout its almost two hundred years of existence, the Brazilian state has witnessed major changes.[3] The Revolution of 1930 initiated the period of Brazil's great industrialization[4] (Baer, 1995: 39). The commitment towards modernization was expressed by political, economic, and public institutions within Brazil. In the political sphere, a new ruling class replaced the old rural (coffee) oligarchy, their leaders, and values. This group was identified by the revolutionary military officers called lieutenants or *tenentes*, and the civilian "liberal constitutionalists," who applied ideals of reform

3. At first Brazil was a monarchy and later adopted republicanism in 1889—it used to be a unitary state and now is a federation. Since the republic, a presidentialist system has been adopted, but it did have a parliamentary system of government for 17 months. Democracy has been the reigning political regime for most of the time, but Brazil had a dictatorship from 1937 to 1945 and recently, there was an authoritarian regime of 21 years.

4. Werner Baer (1995) argues that, differently from industrial growth, "industrialization is present when industry becomes the leading growth sector of the economy and causes pronounced structural changes."

and modernization to Brazil's institutions. According to Brazilian political economist Celso Furtado, they proposed an industrialization of the country through "import substitution," a term that denotes the state's actions to lead to the creation of key, basic industries (Furtado, 1976: 117).

As a result of adopting this policy, Brazil experienced its first wave of uninterrupted industrialization from 1930 to 1945. The breakdown of orthodox economic policies, in the wake of the 1929 international economic crisis, led the administration of President Vargas to expand the state's role in the nation's industrial development. Through direct and indirect interventions, the state enlarged its activities in the promotion of Brazil's economic development.[5] Heightened nationalism and the need for industrialization resulted in calls for centralized planning, the development of a national steel industry, and state-funded technological research—in manufacturing, transportation, and heavy industry. These measures were in accordance with Keynesian and neo-Keynesian policies that governments must stimulate economic activity. This policy recommendation contrasted sharply with previous assumptions and the practice of policymakers of favoring balanced budgets.

Keynes' theories justified the implementation of social welfare reforms by capitalist democracies and authoritarian regimes alike. In the case of Brazil, economic initiatives included: the establishment of Petrobras (Petróleo Brasileiro S/A) in 1953; the opening of Brazil's first steelworks (Companhia Siderúrgica Nacional, founded on April 9, 1941, and whose operations began in 1946) at Volta Redonda; and the body of labor laws issued in 1943 condensed as CLT (Consolidação das Leis do Trabalho).

The adoption of the Keynesian economic model by Brazil coincided with the need for government social policies to alleviate the effects from the massive economic and social tragedies that had occurred in the decades following the stock market crash in October 1929. The convergence of the Great Depression, industrialization, urbanization, industrial worker militancy, and of the accession of an activist to the presidency all worked to expand the state's sphere of influence in Brazil (Topik, 1989: 100). Growing state intervention in the economy marked the Vargas years[6] and continued to be

5. Industrialization during the First Republic did not include capital goods or basic industries. For a detailed account of that period, see Steven Topik (1987). In this article we follow the standard assumption that expanded state interventionism has its origins in the centralized, authoritarian, nationalist, intrusive, Vargas Regime.

6. Getúlio Vargas was the head and the heart of the system. As such, he dominated the political life of Brazil, whether as a president, or in *absentia*. He continued to exercise political power for 24 years, one-fourth of the first hundred years of the Republic.

characteristic of Brazilian development from the early 1930s until the end of the 1980s.

It was this interventionist state—the New State (*Estado Novo*)—that became broadly associated with the Vargas tenure in office (1930-1945; 1951-1954). It was characterized by economic policies that sought to mitigate consequences of the crisis of the 1920s. These policies changed in a more liberal direction during the years of President Dutra (1946-1951). In economic matters, contrary to the Cooke Mission's recommendations (1943),[7] the Vargas administration initiated policies that promoted the nationalization of industries and increased state interventionism. The Vargas government began to draw Brazil into a wave of economic nationalism that was legally endorsed by the Constitutions of 1934 and 1937. Restrictions were applied to the commercial activities of foreign-owned interests in banking, insurance, media (newspapers and magazines), and other industrial sectors. For example, foreigners in the agricultural sector could not own land until they had established permanent residency as farmers or had worked in agriculture in Brazil for at least one year. Restrictions were levied upon the labor market as well. Foreigners were not allowed to constitute more than one-third of a company's employees or to receive more than one-third of the wage salaries in any industrial, commercial, or public enterprise, except under special circumstances permitted by the government (Hill, 1947: 303-04). As in other Latin American countries that nationalized industries, statism and nationalism in Brazil went together. Vargas' *Estado Novo* followed such a pattern by issuing several nationalist decrees. In official dictums, President Vargas declared that "at least twenty percent of all the coal bought by factories must be Brazilian coal. Some alcohol from Brazilian sugar must be mixed with all gasoline. Manioc flour must be mixed with wheat flour. In those ways the government lent a helping hand to struggling Brazilian industries" (MacDonald, 1954: 152).

Protectionism favored the industrialization program of the country and extended the state's activities further into the spheres of business. The Vargas administration established new governmental standards, centralizing the powers of the federal government in political, economic, and administrative matters. These actions were implemented towards the strengthening of the nation-state. President Vargas expanded the government's "machine" with the creation of a series of new ministries (Ministry of Labor, Ministry

---

7. The Cooke mission recommended that the task of industrialization should be left to the private sector, while the government should concentrate on general industrial planning, developing industrial credit facilities, and providing technical education. See Werner Baer (1995: 43).

of Industry and Commerce, Ministry of Education and Health) and nationalizations that allowed the federal bureaucracy to grow. In this manner, there was an institutionalization and formalization of the centralist (political, economic, and administrative) tendencies that had existed for decades alongside alternating periods of decentralization.

It is fair to credit President Vargas with the shaping of almost all state and government institutions that now characterize modern Brazil. Some of these institutions have even proven resilient to the current wave of reforms of the 1990s and are still in place in almost an unaltered state it points out to the fact that because no one prior to Vargas—or after him—has amassed a greater power in ruling Brazil.

Reforms After Vargas (1954-2009)

Successive administrations pursued the goal of transforming Brazil into a modern, independent, and industrialized nation capable of playing an important role in the international scene. Brazilian political elites viewed industrial development as a hallmark of a modern economy. Development became a national goal despite the lack of consensus among politicians and planners on the methods to achieve it. The dispute lay between the nationalist, state-led model, and the free-market ideologies of classical economics. In the administration of President Juscelino Kubitschek de Oliveira (1955-1960), the role of the state was significantly enlarged to promote industrialization, build infrastructure, and encourage foreign investments in Brazil. During this period, nationalism lost ground to a wave of "developmentalism" that was anchored in the *Plano de Metas* (1955-1960). The economic results were impressive. Between 1955 and 1961, industrial production grew 80 percent (steel production, 100 percent) while mechanical industry, electricity, telecommunication, and transportation materials expanded 125 percent, 380 percent, and 600 percent, respectively. Industrial growth was channeled into increases in national and personal income. From 1957 to 1961, GNP grew seven percent and per capita income increased four percent. By the end of the 1950s, the growth of the Gross Domestic Product (GDP) in Brazil had outpaced the rest of Latin America by three-fold. However, the cost of these advances, including the cost of building the nation's new capital of Brasília, was a growing public debt and rising inflation. Eventually, Brazil was forced to break from its membership in the IMF (International Monetary Fund) in a political maneuver intended to protect its national sovereignty against foreign pressures to reform (Fausto, 2001: 239-40).

Getúlio's development model initiated in the 1930s, prove to be decisive for Brazil, as it emphasized industrialization and social inclusion. This economic model persisted for decades and shaped Brazil's economy, in part because of a competent bureaucracy in high levels of state apparatus. Vargas' development model gradually lost its strength beginning in 1979, with the start of the last administration of the military regime, which had begun in 1964, led by President João Batista de Oliveira Figueiredo, until the end of the President José Sarney administration in 1989.

The fall of communism in Eastern Europe on November 9, 1989 was paradigmatic for Brazil. The Soviet Union imploded, ruined by economic deterioration and by Michael S. Gorbachev's renunciation of force to hold it together. The unprecedented event launched a new wave of structural reforms around the world.

At the same moment, a "third wave" of globalization was gaining force and spreading at an incredible velocity. Models that combined free market policies with democratic structures became the accepted form for political and economic organization under globalization. State reform programs around the world adopted these models under the almost universal assumption that a democracy was the only acceptable form of government. Such a political system was considered the best means to ensure a framework of liberties that would provide lasting solutions for the political, economic, and social problems, which many nations faced.

Whichever the country, structural reforms have not led to a cessation of state intervention in the economy, as opponents have proclaimed. Instead, these policies have placed limits on the state, allowing domestic economic structures to adjust to the new realities that globalization has brought. There is clear evidence that pragmatism has been upheld as an important variable to implement changes regardless of ideological constraints. The Brazilian case will be considered from this perspective.

In Brazil, structural pressures-such as the fiscal crisis of the 1980s, along with excessive intervention by the state in the economy and the paradigmatic changes in the international political and economic orders-legitimized the reform policies implemented during the nineties.

One of President Cardoso's main objectives was to pass the constitutional amendments to eliminate the state monopolies, such as oil and telecommunications. Such action had not been possible during the Constitutional revision process in 1993.

Immediately after his inauguration, Cardoso began to concentrate on his economic reform agenda. Continuous amendments to the economic chapter of the 1988 Constitution were necessary to ensure the success of the anti-inflation program. The underlying reason for the successful stabilization plans is that Cardoso's government improved fiscal responsibility by decreasing public expenditures.

Economic reforms advanced rapidly because of the effective coalition that was constructed among Cardoso's political allies. No political force in Congress could oppose the government's voting bloc composed of more than 370 out of 513 Deputies and 60 out of 81 Senators. However, the lack of cohesiveness and discipline endemic to Brazilian politics led to the constant need to guarantee that political allies perpetually cast their votes in favor of the government proposal.

Four major political parties vigorously opposed the reforms of the Cardoso administration (1995–2002). Strong opposition came from the left-wing political parties that included the Partido dos Trabalhadores (PT) and the Partido Democrático Trabalhista (PDT). Luiz Inácio Lula da Silva was the leader of the PT while former Rio de Janeiro Governor Leonel Brizola commanded the PDT. Both men had been presidential candidates in 1989 and 1994, and were defeated by President Cardoso. Other smaller political parties formed part of that opposition forces such as the PCdoB and a far left splinter group of the PT, the PSTU (Partido Socialista dos Trabalhadores Unificado). Both of these parties' representatives originally had refused to sign the 1988 Constitution but became very keen at defending its "social advances" against Cardoso's recommendations for reform.

Outside the official legislative debate, most trade unions and many civil society organizations opposed the reforms. The most militant of the trade was CUT (Central Única dos Trabalhadores/Unified Worker's Union), which had close political ties with the PT. Both the leadership and the rank-and-file of this union were strongly antagonistic to privatization of state industries, as well as to social security, and administrative reforms. Employees' associations of state-owned enterprises were also active in the anti-reform movement. The most vocal employees' groups included those for the Petrobras, the TELEBRÁS (Telecomunicações Brasileiras S/A), and the Banco do Brasil. These companies' employee associations went as far as to pay for advertisements on television that attacked the reform program.

They argued that the reforms were designed to "sell out the wealth of the Brazilian people" and compromise their "national patrimony."

Another source of opposition came from many civil society organizations in Brazil and included such diverse groups as OAB (Ordem dos Advogados do Brasil) Brazilian Bar Association, the ABI (Associação Brasileira de Imprensa) Brazilian Bar Association, and the CNBB (Conferência Nacional dos Bispos do Brasil) National Conference of Brazilian Bishops. Their main argument was that the reforms would seriously jeopardize the social and economic rights included in the 1988 Constitution. They also argued that the reforms would challenge to national interest. Among trade unions, one important exception to the anti-reform stance was Força Sindical, an organization that was largely composed of metalworkers from the city of São Paulo, and was CUT's main competitor.

Although many of the center and center-left parties were divided on the issue of reform, almost all of them eventually came out in favor of it. The most important supporters were the three political parties that had comprised the coalition to elect President Fernando Henrique Cardoso in 1994. President Cardoso was also able to organize a viable legislative coalition that was formed with the PMDB (Partido do Movimento Democrático Brasileiro). The PMDB adopted a hegemonic attitude during the constitution's drafting in 1987 but it had begun to show serious concern over about the wisdom of many of the provisions by 1995. On the right, the PPB (Partido Progressista Brasileiro) [formerly ARENA (Aliança Renovadora Nacional) and currently PP (Partido Progressista-the party that had given legislative support to the military regime-came out in favor of the reforms, attracted to the platform of economic liberalism. Though the PPB clearly was convinced that the reform drive could give the Cardoso administration a political advantage, it fought hard in Congress to prevent the debate from being sidetracked by left-wing pressure. After May 1996, the PPB became increasingly involved in governance and officially joined the governing coalition. One of its members of parliament, Deputy Francisco Dornelles, was appointed to the President's Cabinet as Minister of Industry and Commerce. Pratini de Morais, another member of the PPB, was selected to serve in the Cabinet as the Minister of Agriculture. All the political parties that became allied with the Cardoso government chose to implement a pragmatic strategy to reflect the country's economic reality and address changes in the national and international arena.

Apart from political parties, trade associations, and related organizations assisted the reform efforts because they were extremely concerned with some of the key issues on the agenda such as privatization, tax reform, foreign investments, and the end of state monopolies. FIESP (Federação das Indústrias do Estado de São Paulo) and its national counterpart CNI (Confederação Nacional da Indústria) lobbied the legislature in favor of the reform's passage. In the case of the privatization of the national telecommunication company, a special interest group was organized precisely to argue the case for liberalizing the constitutional provisions that blocked its sale. It was financed by major private enterprises directly involved in the sector. Some workers' organizations like the São Paulo metalworkers' union and its national affiliate Força Sindical championed such reforms.

The political battle over reform divided combatants into two distinct groups: the ideologists versus the pragmatists. The pragmatic nature of Brazil's electorate was best surmised by the Minister of Social Security Roberto Brant when he stated "I never changed my ideology, but voters don't link ideology to political parties. [The] PMDB, PFL, and PSDB could be one (and the) same thing."

Economic Reforms After 1988. Economic liberalization, state modernization, and privatization were introduced into the Brazilian political agenda in an incisive, continuous, and socially legitimate way that had never been seen before. The withdrawal of the state ("desestatização") had actually started during the government of President João Batista Figueiredo (1979-1985), when the state abandoned the statist economic policies. But the big push for reform came through post-1988 structural reforms that included the sale of the telecommunications, oil, and electric energy companies.

Reform defined the 1989 campaign, and it became government priority after the inauguration of President Fernando Collor de Mello. The polarized 1989 presidential election between Fernando Collor de Mello (PRN, Partido da Reconstrução Nacional) and Luiz Inácio Lula da Silva (PT) was a trailer for the struggle that would arise for the implementation of structural changes in Brazil. President Collor was not a militant liberal. On the contrary, his policies were more identifiable with authoritarianism than with neo-liberalism. He practiced economic liberalism during his two years in office because there was a real wish for change in several aspects of national life. These economic measures led to one of the two most important aspects of the Collor administration: the introduction of neoliberalism, and his impeachment for corruption charges. His successor President Itamar Franco, characterized for his reserved stance on these and other national issues, was not a reformer and allowed the agenda for structural reforms to stagnate during his administration (1992-1995). He even tried, without success, to block the privatization of CSN (National Steel Company) as well as the sale of other state companies that occurred during his tenure. The next president to give priority to structural reform was Fernando Henrique Cardoso, whose 1994 campaign was strongly based on the need to implement deep institutional changes in Brazil. Although the Collor government's reform program (the "Big Project") had been largely forgotten,[8] its basic principles were carried over into President Fernando Henrique's administration. Some of the "Big Project's" creators had held top jobs in the economic areas of both Presidents Collor's and FHC's administrations.

Constitutional Way: Changing the Economic Order

Legal frameworks significantly affect the economic performance. In the case of Brazil, the 1988 Constitution favored state capitalism and economic nationalism over a liberalized and internationalized free-market economy. The constitutions set out general principals, and also specific provisions that define national life in ways that most nations address with specific laws, rather than of Constitutional provisions.

After President Cardoso assumed power in 1995, he asked the National Congress to rewrite all the sections in the Constitution pertaining to taxation, foreign investment, energy, telecommunications, mining, social security, labor relations, and the provision of public services. There are five paradigmatic points that were incorporated into the 1988 Constitution that Cardoso's reforms attempted to redress. These were: the constitutional perpetuation of state monopolies in telecommunications; in oil monopolies; the preservation of state enterprises; the limited participation of foreign companies in the country's mineral sector, and the government's continued monopoly of the commercialization of piped gas. It is important to note that Congressional approval to amend the constitution for each of these provisions-during the first six months of President Fernando Henrique's government lead to the economic liberalization, and policies of state reform that today are evident in Brazil.

8. The "Big Project" had been inaugurated in Brazil following the fall of the Berlin Wall in 1989 and is associated with the neo-liberal phase of the economy.

The State Monopoly in Telecommunications (Art. 21, XI). This provision established the state's monopoly of the telecommunications sector as defined in 1988 Constitution. Given the legal weight of its text, the maximum the government could do to liberalize the sector was to allow for its use by firms whose majority control was held by state-owned companies. The constitution legitimized the practices that were already existent in the sector. Since their creation under the military regime, the state telecom holdings of TELEBRAS Telecomunicações Brasileiras S/A (Brazilian Telephone Company) and EMBRATEL Empresa Brasileira de Telecomunicações Brazilian (Telecom Company) allowed the federal government, and certain states, (e.g. Rio Grande do Sul) to be the country's only telephone operators and to assume the role of the private sector.[9]

With the passage of the 1988 Constitution, it became known that Brazil did not intend to open its telecommunications market to private operators because such a move would require a constitutional amendment.

It did not take long for the impact of this stipulation upon national and foreign investors to materialize. A state telecommunications monopoly was seen as the only option, permanent, and inviolable. Paradoxically, this pronouncement occurred at the same time the decrease in state investments. The drop reduced the quality of the services and a technological backlog that state companies could not hide with any amount of publicity.

The State's Monopoly of the Oil Sector (Art. 177). One of the most sensitive issues of the reform agenda was defining, on a constitutional level, the degree of monopoly power that could be exerted by the state oil company Petrobras. From the creation of Petrobras in 1953 until the promulgation of the 1988 Constitution, the state's monopoly in the sector was defined by law. After 1988, it became a constitutional matter that complicated the prospects for any changes. The constitution even stipulated the royalties that Petrobras was to pay oil producing states and municipalities. In some case, access to foreign know-how was possible through the use of foreign state owned enterprises.

The Definition of a State Enterprise (Art. 171). As a symbolic issue, the redefinition of what constituted a state enterprise or national company was another extremely important constitutional change. Unfortunately, the

9. There were some telephone companies where TELEBRAS participated on a minority basis, the main example being *Companhia Telefônica Central do Brasil* (CTBC), which provided services in the Minas Gerais region.

Constitution of 1988 as a legal framework functioned as an obstacle for the efforts to attract foreign capital. Certain aspects of the Brazilian economy, like high interest rates, did encourage the entrance of foreign capital but it was directed to the financial market and not toward productive investments.

The specific rules governing foreign investment created an extended debate in the constitutional assembly. The difference in treatment between foreign and national companies had been limited to a few sectors of the economy that were considered strategic, such as computer sciences (Baaklini and Rego, 1988). The constitutional assembly in 1987 imported the exact stipulations of the computer science law and used them to regulate foreign investment in all sectors.

Participation of Foreign Companies in Mining (Art. 176, paragraph 1). The constitutional prohibition against foreign companies investing in Brazil's mining industry was as important as the laws established for telecommunications and oil. According to the Constitution, all mineral resources belonged to the nation, and their exploration could only be done by domestically-owned companies or Brazilian citizens.

Geologists and mining engineers actively defended its approval and the result was the flight of foreign capital from the Brazilian mining sector. Mining production was negatively affected by this decision to restrict foreign investment. At a time when all Latin American countries were going through the process of an economic opening, the new constitution excluded Brazil from the lucrative opportunities with foreign investors.

State Monopoly on Piped Gas. Another important constitutional change that was proposed ended the monopoly held by the states over the commercialization of piped gas. The 1988 Constitution had passed control of this sector to the governments of the Brazil's 26 states.

With the passage of Cardoso's amendments in 1995, private companies were granted permission to operate in this sector. These changes followed the same legislative trend that other developing countries had taken in the 1990s. Such stipulations included a decrease (or elimination) in the restrictions placed on foreign participation in the sector and a reduction in the power of state monopolies.

The constitutional reform process in Brazil during the 1990s reveals that it was dominated by the classic questions of "who won what, when, and how much." The first and frustrated attempt at a constitutional revision in 1993 was commonly considered a "well succeeded failure." However, it allowed then-presidential candidate Fernando Henrique Cardoso to adopt these incomplete institutional reforms as one of his main platforms in a campaign that eventually would take him to the presidency.

The Cardoso presidency abolished the state oil and telecommunications monopolies, opened commercialization of piped gas to private companies, removed significant legal obstacles to national and foreign companies, and opened the mining sector to international investors. These developments were not reversed under President Lula.

Pragmatism as a Method for State Reform. Despite these reforms, the Brazilian economy is far from having fully liberalized institutions or neo-liberal structures, and the Brazilian state lacks key attributes of a liberal state. There are three basic points that can help explain why reforms have not achieved these ends. First, Brazil is not nor has ever been a liberal society, either economically or politically. Second, the structural reforms instituted during the 1990s were designed as short-term measures to cope with the grave fiscal crisis and to attend to the new, non-ideological scenario enforced by globalization. Lastly, a radical center in the political spectrum has emerged to offset the complete adoption of neo-liberal policies.

The pragmatic character of Brazil's state reform, and the prevalence of liberal ideas among influential political leaders in the Cardoso administration, created the impression of economic and political liberalism. However, the country's economic crisis needed a fiscal adjustment aimed at reducing the public deficit to bearable levels and at allowing the government to recover its investment capacity and ability to manage national accounts. The president, state governors, and party leadership in Congress did not act on these questions of reform with ideological intentions but instead responded to them according to the demands of the grave fiscal crisis.

Reforming the State: A Summary

Modern-day Brazil had experienced four major reforms in its state apparatus in the 1930s, 1964, 1990, and in 1995. The pioneering reform during "Estado Novo" set the basis for an administrative and interventionist state; the reform related to the authoritarian modernization period during the

1964 regime; the "Collor shock" in 1990; and the Bresser-Pereira reform in 1995.

The first reform was characterized by administrative centralization, by state intervention on a number of sectors of national life, and notably by the creation of DASP to eliminate nepotism. At that time President Getúlio Vargas wanted universities to be autonomous and to have administrative freedom under certain national parameters.

The second reform had its major feature in "administration for development," which coincided with the golden period of public administration in Brazil, and the world, that was in force mainly during the 1960s and 1970s. The administrative reform provided for by Law Decree 200 (February 25,

TABLE 2-3. Four Approaches to Administrative Reform, 1930-2009

1930–1945	Administrative reform to implement bureaucracy: DASP
1964–1985	Modernization of authoritarian regime: Law decree 200
1995–2002	Managerial (Incomplete) FHC/MARE (Ministério da Administração Federal e Reforma do Estado)
2002–2009	Governance: More government effectiveness

Source: Peixoto, 2009.

1967) at the end of the President Humberto de Alencar Castelo Branco (1964-1967) administration in March 15, 1967 introduced twice as many modernization elements and, as the first reform, the simplification of the federal administrative machine such as the five basic principles stated in Law Decree 200: Planning; Coordination; Delegation and Deconcentration of Powers; and Controlling. All are based on the idea that the state should be removed from instances where it is a hindrance to private initiative; on the belief in professionalization; on privatization; and on the modernization and debureaucratization of public service. The administrative reform of 1967 contains new administrative mechanisms, and was based on strong political and philosophical principles. It was initiated under President Castelo Branco by Helio Beltrão, who served as a key policy maker for public sector reorganization. The reform depended on the presumption of trust (to trust people and their judgement); detachment from the fetishism of document (to believe in people more than in documents); and the decision to pay a price for simplification and for stimulation, therefore eliminating expensive contrasts. He summarized these ideas saying that "those who decide have a right to a certain margin of error; it is better to run the risks of decentralization than of stagnation." The effort for change and state modernization was followed by other administrations regardless of the political regime, as had already happened in the pre-1964 period.

The other reform thread in the FHC era was the reorganization of the state apparatus, which rested on three fronts: institutional-legal, cultural, and managerial. The first aimed at removing legal hindrances to modernizing public administration. The second involved a cultural change in order to allow a transition from bureaucracy to management, as part of the changing environment in the field of public administration with the adoption of the NPM (New Public Management).[10] The aim of that change was to move from bureaucratic administrations (more focused on processes, controls, and hierarchy) to a more market oriented form of public sector management. In Brazil the NPM principles were part of the Plano de Reforma do Aparelho do Estado (Plan for the Reform of the State Apparatus), launched during the FHC presidency by Luiz Carlos Bresser-Pereira, who served as Minister of State Reform and Public Administration. Finally, public management would deal with administration improvement through modernizing organizational structure and management methods. It must be pointed out that the first reforms were intended to prepare the government to formulate, rather than implement, public policies.

LULA AND THE UNFINISHED AGENDA

On January 1, 2003 Luiz Inácio Lula da Silva became the first metalworker in Brazil and Latin America's history to be sworn in to the presidency. Lula, succeeded the sociologist and PhD Fernando Henrique Cardoso, the first president to be reelected in the Republican era in Brazil. Both are from leftist parties: the PT and the PSDB, respectively; a fact that is new in Brazilian politics over the last 40 years. Both FHC and Lula come from a neo-Marxist background: the first in his intellectual formation, and the second from his union activities, aligned with PT's socialist proposals. Both of them, committed to economic rationality, undertook an agenda of structural reform that changed the face of the Brazilian state.

This agenda was taken up despite resistance from within their own parties. Playing the moderator's role, both presidents move pragmatically in their quest to neutralize ideological positions seeking to shape the reform agenda. They rapidly aligned themselves with the international economic architecture

10. The NPM is a management philosophy used by governments throughout the world since 1980s to modernize the public sector.

and the multilateral finance agencies, notably the IMF and the World Bank, perplexing the orthodox left. President Cardoso's legacy in the field of state reform include structural changes such as public sector modernization, economics, and social security reform. His administration was also responsible for deepening democracy and the market economy, as well as for strengthening the international presence of Brazil through presidential diplomacy and macroeconomic stability, probably its more successful aspect.

Eight years of social democracy improved and enhanced the reform agenda inaugurated in the early 1990's. While Collor's presidency had been dedicated to reintroducing the principles of economic liberalism according to ideas from the Washington Consensus, the expectations created about the new left-wing presidency of Lula da Silva were oriented to immediately reverse such economic policies. To the despair of the radical left within the PT, this did not happen. On the contrary, the new administration deepened the implementation of orthodox economic policies, announcing its intentions during the electoral campaign of 2002, when it launched the "Carta ao Povo Brasileiro" (Letter to the Brazilian People) in which Lula stated that his government would honor the country's financial contracts and obligations. He also stressed his disposition to "preserve whatever primary budget surplus would be necessary in order to prevent an increase in the internal debt that would destroy confidence in the capacity of the government to honoring its commitments." The markets interpreted Lula's promise as a commitment to continuity by enacting market-friendly policies, such as honoring the country's external debt and upholding fiscal discipline. The letter was widely perceived as a turning point in the relationships between the PT's candidate and the markets, which slowly but surely began to change their perceptions of the threat to their interests represented by a possible Lula victory (Panizza, 2006), and continued to have a favorable reaction to the Lula presidency.

Facing an incomplete agenda of state reform, Lula encountered a complex set of challenges as he became president:

- Govern efficiently at the federal level,
- Maintain economic stability,
- Implement the long term promise of implementing a "truly" social agenda,
- Control the PT's radicals while retaining its ideology,
- Carry on the agenda of state reform,
- Promote sustainable economic development, and

- Make a difference against the PSDB by appearing as the "real" leftist political party in Brazil.

Moreover, during his electoral campaign president Lula promised to continue to push reforms in favor of state modernization. Accordingly, he announced a set of institutional reforms: social security, tax/fiscal, trade unions, labor, political, and agrarian reforms. At the end of his mandate, however, the results shown by his administration have been modest in this regard. Out of the proposals, only three (judiciary, social security, and tax/fiscal) were partially implemented. Although strongly demanded by many sectors in Brazil, a strong agenda of state reform is still waiting for a better political moment, probably after the inauguration in 2011 of a new President. The lack of political will by President Lula da Silva to move ahead with a state reform agenda can be explained mainly by his own and his party's vision about the role of the state, which differs sharply from the one defended by President Cardoso and the PSDB.

This statist ideology prevailed on different occasions since the beginning of his administration in 2003. One of the first targets to be attacked was the model of regulatory agencies, such as Agência Nacional do Petróleo (ANP, National Petroleum Agency). The ANP was responsible for regulating the oil sector, and put in place during the Cardoso presidency-commanded by former Chief of Staff Dilma Rousseff. The government sent to Congress a new law regulating the agencies, changing their responsibilities, and diminishing their autonomy. When Congress did not fully approve the new legislation, they sought another way to diminish the power of the regulatory agencies. That was the case with the vitally important ANP, whose new head was former Deputy Haroldo de Lima, a member of the Partido Comunista do Brasil. This appointment suggested that the liberal approach to the public sector may be reaching its end. Another front was to enlarge and widen the scope of the public sector by increasing the number of ministers to thirty-seven, an unprecedented number of cabinet level positions.

Instead of being a reformist government, Lula's two terms have been governments of programs rather than governments of reform. The inability of the Lula-PT years to greatly advance the state reform agenda might have been due to ideological constraints regarding the role of the state.

Conclusion

Deep structural changes have taken place in Brazil since 1990. Through policy measures, laws, and institutional changes, several administrations have gradually reduced or, in some cases, even extinguished the power of state monopolies and have promoted structural reforms in the economic realm, social security, administration, and fiscal matters. In the implementation of these policies, fiscal crises and the unavoidable economic reality imposed by the process of globalization have forced ideological sophistication to be abandoned in the name of pragmatism. The aggregation of these internal and external pressures has prompted Brazil to minimize its pro-state tendencies and enter a new era of pragmatic, liberal-inspired economic policies.

However, these changes have not completely altered the statist model of the twentieth-century. Brazil's leaders remain uncomfortable with pure neoliberalism and prefer what could be called social democratic approach, though not necessarily the one proposed by PSDB.

Reform Agenda for 2010. Brazil will have to continue its search for public sector modernization in the coming years. A new round of structural reform will be crucial to achieve it. The following sectors deserve priority for the reform agenda:

- *Administrative reform* to lower the costs of bureaucracy for ordinary citizens as well as for businesses,[11] reduce the size of the state, eliminate waste of resources in the public sector, and restrain the number of politically appointed positions in government.
- *Judiciary reform* to speed the judiciary system, reduce costs, and enhance social confidence in the institutions of the judiciary.
- *Fiscal and tax reform* to diminish the level of tied revenues in the federal budget; improve the efficiency and make less complicated the tax revenue machinery; and reduce the number of indirect taxes via the consolidation of state and federal taxes into more efficient national value-added tax structure.
- *Labor and trade union reform* to introduce direct negotiation between companies and unions through the labor collective agreements and

11. According to the World Bank reports on bureaucracy (2009) among different countries in the world, Brazil appears in a bad position. Industrialized countries are permanently in search of new measures in order to be more attractive to businesses. They are champions in bureaucratic simplification. The richest countries in the world—USA, Japan, China, Canada, Switzerland, Norway, Denmark, United Kingdom, and Singapore are at the same time the easiest in which to do business. In general it is twice more difficult to open and close down new companies in poor countries than in the rich countries. In the globalized world we are living in, bureaucratic simplification is necessary for survival.

diminishing the level of intervention in those disputes by Labor courts and to alleviate part of the tax incidence over the payroll which almost doubles the cost of legal employees due to this high tax burden. The main laws regulating labor were created more than 60 years ago during the Vargas era and need urgent change.[12]

- *Social security reform* to continue and improve measures seeking to attack fraud and corruption, and reduce payments of undue benefits; to increase inspection in order to inhibit tax evasion and informality in the labor market, enlarging the size of the contributors base; and to regulate the changes in the system approved by Congress in 2003, spreading its new regulations to states and municipalities, as some of those changes require passing and implementing new legislation.
- *Political reform* to improve campaign financing, party loyalty, the electoral system, and the party system.

Finally, it should be noted that reforms have been oriented to enhance the government's capacity to design public policies rather than implementing them. The country needs to reverse this pattern, dedicating efforts on both sides of the coin at the same time: not only designing good policies, but—more important—efficiently implementing and managing them.

From institution building under Vargas, through succeeding policies the leftist 'reformas de base' proposed, but never introduced by João Goulart; the conservative modernization implemented during the military regime; the adoption of neoliberalism forced by globalization put in place by Fernando Collor's administration; the quasi-liberalism adopted during the Cardoso and Lula presidencies—Brazil's state reforms have followed a traditional zigzag path observed in other areas of public policy. Even by flirting with the left, or right, and never getting a determined and continuous course of action in government policies, pragmatism alone cannot ensure lasting success. Principles and values need to be firmly attached to government actions to achieve truly enduring results. The state reform agenda continues to be central to enhancing the development and modernization of Brazil's political and economic institutions.

12. In part due to such an outdated legislation almost half of the labor force is outside the legal system, working in the informality apart from the legislation with no access to social security and other benefits.

3

State Developmentalism: Continuity & Uncertainty

Renato Boschi

Abstract: This chapter focuses on the revival of state developmentalism in Brazil in the wake of market-oriented reforms (1990–2002). The main argument is that more so than the anticyclical policies adopted to face the crisis of 2008, state capacities dating back to the ISI developmental period (1930–1980) together with the emphasis of the Lula government (2003–2010) on social inclusion opened up the internal market alternative to circumvent bottlenecks of growth and employment. The timing and intensity of these reforms was such that lines of continuity dating back to the previous state-sponsored model were maintained, preserving strategic bureaucratic nuclei and patterns of business-state relations, which constitute comparative institutional advantages in the era of post neoliberal globalization.

In contrast with other crises that have recently struck the worldwide capitalist system, the recession that began in the end of 2008 as a result of the deregulation of financial markets did not originate in the periphery of the system. Nor did it drastically affect many of the emerging economies, particularly those in Latin America including Brazil. Furthermore, evidence of recovery has also appeared quicker in Brazil, in contrast to the recession that still looms over the United States and Europe.[1]

Employment rates have surged along with positive and considerable[2] gross domestic product (GDP) growth predictions. The adoption of emergency anticyclical policies by several countries including Brazil is evidence of a possible revival of a more active and interventionist role of the State. This time some emerging economies in Latin America and, specifically, Brazil, pioneered interventionist and developmentalist policies in the wake of the unsuccessful market-oriented reforms guided by the Washington Consensus. In Brazil, Chile, and Argentina center-left governments implemented policies reviving the role of the state, signaling a return to certain principles of developmentalism more typical of the period that preceded market-oriented reforms yet redefined and readapted to new times (Boschi, 2008; Boschi and Gaitán, 2008; 2008a; 2009). In Argentina, the drastic measures adopted to deal with previous crises, such as in 2002, were an early sign of the need to break with neoliberal orthodoxy at the macro-economic level. It was a crucial step for the reactivation of growth along the lines of a neo-developmentalist model (Bresser-Pereira, 2009). In other countries, as was the case in Bolivia, Venezuela, and Ecuador, leftist governments reenacted their own versions of national revolutions and adopted radical measures that resulted in renationalization or reprivatization.

In this context, one must question the role of previous trajectories and the institutional characteristics of the different production regimes relative to the different responses to the crisis. This, in turn, would require an analysis of what role the state might play in various capitalist systems that are currently being reshaped and redesigned, especially in peripheral and in emerging countries (Boschi, 2009). The role of the state in these cases is a lot more central and strategic than it is in advanced countries. (Hall, 2007; Amable, 2003). While recent analyses do not go as far as to deny the importance of dimensions operating at the level of the private sector, they treat the state as a crucial element due to its powerful allocative and regulative capacities (Weiss, 2010). In the Brazilian case, the positive role of state intervention in the configuring of a modality of capitalism that has proven itself to be more coordinated and articulated over the course of time. Beginning with the

1. According to the IBGE the Brazilian economy outperformed other economies. In the second quarter of 2009 compared to the previous quarter, in twelve selected OECD economies, those that had positive GDP growth rates were South Korea (2.6%), Australia (0.6%), Japan (0.6%), France (0.3%), and Germany (0.3%). In this subgroup, only South Korea had a higher growth rate than Brazil (1.9%). At the opposite end, one must remember the scale of the economic retraction faced by Holland (-2.0%) and Mexico (-1.1%). Canada (-0.9%), the United Kingdom (-0.7%), Italy (-0.5%), and the United States (-0.3%) complete the list of selected countries that registered a shrinking GDP (Carta IEDI n. 370, "Produção Industrial em Maio de 2009: Recuperação Gradual." Available at: www.iedi.org.br).

2. A 1.9% GDP growth rate recorded between the first and second quarters indicates that the economy is on an upward trajectory. The unemployment rate has dropped in the last four consecutive months as well. In March it was at 9% and in July it had dropped to 8.1%—rates that are considerably low for a recession ("PIB cresceu 1,9%: a crise era um V," 14/09/2009. Data available at: http://www.ipea.gov.br/003/00301009.jsp?ttCD_CHAVE=12005).

modernizing revolution implemented by Vargas in the 1930s, followed by the brand of developmentalism of the Kubitschek era in the 1950s—which promoted industrialization based on the import substitution model (ISI)—and completed by the enhancement of the State-led economic model and its expansion in the productive sphere during the years of military rule. Rather than solely focusing on the State in general terms—strengthened as it was during this process of industrial revolutionizing throughout the twentieth century—one must pay close attention to the Executive branch, regardless of the nature of the political regime in power. It has been shown to fulfill various roles: the articulator of Weberian bureaucracies that constituted themselves over time (Kohli, 2004; Boschi and Lima, 2002); the shaping force behind work/labor relations; and the articulator of the private and public sectors by means of the creation of a corporative structure of interest representation (Diniz and Boschi, 2004).

The forms of social protection implemented at different points in time are no less important in the consideration of the role of the State. They have evolved from modest yet important social policies aimed at wage-earning workers and those in the formal labor market. They were gradually redesigned and expanded in time and eventually complemented by (also modest) health and pension reforms. These reforms took place in the context of the neoliberal policies of the 1990s to what can be called the "expansion of social frontier" by means of a set of targeted policies aimed at eradicating poverty and reducing inequalities structural inequality is a defining trait in the configuration of Brazilian capitalism. Accentuated by policies that resulted in income concentration throughout the developmentalist period, especially under military governments. This is the result of several factors including a top-down model of transition, which neglected agrarian reform; rapid urbanization due to rural emigration; social exclusion due to the aforementioned social incorporation via labor corporatism. Thus, poverty reduction policies are preconditions to interrupt vicious circles or "negative complementarities." These unsavory results are repeatedly pointed out with respect to the organization of the Brazilian productive regime from the perspective of how corporations carry out their activities (Schneider, 2008). Solving this problem implies the fulfillment of basic conditions necessary to incorporate a vast segment of the population into the consumer market.

In considering the process of development its crucial to keep in mind that the outcome of policies can only be adequately assessed within a long-range time frame. If without a doubt not all the effects of policies are known or even consciously expected when they are first enacted. Recently, the importance of time has been reintroduced systematically in analyses (Pierson, 2004). The decisions concerning policies in this field, in most cases, involve the accumulation of experiences. The production of new ideas capable of asserting themselves, of being assimilated by institutions, and, finally, of being leveraged by support coalitions, thus determining the correction of previous trajectories. Ideas, interests and institutions follow different timings and are interwoven in distinct ways. Understanding this complex articulation has been at the core of discussions within the different contemporary strands of institutional analysis, and, more specifically in those focusing on the comparative analysis of the transformations of global capitalism. In contrast to the emphasis placed on "path dependency," the most recent debates have stressed the importance of correction of previous trajectories. These corrections have been marked by changes in the elites' frames of reference, combined with the timing and capability of certain institutions to make a difference. Central elements in this respect are the patterns of organization of the private sector and its articulations with the state—as one of the dimensions of the production regime—in addition to the patterns of financing, capital/labor conflict resolution; education and skilled labor training policies; and incentives for technology generation (Amable, 2003; Boyer, 2005; Campbell and Pedersen, 2007; Crouch and Farrell, 2004; Crouch, 2005; Deeg, 2005; Deeg and Jackson, 2007; Hall, 2007; Jackson and Deeg, 2006; Thelen, 2004).

In the specific case of the revival of the state and of neo-interventionism as a protection against systemic crises, long term considerations are fundamental in order to grasp the continuity of trajectories in the context of the substantial changes in the international scenario. With the emergence of China as a power, consequent opportunities and restrictions redefine the relative positions of different countries. In the newly defined scenario in which markets must yield to the logic of politics, the possibility of new autonomous national projects (even if they aim at strategies that will allow them to compete in a globalized marketplace) are increasingly linked to how political institutions can process conflict. In this scenario, political institutions play a decisive role since they constitute the filter through which new agendas are produced and implemented in a national context. Thus, policies in these areas will fundamentally depend on how they are conducted, the political interplay between actors in charge of implementing them, the nature of the government coalitions that are forged to support a developmentalist platform, and on previous trajectories—both in terms of the developmentalist model as well as in terms of the timing and manner in which market-oriented reforms took course.

Chile, for example, carried out these reforms earlier, in a more favorable international context and under a military regime whose transition to democracy was gradual and negotiated. At the same time, Brazil intensified the process of industrialization through import substitution, carried out an equally controlled transition, albeit one that more quickly expanded the political universe without restrictions and which was marked by the presence of expressive and organized social forces. In contrast, over time Argentina did not accumulate capacities in line with state developmentalism; it implemented radical reform, underwent a strong productive downturn, became extremely vulnerable to foreign shocks. Recently, it seems to have entered a less tortuous path, showing strong signs of recovery after resorting to unorthodox economic instruments to strengthen the state. In sum, it is a matter of legacies, trajectories, and different timings that today configure different modalities of capitalist development, as well as possibilities for the recovery of growth in the context of post neoliberal globalization. The timing of market-oriented reforms and how they were implemented were more drastic in the cases of Chile and Argentina; its later implementation in Brazil and the social resistance it faced served to preserve elements of its developmentalist past, especially in terms of state capacities. Brazil, despite its tradition of strong interventionism, has operated under conditions of intense competition. The capitalist model, adapted to the functioning of financial markets, and progressively based on publicly-traded stock companies, tends towards internationalization and, most importantly, maintains a macro-economic policy that has rigidly kept intact the foundations of stabilization. The maneuvering space left for development policies thus becomes more geared towards long-term time frames, the creation of institutions capable of assuring the interlocution between the business sector and the state, and the implementation of anticyclical and industrial policies.

In this sense, the main argument of this paper is precisely that the market-oriented reforms implemented in the 1990s were not able to wipe out, as intended, the legacy of the Vargas era. In fact it remains alive in more than one fundamental aspect for the current configuration of Brazilian capitalism. These aspects mainly have to do with the persistence of an institutional matrix established by Vargas, which proved itself capable of articulating the interests of the private sector. It was also able to inaugurate forms of interlocution between these and the state on one hand, and on the other, the prevalence of labor laws that have withstood flexibilization and are still responsible for several rights of unionized sectors of the formal economy. The continuity of this path expresses itself as well in the active presence of agencies created during Vargas' second term, such as the Banco Nacional de Desenvolvimento (BNDES, National Bank for Development). BNDES has played a crucial role in the fostering of productive activity and in the development of the country, and has recently expanded its actions into the regional sphere.

In innovative fashion and, in this sense, in contrast to the concentrating tendencies of the latter-day developmentalist matrix, the social inclusion policies based on combating poverty and reducing social inequality implemented since the Lula government are a watershed, offering a development alternative that is geared towards the domestic market. The ensemble of anticyclical measures have been put in place in the wake of these processes as a follow-up to stabilization—which, in turn, is based on the regulation of the financial system established during the presidency of Fernando Henrique Cardoso.

The first section of this paper focuses on the continuity of the developmentalist paths in terms of the patterns of interaction between the state and the private sector while recognizing the significant role of the BNDES as a development agency. In the second section, I point out the main measures adopted by the current government to face the financial crisis and emphasize within these measures the importance of social inclusion by looking at more immediate consequences. Finally, I will highlight the expansion of the social frontier as the trademark of state interventionism in recent years, and as the main factor in the configuration of Brazilian productive regime—one that simultaneously combines an inward expansion with an outward thrust to compete globally.

Business Interests and Development Agencies

The corporatist structure of business interest representation, set up during the first Vargas administration, constitutes, along with the Labor Legislation, one of the most expressive continuities within the institutional trajectory of Brazilian capitalism. On a positive note, it is possible to show that they established the foundations for organized collective action of the business sector as well as for conflict regulation between capital and labor. This institutional architecture was very controversial and received substantial criticism when it was first implemented. This was due to its potential control of the labor sector, the creation of a weak and dependent business class, and, according to some more recent evaluations, to the fact that this approach is reminiscent of the authoritarian principles of the Estado Novo, and its potential to create obstacles for the flexibilization of the labor market. However, specifically in the case of the organization of business interests as the main mechanism of articulation between the business sector and the state, the structure has changed and adapted to modern times demonstrating its flexibility and propensity to change. Despite competitive or complementary formats of business collective action organization created throughout the years—fragmentation and the specialization of this structure discussed in previous works (Diniz and Boschi, 2004; 2007), a possibly inferior performance if compared to mediation structures in other contexts (Pedersen, 2008; Schneider, 1995; 2004)—its centrality in the organization of the productive Brazilian regime is undeniable.

Generally speaking, which characteristics within the realm of the private sector could provide responses in favor of developmentalism? We could say that pragmatism and adaptive capacity led the entrepreneurs to act extremely fast as they confronted the changes that took place in the institutional framework with the transition of the 1990s. This transition—characterized by an extensive variety of institutional frameworks as the result of the combination of more centralized modalities of coordination with a coordination conducted by the market after the economic reforms—led to a rapid adaptation of business organizations to the new market conditions. With redemocratization, Congress played a prominent role in the formulation of legislation pertinent to business. In this way, the Congress became a target for the collective action of the business sector, through the utilization of lobbies. Business organizations—anchored in a dual structure with compulsory and voluntary modalities of collective action that adapted since the beginning of the industrialization led by the state in the 1930s—was characterized, at that moment, as very complex, combining segmentation with centralization. Again, in a quick adaptive effort, this structure revealed itself to be suited to play a central role in terms of coordination activities in the new productive regime.

Organizations that bring together more traditional developmentalists, such as the *Instituto de Estudo para o Desenvolvimento Industrial* (IEDI, Institute for the Study of Industrial Development) have been producing studies and documents that systematically analyze the situation of the industry; it publishes IEDI Newsletters, current industrial outlook bulletins on the Internet, and systematically advocate for the establishment of partnerships with the government to encourage industrial development. FIESP (Federation of Industries of the State of São Paulo, the most important among regional industry entities) has broken its long tradition of unity around a single candidacy for its leadership and, for the first time, there was internal competition for it. It has moved towards relative autonomy vis-à-vis the state, but still in the direction of the establishment of linkages. CNI (National Confederation of Industry, the highest entity of the business sector in Brazil) went through a process of significant modernization, and created a coordination office for legislative affairs—COAL—which follows up on demands made by the industry to Congress (Mancuso, 2004; 2007). CNI engaged in elaborating productivity and technological application studies and has taken charge of labor relations. A series of sector associations and others organized by productive chains such as ONIP (National Organization of Industry and Petroleum), have also proven themselves to be very effective in the defense of their interests through coordination activities. To sum up, there is evidence, in the associative sphere of the private sector, of an adaptation to modern times. This is especially true from the point of view of the articulation of firms in the productive regime that was established after the market-oriented reforms in Brazil (Diniz and Boschi, 2004).

In the context of creating comparative institutional advantages in terms of the articulation between the state and the private sector, the CDES (Council of Economic and Social Development) was created as a state initiative out of the necessity of more wide-randing modalities of interlocution with civil society as a whole in the new developmentalist model. Far from replicating old formulas and the supposedly authoritarian characteristics of the period when the official corporatist structure was established, this nucleus has functioned as a consulting body whose goal is to formulate directives for development policies. The CDES, a consulting agency at the service of the president created in 2003, is composed of 103 members—90 of them are members of civil society, 13 ministers, and the president. Like other agencies that are part of a network of institutions, the CDES differs from the corporatist councils of the developmentalist period that made them an essential modality of economic regulation for that period (Boschi and Lima 2002)—in the sense that it is not a representative organ of specific categories and, much less, focused on the definition of policies tailored to the needs of different sectors or on the solution of capital/business conflicts. The CDES focuses on the creation of consensus and the establishment of directives for development, providing guiding principles for the different spheres of government. The forum has actually proved itself to perform this function effectively. It can be said that it has been positively accepted within the government despite being a very recent experiment, therefore, making it hard to reach definite conclusions on the subject (Costa, 2006). The emphasis placed on the social dimension is an all-encompassing concern of the CDES. It is in line with the perspective of the Lula government of framing development in terms of equality—as opposed to the developmentalism approach of the 20th century. While the dominant concept during that period was to foster growth and only thereafter distribute wealth, the CDES has as its main principle the reduction of inequality, hoping to reduce the GINI coefficient from 0.569 in 2004 to 0.400 in 2022. Equality should be a guiding principle for all the decisions of the public sector. The goal is to double the share of the national wealth received by the poorest 20% in this time period. In order to achieve this goal, education is a strategic priority in the transition to a new model of development, side by side with the public health system (Sistema Único de Saúde), and the appreciation in value of the minimum wage to follow inflation targets.

Besides the CDES, the National Council of Industrial Development (CNDI) was created in April 2004, and charged with the implementation of the Development Agenda's main objectives. The CNDI is presented as a consultative agency responsible for defining the directives for the industrial development of the country. It subsidizes the formulation of public policies focused on industrial development, infrastructure activities, normalization of measures that allow for greater competitiveness of enterprises, and financing of entrepreneurial activities. Linked to the Presidency, the Council is composed of 13 ministers, the president of BNDES, 14 members of the private sector, and workers. Among the CNDI's development coordination activities there is a plan for investment and systemic innovation in the durable consumer goods industries, and the establishment of links between governmental agencies, universities, and research institutions for partnerships utilizing the sectoral funds from the Ministry of Science and Technology. Finally, in December of 2004, an executive agency was created—ABDI (Brazilian Agency of Industrial Development)—whose objective is to implement industrial development policies. The Agency seeks to "execute and articulate actions and strategies of industrial policy by supporting the processes of innovation and development to the competitiveness of the productive sector" (ABDI).

In addition to the initiatives to support the private sector, it is possible to highlight the concern with creating institutional conditions in the long run—especially those concerning the establishment of relations with the private sector. One can observe the revival in the post-reform scenario of a specific trajectory of development based on a modality of state interventionism that innovates, but that also continues the state developmentalism of the twentieth century. In short, the transition seems to have consolidated itself in terms of a flexible institutional arrangement with regards to the state/private sector relation, with new forums for cooperation and a more modern associative structure, based on the corporatist structures of the developmentalist period. One can also note the engenderment of institutional competitiveness with the creation, on one hand, of an apparatus to encourage development on the industrial policy front, and, on the other, through stimuli to exports and promotion of continental integration, on the foreign policy front.

The state reform implemented during the Fernando Henrique Cardoso government preserves certain nuclei of technical and bureaucratic excellence and maintains development institutions, such as the BNDES. During that administration, while it was in charge of implementing privatizations, BNDES clearly demonstrated that it was playing a role as prominent as during the developmentalism phase. Despite an apparent interruption in the agency's mission—it was responsible for carrying out neoliberal privatization—the continuity of its trajectory is explained by the strict adherence to the constitutional precepts defined when it was created during the second Vargas government, namely the support of projects that encourage job creation. The BNDES then equipped itself and broadened its scope, especially once Lula took office, and more recently its strategic mission has veered towards the regional level, so as to include all of South America.

As pointed out earlier, the economic policy of the Lula government had as a starting point the commitment to maintain the stability achieved with the implementation of the Real Plan during Fernando Henrique's Cardoso first term. The PT government came into power in an extremely restrictive context of strong inflationary tendencies, high levels of foreign debt, and an ill-equipped state apparatus resulting from an unfinished administrative reform, and an intense privatization process. Considering such a scenario, the reorientation of public expenditure was remarkable, with the adoption of a selective modality of interventionism focused on industrial policy, export incentives, and specific support programs for small and medium businesses, among other national initiatives. These were complemented with an extremely incisive initiative in the foreign policy front directed at regional integration. Behind this result, we can find the government's determination to give the BNDES a prominent role, rendering it the nucleus of an institutional network that coordinated development activities. The Lula government sought to redefine the BNDES's role, to turn it into a promoter of stimulus for the private sector without parallel in Latin America, in terms of significance, size, and diversity of functions. This redefinition sought the implementation of an industrial, technological, and trade policy (PITCE). It included a series of new credit lines available to small and medium enterprises and the increase of support to export activities (Boschi, 2008).

The BNDES's function is determined by its provision of credit for long-term investments with lower annual interest rates (9.7%), mainly to small and medium businesses. Three main directives guided the BNDES's actions in the last few years, especially starting in 2005: enhanced agility, with improvements in management routines and procedures; reduction in loan costs; and democratization of credit access. The BNDES's disbursements—the amounts that were actually transferred to businesses—reached R$47 billion that year, a record figure for project financing, 17.5% higher than the R$40 billion in 2004. In the industrial sector, BNDES financing reached R$23.4 billion, growing 48% in relation to the previous year (R$15.8 billion). In the first three years of Lula's government, the BNDES disbursed R$122 billion, R$66 billion (54%) of which were allocated to the capital goods sector, an important barometer of the investment rhythm in Brazilian production (Boschi, 2008).

A recent study investigates the BNDES's role as a development agency, emphasizing the points that support Brazil's inclusion in the small club of advanced countries (Almeida, forthcoming). The objective of the study is not to defend that it is up to Lula's government to make Brazil gain entry to this club, but rather to identify the impact of domestic decisions on the country's recent material progress. According to this author's analysis, the BNDES developed a series of strategies to complement its macroeconomic stabilization efforts and offer coordination mechanisms. BNDES has played an important role in the promotion of a national industrial, technological, and trade policy. Highlighting its role would mean questioning the current idea that the trade and capital market dynamics explain, by themselves, the country's recent economic performance.

In a similar direction, another recent work (Santana, forthcoming) shows the role of the BNDES and of the pension funds, of both public banks and state companies, that have been crucial for the stabilization of macroeconomic variables affecting the labor market and important sectors of the Brazilian industry. In turn, these actors secure an advantage in the capacity to innovate and compete in the global market and establish a space in which their interests can be intermediated and guided towards the formation of new productive coalitions. The BNDES, in addition to establishing itself as the main long-term financing source for the transformation and infra-structure industries, plays a strategic role as a provider of credit lines precisely at times of cyclical variations due to international financial crises. The BNDES is thus able to provide the economy with adjustment mechanisms helping to stave off the harmful effects of crises on investment rates, employment, and growth.[3] According to the data presented in Santana's analysis the BNDES backed credit lines accounted for 20% of the total of credit offered by Banks to the private sector. In 2009 the sum of the credit offered by the BNDES and by other public banks was equivalent to the total value of private banks, that is, about 18% of the Gross Domestic Product (GDP). In all, public federal banks accounted for 38% of the total credit offered by the banking system. The BNDES has maintained its disbursements at a steady rising rate. From 1999 to 2002 it nearly doubled the volume of disbursements. From 2003 to 2008 they increased by 175%. Santana concludes that these state-owned investment and credit institutions constitute one of the institutional legacies that have become the object of a new political interpretation of development. It also runs counter to the hegemonic assessment of the independent role of market forces in the Brazil's recent cycle of economic expansion.

Crisis, Response and Social Inclusion

In a piece written in 1997 comparing the trajectories of Brazil and Mexico in terms of their wealth accumulation and political regimes, Marques

3. On October 7, 2008, just after the beginning of the crisis, the BNDES announced the expansion of its export credit lines to counteract the scarcity of credit in the market. An additional 5 billion reais were offered given the need to finance pre-shipping operations. These resources could be used to acquire capital assets and consumer goods ("BNDES amplia linhas de financiamento à exportação para suprir escassez de crédito no mercado," 07/10/2008).

Pereira and Théret (2009) shows that the policies adopted by these two countries—which were originally based on a rather similar developmentalist tradition during the initial period of industrialization through import substitution[4] divergered directions in the 1970s, and the aftereffects are seen in the ensuing patterns of economic performance. In line with the arguments advanced in this paper, these authors emphasize the importance of the political dimension as a determining factor of economic development, and of the trajectories that are estabilshed in each case: whereas in Brazil the military government furthered the ISI model in order to acquire capital assets, thereby concentrating income, in Mexico the PRI favored a strategy of demanding expansion without rearranging its productive structure. The legacies of the institutional forms of regulation at the time of the ISI model therefore shaped the reactions of each country to the challenges of financial globalization and liberalization: clientelistic salary negotiations, a structuralist approach in managing monetary and financial policies, and economic nationalism aptly describe the Brazilian trajectory. This contrasts with the corporatism, monetarism, and political nationalism of the Mexican case. Building upon this differentiation regarding the processes of political intervention of the state, the forms of social protection, and the nature of the political regime, the authors depict a scenario to understand the current state of affairs: the importance of the political democratic option coupled, with the possibility of growth sustained by the domestic market, accompanied by a perspective of income redistribution as a possible route of development in the Brazilian case, in contrast with Mexico which followed the path of later democratization and externally oriented growth.[5]

The option for targeted policies aimed at the reduction of poverty and social inequality, although an item on the Fernando Henrique Cardoso agenda, had to wait until the Lula government before it became a development priority. This shift epitomizes the strategy of development based on social incorporation and expansion of the domestic market. They comprise an array of policies centered around, yet not limited to, the Bolsa Família, a means-tested income support program created by the Lula government for poor families to keep their children in school. These are complemented by other initiatives aimed at expanding access to citizenship, and to the con-

4. That is, accumulation regimes identical at the macro-economic level, albeit installed by different types of political regimes and contrasting institutional forms of regulation.

5. "The conclusion that must be spelled out at the normative level of this comparative analysis of the long-term interplay of mediating regulatory institutions is that the reduction of social and regional inequalities constitute, in both cases, a fundamental condition of development" (Marques Pereira and Théret, 2009: 42).

sumer market, the most recent of which is access to the banking system as a doorway to micro-credit lines.

Some effects of this policy redirection can be assessed based on the data of the 2007 Household Sample National Survey—PNAD (IBGE, 2007). According to an IPEA report (2008) which analyzes the data produced by the survey, the degree of inequality in Brazil dropped sharply and constantly since the beginning of this century. The exact figure is 7%, meaning that the GINI coefficient dropped from 0.593 in 2001 to 0.552 in 2007, at an annual rate of 1.2%, as shown in Figure 3-1 below.

FIGURE 3-1. Gini Coefficient 1977-2007

Source: Data produced on the basis of PNAD (National Sample of Household Research).

The above mentioned survey employed other indicators as well: the ratio between the average income of the richest 10% and of the poorest 40%, and that of the richest 20% and the poorest 20%. In both cases, the indicators show a considerable decline in the inequality in income distribution from 2001 to 2007: the first ratio declined 5.2%. (IPEA, 2008). In addition, the study shows that this drop, which has been observed since 2001, is the longest lasting one in the last three decades. There have been six continuous years of declining rates of inequality. From 2001 to 2007, the income of those in the lowest income bracket has increased significantly, which in turn lowered the levels of poverty and extreme poverty. The analysis estimates that the recent decline in extreme poverty occurred at a rate three times faster than it would be necessary in order to achieve the Millennium Development Goal, set for 2015, which in fact was reached in 2006 (IPEA, 2008).

Regarding social mobility, the 2007 survey shows that only 27.4% fall in the lowest income bracket (less than R$545.66 net family income per month) (IPEA, 2008). This corresponds to 13.8 million people moving up the social ladder, out of which 10.8 million crossed the threshold separating group 1 from group 2 (intermediate net family incomes between R$545.66 to R$1,350.82 per month); and 3.6 million advanced from group 2 to group 3 (the higher income bracket above R$ 1,350.82). The highest increase in social mobility occured in the transition from group 1 to group 2, representing 74% of those which were able to ascend socially. Mostly, this mobility took place in the Northeast, North and Central-West regions—5.3 million, or 52%, whereas the transition from group 2 to group 3 occured in the Southeast and South regions—2.7 million or 69.9%.

Some of the data concerning the reduction of poverty are also revealing. In this sense, one should note the reduction in the number of people below the poverty line, especially after 2003 (see Table 3-1).

TABLE 3-1. Percent of Population with Net Family Income Below the Poverty Line, 1995–2007

1995	4.0	2002	3.0
1996	5.0	2003	4.0
1997	4.0	2004	2.0
1998	4.0	2005	1.0
1999	4.0	2006	9.0
2000	6.0	2007	8.0
2001	4.0		

Source: IPEADATA, 2009.

According to PNAD (2007) data, employment increased 1.6% from 89.3 million workers in 2006 to 90.8 million in 2007. Furthermore, the real average income of those employed increased 3.2%, reaching its highest level since 1996. The unemployment rate decreased marginally and is now at 8.2%, the lowest level of this decade. There has been an overall increase in the number of so-called formal or protected job positions and a reduction of those attached to the informal market. As a result of job expansion, the degree of informality decreased significantly from 55.1% in 2006 to 54.1% in 2007. Considering only the most reliable forms of employment relationships (paid wages, autonomous labor, employers), informality has dropped from 49.7% to 48.9% in this same period. A result in this reduction of informality has been the increase of the percentage of workers that contribute to the social pension system (this figure has climbed from 48.8% in 2006 to 50.7% in 2007) considering that the number of those contributing has dovetailed with remained the increase of the number of protected workers (IPEA 2008).

The graphs below (Figure 3-2) exemplify the above mentioned tendencies, which were, already in progress before the onset of the crisis.

FIGURE 3-2. Employment Data, 2001-2007

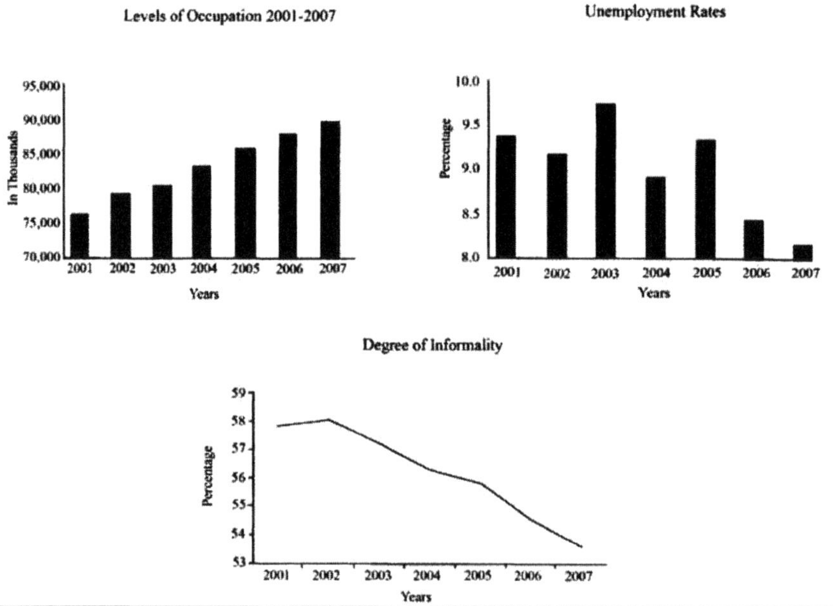

Source: IPEA, 2008a.

It is in the wake of these previous policies and the establishment of an institutional framework through time that it is possible to understand the effect of anti-cyclical policies adopted to weather the crisis. These policies aim to secure and expand excluded sectors in the consumer market, and the industrial sector's production of durable goods oriented towards (but not exclusively to) the domestic market, while at the same time maintaining levels of employment through concessions of fiscal incentives as shown below.

The financial market crisis certainly had an impact on the Brazilian economy, and in certain regards, it influenced aforementioned positive results. When the crisis struck, the country was on a roll in terms of employment compared to the last 30 years, with an unemployment rate of approximately 6%. Still, the burst of the real estate bubble caused by the subprime market caused Brazil 800,000 formal job losses in the span of only three months.

The newly instituted Bolsa Família program helped to prevent people from losing jobs and falling back into poverty. On average, from October 2008 to June 2009, the poverty rate decreased 2.8% compared to the same period the previous year. In this period, 503,000 people were removed from poverty and inequality dropped 0.4%. According to the IPEA, this is why that one year after the peak of the crisis, poverty and inequality rates remained at almost the same level as before 2008. Thus, the real outcome of the crisis can be said to have been a sudden slowdown in the reduction of poverty and inequality, something that had been occurring quite rapidly in the last years, with an average of 5 million people moving out of poverty each year.[6]

Among the main anticyclical policies adopted I would like to highlight the following:

A minimum wage real (above-inflation) increase of over 6% effective March 2010 note that 2/3 of all pension benefits are equal to one minimum wage;

All benefits beyond the minimum wage were adjusted according to past inflation with no loss in purchase power from 2008 to 2009;

Expansion of directed credit, especially of credit lines offered by public financial institutions, such as the BNDES, Caixa Econômica, and Banco do Brasil;

Creation of two new taxes on individuals, increasing available government funds;

The addition of 1.3 million people in the Bolsa Familia program;

Increased efforts in the implementation of investment projects established by the Growth Acceleration Program *(Programa de Aceleração do Crescimento*, PAC);

Reduction of the annual primary budget surplus target, previously established at 4.3% and reduced to 2.5%;

Launching of the Minha Casa, Minha Vida (My House, my Life) housing program which includes the construction of 1 million homes for people with incomes below 10 minimum wages. This program will require investments amounting to R$34 billion and will try to keep the housing sector moving at a strong pace. According to estimates made by the Caixa Econômica Federal, 800 thousand jobs will be created this year.

Maintenance/expansion of public expenditure with employees, social programs, and direct activities of the state and,

---

6. "Políticas anticíclicas protegem base da pirâmide," 09/09/2009 (http://www.ipea.gov.br/003/00301009.jsp?ttCD_CHAVE=11914).

> Reduction of the Tax on Industrialized Products (Imposto sobre Produtos industrializados-IPI) in several sectors, among them, the automobile industry.[7]

In the realm of economic policies, the reduction of the IPI in sectors such as home appliances, construction, and automobile industry was responsible for preserving, directly and indirectly, up to 60,000 jobs and for 13.4% of car sales in the first semester, which translates to sales of 191,000 cars.[8] As a result, these numbers show that the anticyclical policies worked effectively—they stimulated spending, increased sales, energized the economy and made the consumer spend savings at a time when the uncertainties provoked by the crisis made it difficult to do so suggested otherwise. Therefore, the IPI reduction in these sectors was especially important in energizing the economy.

The anti-cyclical policies taken by the government also had a positive impact concerning employment, insofar as more than half of the jobs lost were recovered, which provided families with greater purchasing power as well as stimulus for growth. Last May, the rate of unemployment dropped to approximately 9% in the six main metropolitan regions of Brazil—São Paulo, Rio de Janeiro, Belo Horizonte, Salvador, Recife, and Porto Alegre. Large companies such as Vale and Embraer announced significant cuts in personnel and output. But, to the surprise of many analysts, the job market turned out to be the life line of the Brazilian economy.

The social programs supported by the government, such as the Bolsa Familia, the above-inflation increases of the minimum wage, and the PAC (even if slow in its implementation), have rescued Brazil from recession while protecting a fraction of the population that would have otherwise been excluded from the formal economy.

Given Brazil's quick recovery from the international financial crisis, on September 22, 2009, Moody's credit rating agency promoted Brazil to investment grade. To date, Brazil has achieved investment grade according to three credit rating agencies: Standard and Poor's, the Canadian agency Dominion Bond Rating Service, and the Japanese agencies Rating and Investment Information, and Japan Credit Rating Agency. It's important to realize the fact that Brazil was the only country to receive the rating upgrade during the crisis.[9]

7. "PIB cresceu 1,9%: a crise era um V," 14/09/2009 (http://www.ipea.gov.br/003/00301009.jsp?ttCD_CHAVE=12005).
8. "A mão visível do governo," 02/09/2009 (http://jbonline.terra.com.br/pextra/2009/09/02/e020927895.asp).

Concerning industrial performance, IEDI's newsletter nº 371, "Industrial Production and Jobs: More Positive Signs with Distinct Regional and Sector Characteristics," had predicted a significant improvement of industrial production, pointing out that, if the external scenario remained favorable as it has in the previous months, recovery could come and the level of the production reached before the crisis accentuated. The recent evolution of production, although it has shown a less robust growth rate and rather negative levels in the last five months, indicates, nevertheless, a marginally positive tendency. However, differentiated regional performances still persist.

In fact, production in some states has started to improve, as is the case of São Paulo. Comparing the months of March and April, industrial production in this state increased 2.4% (with seasonal variations accounted for) after growing 1.1% in April. Evidently, this does not mean that industries in São Paulo have returned to pre-crisis levels of production. Compared to May 2008, there has been an 11.6% decrease in production, and in the accumulated index for the first five months of 2009, industrial output in the state of São Paulo decreased 14.6%. However the 2.4% increase in May might be the first indication of industrial recovery in São Paulo. It's an important development, with implications for the rest of the Brazilian industry, since the state's industrial complex accounts for a good portion of the demand for products from other regions of the country. IEDI's preliminary assessment, based on output patterns for May 2009, indicates the industry's positive reaction to the crisis. This reaction is buttressed by improved credit conditions, the fiscal unburdening provided by the IPI cuts, and by the domestic market's enhanced demand capacity. Therefore the anticyclical policies announced by the government—postponement of tax reductions for automobiles, motorcycles, home appliances, construction material, trucks, wheat flour for bread, and tax cuts for capital assets, and, most important, the reduction of credit costs provided by the BNDES for the acquisition of machinery, and equipment—should favor the industry's response.[10]

9. According to Moody's, "the chances that Brazil's rating continues to improve are reasonably high" since "economic conditions seem favorable to constant reductions of public debt indicators, given the perspective of growth in the short term and the probability that macroeconomic conditions will continue warranting one-digit interest rates, a condition that fundamentally changes the dynamics behind the debt." Moody's positive outlook adds that "the absence of fundamental macroeconomic inbalances in the Brazilian economy is a favorable condition given that it places the country in good standing in relation to other sovereign creditors in the same rating category yet with greater fiscal and foreign challenges." Brasil torna-se Grau de investimento pela Moody's. Available at: http://www.fazenda.gov.br/portugues/documentos/2009/Nota-Moodys-220909.pdf

10. Carta IEDI n. 370—Produção Industrial em Maio de 2009: Recuperação Gradual (www.iedi.org.br).

Industrial output, after the 20% drop between September and December 2008, already shows a positive growth rate of 7.9%, between December 2008 and June 2009, according to data that includes control for seasonal variations produced by the PIM/IBGE (Constanzi, 2009) (See Figure 3-3).

FIGURE 3-3. Industrial Output, 2007-2010 (2002=100)

Source: Monthly Industrial Survey *(Pesquisa Industrial Mensal, Produção Física)*, IBGE, 2009.

CONCLUSION: ESTABLISH A VIRTUOUS CIRCLE?

Development involves long-term processes that are best analyzed in hindsight, since there are uncertainties about the impact and direction of change. In certain aspects, especially those pertaining to structural dimensions, we can speak of path dependency in terms of institutional choices taken at the outset of any process. This includes, those which begin to generate increasing returns for the federal institutes, bureaucracies, and political institutions capable of ensuring governability, and enhancing the executive's effectiveness. In other aspects, as in the case of the types of social security associated with a certain productive regime, it would be more appropriate to speak of a trajectory that is influenced by changes or reorientations in policies, even in a radical fashion, according to changes in the elites' reference points. We can affirm that, depending on context, a single factor can be an obstacle or a stimulus for development.

In the Brazilian case, as I have attempted to show, the long-term analysis indicates, on one hand, the path dependency of state institutions in terms of their role as the coordinator of economic activities, and on the other, the continuation of a trajectory that has undergone adjustments over time in terms of social and inclusion policies. Finally, a factor such as the size of the population can shift from being considered an obstacle to development, as was the case not too long ago, to becoming a facilitator for development within a new outlook, as it seems to be the case now. The late buildup process of the state apparatus in the 1930s—actually the result of a political rupture with the oligarchic agro-exporting model—continuing with the progressive import-substitution industrialization, was combined, however, with a process of social exclusion and income concentration. Under authoritarian governments and democratic interregnums, this logic was pushed forward by the ruling elites in an outlook of growing foreign debt, and high inflation that ended up exhausting this type of development predominant until the end of the 1970s. Concurrently to the political regime, there is the transition to a competitive and pluralist democracy, characterized by the expansion of the political spectrum. The neoliberal turn led to a resizing of the state and of state interventions, which combined market regulation and orthodox macroeconomic policies. The financial system, which had undergone reforms in the 1970s, was improved and regulated during the implementation of the Real Plan. However, structures and models from the previous model—especially those relating to the articulation of the state with the private sector, as well as those related to development and productive activities—remained in place.

A party with roots in the labor movement emerges democratically in the political scene and, after reaching the presidency, implemented developmentalist policies while maintaining the principles of monetary stability established by the previous government. It did this through the administration of the interest rate, exchange rate, and public spending. The main difference between the two governments is the latter's prioritization of poverty reduction and social policies. Utilizing this framework, we can evaluate the impact of the international crisis and the emergency policies adopted to manage the economic slowdown. What can be called the "expansion of the social frontier," besides a striking feature of the new outlook, is the doorway to a new development model based on the possibility of domestic market expansion. This is without overlooking the insertion in foreign markets, ensured by an extremely diversified and complex export portfolio, of which primary goods and agro-exports are but a few of its components. Combining these tendencies with a foreign policy characterized by a strong orientation towards regional integration, it is possible to foresee the establishment of a positive context for development in Brazil. The rich energetic potential that opens up with the exploration of the pré-sal and ecological resources demands action in the realm of regulation and implementation of strategies for sustainability. This scenario not only further empowers the comeback of the state as the central actor in a new development model, but also makes it the nucleus of the productive regime. Problems will certainly exist, especially in governing the intense conflict among traditional oligarchies, big rural landowners, and conservative sectors in general. It is precisely in this scenario that politics can make a difference, playing an open game that simultaneously articulates uncertainties and possibilities.

4

New Directions in Public Policy and State-Society Relations

Glauco Arbix and Scott B. Martin

Abstract: This chapter takes as its point of departure the notion that an incipient new development model is taking shape in Brazil. This model recovers the state as a focal point, but in a manner quite distinct from the heavy-handed, often dirigiste role of the developmentalist state of what some have insightfully termed the period of the state-centered matrix. The visible outlines of this new model, though incipient, suggest its compatibility with political democracy and open economies. A central argument of this chapter emphasizes the new synergies that have emerged, to some extent by design, and to some extent by virtuous accident, across economic and social policy—traditionally two very distinct spheres of public policy in Brazil in terms of aims and institutions.

This decade's rapid growth of many large developing countries, and the critique and political backlash against neoliberalism, have begun to reinvigorate age-old debates about the prospects and "state of the state."[1] Debates about the declining state—until recently common in the literature about globalization—have shifted. Without a doubt, states in many developing countries have altered dramatically their real policy capacities and institutions as well as relationships with civil society. In part this was done in

1. This paper draws on ideas first presented in Arbix and Miranda (2009).

response to globalization, but also in reaction to changes in national political systems. Since the 1990s, in Brazil as in many developing countries, states no longer seem to wear the straitjacket suggested by neo-classical orthodoxy. In fact, it could be argued that states have never really been in retreat anywhere in the world, even in their weakest moment. Still, they have definitely undergone major transformations that make them quite distinct from the pre-neoliberal, pre-globalization "states of old," with their statism and dirigisme.

We propose to explore the shifting roles and forms of intervention of the contemporary Brazilian state, with a focus on theorizing and re-conceptualizing evolving approaches to economic and social policy that are captured neither by the market fundamentalist/neoliberal or old (or revived) "developmental state" or *desenvolvimentista* paradigms. A more synergistic, two-way pattern of state-market relations seems to be emerging in Brazil, centered on state roles of promotion of competitiveness and innovation. At the same time, the state has assumed a heightened role in social policy oriented toward combating poverty, making inroads against inequality, and promoting market incorporation of underprivileged citizens. Thus far, the response to the global crisis that began in 2008 suggests a deepening of these trends as well as the resiliency of emerging practices and institutions.

In the next section, we will briefly situate our discussion within the context of (1) recent debates about the state concerning impacts of globalization and the apparent decline of the neoliberal paradigm as well as, (2) recent efforts to characterize these patterns or promote alternatives to neoliberalism using the conceptual apparatus of developmentalism. Following that, the heart of the paper will explore the emergence and evolution since the mid-1990s of what we identify as new state capacities in the areas of fiscal policy, competitiveness policy (toward trade, industry, and science and technology), and social policy, including reform and expansion of traditional entitlements together with expanded targeted social assistance. Along the way, we discuss the synergies across these revived and re-oriented state roles; how they diverge from developmentalist practices and concepts (particularly under the military regime); how they emerge out of the democratization process and policy learning; and how together with other developments they seem to have helped produce a new model of income-redistributing and equity-enhancing growth. Toward the end, we discuss why the enticing alternative label of "social democratic," quite often applied to the Lula government, may be misleading or incomplete given divergence from what that concept has meant, including in recent influential research on "peripheral social democracy." We conclude with a call for recognizing that Brazil's recent evolution is not well captured by any of these labels, and the need for a conceptual apparatus that will enable us to analyze and explain the emergence and possible consolidation of a "neo-activist" state form (to borrow Weiss's term) that does not yet have a ready-made conceptual paradigm among social scientists. This state takes on an enabling position of moderate, pro-market intervention via an active competitiveness policy, joined closely with a much stronger role in providing social services and benefits. It is also increasingly linked to fostering market inclusion for the previously underserved and excluded, in addition to transferring income in targeted fashion to increasingly broad segments of the poor and extremely poor.

GLOBALIZATION, STATES, AND DEVELOPMENT: FROM NEOLIBERALISM TO NEODEVELOPMENTALISM?

If much of the decade of the nineties was marked by considerable preoccupation about globalization-induced "convergence" toward a narrow minimalist neoliberal or market fundamentalist state, the past decade or so has been marked by powerful empirical and theoretical refutations of such determinism. This has been applied to both advanced and developing countries[2] as well as interesting discussions about varieties of capitalism in the North (Hall and Soskice eds., 2001), and alternatives or successors to neoliberal versions of capitalism for Latin America and the global South (e.g., Huber ed., 2002). The sense of a palpable (if not necessarily definitive) decline of neoliberal policy and doctrines, and the associated Washington Consensus is widespread, in part given the backlash generated against those policies at the national and international levels. Within that general intellectual and policy milieu, some scholars (e.g., Weiss ed., 2004; Weiss forthcoming), have begun to creatively explore how states seemingly are carving out new roles, and development strategies that are both post-neoliberal and post-developmental. Meanwhile, some analysts in Brazil (Bresser-Pereira, 2004 and 2006; Sicsú and Renaut eds., 2004), reflecting the tremendous hold that developmentalist thinking still has in certain intellectual quarters, have begun to discuss—in part as pro-

2. Restricting the focus to studies centering mostly on the global South, we can cite Weiss ed. (2004) regarding states in general, and with regard to social welfare polices in particular, Glatzer and Rueschemeyer, eds. (2005) and Haggard and Kaufman (2008).

posed doctrine and in part as description of the emerging empirical reality they seek to analyze and promote—a "novo desenvolvimentismo" with roots in the "old developmentalism." For his part, the current Finance Minister, Guido Mantega, spoke in September 2007 of a "social-desenvolvimentismo" that he believed was emerging under Lula.[3]

The problem with attempts to revive or re-orient the developmental state concept, in our view, is that it conflates very distinct experiences, across time and disparate countries. By associating state behavior narrowly with economic performance, especially growth of Gross Domestic Product (GDP), it tends to obscure the real debate that needs to occur about recent transformations. It reduces the diverse dimensions of state action and capacity—their roots in society and in institutional relations—to the simple movement of the economy, in particular the macroeconomy. Thus, the new profile of the state would be narrowly defined by its capacity (in reality, its success) to deliver better economic performance.

The debt crisis of the early 1980s, which resulted in the corrosion and collapse of the economy of Latin America, and Brazil in particular, was the first great blow to the developmentalist edifice constructed over the 1950s and 1960s and still operating—albeit with greater difficulties—in the 1970s. During the nineties, economic opening and privatization processes were key turning points that ended a long cycle of protectionism. Also affected was the direct presence of the state as a producer of goods and services, and as heavy-handed regulator creator of private firms and entire sectors. The structural changes promoted during the course of the 1990s took place within a process of global integration, marked particularly by the newly founded World Trade Organization and international financial liberalization. In terms of the structural characteristics of the national state, these global changes produced a point of no return, in Brazil and elsewhere. At the same time, the transformations produced new configurations that by no means approximated the most orthodox pro-market models or prescriptions. They were based on the idea of an inert state, responsible only for setting basic rules and broad regulations for private markets, and notable reactive in character. In fact, we argue—for the Brazilian case, though the argument could be extended to many other countries— that the state never did withdraw altogether, even though various foundational elements were irreversibly altered, and in due course, new elements were added, such that

3. Interview with Radiobrás, September 12, 2007, reported in Edla Lula and Daniel Lima, "Brasil entrou no novo ciclo econômico do social-desenvolvimentismo," Agência Brasil, September 23, 2007.

in its current form it bears little resemblance to either orthodox market fundamentalism or the developmental state.

State Capacity and Social Policy: Contrasts with the Old Developmentalism

We argue that the contemporary Brazilian state has evolved, within the broad context of economic opening and political democratization. Even as old forms of state capacity associated with the country's particular version of "developmentalism"—particularly but not only in its late, military regime phase—have been undermined by market reforms and by economic opening, new forms of state capacity have emerged and taken shape. This has not been a "neat" or coherent or linear process, but nonetheless, when one steps back from the process of change (a subject we tackle in the following section) to focus on its concrete manifestations today, it is difficult to understate the extent of the transformations. State capacity has, in short, been transformed and adapted, rather than simply declining. Additionally it has taken on new characteristics not captured by the developmentalist or neoliberal paradigms (or that of populism, however that contested concept might be applied).

It is rather easy to quickly relate the process by which the main developmental capacities of the old military-developmentalist state were dismantled, or suffered serious decline, in the 1980s and, particularly 1990s. Emerging in the broader context of fiscal crisis, continuous stabilization crises, and extremely high levels of inflations amidst the exhaustion of the ISI model, extensive privatization of state-owned enterprises under Collor (1990–1992) and, particularly, Cardoso (1995–2002) undermined the state capacity to shape productive investment in steel, petrochemicals, and mining. The power deriving from a centralization of fiscal authority in the federal government was undermined not only by the general atmosphere of crisis, but also by the fuzzy fiscal federalism of the 1988 Constitution. Furthermore, there were successive financial crises and initial difficulties in working out the rules of fiscal federalism, such as the "fiscal war," over state-level incentives to attract investment. Rapid and indiscriminate trade liberalization from the Collor government onward, in the broader context of privatization and persistent fiscal crisis, weakened the once considerable ability of Brasília to promote—through sectoral industrial policies involving subsidies, protection, and investment incentives—domestically owned firms as either "national champions" or important firms that could work in close alliance with multinationals (e.g. auto parts).

Of course, the coercive capacity of the military-developmentalist state—one of the main attributes of the state in that era—was debilitated by democratization and a shift in the balance of relations between civil and military authorities, as well as other processes of a more socio-structural nature.

The fiscal sector was one of the first of the key areas in which state capacity has been reconstructed over the past two presidencies. Numerous elements beyond the starting point of macroeconomic stabilization under the Real Plan—a de facto renegotiation of the fiscal pact between federation and states, incremental tax and social security reforms, administrative reforms, tight-fisted monetary policies including primary fiscal surpluses—have contributed to this process of restoring the state's key capacity to tax, spend, and invest. It is well known that Brazil has one of the highest tax to GDP ratios in the developing world; scholars have also noted how crucial fiscal health and fiscal capacity are in offering either a more permissive or a more restrictive environment for social policy (Haggard and Kaufman, 2008). With the Real Plan, not simply did the state gain a better handle on management of various large fiscal burdens such as social security and management of subnational sovereign debt, but it was also able to maintain a large tax base ("revenue extraction capacity," if one wishes to be more abstract), through periodic—typically incremental—tax reforms, even amidst persistent cycles of crisis, stabilization, and recovery including the late 1990s recession. As finances improved and growth picked up, this extractive capacity has restored the state's ability to undertake key investments in infrastructure, social services, and science and technology. Policy orientations placed these as high priorities.

A second key area of renewed and transformed state capacity combined with a substantive reorientation in substance is in trade policy (broadly conceived) that is tied to the general theme of competitiveness policy which is a key element of the new market-friendly Brazilian state activism. While extensive protection has been left behind since the trade liberalization of the early 1990s, and indeed the World Trade Organization (WTO) and other international trade commitments create further general constrains, the federal government has taken on and steadily expanded its role in trade promotion in the Cardoso and particularly the Lula governments. This primarily takes the form of an aggressive promotion of these very bilateral and multilateral free trade agreements within and beyond the Americas (and opposition to those, such as the now defunct Free Trade of the America proposal of the 1990s and early 2000s) as well as energetic defense of perceived Brazilian interests within multilateral trade negotiations. Of note is, that unlike the more straightforward economic nationalism of developmentalism's yesteryear, this involves an ambitious and elaborate effort to cultivate foreign market access for Brazilian goods as well as increasingly for foreign direct investment (FDI) abroad by Brazilian firms [where for instance Brazilian firms were responsible for 14 mergers and acquisitions in 2008 (Arbix and Miranda, 2009)]. One result of this policy has been a very strong and healthy diversification of Brazil's foreign trading relationships over the past decade or so, in particular in terms of a relative diminution in its trade dependence vis-à-vis traditional Northern partners among the OECD powers and relative increase in its ties with the global South, most notably China but also sub-Saharan Africa and other regions outside the Americas. This has been closely related to a diversification in the range of exports in terms of sectors, degrees of value added, and types, which include not just simple commodities, but also value-added commodities such as ethanol as well as manufactured goods across an increasingly diverse range.

Moreover, while the country has perhaps not been as aggressive as some East Asian countries in trying to use all the remaining tools of permissible selective protection at its disposal within a post-WTO world,[4] Brasília has not shied away from a sometimes aggressive defense of measures such as the automotive regime of the mid to late 1990s (forcing multinationals to invest directly in the country if they wished to receive lower tariffs on imports) or successfully challenging US cotton subsidies within WTO mechanisms (Evans, 2005b).

In all these cases, whether pursuing multilateral or bilateral trade disputes, or negotiating new trade deals (e.g., taking a much greater role in the Doha round than in the previous Uruguay round of global trade talks), or channeling lines of credit through the BNDES, trade promotion involves increasingly closer relationships of consultation with firms and sectors who can benefit quite tangibly and directly from specific expanded market opportunities.

In sum, even within a context of openness that policy elites across the last two presidencies have not just accepted but actively embraced in a historic shift for Brazil—the state has not taken this a simple cue to retreat into a

4. For a good analysis of what "policy space" might remain within WTO rules for competitiveness and other policies on the part of developing countries, see Gallagher ed., 2005, in particular the essays by Alice Amsden and Peter Evans.

passive "laissez faire" position of accepting Brazil's inherited comparative advantage or current structure of imports, exports, and trading partners.

Besides trade policy understood broadly, competitiveness policy has two other key, closely related dimensions—industrial policy and science and technology, or national innovation, policy. In both these areas, one finds an increasingly pro-active role of the state, mainly within the Lula government but to some extent building on some institutional innovations from the Cardoso administration, with respect to (1) strategic policy formulation and related creation of new institutions for such purposes; and (2) development finance.

In 1999 the Ministry of Development, Industry, and Commerce was created. This was a step that would loom as more significant after Lula took office in 2003, and began to place greater emphasis on formulating an active competitiveness policy. Yet the initial institutional move placed significant responsibility for both trade policy and policy toward industry, commerce, and services into a single cabinet-level agency.

It is difficult to trace a fully coherent and rational arc in the process of creation of policy designs and institutionalities for industrial policy under Lula. Rather, the process seems in part an experimental one of trial and error—and thus arguably of policy learning among cabinet and mid-level officials—in which, over time, the degree of coordination among agencies and of explicitness in goals (through a more "results-based" approach) as well as ambition of goals have all tended to increase. In the early years of the first Lula government, when concerns about macroeconomic stability and structural reforms that would cement the government's credibility with the international financial community prevailed, the Conselho Nacional de Desenvolvimento Econômico e Social (CNDES) was established in 2003. Its role has been primarily consultative, rather than becoming a kind of national negotiating forum that extends nationally the principles of the sectoral chambers or regional chamber of the greater ABC region comprising Santo André, São Bernardo do Campo and São Caetano do Sul (which some at the time might have hoped or, depending on their perspective, feared). Nonetheless, in bringing in not only business associations but also labor unions and other civil society organizations into a broader debate about national development priorities, the CNDES at least set an important early tone of dialogue and societal, particularly business, participation in a process of promoting a public-private alliance for development, which has remained and grown in subsequent years.

Created in late 2004 and early 2005, the Agência Brasileira de Desenvolvimento Industrial (ABDI) is a networked institution, formally under the Ministry of Development, Industry, and Trade, that brings together in its governing deliberative council federal ministries and funding agencies, private sector representatives from inside and outside the official corporatist business structure, labor (CUT, *Central Única dos Trabalhadores*), and universities to promote technological and economic development in sectors of Brazilian industry. ABDI has played a leading role in seeking to develop an industrial policy and helps identify and guide investment decisions in technological research, innovation, and industrial development. The comprehensive framework that the ABDI has developed under its *Política de Desenvolvimento Produtivo* (PDP, Policy of Productive Development) stresses the importance of public investment and support to build capability in infrastructure, capital goods, exports, and technology firms (Trubek, 2008). One interesting aspect of the PDP is that it set in 2007 a series of concrete measurable benchmarks, or "macrometas," for 2010 in terms of desired improvements in the country's ratios of fixed investments, share of global exports, share of private R&D in total GDP, and number of exporting micro and small enterprises.

Another new institution, also created in January 2005, is the Conselho Nacional de Desenvolvimento Industrial (CNDI, National Council for Industrial Development); an inter-ministerial body comprised of all the main ministries with responsibilities for economic, social, and environmental policy, other development-related agencies [including the IPEA (Institute for Applied Economic Research) with its advisory function and BNDES as national development bank] along with 14 representatives from civil society. Its primary function is to "propose to the President national policies and specific measures to promote Brazil's industrial development."[5] The Council plays important roles of agenda-setting as well as coordination and mediation of disputes among ministries that may bring to the table different bureaucratic, partisan, or other types of interests as well as potential competing ideas and priorities.

Along with the creation of new institutions, traditional institutions have been strengthened. Of note, particularly with regard to science and technology, or national innovation, policy is the strengthening of (1) the Ministry of Science and Technology's funding agency for public, private, and mixed

5. Ministério do Desenvolvimento, Indústria e Comércio Exterior, http://www.mdic.gov.br/sitio/interna/interna.php?area=1&menu=558.

projects of applied and basic research, FINEP (Financiadora de Estudos e Projetos) and (2) state-level foundations and technology institutes that play similar roles at the subnational level. With promotion of firm-level innovation now articulated as a major policy goal under the 2005 National Innovation Law, the FINEP's funding has increased substantially and also its emphasis on lending directly to firms has been enhanced significantly. In addition, funding for the federal university system has increased generally and in terms of support for dynamic high-tech sectors in particular, including the creation of new universities such as the Federal University of the Greater ABC Region, and there is much evidence of heightened university-firm linkages in terms of fostering innovation. In addition, the long-standing national development bank dating from the advent of developmentalism in the 1950s, the BNDES, has recently enjoyed a higher profile, revamped role for which even the liberal *The Economist*[6]—usually no fan of industrial policy—has delivered grudging praise. The Bank's assets stood at US$120bn as of end-2008, according to the magazine, and its annual lending portfolio is now larger than that of the World Bank (Trubek, 2008), at around US$100bn. Noting that "[I]n the past its funds were sometimes handed out according to political expediency, to dying companies and in pursuit of a patchily successful industrial policy," *The Economist* notes the BNDES' recently expanded role as a venture capitalist and direct provider of trade finance during the recent credit crunch as well as its "slim" administration comprised of "career civil servants" that has engaged in "less political lending of late."[7] All of the areas of improvement noted by the article relate to problems that have plagued the BNDES, a quintessential institution from the developmentalist era, and that seem to have been overcome or at least been addressed in large measure.

The BNDES' heightened role as a venture capitalist is of particular importance because it reflects not just a new policy instrument but also a strategic shift toward greater emphasis on promoting innovation in nascent or promising new sectors as well as traditional lending to established firms and sectors. And while this role no doubt grew in the context of the quite agile stimulative and anti-crisis posture that the Brazilian state in general has displayed with respect to limiting the impacts of the global recession on the country's growth

6. "Central Planning: Rediscovering the Charms of BNDES," *The Economist*, April 16, 2009.

7. The magazine's only two caveats are that "the government still has a thing about helping to create big companies that can conquer rivals abroad" that is reflected in BNDES policies (a debatable point in terms of wisdom of policy priorities) and that its enhanced role as trade financier and venture capitalist has to do with wider capital market inefficiencies and insufficiencies in Brazil.

(a topic to which we turn below), this evolution has been underway for a number of years under the Lula presidency. We reproduce the following summary from Trubek that builds on the work of several Brazilian specialists:

> BNDESPAR is the investment bank arms of BNDES whose goals include support for technological innovation, small business, and start-ups producing innovative and competitive products; the creation of a seed money and venture capital market; and support for the acquisition of foreign assets by Brazilian firms. BNDESPAR both operates like a private equity fund and venture capitalist and supports other institutions that perform these roles. BNDESPAR can make direct investment in start-ups and unlisted companies; participate in their management; and affect corporate strategy and governance. In some cases, BNDESPAR requires that firms receiving its support submit innovation plans. It also encourages the firms it supports to secure private capital through IPOs. But the bank also supports closed investment funds that provide private equity and venture capital especially for small and medium size firms. BNDESPAR invests in privately managed closed funds that are targeted at specific sectors and attract substantial private funding: currently these funds have raised $4 for every $1 committed by the Bank.

This novel role for the BNDES in terms of close public-private collaboration in support of private entrepreneurship and innovation is characterized by Mattos and Coutinho (2008) as a new "model of risk-taking" that the Brazilian state is arguably taking on. The authors insightfully contrast this new type of state role in industrial policy with the states' industrial policy role as "owner of state-owned enterprises" and "picking winners" under developmentalism as well as the neoliberal model of "privatization."

A fourth area where state capacity was weakly developed under military (and earlier, pre-1964 versions of) *desenvolvimentismo* and has become much more so since the 1990s is in social policy. Despite some modest expansions of social security benefits, health care access, and local educational spending requirements under the military regime,[8] Brazil's welfare regime remained highly segmented and (like the economic model itself) regressive in its impact on income distribution during this period. Newly created programs such as FUNRURAL as well as terms of access for newly incorporated groups in the social security system were riddled with patron-

---

8. This discussion draws on Haggard and Kaufman (2008: 100-03). The notable extensions of coverage included: the extension of noncontributory pensions to some peasants and rural poor under the newly created *Fundo de Assistência ao Trabalhador Rural* (FUNRURAL) in 1971; the 1979 expansion of rural clinics in the Northeast under the Programa de Interiorizacão das Acões de Saúde e Saneamento (PIASS), and extension of access to emergency heath-care for all citizens; and a 1983 constitutional amendment mandating that states spend at least 15% of all federal transfer on education.

age for the official ARENA (*Aliança Renovadora Nacional*) party, and "cash benefits to the rural and urban informal sectors—about one-half the minimum wage . . . remained minimal compared to those going to the civil service, other formal sector workers, and (of course) the military itself" (Haggard and Kaufman, 2008: 101-02). Filgueira and Filgueira (2002: 138-39) characterize Brazil's welfare regime through the end of the 1970s as "dual . . . with an almost universal development of primary education and a significant though stratified degree of health coverage . . . [exacerbated by] the problem of territorial heterogeneity. . . . [S]ocial protection systems [such as this] cushion social segmentation only for those sectors incorporated into modern frameworks of protection. These systems exacerbate stratification between the latter and those not fortunate enough to be part of such frameworks." In addition, of course, the military regime heightened the coercive elements of the state-corporatist structure of labor organization and labor relations (which was extended to agricultural wage-laborers), which helped allow for a model of de facto flexible external and internal labor markets.

The process has been uneven across policy spheres, and full of its fits and starts, but gradually under Brazil's nearly quarter century as a "new democracy" a system of social protection has taken shape and expanded, with particularly decisive strides made since the late 1990s and under the current government. One of the most notable elements of the initial period of the Nova República (under Sarney, Collor, and Franco) was the relative absence or failure of concrete social reform despite the rhetorical emphasis on social inclusion, as documented and analyzed at length by Weyland (1996). Yet there were important constitutional provisions in the 1988 document, inserted through active pressure from civil society, the labor movement, and politicians seeking to cater to these interests, that expanded general, if vaguely defined, rights in access to education, health care, and social security. In addition, specific benefits were created or extended in the Constitution (or in subsequent legislation by the Sarney government), such as sick leave, maternity leave, and unemployment insurance. These principles became important as they established normative goals as well as in some cases institutional templates (in particular, devolution of resources and responsibility to subnational governments) that influenced concretely subsequent reform efforts. Meanwhile, there was contradictory movement in regulation of labor markets and labor relations, as expanded worker benefits, as well as rights to strike and freedom of association created in the 1988 Constitution, were limited in practice by the absence of subsequent implementing legislation or subsequent legislation that interpreted them narrowly. Meanwhile, the labor market reforms of the Cardoso era were "flexibilizing" in nature (i.e, seeking to create more market- and employer-friendly labor norms), even if the government did not achieve as much as it sought due to opposition from unions and their political allies in the opposition.

While the Cardoso government chipped away at some of the social and labor market protections of formal-sector (mostly private-sector) workers in terms of individual labor and social security, it also pursued or furthered important health and education reforms that expanded access to previously uncovered or underserved groups at the same time. There was considerable pressure from below from the *sanitarista* movement on health care, building on the 1988 constitutional provisions and ordinary legislation adopted in 1990 implementing decentralization to municipalities as well as strengthening the Ministry of Health and weakening INAMPS. Responding to this pressure and through a series of executive decree, the Ministry of Health oversaw a large-scale reorganization of the health care system over the course of the 1990s: "By 2002, almost all of Brazil's 5560 municipalities had met the regulatory standards for primary-care services, and about 560 of these receive funding for all services in their jurisdiction" (Haggard and Kaufman, 2008: 285, citing Arretche, 2004).

In education, there was a modest "reallocat[ion] of resources within the primary-education sector and recasting [of] the regulatory and oversight function of the ministry of education" (Haggard and Kaufman, 2008: 285-86; see also Draibe). At the same time, proposals to impose fees and cut wages in higher education were beaten back by political and labor opposition. Meanwhile, the government managed to gain passage from Congress of legislation expanding, under the military-created FUNDEF (*Fundo de Manutenção e Desenvolvimento do Ensino Fundamental*), federal transfers to primary education—which is a state and local responsibility—with mandated shares for teaching pay. Of note about both of these modest but significant health and education reforms was that not only did they expand services to previously excluded or underserved regions and populations, but they also did so *without* focusing on a "neoliberal" social policy orientation centered on privatization, private care or insurance, vouchers, and the like.

Much the same could be said about the two-stage social security reform during the Cardoso and Lula governments. It was, as Haggard and Kaufman (2008) underline, "gradual and parametric," focusing not on privatization and individual accounts (*ā la* the then quite internationally and widely diffused "Chilean model" of pension reform) or even "multi-pillar," creating parallel private systems. Instead, reform focused on shoring up and rationalizing the public system, equalizing benefits across the public and private sectors, and avoiding anomalies that allowed for multiple pensions for certain occupational groupings. To be sure, even these limited reforms were contentious, and in particular the more ambitious and draconian 1995 proposals by the Cardoso government had to be scaled back considerably to secure passage by 1998, given the strenuous opposition of well organized pensioners and unionists as well as from the political opposition led by the PT.

The most notable innovation in social policy, of course, has been in terms of targeted social assistance to the poor. This began to occur on a significant scale through the conditional cash transfer scheme known as Bolsa Escola, adopted in 1997 and building on experiences in subnational governments from both the PT (Workers Party) and PSDB (Brazilian Social Democratic Party) as well as on parallel experience with other smaller-scale conditional cash transfers at the federal level (Soares et al., 2007). The program, which is based on various human development conditionalities tied to school attendance, vaccinations, nutritional monitoring, and pre and post-natal tests, has subsequently been extended enormously by the Lula government, from the 4.5 million families it reached by 2002 to a total of 11.6 million in 2005 (and from 0.15 percent of GDP in 2002 to 0.4-0.5 percent as of early 2009);[9] as a response to the global recession, it was announced in early 2009 that the program would be extended to an additional 1.3 million families (ILO, 2009). Studies have found that is has had positive impacts on reducing dropout rates and on raising family income (Morley and Coady 2003, cited in Haggard and Kaufman 2008: 287) as well as on reducing poverty (see below) and inequality (Soares et al. 2007).[10]

Of particular importance from a state capacity-building perspective is the degree of institutional innovation and efficiency of this scheme in terms of its careful and highly progressive targeting (even better than that of CCTs, or Conditional Cash Transfers, in other countries according to research by Soares et al. 2007), its decentralized implementation through municipali-

9. 2002 data are reported in Haggard and Kaufman (2008: 287), 2005 data by IPEA, and the new expansion announced in 2009 reported in International Labour Organization (2009). Percentages of expenditures on cash transfers in GDP are estimated by ILO (2009) and Soares (2007), respectively, and do not reflect the most recent expansions.

10. By breaking the fall in the Gini over the 1995-2004 into factor components, the authors reach the conclusion that conditional cash transfer schemes (centralized in the Bolsa Família from 2003) accounted for 21% of the total drop.

ties, and its minimization of leakages and overhead costs (82% of spending reaches beneficiaries' pockets, it has been estimated (IPEA, 2006).

Another important development is the expansion of coverage of the social security system, which has steadily grown from 54.4% of the economically active population in 2002 to 59.6% in 2008, according to IPEA. Unlike some previous expansions that took place by bringing in non-contributors through the Seguro Especial or "special public pension" for non-contributory rural workers (and thus contributing to the fiscal problems of the *Previdência* or Social Security system), this expansion has occurred almost entirely through bringing in new contributors to the system or already covered individuals shifting to contributory status.

Moreover, health and education spending as a share of GDP have grown considerably in recent years, magnifying impacts of institutional reforms instituted in the latter 1990s. After gradual expansions that began in 2000 and brought spending up to approximately 1.8 to 1.9 percent each in 2002, outlays have approximately doubled to 3.65 and 4.05 percent, respectively, by 2008. While it is difficult to quantify evolution over time, spending on job training and labor market assistance reached 9.38 million families as of 2008; micro-credit benefited 2 million families under the PROGER (Program for Employment and Income Generation) as of 2007, while unemployment insurance was received by 6.9 million families in 2008. Total social spending, at the federal, state, and local levels, as a share of GDP, has grown considerably from the 1980s to 1990s and then into the current decade (see Table 4-1).

TABLE 4-1. Public Social Spending as Share of GDP, 1980–2005

Year	Share of GDP (%)
1980	13.9
1985	13.3
1990	19.0
1995	19.2
2005	21.9

Source: Based on data from Médici and Maciel (1996), and IPEA.

The combined impact of institutional reforms in existing entitlements coupled with institutional innovations in the form of cash transfers, together with fiscally sustainable increases in spending for both types of programs, is the creation of a considerable network of social protection that has not existed previously in Brazil. And while Brazil's "welfare state" still has segmented qualities, benefiting the better organized and remunerated in the formal and public sectors disproportionately, this segmentation is now much less acute than it has been for decades, and perhaps since the creation of the country's first social benefits many decades ago.

While it is related to economic policy more than social policy, we also must not forget the impact of the successive annual increases in the minimum wage, which have raised its purchasing power considerably after many years of real decline. Combined with formal-sector job creation (which has occurred despite these measures and standard neoclassical economists' views about the job-destroying impacts of minimum wage rises), this measure has contributed significantly to income gains at the lower end of the income spectrum.

As a result of the acceleration of economic growth—under conditions of low inflation, a real increase in the minimum wage, and strong social policies—the decline in poverty and inequality has been substantial. The Fundação Getulio Vargas (FGV) calculates a widely cited index in Brazil that measures evolution of income distribution based on "consumption potential," through a division of people into classes A-E, with classes D and E referring, respectively, to the poor and the extremely poor.[11] Based on this methodology, in 2003 the number of Brazilians in poverty and extreme poverty was 54.85 million. By 2008, the number had fallen to 40.37 million. By 2009, at the height of the financial crisis, overall poverty had risen only slightly 41.64 million, while the numbers of absolute poor (Class E) had continued to fall, from 16.02 to 15.32 million (Neri, 2010:12).

Altogether this means that between 2003 and 2009 around 29 million Brazilians escaped poverty and moved into class C, which is generally referred to as the "new middle class" by the FGV. Taken altogether, the top three income strata—classes A, B, and C—grew by 35.7 million from 2003 to 2009, while classes D and F together fell from 96.2 to 73.2 million over the same period. That "new middle class" found in Class C represents slightly over half (50.5%) of the Brazilian population (Neri 2010: 38). The social, economic, and political consequences of Brazil's "becoming a middle-class-majority country" remain to be studied and analyzed.

Overall, the country's Gini coefficient has been declining sharply from its historically extremely high levels since 2001. Inequality began to drop in

11. Monthly household income classes are defined in US$ as E (0-316), D (316-569), C (569-2,843), B (2,843-3,707), A1 (3,707-5,496), A2 (5,496 and above). FGV methodology. Cf. Neri 2010: 44); US$1= R$1.7 (Average, November 2010).

1998 but then rose again over the period when Brazil felt the worst impacts of a financial crisis in 1999-2000, then began its steady downward path.

What seems to be taking shape in contemporary Brazil is a new development model of "growth with equity" that relies not just on export demand but also increases in domestic consumption that build on more buoyant incomes, labor markets, and government income transfers. This more balanced relationship between internal and external demand stimulus would seem to be at least one of the factors that has contributed to Brazil's more rapid recovery from the global recession than that of its Latin American neighbors. Another factor relates to our point about expanding and re-oriented state capacities; in response to the global recession, the government has taken a number of measures—increase trade financing via BNDES and expanding Bolsa Família coverage, as noted above, as well as expanding consumer access to credit for purchases of white goods and consumer durables—to blunt the impact of global trends and bring the country quickly out of what proved to be a very brief and mild recession. In addition, the newly expanded network of social protection had its own automatic counter-cyclical or cushioning impact.

The combined impact of short-term measures and the benefits of longer-term changes in social policy—together with the country's high level of reserves and other policies of macroeconomic stability—clearly demonstrates a capacity for crisis management that the Brazilian state has historically lacked in response to external shocks, such as the oil shocks of the 1970s, debt crisis of the 1980s, or even (in terms of rapidity of adjustment) the financial crisis of the late 2000s. It will be important, of course, to see if the trends of steady, significant decline in poverty and inequality continue unabated or instead experience at least a "pause" given the brief recession and decline in annual growth projections in 2009, when such numbers become available. But there are certainly strong grounds for optimism that social impacts have been much more limited than was initially feared.

What stands out, in a state capacity-building perspective, in the creation or expansion of these key equity-enhancing social programs and policies is the degree to which they have been largely free from the widespread fraud, corruption, and clientelism of Brazil's notoriously patrimonial state, even amidst high-level scandals touching deep into the halls of power in both the current and previous administrations. De-centralization has much to do with that, and the bases for decentralization were initially set by the much-maligned 1988 Constitution, though careful program design and monitoring are required to avoid traditional local patronage from siphoning off resources. While this dimension of the reforms has perhaps not been as fully analyzed and explored as it might, there is a notable degree of transparency, administrative competence, and even-handedness that was lacking historically in the provision of Brazil's social services.

Brazil's developmentalist-era state was known for promoting an income-concentrating economic model and for promoting a pattern of limited transfers almost exclusively to key organized constituencies that left out the bulk of the truly needy and was largely regressive in its distributive impact. In the current decade we bear witness to an economic model that has broadened employment, promoted wage growth, and expanded consumption in the bottom half of the income spectrum. It is reinforced by an emerging new pattern of social spending that has greatly improved positive impacts on income poverty (and arguable other aspects of poverty); together, the two have helped lower inequality, as measured by the Gini, considerably. Moreover, while some may attribute Brazil's economic success up to the current crisis primarily to the global commodity boom[12] our discussion above of the diversified sectoral profile of Brazilian innovation and exports paints a different picture. On the more narrow but significant question of the impact of commodity prices on drops in inequality and poverty—an issue sometimes raised by skeptics about the durability or uniqueness of Brazil's recent social gains—Huber (2002) finds statistical evidence from regression analysis that the positive impacts of public spending on inequality and poverty (including absolute poverty) of the Lula government and other governments she similarly categorizes as "social democratic" in Latin America (Bachelet and Lagos in Chile and Vásquez in Uruguay) are robust even when controlling for the commodity boom.

Beyond the politically charged issue of who should take the most credit among the past two governing parties and presidents in Brazil, we wish instead to emphasize the importance of institutional continuity and deepening from the late 1990s to the present. There has been a cumulative impact of economic and social reforms that were begun at an earlier moment under a different economic environment and that have been carried forward, in some cases re-oriented (as with a greater emphasis on competitiveness policy and

12. Huber also finds that "new left" governments of all types, including populists such as Kirchner in Argentina and Chávez in Venezuela, evidence superior performance on poverty and inequality reduction—measured cross-nationally or within-country—than center-right governments. Of additional note is her finding that, when one controls for the commodity boom, social democratic governments tend to produce greater declines on poverty and inequality, raising the prospect that these gains may be more "fiscally sustainable" (Huber, 2002).

aggressive trade diplomacy), and backed by greater resources in a global and domestic environment that has been more permissive (at least until September 2008). The cumulative impact has been to rebuild a state whose Leviathan-like role in economic life and social affairs under developmentalism had deteriorated to an incapacitated position of extreme weakness by the late 1980s and early 1990s, riddled with conflicts and inefficiencies and incapable of mediating conflicts between contending social and political forces and of building consensus toward a new development model looking forward that was compatible with the country's still-nascent democracy. Surely problems of corruption and malfeasance continue to plague governments at all levels. Yet by the historical yardstick of where the country was in the quite recent past, the progress that has been achieved in rebuilding the state since the mid-1990s is remarkable. There are significant evident synergies between historic progress in fiscal stability, a competitiveness policy that promotes innovation and diversified sectoral transformation, and policies of greater inclusion through transfer payment as well as services that expand human capital.

Of particular note, we stress, is the degree to which the emerging development model reflects a much more mature relationship with organized interests and the citizenry. This relationship involves a new state role of channeling conflict, building consensus, creating spaces of negotiation and consultation around key issues, and seeking finally to join the vibrancy of a dynamic civil society and electoral competition evident for several decades with major strides toward much-delayed social inclusion in more recent years.

A "Social Democratic" Breakthrough?

If we find the major analytical categories that authors apply to contemporary Brazil's development trajectory all wanting—the developmental state or developmentalism (in whatever "neo" guise) or neoliberalism—the question remains, how then can we best categorize and conceptualize this trajectory? In this concluding section, we will consider yet another category or label that analysts sometimes apply to Brazil, particularly under Lula, which is that of "social democracy" or "social democratic" (e.g., Lustig 2009; Sandbrook et al. 2007: 238-42; Castañeda, 2006). Is Brazil experiencing a "social democratic breakthrough?" While it is tempting to make that argument, and the country's recent trajectory bears some important resemblance to hallmarks of social democracy, particularly in its manifestations in the global South (Sandbrook et al., 2007), ultimately we believe that considerable caution must be exercised in applying this concept too readily.

It is important to make some conceptual distinctions here. First, social democracy as a concept (with a small 's' and small 'd') for characterizing a particular model of development or mode of state-society-market relations needs to be distinguished from Social Democratic (with a capital "S" and capital "D") parties, the Socialist International, and other political forces that seek to embrace explicitly that partisan and ideological label and all its historical associations. Objectively, many "social democracies" are not based on the political predominance of parties that use, or even accept, the "Social Democratic" label, or have membership in the Socialist International. In Brazil, the matter is complicated, because the PSDB has claimed that mantle (particular in its "Social Democracy lite," "Third Way" variant à la Tony Blair's New Labour in the UK) despite its lack of organized links to unions or other forces in civil society (long seen as intrinsic to social democracy), and because it has positioned itself in government and opposition more toward the center as opposed to the PT's more center-left stance. While it has long espoused some ill-defined version of "democratic socialism," the PT, for its part, has never accepted the social democratic label and has tried to distinguish itself from both Stalinism and classic, pre-Third Way, European-style Social Democracy, which its sympathizers and militants seem to associate narrowly with a distasteful top-down, bureaucratic, and reformist style of governance. Nonetheless, in terms of the Lula government's orientations in office, and the party's experience in government at subnational levels (e.g., Nylen, 2003), it would seem that the party's efforts to pursue social reforms that advance equality and participation within a framework of democratic capitalism suggest more similarity with what some might see as a "classically social democratic orientation" (in its early phases of deep, broad social reforms) than they themselves recognize or admit.

Moreover, it is also important to make an analytical distinction between party and president, given the tensions that have been evident between party and the executive at times, not to mention PT defections from dissident elements to Lula's left. The party itself still maintains references to socialism as an important unifying ideological element, without many practical translations into programmatic/policy prescriptions, however. Indeed, one might argue, at an analytical level and among Brazilian and perhaps also Brazilianist scholars, the category as a useful, long-standing approach to social scientific inquiry (e.g, Przeworksi, 1985; Esping-Andersen, 1985;

Huber, 2002; Rueschemeyer, Stephens and Stephens, 1992) has unfortunately been spoiled by how the term has been appropriated (or misappropriated) in political praxis, where it is bandied about readily as a simple "label" devoid of deeper analytical content.

Second, it is widely noted that Brazil and other countries in the region and developing world more generally seem to lack the structural prerequisites of social democratic governance—namely, a large industrial working class, organized into strong peak labor confederations (e.g., Roberts, 1998). This makes, it is argued, structurally impossible the links to a programmatic left party (or parties) dedicated to social transformation through economic, social, and political reforms, not to mention the kind of peak bargaining of organization of labor and capital with the state, that used to be quintessential to European social democracy (e.g., Esping-Andersen, 1985; Przeworski, 1985). However, contrasting with these views is the concept of a specific version of social democracy arising historically in certain countries or locations of the global South—peripheral social democracy (Sandbrook et al., 2007). This analytical approach emphasizes the key role that is played, instead, by associations of rural laborers, the urban poor, and other non-industrial proletarians in terms of providing a social base as well as organized sources of continual pressure on reformist and left parties seeking and holding political power and to use the state as a lever for reform. It is in this sense that Sandbrook et al. (2007) argue that Lula's government is "social democratic" (while a "social democratic regime" has not yet emerged, in their view). Of interest in their analysis is the fact that in all the countries or territories to which they apply this label over the course of decades of development, there were *at least two* competing parties who attempted to appeal to an organized, mobilized civil society (typically *none* of which called itself "social democratic") and to occupy what we have called above the "reform space" within the national political universe.

We see important similarities but more fundamental differences between Brazil's recent development and the model of peripheral social democracy on three fronts—its social welfare model, its patterns of interest intermediation and of governing parties' relations with core constituencies. In terms of social policy, the rapidity, depth, and scope of the expansion of social services and benefits, discussed in previous sections, reminds one of periods of rapid inclusionary social reforms in earlier historical moments in the cases discussed by Sandbrook and co-authors, with the attendant rapid increases in performance on social indicators that the authors underline. However, the social programs of today's Brazil are still far from universalistic in coverage or in terms of their underlying principles and indeed ethos of access. They are, for the most part, targeted and means-tested programs, directed at poverty as carefully measured and below certain income thresholds, albeit expanding to larger segments of the poor over time. In this sense, they respond to the critique (not unique to neoliberalism but strongly associated with it) about "welfare state" approaches to social policy that has guided the social policy orientations of international financial institutions and developing country governments across the political spectrum. Institutionally as well as in the political imaginary, Bolsa Familia is a "program for the poor," and not part of some more broadly institutionally comprehensive set of goods and services that near-poor or even middle-class Brazilians can access. This is true even if more poor Brazilians in the rural sector or urban-informal economies have been brought into the social security system and other programs (as discussed above) that were traditionally limited to formal-sector workers. Indeed, what seems to be distinctive about Brazil's conditional cash transfer scheme from other modalities of the same concept of targeted transfers tied to behavioral modification conditionalities for recipients pursued in a range of different countries in the Americas is mostly the generosity and scope of the program as well as its high level of cost-effectiveness.

So, to be sure, there have been gains in universalism as well as coverage and generosity, particularly compared to the highly segmented and stratified social welfare model of the previous era, but Brazil's "welfare state" still remains segmented. This is significant insofar as it potentially undermines social solidarity in the sense that, in a future downturn or under a future government of a different political orientation, citizens from various social classes will not necessarily perceive "a cut in my benefits as a cut in all our benefits." This political logic, key to the underlying social consensus or social contract that tends to underlie a social democratic version of social policy and a welfare state, is still quite lacking in Brazil. There formal-sector entitlement programs and those for the poor are perceived and experienced (because they are administratively structured and politically "packaged") as separate. It is still too early to say, particularly vis-à-vis fickle middle-class Brazilians where Lula's support has waned or among business elites who accept social transfers as long as they do not impact on state finances or growth, that an "inclusionary social contract" has emerged and been consolidated in Brazil.

The differences are also more striking than the similarities with respect to social democratic patterns of interest intermediation, based on mechanisms of inter-group and cross-class consensus building and negotiation and an ethos of class compromise. As noted above, channels for participation of unions, civil society organizations, and business associations in dialogues, and in some cases negotiations, about aspects of economic and social policy have grown under the Lula government. As examples we would cite the Council on Food Security and National Council on Education, Science and Technology. However, tripartite mechanisms of concertation regarding incomes policy, wages, and the like have not been forthcoming, and efforts at labor relations and labor markets—initiated with much fanfare in the first Lula government through extensive tripartite consultation in the National Labor Forum (a tripartite labor-business-government body operating in 1993 and 1994)—proved stillborn as the government backed off them in response to opposition from both within and outside the governing coalition. Those who expected greater high-level negotiation and reform with respect to labor issues have been disappointed. State interaction with organized civil society, while exhibiting the gains in access, transparency, and frequency noted earlier, still reflects a more diffuse pattern of interest intermediation, with multiple and competing channels and points of access and more arms' length pressure, than we would expect from the stronger, more sustained, and more authoritative channels of access to decision-making under social democracy, as characterized by Sandbrook et al. As a national governing party (or more precisely lead force in a multi-party alliance), the PT has become more of a "state party"—and to some extent more of a "catch-all" party and become more distant from its social movement and labor movement roots (see Keck, 1992). This evolution is fed by several converging "streams"—the weakening of its urban-industrial base in the Southeast and perhaps South, the strengthening of its (or rather Lula's) base in the Northeast and North that have disproportionately benefited from its anti-poverty policies mainly because of their greater objective level of poverty, and the tendency for many from the party's "movement base"—labor leaders, activists from urban movements, etc.—to move into executive positions (leading to concerns among some about "loss of cadres" and "subordination of party to state") as well a tendency for many of the groups and associations to face a difficult choice between a certain political subordination to the PT/state or moving into a position of open opposition, dissidence, or splitting off. Some of this is a natural by-product of a party closely tied to organized civil society moving into national power for the first time, yet to some extent it may be questioned whether there has been enough maturity on both sides to maintain an arms-length relationship of mutual respect (which historically the PT and movements managed to maintain through careful institutional separation of roles as the party developed out of movements, rather than vice versa) and respect for the right to combine political support with principled opposition issue by issue.

In sum, Brazil's development trajectory seems to occupy some kind of intermediate space, where perhaps it is appropriate to speak of hybrid categories, but not of it exhibiting, or moving clearly towards, broadly encompassing "models" such as neo-developmentalism or neoliberalism. This does not mean that we adopt a theoretical position that "Brazil can't be compared" because it is so *sui generis*, either generally or contemporarily. Nor should it understate the extent to which we see the emergence and some steps toward the possible consolidation of a new type of state, which takes on an enabling position of moderate, pro-market intervention via competitiveness policy and a much stronger role in providing social services and benefits that is increasingly linked to fostering market inclusion for the previously underserved and excluded and not simply transferring income in targeted fashion to the poor.

Whatever precise terminology might be most appropriate—a debate we seek to open without attempting to resolve here—the final question that calls out for greater analysis are the conditions under which this emerging model can be consolidated or not. Brazil has had two strong presidents with outsized personalities over the past 15 years who have left a big impact, and between the two there are complex patterns of continuity and change, but above all key underlying reform continuities that are frequently not appreciated by analysts or, in particular, political actors. The policies they pursued in office have not necessarily represented uniform, consensual positions within their respective parties, and their policies have reflected complex relations both between executive and governing party as well as between executive and coalition partners within the cabinet and congressional base. This is likely to continue to be the case, and thus much will depend on whether current directions and recent institutional innovations in both economic and social policy will survive electoral succession—whichever party's candidate emerges victorious. The candidates of the two major parties may each have motives for wanting to distance themselves in office from their predecessors of whatever party, and coalitional politics in the next government could become more complex on the left with the existence of opposition candidacies on the PT's left flank. This is all not simply a matter of politics of the state, but also—as we have tried to argue in this essay—politicians' interplay with key constituencies and organizations as well as the electorate and civil society more generally in a more open, democratic context.

5

Crisis and Beyond: Responses and Prospects

Eiiti Sato

Abstract: This chapter argues that prospects of a successful Brazilian economy are good in the short term, but in the long run there are some structural problems to overcome. The main reason is that short term conditions have not been accompanied by long term structural investments. Investments in infrastructure as well as in some key areas of technological development depend on government initiatives. Furthermore, Brazilian economic policy has been remarkably anti-globalization—i. e., against integration to global markets. The chapter explores these structural problems, and concludes that the current world crisis will not greatly change Brazil's chances to benefit from an emerging cycle of growth in the international economic order.

Setting the Problem

The Brazilian government has been optimistic regarding the overall situation of the Brazilian economy. Even analysts from other countries and international organizations have been quite optimistic about the Brazilian capacity to handle the current imbalances and challenges brought about by the world economic crisis. The present analysis argues that the current optimism regarding the Brazilian economy is reasonable only in the short term. In the long run, the perspectives associated with a new cycle of growth do not seem very bright for the Brazilian economy. The main reason for this contrast is that important aspects of the macroeconomic conditions of the Brazilian economy are relatively well balanced, but weaknesses remain in important structural aspects amid increasing international competition. Compared to leading industrial economies as well as to other emerging countries during the last two decades, Brazil did not make the investments in key areas needed to keep up with technological advancements.

Keynesian economic policies can be adequate to manage business cycle variations, and consequently to cope with crises such as the ones that the world economy has been going through since 2008. Nevertheless, a Schumpeterian approach seems to be much more appropriate to understand the overall possibilities for an economy to be successful in the aftermath of a crisis, because history shows that every systemic crisis has been associated with structural changes in the world economy. Keynesian theory is important—even fundamental—to understand the problem of economic equilibrium, but Schumpeter's views are essential to understand the process of economic growth and the succession of long term economic cycles based on structural changes in the world economy.

Peter Drucker summarizes the main differences between these two approaches: the Keynesian view is based on the idea that money and credit (the symbolic economy) are independent and even determine the production and distribution of goods and services (the real economy). The Schumpeterian approach is based on the view that growth and change form an essential dimension of economic life, and as a consequence technological innovation, economic disequilibrium, and crises should be considered as intrinsic components of the economic process (Drucker, 1986: 104).

According to Drucker, in such a process the capacities for innovation and entrepreneurship inevitably produce changes that from time to time appear as a deep crisis. This indicates that a new long cycle of growth based on new patterns of technology is about to start or has already started. In this way Drucker argues that Keynes' approach is really essential to cope with unemployment, inflation, and stagnation or recession—but crises cannot be seen only as momentary imbalances and misbehavior of some economic variables such as inflation, unemployment, or shortage of liquidity. When crises such as the one that affected the world economy in 2008 are deep, anticyclical measures are not enough. It is necessary to look at structural factors related to technological changes and at the mechanisms and institutions through which economic activities are conducted.

Schumpeter says that economic growth is basically a turbulent process (Schumpeter, 1982). Schumpeter's best-known phrase is "creative destruction." As new economic activities are created, they often replace older ones; for example, automobiles replaced horse and carriage transport. The gain represented by new automobile output and the new businesses associated with, as well as the wealth embodied in new homes built in automobile producing areas, is offset by the loss of the horse industry, and its associated businesses and homes. Currently, the difference in environmental impact also would be taken into account in a Schumpeterian accounting of the net gain or loss to an economy from economic growth. Thus, if economic figures show that within a period of time the world GDP has increased by 100%, one cannot simply conclude that the size of the world production has doubled without considering the fact that probably the structure of the world economy has changed too, including products, firms, institutions, and patterns of trade and investments. The economic system should be seen as a dynamic process characterized by the constant interplay of two contradictory forces: on one side most actors are strongly engaged in promoting growth and change, while on the other side, other actors demand order, stability, and the demand for security.

The positive aspects which assure a comfortable position for the Brazilian economy regarding the current problems in the world economy are basically those related to macroeconomic variables: the low rates of inflation, the large amount of foreign reserves, the absence of any significant pressures on the economy generated by foreign debt, and the sense of realism which has prevailed among those who had to manage the Brazilian monetary system during the last decade. Since 1994, when the Real Plan was launched under President Itamar Franco, monetary stabilization has been the most important aspect of economic policy in Brazil, bringing about the many benefits deriving from a more stable and predictable economic environment.[1]

There are very few reasons to think that the immediate aftermath of the world financial crisis will be expressive for Brazil compared to other economies. Nevertheless, in the long run one cannot be so optimistic. Some structural problems regarding the relationship between the government sector and private business still persist, and some of these problems actually have

1. The Real Plan was issued in February of 1994 by president Itamar Franco. It established the real as the Brazilian national currency. The law that established the Real Plan was designed to bring down the high rates of persistent inflation. The Plan included also other measures to assure fiscal balance, a more effective role for the Central Bank in managing liquidity in domestic markets, and the gradual opening of the economy to foreign trade. See http://portalexame.abril.com.br/economia/15-anos-plano-real-seus-protagonistas-481015.html.

been aggravated during the years since the Real Plan was issued and implemented.

This chapter explores these structural problems and shows that the current world crisis will not greatly change the prospects for Brazil no matter how the current crisis affects the international economic order. It indicates the three basic developments that make it difficult for the Brazilian government to issue long term policies: (1) the "fiscal trap," (2) the dominance of political disputes in determining public investments, and (3) the lack of a long term industrial development policy coherent with world trends for goods and services. These problems were made more difficult by anti-globalization sentiments among policy makers.

First, the "fiscal trap" is understood as the imbalance between the rising demand for increasing public expenditure and the insufficiently increasing revenues that therefore do not pay for this expenditure. The demand for increased public expenditure is facilitated by political and judicial systems that drain a great deal of the scarce resources, which should be invested in the modernization of public services. A great deal of expenditures with pensions, and refunds based on alleged unfairness derived from government measures often depends on dubious interpretation of the law. Judicial decisions can also produce unexpected problems in the public revenues by granting tax exemptions also based on dubious legal interpretations. An instructive example is the amount of welfare grants and pensions paid to retired workers and individuals entitled to receive a variety of welfare benefits. This produces a deficit, which is increasing yearly. In 2008, the deficit between the contribution paid by individuals, firms, and other organizations and the pensions and other forms of social welfare disbursement attained R$42.9 billion (almost US$24 billion).[2] For those workers who have retired from public service, figures are even worse. According to Brazilian laws there are several cases in which a retired public officer earns a pension which is higher than the salary paid to an officer in similar position but who is not yet retired.[3]

Second, the dominance of political disputes in determining public investments increased when political power moved from military to civilian hands, and investments in economic development dwindled dramatically.[4] The Military administration's main concern was national economic devel-

2. See http://www.estadao.com.br./estadaodehoje/2010020/no.
3. Figures released by the Ministry of Welfare show that by the end of 2008 there were 6 million people regularly working for the Brazilian state (Federal, State, and Municipal levels), and 3 million retirees and pensioners (Ministério da Previdência Social, 2008: 45).

opment and improvement of social conditions to avoid communism and social unrest. They emphasized investments in infrastructure. The military left power in 1985. Politically, the process of transferring the power from military hands to civilian hands was called "democratization," but, under civilian administrations, political disputes over privileges and preferences of political parties regarding electoral and individual interests rather than the modernization and efficiency of public services determined the allocation of public investment.[5] Public investments dwindled sharply, making harbors, roads, energy plants, and research institutions increasingly inadequate to match the highly dynamic demands of competition in world markets.

Third, the lack of a long-term industrial development policy coherent with world trends for products and services reflects the fact that since the 1980s, the Brazilian government virtually has abandoned investments in technological development. Here the term technological development does not mean R&D (Research and Development) to create new products and new industrial processes. Investments in this area of technological innovation are mainly financed by industrial corporations and by private capital.

In this paper, "technological development" refers to public investments in universities, laboratories, and the many scientific and technical institutions that provide support for industrial activities.[6] It also refers to investments in areas that the government wishes to develop, but in which private capital hardly can play a significant role, such as the development of alternative sources of energy, the improvement of defense industry, and the exploration of outer space technology. Furthermore, biased policies and initiatives can be damaging to industrial development. In 1984, the Brazilian Congress, stimulated by nationalistic sentiments, approved a law by which the import of computers and related products was prohibited for seven years. Exceptions were to be examined by a Special Secretariat attached to the President's Cabinet. Nevertheless, the national computer industry did not develop as much as expected by the government authorities and Brazilian

4. The military seized power in 1964 and remained until 1985. Every military administration—from Castello Branco (1964-67) to João Figueiredo (1979-85)—had issued a "development plan" defining priorities, resources, and strategies to attain development goals.

5. Since 2009, Brazil has 37 Ministries which are distributed basically among Senators and Deputies from political parties which support the president: PT (Political party of the president) holds 17 Ministries; PMDB holds 7; PSB holds 2; PP (Progressive Party), PV (Green Party), PCdoB (Communist Party), PDT (Democratic Labor Party), and PR have one Ministry each. Only seven positions which have Ministry status are held by people who are not clearly engaged in political parties.

6. There is a set of institutions that form a sort of "technological infrastructure" in modern economies. These institutions provide essential services such as preparation of skilled manpower, metrology, protection of intellectual property, laboratories to support scientific and technological cooperation, international certification, participation in joint research programs, etc.

industry was severely affected, becoming outdated, and the economy as a whole lost competitiveness.[7] Restrictive policies such as the one implemented in the mid 1980s prohibiting the importation of products like computers in order to develop a national industry have been abandoned since the 1990s.

These three problems together created a social and economic environment that became more likely to foster stagnation instead of creativity and innovation. Even in areas like the production and use of ethanol and other biofuels, Brazil is a follower rather than a leader. Furthermore, the technology used to produce bio-fuels is an old technology, and is not a new alternative for the future, because the technology is essentially the same as the one used in engines powered by gasoline or diesel from petroleum. The main research centers worldwide are now developing new concepts of engines, and also are under pressure to develop new technologies more adequate to large populations, particularly in countries like China and India, which are facing the challenge of providing large scale increases in their consumption without damaging the environment too much.[8] The anti-globalization sentiments among policy makers had mixed effects on the Brazilian economy. Brazil had less integration into global financial markets than many other nations not only because of its longstanding inflationary experience, state oriented views of the bureaucracy, and nationalism, but also because monetary authorities in Brazil have constructed a domestic financial regime favoring control rather than free flow of capital. Consequently, Brazil did not get many of the benefits derived from the soaring financial markets of the fifteen years previous to the crisis. On the other hand, Brazil did not suffer many consequences of the 2008 crisis when the falling prices of financial assets hit the more globalized economies, because to a large extent the country had stayed relatively apart from the global financial competition.

Macroeconomic Variables and Keynesian Policies

When 2009 was ending, the worst moment of the world financial crisis seemed to have already passed, and stabilization and growth was slowly

7. See the analysis of the Brazilian computer industry in mid 1980s presented by C. Frischtak in Rushing, Francis W. and Brown ed. (1986: 31-69).

8. Analysts say that the Conference of Copenhagen was a failure because no significant agreement was attained, but it showed largely enough that environment has moved to the forefront of the issues the world is concerned with. The United Nations Climate Change Conference (COP-15, Dec. 7-18th, 2009) brought to Copenhagen presidents and prime ministers from more than a hundred countries and registered more than 25,000 participants from almost every country in the world.

becoming a prospect even for the US, Japan, and large European economies. Nevertheless, it was not yet clear whether such a prospect of stabilization and growth was part of a new emerging long cycle of growth, or was a simple succession of random growth bubbles derived from Keynesian policies implemented by governments to cope with falling markets and unemployment.

Brazil was one of the economies least affected by the consequences of the financial crisis. Growth halted and unemployment increased but not as much as in countries like the US, Japan, Germany, and most emerging economies. In the first quarter of 2009 among emerging market economies, only China, India, and Indonesia did not suffer a reduction in their GDP. Brazilian GDP fell by 1.8%, but the figure was pretty small when compared to Japan (-8.8%), Germany (-6.9%), France (-3.2%), the US (-2.6%), Mexico (-8.6%), and South Korea (-4.3%)(UNCTAD, 2009). In former crises the overall situation was the reverse, i.e., Brazil usually suffered the consequences of any turbulence that was taking place in the world economy much more than did major economies. Two main reasons can be pointed out to explain the relatively good condition of the Brazilian economy on the eve of the 2008 financial crisis: the soundness of the main macroeconomic variables, and the relatively low level of integration to the world economy.

Since the oil crisis in the 1970s, the Brazilian economy went through a long period of persistent inflation and economic instability. Only the implementation of the Real Plan in 1994 created the basic conditions for a stable monetary system necessary to produce an economic environment more appropriate to foster business, investments, and foreign trade. By the end of 2002 when Mr. Lula da Silva was about to start his first term as president of Brazil, there was a great concern that his administration would abandon the Real Plan and monetary stability as a crucial part of the economic policy for the country. Fortunately this did not happen and when the 2008 financial crisis came about, the Brazilian economy had already accumulated some important assets. A persistent balance of payments surplus has permitted an increase in foreign reserves to more than US$200 billion, which meant that the level of reserves was higher than the total foreign liabilities. Furthermore the largest part of such liabilities already had been well negotiated during the late years of the Cardoso administration, which ended in 2002. The negotiations established a very comfortable schedule that virtually eliminated the pressures represented by foreign debt.[9]

9. According to official figures provided by Brazilian Central Bank in December 2008, the Brazilian reserves were around US$205 billion while foreign debt totaled US$195.8 billion from which only 22% referred to short-term bonds.

Another important reason for the good condition of the Brazilian economy in 2008 is that since the Real Plan was issued in 1994, monetary policy has given a strong support to the banking system. Except for the turbulences of a few months associated with the 1999 reform of the Real Plan, the Brazilian economy had already enjoyed a period of stability for almost 15 years.[10]

Historically, the Brazilian banking system has been essentially private and even the state owned banks have been bound to follow the same rules applied to private banks: both suffered little influence and pressure from the government authorities. The main privileges assigned to public banks have been the current accounts of government agencies and funds owned by public companies that are allocated to public banks.

The Brazilian monetary crisis of 1999 shook the national financial system by severely reducing the value of bonds, stocks, and other financial assets. Nevertheless, the government response was quite effective. A large program of mergers and acquisitions was produced under the sponsorship of the Federal Government. It provided enough funds, and new rules were issued to make the banking system safer and less vulnerable to variations in the business cycle. The reform of the banking system of 1999 avoided panic, financial assets very quickly regained the confidence of the public, and profits of banks continued high. It is possible to say that banks and other financial institutions actually did not suffer any critical harm from the 1999 Brazilian monetary crisis, but rather gained maturity and increased their importance to the national economy as a whole. The overall result was that the Brazilian economy became more stable and inflation went down consistently to a level of one digit per year.[11]

During these years the interest rate in the Brazilian financial market remained much higher than in any other stable economy, attracting domestic and foreign capital. By December 2005, the interest rate managed by Brazilian Central Bank was 18.0% while the inflation rate was only 5.69%. When the world financial crisis broke out in mid 2008, the interest rate in Brazil was still very high (12.92%).[12] A considerable part of the assets of the banking system was composed of Brazilian Treasury bonds issued to finance

10. When the Real Plan was issued in 1994 the exchange rate was fixed (R$1.00 = US$1.00), and was allowed to oscillate within a narrow band. The exchange rate was considered as the "anchor" to keep economic stability. By the Real Plan reform in 1999, the Central Bank abandoned the system to the US dollar, adopted a floating exchange rate system, and the interest rate managed by the National Monetary Committee became the basic instrument to cope with inflationary pressures.

11. From 1990 to 1994 (included) the inflation rate in Brazil was very high (764.0% per year). The *Real* Plan brought the inflation down to the level of 8.6% (average 1995-2000), and in 2005 inflation registered was 5.69% (*O Globo*, 2006: 27).

12. Figures are released by Brazilian Central Bank (http://www.bcb.gov.br/?copomjuros).

public debt. These bonds were very safe assets, especially when compared to the US sub-prime market. Under such a circumstance the interest rate put some pressure on the public debt, but at the same time it acted as a sort of guarantee for the banks by providing a good profit within a stable and safe environment for financial assets. As a result, one can say that for almost a decade before the 2008 financial crisis the Brazilian banking system earned enough profit to be able to meet the turbulences and downturns of business cycles without great concern. Furthermore, the high interest rates could be reduced considerably, thus serving as an additional and effective instrument of monetary policy to offset the recession produced by the world crisis.

The evolution of foreign trade also was favorable to the Brazilian economy. The two decades of persistent growth of the world economy have permitted an increase of exports to both traditional and emerging markets. Traditional markets such as the US and Europe were joined by emerging markets from Asia and from other regions, substantially increasing the demand for industrial goods as well as for commodities. In such an environment of growing demand, the size and diversification of the Brazilian economy allowed the nation to benefit from world economic growth. On the other hand, the Brazilian economy had a long tradition of restricting imports by taxation and by exchange rate mechanisms. The relatively low level of imports combined with an increasing demand for the nation's exports gave the Brazilian economy a consistent trade surplus, increasing foreign reserves to a level that made its foreign debt almost irrelevant. Even the soaring prices of oil in world markets in the years previous to the 2008 crisis did not represent a substantial pressure on Brazil's balance of payments, because in recent years domestic oil production has increased enough to meet domestic consumption.

Despite the fact that foreign trade increased substantially during the last decade, it did not lead to a strong dependence on trade to promote stability and growth. Foreign trade still represents only 1/5 of the Brazilian GDP.[13] Particularly since president Lula da Silva inaugurated his first term in 2003, most critics of the Brazilian economic policy have been arguing that the sluggish performance of the Brazilian economy, when compared to other emerging countries, was due to a hesitant attitude regarding integration to world markets. Their argument is that Brazilian economic growth strategy has been too much inward looking, despising the dynamism of world mar-

---

13. World trade figures show that Brazilian participation in world merchandise exports remained roughly at the same level since the 1980s (1.2% in 1983, 1.0% in 1993; and 1.3% in 2008) just following the rate of growth of the world trade (*WTO Statistics 2009*, Table I.6).

kets.[14] Critics also say that politics and ideology have been inappropriately dominant in commercial policy that gives too much importance to trade agreements with poor economies rather than to the main world markets. Generally trading with poor economies is difficult, expensive, and produces small results when compared to large world markets. Nevertheless expectations are that these countries give their support to Brazilian government demand for a permanent seat in the United Nations Security Council. In fact fiscal mechanisms protected Brazilian domestic markets from other economies which were much more productive and competitive. Consequently, Brazil was not forced to increase its productivity to meet efficient competitors from these economies, and trading with poor countries reduces the need for productivity and competitiveness.

During the last two decades the rates of growth of other emerging economies—particularly from Asia—were substantially higher than that of Brazil. Countries like South Korea, Chile, and Mexico, frequently are mentioned as good examples of countries that have adopted a desirable strategy of economic growth with a strong integration into the world economy. Their economies have been severely impacted by the 2008 financial crisis. Ironically such a low level of integration to the world economy became an asset for Brazil: in the short run, the Brazilian domestic market was large enough to reduce the effect of the world recession. In this regard, the case of the car industry can be instructive. Due to the relatively low level of dependence on world markets, Brazil's simple tax reduction on vehicles and auto parts avoided a recession in this quite influential industrial sector.[15] In other sectors that are more dependent on exports such as mining, shoes, and commodities, the effects of the world recession could not be avoided.

Despite Brazil's success in mitigating the short-term effects of the 2008 financial crisis, in the long run the nation's prospects are not so positive. Brazil probably will not become a leading economy in the near future. Important investments in economic infrastructure as well as in science and technology are essential to raise productivity and competitiveness; they

14. In 1983, China's share of the world exports was similar to Brazil's share (1.2%) but in 2008 China's share of the world exports had attained 9.1% and South Korea's share increased from 0.5% to 2.6% (*idem*).

15. The figures released by the Brazilian Association of Producers of Cars and other Vehicles (ANFAVEA) show that in the first four months of 2009 the exports of cars, other vehicles, and auto parts have dropped by almost 50% when compared with the same period of 2008. Nevertheless exports represent only about 20% of the total sales of the car industry in Brazil. This fact explains why a tax reduction was a measure enough to stimulate domestic demand to fairly offset the decrease in foreign demand (http://www.anfavea.com.br/tabelas.html).

have been neglected systematically for more than a score of years. In the past public investments were essential, for example, to establish the steel industry and to create a national airplane industry. Even in agriculture public investments were essential to develop varieties of crops well fitted to Brazilian climate and soil; and to combat plagues to make Brazilian agriculture efficient and competitive.[16]

Crisis: The Long-Term Prospects

History shows that in modern times Schumpeter's analysis is correct: after every deep crisis the dynamism in the world economy reappears based on new technological patterns. It is not the case that war and crises are the best stimuli for innovation, but just simply an observation that after deep crises and great wars lots of innovations have appeared. This happened after the great depression of the 1930s, and it occurred also after the oil crisis of the 1970s that brought about the third world debt crisis of the early 1980s but also stimulated competition and innovation particularly in information, transport, and communication technologies. There is no reason to suppose that the aftermath of the current crisis of globalization will be different in general, but specific new trends are increasingly apparent. These are: (1) the relative weight of the economies that were small when international economic rules were established in the 1940s and 1950s is likely to be better represented in the world regimes and institutions; (2) international regimes probably will be more robust and binding, particularly regarding world financial transactions; (3) the new economy which has been emerging since the end of the last century is going green, i.e. more technologies are being created or transformed fostered by concerns with environmental impacts. These trends are particularly important to a country such as Brazil whose interests are various and worldwide.

Economies in World Regimes

There is a widespread consensus regarding the fact that institutions and practices, which were designed after the 1930s crisis and World War II, pro-

16. The CSN (Companhia Siderúrgica Nacional), the first steel industry in Brazil, and the CTA (Technological Center of the Brazilian Air Force), essential to the national airplane industry, were established in the aftermath of the World War II. The EMBRAPA (State Company for Research in Agriculture) was established in 1972 under the military regime. Simon Schwartzman gives a comprehensive view of the main facts and investments in science and technology in Brazil in the 20th century (S. Schwartzman, 2001).

duced a long period of a relatively peaceful world as well as of economic growth without parallel in the history of modern times. To a large extent these achievements were products of an international economic order that reflected a particular hierarchy among nations. While traditional European powers dwindled economically, politically the overwhelming power of the US was central to molding the emerging new world. The Cold war represented a remarkable feature of the world politics for decades, and in many aspects the cold war bipolarity reinforced the primacy of the US's economic power. The Soviet Union, while competing with the US in ideological and strategic terms, left free room for the US's predominance in the world economy. Even the process of European integration was fueled by the US capacity to finance trade and reconstruction. For example, in the late 1940s and early 1950s the Marshall Plan had played an important role in this process. Available figures show that in early 1950s the GNP of the US was bigger than the GNP of the other six great powers altogether, and the two Conferences which have settled the basis of the peace after the end of the war were attended by the "Big Three" referring to the US, Britain, and the Soviet Union.[17] The establishment of the main post-war institutions largely reflected that particular distribution of wealth and power.[18]

Nevertheless, the world scene has changed substantially. The cold war is gone, and due to the fact that economic growth is essentially an uneven process in the long run, the world distribution of wealth and power also has changed substantially.[19] As a consequence, similarly to Britain's economic history in the late nineteenth century, after the 1960s the US economy continued to grow, but its rates of growth were much lower than in other regions.

At the time of the Bretton Woods Conference in 1944[20] the US Treasury possessed more than 70% of the world gold reserves, and the arrangements that were settled at the Conference reflected these figures.[21] Benefited by the US views on world security and economic strategies, Western European

17. According to Paul Kennedy, in 1950 the GNP of the US was US$381 billion while the GNP of Britain, France, Italy, West Germany, Japan, and the USSR together totaled only US$356 billion (Kennedy, 1988: 475).

18. The United Nations dates from 1945; the Bretton Woods institutions, 1944; the GATT, 1947; the NATO, 1949. Other institutions created in the 1950s even at the regional level in Europe and elsewhere were also strongly influenced by the world economic and political scene in which the leadership of the US was an essential factor.

19. In the late 1950s "development theories" became an increasingly popular issue among economists and one of the more influential though criticized book was The Stages of Growth written by W. W. Rostow who argued that the US was the only economy which had at that time attained the 5th stage (mass consumption economy) but any other country could follow the track and attain the same level of industrial production of the US (W. W. Rostow, 1960).

20. Henry Nau gives a large account of the central role played by the US in the post-war era (Nau, 1990).

countries regained momentum and were followed by Japan. In twenty years time they reconstructed their economies and modernized their industries and became serious competitors with the US in terms of economic efficiency. Later other economies, particularly in Asia, followed the same path. Even in Latin America some poles of growth and modernization showed up. It is very symbolic that by the end of the 1950s the US gold reserves had dropped to less than 50% of the world gold reserves.

Many other facts and figures show the many changes that took place in the patterns of distribution of wealth and power. Currently most of the international regimes in both political and economic matters no longer reflect the weight of countries and regions in the world scenario. As a consequence, the agenda of international organizations frequently is outdated or simply does not fit the interests of governments and societies. Another consequence is that many important international issues have been negotiated and managed outside of the institutions created by the Bretton Woods agreement. Initiatives such as the G-8, the G-20, and the Global Economic Forum, as well as bilateral talks and meetings for specific purposes, became more frequent and more effective in world diplomacy. The OAS and the World Bank lost momentum, and the IMF and the GATT substantially changed their purposes and modes of operation.

The interaction between political and economic conditions led Brazil to attempt to play a more significant role in the regional and world politics and economy. Particularly in South America, the size and the weight of Brazil became increasingly important in shaping the process of regional integration. Nonetheless, Brazil is aware that it has frontier lines with every South American country except Ecuador and Chile, and potentially populist leaderships always tend to elect a foreign country as the enemy to be blamed for any failure in domestic politics. Since the 19th century in various circumstances, Brazil was identified as a regional imperial power to be checked by Spanish speaking neighbors.[22]

21. In early 1960s Robert Triffin wrote a thoughtful paper raising the problem of the stability of the Bretton Woods dollar based monetary system in an environment of declining gold reserves of the US Treasury (Triffin, 1960).

22. A permanent concern of Rio Branco, who commanded Brazilian foreign policy between 1902 and 1912, was largely focused on how to avoid an imperialist label for the country. Even before 1902 Rio Branco had occasion to show that discretion and low profile politics should be more adequate to live peacefully in the region. After his victorious performance in the territorial arbitration process in Washington between Brazil and Argentina in 1894, Rio Branco decided not to go to Rio de Janeiro on his way to London where he occupied a diplomatic position. He knew that his countrymen had prepared a big celebration for him: "He did not accept the invitation to come to Brazil to be honored by his countrymen. For him such an homage looked like an unnecessary public exhibition and a discourtesy to Zeballos (the Argentinian negotiator) and to Argentina," wrote Álvaro Lins (Lins, 1962: 213).

At the global level the scenario for Brazilian diplomacy is also blurred and the issue of reform of the United Nations (UN) is very instructive: the possibility of Brazil becoming a really influential power in the world system has to be seen against an unpredictable interplay of ambiguous and rather contradictory forces. Domestically most critics of Brazilian diplomacy argue that the country has been wasting too much time and energy by fighting for a permanent seat in the UN Security Council and by trying to be a leader of the developing world. Furthermore resources available for foreign policy are too scarce to support large and expensive commitments in the international arena, and it is not clear yet to what extent such an involvement with world politics will effectively help the promotion of Brazilian interests.

A World of Robust International Regimes

To a large extent the recent world financial crisis can be understood as another product of the mismatch between the existing regimes and the new actors and new technological patterns which have substantially changed the ways of doing business in the world economy. The succession of trade cycles and crises in the 20th century has shown that freedom to create opportunities for gains must be balanced by international norms to prevent predatory competition. With respect to this phenomenon it seems instructive to look at history to assess current concerns regarding the international financial regime that present some parallels relative to what had happened in the post-war years.

The Bretton Woods Conference is generally associated with post-war reconstruction. The participants of the Conference were concerned with what to do when the war came to an end. The main concerns underpinning the Bretton Woods negotiations had their origins in the 1920s hyperinflation and the 1930s economic downfall; reconstruction and growth were not the prime concern.[23]

Basically the 1929 collapse was an unprecedented experience. The bitter memories left by the 1930s crisis included the perception that the volatility of the financial system exacerbated the falling markets instead of dampening their causes and effects. Governments and economists were still completely lacking in experience, monetary authorities did not have any instrument to address financial crises before this time, and the pre-Keynesian theories did not include any role for the government. The fact is that the

23. See de Vries (1972). Particularly regarding US/UK negotiations within the Conference see Gardner (1956) (Kindleberger, 1987: 117-96).

widespread view among economic authorities and analysts at the time of Bretton Woods Conference was that the "herd behavior" of the financial agents was crucial to the process by which the 1930s crisis virtually went out of control. In their view the "herd behavior" derived essentially from the unregulated markets of stocks, bonds, and other financial assets. Charles P. Kindleberger gives a detailed account of the process by which the 1929 crash turned into a depression showing that a succession of "panics" in different areas and different moments shrinking bank deposits and credits, cutting the prices of commodities, and reducing confidence in financial assets had led finally to the generalized crisis through the 1930s.

Purposes and Goals

The Bretton Woods Conference took place in July 1944, but did not become operative until 1959, when all the European currencies became convertible. Under this system, the IMF and the IBRD were established. The IMF was developed as a permanent international body. The summary of agreements states, "The nations should consult and agree on international monetary changes which affect each other. They should outlaw practices which are agreed to be harmful to world prosperity, and they should assist each other to overcome short-term exchange difficulties."

Against such a background it seems easy to understand why the establishment of a stable monetary system was associated with mechanisms to control the flow of capital. The Bretton Woods arrangements established that governments could manage large capital flows among countries. International private capital flow should be restricted to direct investments and to bonds issued under the supervision of governments and institutions such as the World Bank. In short, what Bretton Woods did regarding financial flows was replace the free flow of capital regime for a regime based on regulation and control.

Similarly one can say that today the free flow of capital regime is about to be replaced by mechanisms designed to limit and to control the flow of money among financial markets. Even in the heyday of the Bretton Woods system there were leakages in the international financial flow regime, such as the Eurodollar market that started to grow in the 1950s. All European currencies became convertible in 1959. During the 1970s, the financial regime established following the Bretton Woods agreements became unsustainable and started to be changed dramatically. Two landmarks in such a process are the abandonment of the convertibility of the US dollar to gold, and the formation of a huge petrodollar market. The deregulation of the financial system was fuelled not only by savings from oil markets but also by new technologies that created opportunities for business and gains based on the increasing world wide integration of financial markets.

The 1980s are called "the lost decade" because of its slow economic growth and financial crises. Although none of these crises produced a systemic impact on the world economy because they did not threaten central economies to an extent that would force them to change their institutions and practices (Stiglitz, 2003).[24]

The title of Joseph Stiglitz' book—*The Roaring Nineties: a New History of the World's Most Prosperous Decade*—reveals the widespread perception regarding the remarkable performance of the world economy. Actually, looking back now it seems quite clear that there were many fragilities in the financial markets, but no one can deny that in an environment in which fortunes were mushrooming any critical comment would sound really awkward. Alan Greenspan was one of those who had made critical comments regarding financial markets, but obviously due to his position as president —or even as former president—of the US Federal Reserve System he could not say too much without provoking a "herd behavior" reaction in the market.[25] In such an environment in which a great deal of individuals, firms, and nations were getting richer, one can hardly think that anyone would propose any kind of change for the financial regime, especially to limit and to control the flow of funds.

The 2008 financial crisis brought about a radical change in the perceptions of opportunities and financial flows. The dominant new perception was that together with emergency rescue measures, governments and international organizations should produce mechanisms to limit and control the size and reduce the volatility of capital flows by providing a set of rules and norms with the necessary means to assure the compliance of individuals, firms, and governments. These norms and rules should fall not only on the process of issuing bonds, stocks, and other forms of financial assets which are traded, but also on the institutions and their procedures, particularly on stock exchanges, banks, and monetary institutions.[26]

---

24. From 1990 to 2005 world trade increased by a consistent rate of 6% yearly and the world production around 2.5% a year (statistics from WTO reports). From 2003 to 2007 the average increase of the world production was 3.3% a year, and the world exports were increasing by a rate of 7.6% per year (UNCTAD, 2009).

25. Alan Greenspan was the president of the Federal Reserve System from 1987 to 2006.

For a long time the world financial market included a relatively small number of financial centers—basically the US, main European economies, and Japan—but globalization from the 1980s onwards brought into the world market tens of emerging economies in which bonds and stocks could be issued, bought, and sold. As a consequence, opportunities have increased but risks and sources of instability also increased, and the world financial market became more anarchical.

Before the crisis broke out some isolated measures to control the flow of capital were taken by countries as Chile and Brazil, but isolated measures in an anarchical environment tend to produce very limited effects, particularly on small economies.

Banks and financial institutions operating in countries where authorities permit individuals and firms to keep secret accounts under the argument of privacy are a target of more regulation and control. These financial institutions, known as "fiscal havens," as well as the governments which shelter them, have been under siege since terrorism went to the forefront of the international political agenda. The fiscal havens also have been used to facilitate drug-dealing, corruption, smuggling, and to all sorts of illicit practices. They are essential instruments for transferring funds and keeping laundered money. The 2008 financial crisis gave an additional push to tighten the siege on "fiscal havens" because the amount of illicit money was soaring and regulation hardly can separate money from legal and illegal origins. Both can influence financial markets. Even countries such as Switzerland, where the banking system had a longstanding tradition of keeping secret accounts are changing their laws.

Currently, initiatives of cooperation to create mechanisms of regulation of the financial markets are on the way in most international organizations. These negotiations reflect the increasing multipolarity of the world economy. In the last decades, the emergence of Asia is only a highlight of a more complex and profound change in the structure of the international economic order.[27]

---

26. The *Pittsburgh Summit of the G-20* (Sept. 24-25/2009) produced a statement in which the necessity of a more robust international regime for banking and financial operations is stressed several times. Various measures were suggested ranging from regular meetings of the G-20 to the establishment of international bodies such as the Financial Stability Board (FSB) to enhance the grip capacity of the international economic cooperation framework.

27. In the early 1980s, US exports represented 12% of the world exports, Germany's 9%, and China's only 1%; in 2005, the US exports reduced their participation to 8.9%, Germany's increased to 10.5%, and China's increased to 7.5%, becoming the third largest exporter. South Korea is another instructive case: from almost negligible participation in the world exports in the early 1980s, the nation increased its participation to more than 2.5% overtaking by far countries such as Brazil and Mexico (WTO, 2007).

Earlier attempts to change the trade aspects of the international economic order suggest that when coordination in the international level becomes difficult a more binding regime tends to appear. When the GATT was created in the late 1940s the US economy was largely dominant. To foster international trade the first initiative was to create an International Trade Organization (ITO). It was to be an organization rather similar to the World Trade Organization (WTO) of our times. William Diebold in an essay published in the early 1950s—just after the decision taken by the US authorities to abandon the ITO—showed that the ITO seemed too binding to the US interests, who replaced it by the GATT (Diebold, 1952). It is interesting to note that the 52 countries other than the US which signed the Havana Charter establishing the ITO in 1948 did not say anything or take any initiative when the ITO was buried.

Forty years later the US largely had lost its predominance over other economies, and during the Uruguay Round (1986-94) trade negotiations had reached a complete deadlock. The US, the European powers, and even some emerging economies had different views about several issues regarding trade. In the end the stalemate was broken on January 1, 1995 by creating the World Trade Organization (WTO) which was weaker than the former ITO. The WTO was called "the GATT with teeth" meaning that the trade regime became more binding. This, and other developments making requirements for economic and financial reporting similar among nations, suggests that globalization is progressing by establishing binding regimes based on cooperation and compliance.

Another reason why Brazil did not suffer much from the 2008 crisis is because to a large extent the country had stayed relatively apart from global financial competition. For many reasons monetary authorities in Brazil have constructed a domestic financial regime favoring control rather than free flow of capital. Brazil's long inflationary experience, its tradition of state oriented views of the bureaucracy, and its nationalism are among the more important reasons. In this way it seems that a more binding regime with norms and rules can fit the Brazilian experience much better than the free market regime.

CLEAN TECHNOLOGIES: THE EMERGING PATTERN FOR INDUSTRY AND ENERGY

Economists interpret technological changes as cyclical, i.e. when some remarkable technological innovation occurs, industry and many forms of economic activity also change, creating new products and processes, and defining new patterns for markets and opportunities.[28] The first stages of the industrial revolution created the necessary conditions for the European and the US expansion in the 19th century based on a largely liberal economy. Actually the US had considerable intervention in the economy at the State level, and there was Federal action to provide infrastructure, such as railroads, and intermittent Federal and State granting of charters and regulation of banking. Nevertheless these interventions differed from actions taken after the 1930s crisis and World War II. It seems enough to mention the fact that in the 1930s government revenues in the US represented only 4.5% of the GDP, and that after the New Deal experience government revenues increased consistently and continuously to achieve nowadays 1/4 of the GDP.[29] Furthermore, the nature of government intervention in the economy during the New Deal included the creation of various agencies and financial mechanisms to give the population widespread instruments of welfare, incentives to industrial innovation, investments in urban development, etc.

The New Deal focused on domestic needs. US policy increasingly dealt with international needs, beginning in the 1940s. In 1970, the US became a net importer of oil, and the soaring prices of oil in the 1970s led to the transfer of huge amounts of savings amassed by oil exporting economies to private financial markets. Banks and other private financial institutions had their safe boxes full of money—notably petrodollars—and governments, particularly from indebted third world countries, started to borrow heavily from private banks. Deregulation of capital flow emerged as a natural solution.

The difficulties derived from the oil crisis led to the adoption of new strategies of economic development by individuals, corporations, and state owned organizations. These led to new technologies for computers, information flow, and transport.

28. The classical author regarding this view is obviously Joseph Schumpeter (1911) who inspired most approaches which give importance to technology as a factor of development and economic growth. Among such authors are Peter Drucker and Michael Porter. See Schumpeter, 1982.

29. Statistical figures available in the page of the Executive Office of the President of the United States. GPO Access. See http://gpoaccess.gov/eop/tables08.html.

Capital markets also flourished not only based on petrodollars but also on the possibilities opened by new information technology that permitted integration of the main world stock markets in real time. These developments benefitted Asian nations more than Brazil and other Latin American nations that did not actively take part in the globalization process.[30]

A new aspect of international trade is the search for new patterns for products and production processes that have less damaging effects on the environment. These are needed because the patterns of consumption currently existing in affluent societies cannot be extended to hundreds of millions of people without provoking an exhaustion of essential raw materials and serious environmental problems. For example, if only in China and India every year 2% of their population are integrated to the global standard of middle class, every year there will be some additional 20 million cars running (equivalent to almost the automobile fleet of a country like Brazil), consuming fuels, discarding used tires and other auto parts, and discharging a quantity of pollutant gas into the atmosphere. The same kind of argument can be applied to other aspects which compose the standard of living in terms of desirable comforts: food, clothing, air transportation, personal hygiene, education, leisure, etc. More than half of the world population still has a standard of living well below that of a typical middle class Western nation. For example, the carbon dioxide (CO_2) per capita emissions in industrial societies are at least five times higher than the average of developing economies.[31] Nevertheless, there is a widespread consensus that it is a legitimate demand of any society for individuals to have access to all goods and facilities which are available to people living in modern societies.

Another source of pressure to change technology is the desire for economic security. To a large extent a modern standard of living still relies on oil and other non-renewable natural resources that are unevenly distributed among regions and countries. While wealthy industrial societies such as Germany and Japan are lacking in some essential raw materials, other economies—such as most members of OPEC—have large reserves of natural resources but do not have the economic infrastructure needed to produce industrial goods from these resources. Since the 1970s the perspectives of

30. In 1983, South and Central America represented 4.4% of the world merchandise exports, and in 2007 the share of South and Central America dropped to only 3.7%. In the same period Asia (Japan not included) more than doubled its share of the world merchandise exports from 11.1% in 1983 to 22.7% (*WTO Statistics 2008*, Table I.6).

31. According to UNCTAD, in 2006 the per capita carbon dioxide discharged into atmosphere every year in industrialized countries was equivalent to 10.9 tons while in India the individual carbon dioxide emission was only 1.1 tons (UNCTAD, 2009: 136).

natural resources shortage, particularly petroleum, have been haunting the world economy, and the fears of shortage of an essential commodity such as oil recently worsened due to an increasing nationalism and religious fundamentalism in the Middle East. In such an environment industrial countries have been strongly stimulated to develop products and forms of energy less dependent on petroleum coming from unstable states easily influenced by political forces resistant to international integration.

Against this political and economic background, large and well-funded research programs in the field of production and use of energy have been developed for wind, solar, and all forms of alternative energy, as well as for all means to reduce the consumption and to increase the efficiency of industrial plants, equipment, and even architectural design. The leading countries in such efforts have been the US, Japan, and Western European countries. They are investing heavily in developing the use of solar energy despite the fact that they are geographically situated in regions poorly gifted with sunlight, while China is dramatically increasing its investments in clean energy.[32]

The same concern regarding energy production and consumption can be seen in terms of reducing the waste by recycling and management of industrial by-products and discarded objects and materials. In the long run the life in large cities will be virtually unbearable unless some changes are introduced in the current patterns of consumption.

In many ways international regimes already reflect these concerns. Trade regimes have introduced environmental clauses basically derived from commercial controversies involving fishing, forest products, and from various forms of waste production and discard. Allegations of protectionism hidden behind environmental arguments should be considered as effective in some specific cases, but the dominant view in the international community is that by any means environment protection at large should be included in the every day life of the world population. Environmental clauses are already included in trade regimes and it seems likely to expect that other international regimes will also move in the same direction. Brazil, however, has kept a predominantly defensive attitude in most negotiation forums, arguing that allegations regarding environmental requirements and intellectual property rights are hidden forms of protectionism of industrial countries.

32. China, which has been pointed out as a leading economy for the next decades, is also increasing dramatically investments in clean energy. F. Zakary states that today China has the largest investment program in clean energy mainly solar technology (Zakaria, 2008).

Domestically, the volume of R&D investments in most areas of alternative sources of energy have been small in both private and public organizations, suggesting that in the emerging cycle of growth Brazil is bound to lag behind other nations.

In the next pages this essay concludes by attempting to capture some of the trends in the Brazilian economy vis-à-vis the perspectives that seem to be emerging from a new cycle of growth in the world economy.

BRAZIL AND THE NEW CYCLE OF GROWTH IN THE WORLD ECONOMY

Brazil and the Management of Short-term Problems

As discussed in the early pages of this essay, Brazil went through the 2008 crisis much better than most countries. Inflationary pressures were low and the domestic financial market did not depend heavily on international bonds and stocks that were turning sour. Domestic public debt was relatively high (around 50% of the GDP) but for years it had been quite well managed in financial terms, and it has been an important support for the banking system to go through the crisis. Moreover, unlike banks in many other nations, Brazilian banks had a great part of their assets in very safe Federal Treasury bonds.

This supports the predominantly positive views of Brazilian economic policy that are held even by those who criticize president Lula da Silva's administration. Those who are more optimistic tend to see the crisis as a threshold of a new era in which Brazil will play a role as an important power in the world scene. Nevertheless, when we look at structural conditions instead of focusing on macroeconomic variables of the Brazilian economy, the outlook for the near future indicates only a limited benefit for Brazil in a new cycle of economic growth, because of its limited investment in technology and modernization.

Bad Management: Inadequate Infrastructure

There are visible deficits in almost every sector of Brazil's economic infrastructure. Transportation systems are not only insufficient; the poor quality of roads, services, and equipment can be observed everywhere. In a large country like Brazil, transportation of goods and people is essential to link regions, markets, and the different phases of the production process. For example, in a large city like São Paulo public transportation is very precarious and instead, people use their own cars. As a consequence, the everyday life of the population is plagued by horrific traffic jams in which hundreds of thousands of people waste their time, and tons of unnecessarily burned fuel are discharged into the atmosphere. In this way a comparison between Greater London and São Paulo is instructive. The area of both cities is approximately 1,550 km^2, but the population of São Paulo is substantially larger: São Paulo has a population of 11 million inhabitants while Greater London has a population of 7.5 million inhabitants. São Paulo has the best metro system among Brazilian cities, nevertheless when compared to London the differences are dramatic. By the end of 2009, the São Paulo metro system had only 61.3 km of rails uniting 55 metro stations while the London underground system was around 400 km long and had 270 stations so that, unlike São Paulo, in London people can go everywhere in the city without using their own car.[33]

A more accurate account of the high costs of the losses derived from the poor infrastructure of a city like São Paulo includes other effects that are the result of precarious infrastructure, such as frequent floods even when the rains are not so heavy, and car crashes in numbers far above the figures of industrial countries with a proportionally greater number of vehicles. Obviously the list is too long to be presented, but it seems enough to say that inadequate infrastructure leads to waste, environmental damages, additional costs, and low productivity. In fact, since the 1970s any significant investment has been done only to cope with some kind of imminent collapse.

Technological Development in the Emerging Cycle of Growth

The sources and uses of energy in Brazil may define its ability to control its economic growth. Brazil imports electricity and natural gas. The need to secure these resources influences government loans to supplying nations, adjustments in prices for their products, and explains Petrobras' investments abroad. Furthermore, the technological development in energy alternatives is worth discussing because energy systems are critical in defining products and processes. The US has invested in the production of energy from alternative sources, while in Brazil investments have been made in technologies from the past. Public policy in this regard is basically oriented

33. Figures available in official pages of the cities of São Paulo and London: http://www.capital.sp.gov.br/portalpmsp/homec.jsp (Sao Paulo); http://www.london.gov.uk/thelondonplan.jsp (London).

to constructing large energy plants based on traditional forms of energy (hydroelectric, nuclear, and gas or carbon powered plants).

Perhaps the Brazilian government should pay more attention to uncertainties of the market that can worsen if a significant technological breakthrough occurs.

Modern Society, Obsolete State

The case of insufficient investment in infrastructure, energy, and technology for the future shows that the greatest liability of the Brazilian nation continues to be the malfunction of the state. Every aspect ranging from needs of the every day life to harbors, public education, and technological innovation that depend on some kind of government initiative simply do not work properly. Modern life depends on many systems—generally interconnected—most of them funded and managed by public authorities. Private companies can provide buses to transport people in a big city, but some kind of public authority will be needed to organize and to manage the whole system. Private firms usually make roads, but the money to build the roads comes from official agencies established by the municipalities, states or federal government. Education at any level can be provided by public schools and universities or by private institutions, but in either case government authorities will be always playing an essential role by establishing and enforcing rules and requirements, and in most cases providing funds to assure the quality and even the access to education for the poor. A great deal of the modern technological development depends directly on government initiative either because there are implications for defense and other strategic aspects and/or because the amount of money as well as the time needed cannot be provided by private sources through allocation by an unregulated market.

Sound macroeconomic conditions though essential are not enough. In Brazil civil society and the market are quite active and strong, but the state is obsolete and has been working very badly in most areas. To make things worse, the judiciary system has a longstanding tradition of being completely self-centered and most of the time dedicated to protecting those who in some way have done something wrong to individuals, firms, and institutions. Not only corrupt politicians and dishonest businessmen tend to feel safe under the judiciary institutions, but generally the laws are largely lenient even with those who commit crimes such as drug-dealing, robbery or smuggling.

When individuals and organizations are oriented to misbehavior, and innovation and creativity are not properly rewarded, society declines inevitably. Unfortunately it seems that in many aspects this is what is happening in Brazil.

6

BUREAUCRATS, PARTIES, AND INTEREST GROUPS

Maria Rita Loureiro, Cecília Olivieri,
and *Ana Cristina Braga Martes*

Abstract: The chapter discusses the relationship between politics and bureaucracy in Brazil. Based on studies on the emergence and consolidation of the bureaucracy developed in the context of the wider debate on the relationship between state and society, the text examines the ties built between the government bureaucracy, political parties, and interest groups. The chapter emphasizes the significance of understanding the nature and scope of the power of bureaucrats in the general structure of the state, especially those coming from the functions of the Executive and Legislative, the relationship between them and their links with political parties and interest groups. Understanding the bureaucracy in Brazil is therefore inseparable from debates about the hypertrophy of the executive over the legislature and the weakness of the governing function of political parties, not only in authoritarian times, but also in democratic periods. The text takes up issues such as patronage, bureaucratic insulation, corporatism, and meritocracy, seeking to understand them in the logic of the political system and its challenges to the democratic order.

Politicians make decisions and bureaucrats merely administer. This view, which bears the stamp of common sense, is to be found in various public administration texts. However, in one of the most insightful studies into the role reserved for these two groups of players in contemporary democracies, Aberbach, Putnam, and Rockman (1981) show that, in all seven of the developed countries studied, the public bureaucracy is an integral part of the decision-making processes of the Executive branch, and furthermore that the Legislative branch wields power over the bureaucracy.

Bureaucrats have played an active part in decision-making processes in contemporary democracies.[1] Even when only prioritizing procedures or even the technical dimensions of problems, bureaucrats make relevant contributions because the state acts in different areas and deals with ever more complex issues. Contemporary authors have highlighted the bureaucratization of politics and the politicization of bureaucracy. Both adopt hybrid action strategies: politicians base their decisions on technical criteria while bureaucrats reinforce their political roles by mediating the interests of specific clientele groups and the signals sent out by the politicians.

Studies on pluralist democracies have paid considerable attention to the participation of bureaucrats in the decision-making process. Charles Lindblom emphasizes the way they operate, particularly when public policies are being implemented. According to the author, such policies are generally approved by the legislature in a general and vague way that requires the intervention of the bureaucrats in working out details and specifications. The involvement of bureaucrats with the decision making, which is seen by Lindblom as inevitable or even sometimes desirable in the contemporary world, occurs because those who are governing lack time and are not closely familiar with the specialized subjects that characterize most governmental action (Lindblom and Woodhouse, 1993).

In Brazil, bureaucracy not only forms part of the decision-making process, but is in fact one of the most important players. It has played a prominent role in the definition and conduct of public policies in authoritarian as well as democratic periods when parties and organized social groups recovered their capacity to influence or participate in government. In an influential analysis of Brazil's party system, Campello de Souza (1976) indicates how the roots of the crucial problems of Brazilian political parties—enormous institutional fragility, an inability to participate effectively in the preparation of public policies and the generalized persistence of clientelistic practices—lie in the type of relation that has been established between them and the government.

Bureaucratic power is never exercised on the basis of its own resources alone. The power of the bureaucrats depends on the backing of or delegation by some strategic political player seeking to sustain positions as policymakers. In other words, bureaucracy only plays a directing role in govern-

1. As Woodrow Wilson stated, "The administration is outside the political sphere. Administrative issues are not political issues" ("The study of administration," *Political Science Quarterly* June, 1887).

ment based on the granting of power by other political players or, in extreme situations, based on the usurpation of this power (Martins, 1974).

Stating that bureaucrats are relevant when it comes to government decisions does not mean ignoring their institutional dependence on political authority, or denying that the ultimate responsibility for decisions belongs to the politicians, as Max Weber pointed out. But affirming the institutional dependence of the power of the bureaucrats on politicians does not mean reducing bureaucracy to being a mere instrument of the executive branch. The assumption that there is separation between the administrative area and the political area is a legal formula that helps us understand the roles and responsibilities of each of these players, but which does not detract from the political nature of the role and activities of bureaucrats (Miliband, 1983: 143).

Brazil and the United States share such political institutions as a presidential system, a federative structure, and an administration open to lateral entries.[2] But relations between bureaucracy, the Executive, and the Legislative branch are very different in the two countries. In the United States, despite the fact that the bureaucratic apparatus is under the functional responsibility and within the structure of the executive, its main "master" is the Congress. In other words, delegation of power to the bureaucracy, and consequently its backing, comes mainly from the legislative branch, albeit not exclusively. This is what gives rise to distinctive aspects of the relation between politics and bureaucracy in the United States: members of Congress have the means of controlling the actions of the bureaucrats, and political parties have exercised both their representative and governmental functions, regardless of the expansion of the functions of the Executive and of its bureaucratic apparatus.[3]

To better specify the relations between politics and bureaucracy in Brazil, this chapter reviews major studies on the emergence and consolidation of the bureaucracy as a relevant player in the decision-making process and the links that have been established historically between it, the Executive, political parties, and interest groups. It looks at the broader debate about rela-

2. Bureaucracies that are more permeable to lateral entries are those in which some of the top echelon positions can be filled by professionals who have not necessarily had a public career, i.e., they did not climb the respective rungs of the hierarchical ladder, but were indicated for the position as a result of their previous activities outside the public sector.

3. From the theoretical point of view it is necessary to differentiate two essential functions of the parties in a democratic order: the representative function, in other words, representing the various different interests of society, and the government function, i.e., the capacity to determine or influence government decisions through the formulation of projects for the country, imposing direction on public policies (Campello De Souza, 1976).

tions between state and society by focusing on the processes that led to a strengthening of the decision-making role of the bureaucracy vis-à-vis other political players, and hence its impact on democratic order. This perspective cannot be disassociated from the issue of hypertrophy of the Executive relative to the legislature, the weakness of the governmental function of political parties, and the problem of the state's relations with interest groups—both in the sense of the attempt made by private groups to take over governmental organs and, in the opposite sense, of the cooptation of these groups by state agents.[4]

Generally, the literature about bureaucracy in Brazil is not very extensive when compared with the literature in the United States. It consists, above all, of case studies of government agencies and works on two of the few more consolidated public careers in the country; the armed forces and the diplomatic service. Furthermore, this literature refers above all to the authoritarian periods, since the blocking of the democratic paths of political participation redirected political activity to within the state's bureaucratic apparatus. Also, unlike the North-American literature, the main focus of which is on the effectiveness of the democratic controls over bureaucracy (Wood and Waterman, 1994), studies in Brazil have favored an analysis of the relationship between state and society. In other words, the focus on the bureaucracy in Brazil has been a by-product of the concern with the central role played by the state in Brazilian society.

Despite nuances and variations in emphasis, two main analytical strands dominate in these studies. The first approaches bureaucracy from the point of view of the class-driven nature of government—and it emphasizes the macro-structural transformation processes which Brazilian society experienced after the 1930s, which led to centralization of power in the federal executive and expansion of the state apparatus and public bureaucracy. The second strand favors the study of bureaucracy from the prism of its links with political institutions. Its central theme can be summarized as a discussion about the dilemmas between bureaucratic insulation versus clientelism and patronage.[5]

4. We use the expression "governmental capacity," as used by Campello de Souza (1976: XXII): "the capacity to formulate and implement a broad spectrum of public policies."

5. As José Murilo de Carvalho indicates, "the concept of clientelism was always used in a loose way." Generally speaking, it indicates a type of relation between political players that involves the granting of public benefits in the form of jobs, tax benefits, and exemptions, in exchange for political support, above all by way of the vote. In turn, patronage in Brazil refers, above all, to the distribution of public jobs for political convenience purposes, especially too for votes. For more details about the difference between these political relations, including "coronelismo" and "mandonismo," see Carvalho (1997).

Three caveats are in order. First, this essay does not ignore the discussion in today's democratic theory relating to the crisis in representative institutions and to the decline in political parties. The latter have been considered incapable of expressing all the splits that exist in contemporary societies. They are also losing space within the context of growing media communication or the return of charismatic leaders (Przeworski, Stokes, and Manin, 1999; Novaro, 2000; Lavalle, Houtzager, and Castello, 2006). However, parties are still the mediation institutions *par excellence,* between society and the state. In Brazil, for example, analyses of post-1985 governments underline the centrality of parties in the organization and functioning of the Executive and its relations with the legislature (Meneguello, 1998). Furthermore, theoretical works effectively argue that representative democracy is firmly founded on parties (Urbinati, 2006).

The second clarification refers to the concept of bureaucracy. The political player we highlight—which we call "bureaucracy"—comprises incumbents of the top echelon, or the directors of the direct and indirect administrative bodies of the Executive. These people may be both career civil servants (who comprise the stable body of government) and professionals from outside the public sector (recruited from private companies, non-state entities, such as universities or research centers and from trade unions and civil society organizations) who temporarily undertake activities as directors in governmental bodies.[6] Therefore, when we refer to bureaucracy we are talking about the individual players or "informal groups" who occupy top echelon positions, and we refer to state agencies or organs as the bureaucratic apparatus.[7]

Finally, the literature discussed in this work refers exclusively to the economic policy decision-making process. This restriction is justified by the fact that most of the studies about the expansion of the central state bureaucracy in Brazil concentrate on the way the developmental national state is assembled and, therefore, on the agencies charged with regulation, funding and economic planning. Despite this limitation we believe that questioning the links between bureaucracy and politics is also pertinent to other public policy areas.

6. Although not extensive, there is some literature in Brazil that analyzes the recruitment process of those who come from outside the state to occupy positions in the public policy decision-making organs (see Schneider, 1994; Loureiro, 1997; Olivieri, 2007; D'Araujo, 2007).

7. Examples of informal groups that took part in the top echelon of public bureaucracy at different times in our history are the members of the Vargas Economic Assistance group in the 1950s; they were the originators of groups formed with nationalist and developmental ideas (D'Araújo, 1982). Also the economic team that prepared the Real Plan in 1993-94 comprised groups of former colleagues from the Economics schools in Rio de Janeiro (Loureiro, 1997).

CAPITALIST STATE, SOCIAL CLASSES, AND BUREAUCRACY

A series of studies carried out predominantly throughout the 1970s and 1980s and growing out of the Marxist tradition, share a class-based approach to the state. Often influenced by the interpretative current expounded by Italian theoretician Antônio Gramsci, this strand of analysis starts by highlighting the absence of hegemony in the bourgeoisie in Brazil and the latter's inability to prepare a political project for the nation. They try to understand how, given this absence, the state assumes the function of the promoter of development through industrialization. That is, the focus is on the central role assumed by the state after the 1930s in constructing the national developmental project within a context that is marked by an absence of hegemony in the entrepreneurial class and by social fragmentation. Notwithstanding their internal differences, some authors in this strand more clearly express the analytical characteristics of the strand as a whole.[8]

Draibe (1985) analyzes the role of the state in the industrialization process and the "metamorphoses" which the bureaucratic apparatus underwent throughout this process, noting the "courses" adopted by its directorial nucleus under the influence of different political forces. Emphasizing social class differences, on the one hand, and the formation of the bureaucratic structures of the state on the other, the action of bureaucrats is seen from the point of view of the degree of autonomy of the state relative to social classes. The autonomy is not viewed as full or absolute, but is founded on the unstable field of inter-class relations and decisively rooted in the multiplicity and heterogeneity of political forces. This heterogeneity and the incapacity of the bourgeoisie to exercise hegemony allow the state to act with a certain degree of autonomy, according to this author. Put another way, the relations between the classes not only marks out the limits but also the direction of the state's autonomous action.

Economic conflicts impinging on decision-making bodies intensify the political dimension of supposedly technical resolutions. Top echelon technicians act politically when they arbitrate or negotiate interests in localized confrontations and constitute one of the many forces that seek to make their points of view prevail in public policy decisions. The force of the tech-

8. There are countless pieces of work on the expansion of the bureaucratic apparatus of the national developmental state in Brazil (its regulatory agencies and economic planning) after the 1930s, such as Dalland, 1968; Cohn, 1968; Ianni, 1971; Wirth, 1970; Lafer, 1970; Singer, 1974; Benevides, 1976; Bresser Pereira, 1977. Our intention here is not to review all this literature but to highlight those studies that raise the question of the links between politics and bureaucrats or, in other words, the role of the bureaucratic elite within the political system.

nician derives from the incapacity of the economic interests to impose themselves to the same extent as the market's regulatory forces. Brought directly within the sphere of government, the different interests face each other in public sector arenas, and the alliances they help establish within each organ are ephemeral because they were built around isolated projects or one-off measures. This is the more independent and politicized action space of bureaucracy. Given the inter-penetration of policies and their growing degree of complexity, the special knowledge of the technician and his domination of the content of decisions enable him to operate as the pivot in the alliances between interest groups and inter-bureaucratic articulation (Draibe, 1985: 43).

Examining the subsequent period, Martins (1985) focuses on class structure to understand the expansion of the capitalist state and the transformations in bureaucracy arising from this expansion. For Martins, the nature of the role of the state and its fragmentation into various organizations with different degrees of autonomy come from social disarticulation, from the nature of the class structure in continuous transformation, and from the presence of international players controlling parts of the production system. Therefore, what allows the state to convert itself into an historic agent of transformation is not its relative autonomy vis-à-vis the dominant class, but "the autonomy of the political dimension vis-à-vis other instances of the social structure." The autonomy of the politician precedes and conditions the autonomy of the state and refers to a given way of development, which in the case of Brazil is characterized by social disarticulation.

Although the analysis of bureaucracy only acquires a fuller meaning when it is referred to the state's class dimension, it is not only by identifying the classes that directly benefit from the state that the top rung on the ladder of power can be found or that the nature of the relations between state bureaucracy and the owners of capital can be clarified. This is why Martins analyzes the expansion of the state as a concrete way of evaluating the development of capitalism in Brazil. To do so, he emphasizes two dimensions of state action; its extractive capacity and the expansion of its corporate activities. He concentrates on three agencies—Banco Nacional de Desenvolvimento Econômico (BNDE) *[National Economic Development Bank]*, Conselho de Desenvolvimento Industrial (CDI) *[Industrial Development Council]*, and Carteira de Comércio Exterior (CACEX) *[Foreign Trade Portfolio]*. These agencies operate in strategic areas: public funding, encouraging industrial investment, and the promotion of foreign trade.

The way in which each of these agencies is involved in the state apparatus (on the fringe, at the core, or in specific sectors of government) marks in a decisive way the functioning conditions, nature, and volume of funds that they handle, as well as the reach of their action. For Martins, it is not delegation of the attributions of political power that confers degrees of importance on each agency, but the power resources they manage to bring together and maximize via their actions and the choices conferred by the nature of their respective involvement with the state apparatus. Through their placement in or out of the government sector these agencies develop behaviors that are more or less autonomous and innovative.

These examples thus illustrate that pluralism in Brazil does not happen at the level of society, but within the scope of the state, as the actions of the agencies end up substituting the political parties. In other words, interests in society are so dispersed and disorganized that they are only structured by the organization provided by state institutions. According to the author, this situation partly explains the differences in the logic that exists in the state apparatus and, on the other hand, tends to accentuate its segmentation even more and disorganizes it internally.

Also focused on the post-1964 authoritarian regime, Werneck Vianna (1987) carried out a case study of the National Monetary Council (CMN), and from the transformations in this decision-making agency this author points to the character and role of the Brazilian state coordinating the direction of capitalist expansion by planning and organizing it.

Two theoretical perspectives allow this author to understand the CMN as an intermediation body for segmented corporate interests: that of state corporativism, which in the words of Schmitter (1971) is linked to highly centralized, bureaucratic political regimes that have weak parties; and the analyses of O'Donnell (1975) of the so-called bureaucratic-authoritarian state. This theoretical reference point also leads to interpreting the institutional transformations in the CMN between 1964-74, from a monetary regulatory body (as it was intended to be when it was created in 1964 and, therefore, a corporate chamber for accommodating the specific interests of the financial sector) to a national coordination body that centralized all economic policies between 1969-74 under Minister Delfim Neto.

As the CMN started to filter and select demands from groups, its actions were not mere bureaucratic routine but political acts by means of which interests were negotiated and channeled to within the state. Different bureaucracies attended the various clienteles, thereby helping to segment claims and make the state capable of dealing with different pressures and even with opposing demands. The bureaucracy does not just act as an intermediary of interests. It also selects them and organizes them politically.

In short, the group of texts selected as expressing the first analytical strand assumes that the structural characteristics of the bureaucratic apparatus (heterogeneity, the disarticulation of organizational structures and public policies) come from a lack of hegemony of the dominant class and the consequent absence of a unifying political direction. In other words, the state internalizes the diversity of the political conflicts in its various organs, institutes, government corporations, and companies. Bureaucracy becomes hostage to a set of interests. But, at the same time it emerges as beneficiary, when through them it promotes its own specific forms of power (for example, issuing regulations, deciding about financing, and the like) and thereby gains some degree of action autonomy. In other words, the structure, organization, growth, and directions of the state can be explained to a considerable extent as a function of the forms of expression of the conflicts between the classes. In the last analysis, the autonomy of the state and the bureaucrats comes from the cracks in this disarticulated set of organs, given the weakness of the classes to impose a single and coordinated direction on the state as a whole.

The majority of these works refers to the authoritarian period, when the tendency to transfer the political struggle to within the bureaucracy and thus to the executive branch expanded. But it is interesting to note that the same movement occurred in the democratic period between 1946 and 1964, which was analyzed by Draibe. The author shows that even under democratic rules, the executive maintained the extent of the power of the bureaucracy, its role as the promoter of industrialization and the heterogeneous and autonomous action of its bureaucrats, with parliamentarians being relegated to a position of spectators.

AUTHORITARIANISM AND BUREAUCRATIC RINGS

Cardoso (1975) discusses the ways in which the interests of the dominant classes are articulated within the government apparatus, building on a critique of the above analytical perspective. This author marks the transition from the first to the second interpretative strand. Focused on the relations between the state and society in the context of the post-64 authoritarian regime, Cardoso formulates the concept of bureaucratic rings because he considers that the concept of the bourgeois state is not enough to explain the policies implemented by the state of the "Revolution of 64." In other words, to the extent that political conflict and power struggles cannot be deduced from the abstract determinations of class, they must be analyzed in their concrete forms of expression. Not only the parties, but state organizations are used by groups as means to the exercise of power.

This leads to rethinking the political system in terms of rings that cut horizontally through the public and the private realms. The relation between state and society is mediated by bureaucratic organizations. The interests of civil society thus gain space within the state. The bureaucratization of the axes of power and the correlated politicization of bureaucracies leads in turn to rethinking democracy in the sense of creating counterweights to the tendencies that arise from the nature of large bureaucratic organizations—manipulation, absence of transparency, lack of responsibility, and even a perverse form of authoritarianism (Cardoso, 1975: 182-85).

The rings are circles of information and pressure (therefore, of power) constituted as mechanisms to allow articulation between sectors of the state and sectors of the social classes. Under the protection of the political society, they ensure at the same time a cooptation mechanism to integrate within the decision-making positions of leadership members of the employee, businesspeople, and military classes who become participants of the political arena, but they join it *qua personae* and not as "representatives" of their class corporations. They are called "bureaucratic" precisely in order to underline where their headquarters need to be located in the state apparatus. This does not differ greatly from how the military regime allowed private interests to participate in the emergence of instruments of political and bureaucratic struggle within the state apparatus. According to Cardoso, the idea of corporativism is unsuitable for characterizing the relation between state and class because it presupposes something that does not exist in the rings, the organization of the classes and their representation, even though this takes place under state control (Cardoso, 1975: 208-09).

PARTIES, BUREAUCRACY, AND THE POLITICAL SYSTEM

This second analytical strand considers bureaucracy to be a central player in the decision processes of economic policies in Brazil and approaches the bureaucratic phenomenon from its links with the structure of government, the party system, and clientelism. According to Campello de Souza (1976), the main author dealing with this problem, the dominant presence of bureaucrats in the decision-making arenas of public policies comes from the historical incapacity of political parties to assume their governmental attributions. In turn, this is related to the preponderant role the state exercised in the Brazilian political system from the 1930s and even in the 1946-1964 democratic period.

The centralization of the power of the authoritarian state in the period from 1930 to 1945, along with the creation of ways of representing society interests via state corporativism, meant that the corporate structures reduced the governmental function of the parties, while the growth in power of the bureaucratic apparatus responded to the logic of centralization. In other words, incapable of exercising their governmental functions and restricting themselves to the representative function, the parties were left to defend short term or particularistic interests that were concerned only with paying for the support they received and guaranteeing their power (Campello de Souza, 1976).

So, clientelism is not a specific characteristic of the Brazilian political system, or even a stage in its development, as often argued, but a way of controlling the political resources to be used by the parties, which are trying in this way to generate power for themselves and consolidate their position as institutions. Given the extent of clientelism in Brazil's political system, the essential thing is to explain the degree by which the Brazilian parties feed indiscriminately on clientelism, making it a strategy for acquiring and consolidating power.

In other words, as the parties were unable to consolidate their governmental function of preparing and defending government projects, the bureaucrats performed the role in the decision arenas that the parties did not. In turn, the exercise of the governmental function by the bureaucracy relieves the parties of this process, increasingly relegating them to the function of representatives of particularistic clienteles or groups in society and reinforcing their practice of merely reproducing positions of power—reelection and the raising of the necessary funds. As a result, a vicious circle keeps the parties further and further away from discussions about government programs and projects for the nation, making the bureaucracies the most important channels for transmitting the interests of society to within the state.

The most crucial political implication of this process, in which bureaucrats assume decision-making functions in the vacuum left by the parties, is the maintenance of the fragility of democratic institutions. As that author so lucidly stated, the development of a democracy depends on the institutionalization of a party system that is capable of "guaranteeing both the stability and effectiveness of the function of governing and the strength and authenticity of the function of representing various different interests" (Campello de Souza, 1976: 50).

Other authors had already presented elements that stated the argument of Campello de Souza. Examining the developmental economic policy in Brazil in the democratic period from 1947 to 1964, Nathaniel Leff, for example, observes a considerable autonomy of the government agencies and states the importance of the technicians vis-à-vis parties that were not there to aggregate interests and formulate broader projects for the country. Not only did Congress refuse to become involved in more complex subjects, but the technicians also had a monopoly on the formulation of economic policy, the context of which increasingly focused on problems like inflation, the balance of payments, and the need for public investment (Leff, 1977: 132-33).

Writing subsequently, Sola (1998) also shares the perception of Campello de Souza. When analyzing the weight of economic ideas on political decisions in the 1946-1964 period of democracy she emphasizes the role that technicians played in the state apparatus, despite the divergences or controversies that existed between their main representatives. Examining the role of nationalist technicians in the political system, that author also shows that they were not articulated via the parties but by other institutions (such as clubs, research centers, professional or corporate associations), which served also as recruitment channels for public sector employment positions.

The economic assistance office in the second Vargas government illustrates not only the role performed by the bureaucracy in the democratic period, but equally the way it functioned, insulated from Congress and party pressures. Responsible for preparing the most important projects of this government—Petrobras, Eletrobrás, the National Coal Plan, CAPES, the National Immigration Institute, the National Agrarian Policy Committee, the Industrial Development Commission, Banco do Nordeste do Brasil, and many others—the Assistance Office consisted of technicians of a nationalist orientation working under Rômulo Almeida, all of whom opposed the actions of the Brazil and United States Mixed Commission, which were taken to represent the interests of North-American companies, at the very heart of the Vargas government (D'Araújo, 1982: 136).

Therefore, here we reiterate not only the exclusion of Congress and the parties from major national decisions, but also their deligitimization in a period of democracy. Below, we examine the other authors of the strand that favors links between parties and the bureaucracy. We are grouping them into two different sub-groups, since they do not view this relationship in the same way. The first indicates bureaucratic insulation as a possible way of overcoming clientelism and avoiding interest groups taking over the bureaucracy, without raising the problem of its implications for democratic order. The second group, in contrast, emphasizes the problems that the insulation solution poses for democracy.

Clientelism vs. Bureaucratic Insulation

Given the high degree of clientelism and patronage in the Brazilian political system, some authors hold or assume that to govern in a rational and efficient way it is necessary to delegate decisions to the bureaucrats and technicians. Concerned with characterizing what she defined as the dilemma of politics in Latin America, Geddes (1996) shows that from the point of view of the politicians, the insulation of the agencies to protect them against clientelistic pressures generates a dilemma. If, on the one hand, it makes it possible to achieve greater effectiveness in public policies, on the other it may lead to the government losing support in Congress. In other words, if a government is only guided by the logic of drumming up support in its recruitment for public administration, it may weaken its own capacity for shaping policies—or, at the opposite extreme, giving too much power to its technocrats may lead to its decision-making capacity being obstructed because of a lack of support in Congress.

Gouveia (1994) analyzes the power and the action logic of public bureaucrats in Brazil, taking as subject the group of technicians who took part in the Commission for Reorganizing Public Finance at the beginning of the 1980s. The author's hypothesis is that these bureaucrats, unlike the groups that propagate corporate interests, knew how to construct a self-protection system that was permanent, regardless of any party political changes. They fully identified with their situation as employees as well as with the ethos of public interest. As many entered the career after 1964, at a time when there was a depoliticization of society and an absence of public debate, they developed no strong ties with the parties. So this group, which was involved with the reform of the public financial institutions, was characterized by great external isolation, by strong internal loyalty, and by points of view formed in their professional practice.

Similarly, although using a rational choice theory approach, Geddes concludes that insulated agencies improve the performance and increase the capacity of the state. Insulation, or the constitution of "pockets of efficiency," was a necessary political resource for guaranteeing and maintaining political commitments, bearing in mind the economic development projects.

Insulation and Democratic Deficit

Unlike Geddes and Gouveia, who do not discuss the power bases of the insulated bureaucracy and thus assume it is neutral, and imply advocacy of insulation as a strategy for increasing the efficiency of state action, Nunes (1997) and Diniz (1997) question the consequences and the extent of insulation. They argue that if insulation helps avoid personalism and patronage in the name of a more technical approach, it also reduces the scope for formulating policies, which means the exclusion of political parties, Congress, and popular demands.

Nunes shows that the introduction of modern capitalism in Brazil interacted with the creation of a syncretic institutional system, in which several different principles for structuring relations between society and political institutions operate—clientelism, corporativism, universalism of procedures, and bureaucratic insulation. The institutionalization of these four, he says, progressed gradually throughout the twentieth century, as state institutions were constituted, particularly those dedicated to social and economic intervention and the modern relations of citizenship.

Bureaucratic insulation was developed in the 1950s to promote national development, so that the administration of economic policies and strategic decisions ended up being carried out outside the parties. The culmination of this process came in the government of Juscelino Kubitschek (JK) with the creation of two main agencies linked to planning and carrying out the Targets' Plan: Executive Groups and The Development Council. Both agencies forged an alternative path to that of traditional bureaucracy and the universalism of procedures. Created by decree, the Executive Groups totally ignored the parties and Congress. Kubitschek insulated these agencies, while at the same time using clientelism and the promise of employment. He prevented the DASP from holding civil service public entrance exams, encouraged hiring people who had not passed these exams, and made clientelistic nominations.[9]

Diniz, referring to the work of Nunes, also deals with the concept of bureaucratic insulation and attributes a role to the parties that is similar to the one emphasized by Campello de Souza. Heavily involved with a political system marked by centralization and by a "bureaucratic monopoly over decisions, political parties became tributaries of state power, deprived as they were of governmental functions and therefore of the effective capacity to have an influence over the decision-making process" (Diniz, 1997: 19).

Diniz questions the impact of bureaucratic insulation on the basis of an analysis of the responses of the first two governments of the New Republic to the crises of the 1980s and 1990s—foreign debt crisis, inflation, redemocratization. Because of the high levels of voluntarism in the state elite, principally in the economic area, insulation not only creates a democratic problem (relieving Congress and the political parties of the main government decisions), but also a problem of governmental effectiveness. The capacity of the government to take decisions unilaterally does not coincide with its capacity to articulate and negotiate the costs and gains of the measures taken towards economic restructuring and state reform.

Analyzing the democratic transition in Brazil under the New Republic, Sola (1998) also emphasizes the confinement of the decision-making arenas when faced with the pressures of competitive politics, the growing opacity of interests there represented and the high level of decision-making autonomy enjoyed by the economists in power. Referring also to the democratic period, Loureiro (1997) reinforces this perception, showing the monopoly that certain bureaucratic segments had over decisions in the area of macroeconomic policy. This monopoly refers not only to the career employees working in the ministries of Finance and Planning and the Central Bank, but above all to the group of economists who were renowned in university circles and the financial markets who were recruited temporarily for commissioned posts in the top echelon of the federal Executive.

In short, the economic bureaucracies in democratic governments also acted as policymakers in decision-making arenas that were restricted and insulated from the participation of the parties and Congress and therefore

9. Also in the JK government the way the executive or parallel administration groups functioned is marked by the undisputed hegemony of the technicians vis-à-vis other political players and their autonomy vis-à-vis Congress. Hence the observations of Luciano Martins about them: "Kubitschek himself declares that the technicians had (during his government) absolute freedom to prepare the plan. The available data seem to indicate that technocracy not only represented the most important role in the preparation and performance of the Targets' Plan but that it managed to have the political controls to which it had been previously submitted relaxed" (Martins, 1974: 427).

"protected" (by presidential backing or by a strong minister) from broader interests in the political spectrum.[10]

FINAL CONSIDERATIONS

The arguments and authors discussed above point out the importance of bureaucracy as a fundamental player in the decision-making process in Brazil even when the authors differ in regard to the source of bureaucratic power. If, in the first strand, the power of the bureaucracy comes from the socio-economic interests it represents within the state apparatus, in the second its power derives above all from the strategic decision of the heads of the Executive to choose bureaucrats to fill management positions in the public service, with the fundamental objective of guaranteeing that they direct and control the administrative apparatus. In both cases the bureaucrats are elevated to positions of great political and administrative power—and this situation generates the two situations indicated by the literature we analyzed: the taking over of sectors of the state by the socio-economic interests that the bureaucracy "represents" and the potential the bureaucrats have of becoming autonomous, relative to the politicians that named them and to interest groups themselves.

So, this analysis refers back to discussions about the role that the bureaucracy plays in the Brazilian government. Generally speaking, debates about the functioning of our political system indicate that its main characteristics—presidentialism, a multiparty state, and federalism—form part of what has been appropriately called coalition-based presidentialism (Abranches, 1988: 21-22).

In addition to the proportional representation electoral system, the fragmented nature of the Brazilian multiparty system has created a situation in which the political party of the President never manages to obtain, in isolation, a majority of seats in Congress, thus demanding alliances with several other parties in order to govern.

10. A report by a journalist who was behind the scenes when the Cruzado Plan was prepared in the Sarney government in 1986 reveals just how far the parties and members of Congress were from the decision-making arenas of economic policies: "Various circumstances suggested to Ulisses Guimarães (then president of the PMDB, the main party supporting the government) that it would be convenient to adopt an attitude of prudence and caution. Although there were many members of the PMDB among the "fathers of reform" the truth is that until the night before there was no party articulation supporting their actions within government. All the party agencies and organs were left on the sidelines; how could they assume a ready-made proposal that had been set up under these circumstances and that, because of its technical level and nature of something new, was difficult to understand and evaluate" (Sardenberg, 1987: 289).

If the view of coalition-based presidentialism is practically consensual, the same is not true with regard to the effects of these institutional features on the dynamic of the political system. For some authors, this combination is problematic or even "explosive" and generates enormous difficulties for the president when it comes to governing—in other words, a serious state of ungovernability (Abranches, 1988; Mainwaring, 1993). Other authors reach an opposite interpretation. Coalition-based presidentialism in Brazil provides the president with institutional resources—the authority to legislate by means of provisional measures and to control the budget—which allow him to concentrate power and thus guarantee governability. Following the latter interpretation, the regulatory norms of Congress, by emphasizing the role of party leaders, are also guided by the same logic of concentrating power (Figueiredo and Limongi, 1999). Other authors argue in favor of the governability theory of the Brazilian political system, not because of the concentration of power, but due to the continuous negotiations between the executive and legislative branches, which include negotiations about occupying key positions in the federal bureaucracy.[11]

The view that the current institutional characteristics of the Brazilian political system do not prevent governability, provided the Executive and Congress have the capacity to negotiate with each other in order to construct coalitions, helps our understanding of the articulation between bureaucracy and politics. The bureaucratic apparatus performs a decisive role in the functioning of politics since it constitutes the material basis for the exercise of government, not just in the formulation and performance of public policies (as in any contemporary society), but also because its positions are used as exchange currency for guaranteeing congressional support.

However, as has already been pointed out by Geddes (1996), the use of a large number of the administration positions as exchange currency by the government to obtain support in Congress creates a crucial dilemma for the President. Granting positions to coalition parties leads to decreased control over part of the administrative apparatus, but this control is necessary for carrying out government policies and programs. If, on the contrary, the President favors a strategy of non-negotiation or the insulation of bureau-

11. With regard to the debate about how the Brazilian political system functions, see the important work on systematization by Vicente Palermo, who provides four different interpretations: a) the theory of "ungovernability" by concentrating power; b) the theory of governability by fragmenting power; c) the theory of governability by concentrating power; and d) the theory of governability by negotiation, with which he identifies (Palermo, 2000).

cratic positions under pressure from the parties, this may result in a decision-paralysis situation caused by congressional non-collaboration.

Historically, democratic governments in Brazil have tried to get around this dilemma by using different strategies. In the 1950s, Vargas and Kubitschek segmented the bureaucratic apparatus by separation, having on one side the ministries and positions that were open to negotiation and on the other the "protected" or insulated areas—such as the economic development agencies, which became known as "islands of excellence" (D'Araújo, 1982; Benevides, 1976; Lafer, 1970).

In more recent times, the Cardoso government, in addition to segmentation of the bureaucracy, also used the strategy of naming, for those ministries granted to parties from his support base in Congress, an executive secretary (or vice-minister) he trusted or who was loyal to the central nucleus of government constituted by the ministry of finance. The mission of this top employee, also known in the slang of the time in the esplanade of ministries in Brasília as "the president's man," was to monitor the decisions taken by the ministers who were indicated as a result of the party coalition agreements, thereby guaranteeing that they did not move too far away from the direction established by the governmental nucleus (Loureiro and Abrucio, 1999). In the Lula government the activities of internal control, put into effect in the different ministries under the command of the Federal Control Department of the Office of the Comptroller General, can be understood as being another type of mechanism. Through this office the President can get around the risk of his government projects becoming unviable because of the negotiation of positions in the bureaucratic apparatus in order to obtain political support (Olivieri, 2010b).

The above analysis suggests new lines of research on the theme of relations between politics and the bureaucracy in Brazil.

First, the power of the bureaucracy has never been usurped from politicians, who granted it even in authoritarian regimes. In other words, politicians, however much they reinforce the decision power of specific bureaucratic agencies, always make bureaucracy dependent on political authority. Therefore, we cannot talk about technocracy in the strict sense of the word; it is enough to say a type of power that derives exclusively from technical competence or from specialized knowledge.[12]

The fundamental point is to understand the nature and the reach of the power of the bureaucrats in the general structure of the state, especially that coming from the main functions of the Executive Branch or the Legislative

Branch, from the relationship between both and their links with the parties and the interest groups. In short, understanding bureaucracy in Brazil as the policymaker is inseparable from debates about the hypertrophy of the Executive relative to the Legislature and the weakness of the governmental function of the political parties.

Studies that analyze the relationship between bureaucracy and the political system in democratic periods, especially post-1988, are rare. The literature is generally full of material indicating how politics becomes confined within the state in authoritarian regimes, in other words, disputes for power projects become internalized within the bureaucratic apparatus and bureaucrats play a predominant role in defining and implementing such projects. So, in asking for more research in this area, one of the inferences that can be drawn from this analysis is the following: in the post-1988 democracy period also, fundamental decisions about public policies are in the hands of the executive branch and the bureaucracy is still its main policymaker, since the central characteristic of Brazilian political parties still seems to be an incapacity to exercise the functions of government.

Another topic that merits additional studies refers to the possible connivance, even in democratic times, of Congress, the parties and organized society with the expansion of the power of the bureaucracy. It is perhaps even possible to talk of the existence of an inclination in favor of the power of the bureaucracy on the part of political players, either because of their weakness (their institutional and/or political incapacity to oppose the decisions of the Executive) or because of their interest in creating particularistic, clientelist or corporativist ways of influencing the decisions of the bureaucracy and the executive branch of government.

Finally, but no less relevant, the time is ripe for new research into the power of the bureaucracy and its relations with politics in Brazil to be carried out in other areas of public policy, especially in the social policy area.

---

12. For the discussion about technocracy see the classic study by Meynaud (1964) and on the role of technicians in the decision-making process in Brazil in the 1946-64 democratic period, see Sola (1998). Bresser-Pereira (1972) considers techno-bureaucracy or technocracy as the new dominant social class in the new way of producing that would succeed capitalism, characterized by the predominance of technique and by statism.

7

POLITICAL REFORM: A "NEVER-ENDING STORY"

David Fleischer

Abstract: After analyzing the attempts at political reform during the presidency of Fernando Henrique Cardoso (1995-2002), the further attempts at adopting such reforms during the term of President Luiz Inácio Lula da Silva (2003-2010) are examined. The reforms adopted during the Cardoso period were: a constitutional amendment in 1997 allowing one consecutive reelection of the president, governors, and mayors; a 30% quota for women candidates on the PR lists for deputy; the adoption of electronic voting machines; and blank ballots being counted as null votes in elections as of 1998. Two examples of judicialization of politics were examined where the Supreme Electoral Court (TSE) and Supreme Federal Court (STF) imposed changes in election rules. In March 2002, the judiciary determined that election coalitions be verticalized. In 2007, "party loyalty" was imposed that prohibited politicians from switching parties after they had been elected. Traditionally, these reform "packages" are presented in odd years because the long election recess in even years reduces the congressional calendar. Thus, it is possible that yet another attempt at political reform might be attempted in 2011.

In May 2001, the Bildner Center convened a symposium to examine Brazil's reforms since the mid 1990s. The papers presented at this meeting were collected in a volume published in 2004 (Font and Spanakos, 2004). My chapter in that volume examined Brazil's progress on "political reform" that I then defined as [President] Cardoso's "missing link"—indicating that he had not been able to implement certain reforms with the result that he was unable to obtain the approval of some of his other proposals (Fleischer, 2004a).

Now, eight and a half years after my analysis in 2001, I propose to address this question again—that is, what, if any, political reforms have been achieved during President Luiz Inácio Lula da Silva's (Lula) nearly seven years in office (2003-2009)? The answer is "not much progress achieved"—thus the subtitle of this paper—"A never-ending story."

This paper will address "political reforms" of Brazil's election and political party legislation, but will not deal with the broader topic of "reform of the State" (Abranches, 1996; Seixas and Proença, 2005)—that involves the relations among the three powers of government (Vianna, 2002); institutional reforms, such as the Judiciary Reform approved in 2004 (Renault and Bottini, 2005; Sadek, 2002 and 2004; Tavares Filho, 2005); federalism relations; tax and fiscal reforms; reform of labor laws; among others.

Political Reforms, 1995-2002

In my 2004 book chapter (Fleischer, 2004a), I catalogued several political reforms that had been enacted during the Presidency of Fernando Henrique Cardoso (1995-2002). The first and perhaps the most important change (the Reelection Amendment) was approved in 1997 and allowed Cardoso and the 27 governors (elected in 1994) to stand for immediate reelection in 1998 (Fleischer, 1998). In sequence, this change allowed the Mayors elected in 1996 to stand for reelection in 2000 (Fleischer, 2002; Viana and Coelho, 2008).

In 1995, Congress approved a 20% quota for women candidates on party lists for Brazil's open list proportional elections (for federal and state deputy, and city council). Because of Brazil's open-list PR system this change had very little impact on the number of women elected to the Chamber of Deputies. Actually, in 1998, fewer women were elected deputy than in 1994. Since then, this quota was increased to 30%, but with negligible results (Araujo, 2001).

In the 1996 municipal elections, the TSE (Tribunal Superior Eleitoral - Supreme Electoral Court) used a new system of electronic voting machines instead of traditional paper ballots for the first time in about 40 towns and cities. The result was considered successful and was expanded in the 1998 general elections to include about 60% of the electorate and was used exclusively in five states—Brasília, Rio de Janeiro, Alagoas, Roraima, and Amapá (Silva, 2002).

In August 1997, Congress decided that blank votes for deputy would be considered "null" [not included in the total of "valid" votes], as in majority elections (President, Governors, Senators, and Mayors). Since 1946, blank ballots had been included in the total of "valid votes" and thus "inflated" the vote total for the calculation of the election quotient. Analyzing the results of the 1994 elections, most party leaders decided that this change would have little impact in 1998, and might even facilitate the reelection of their deputies, because they figured that without the blank votes, the total "valid" vote would be less and thus the election quotient in each state would be smaller. The election quotient in each state is determined by dividing the total "valid" vote by the number of seats (deputies) representing that state. If the total valid vote were reduced (by excluding the blank ballots), the smaller total would produce a smaller quotient.

However, these "projections" did not take into consideration two important factors: (1) from one election to another (four years), Brazil's electorate expands by about 10%; and (2) because of extensive use of the new electronic voting machines in 1998, the number of blank and null votes declined significantly (Table 7-1). The result was a larger valid vote total in 1998 than in 1994, and thus larger elections quotients in all states.

The results of the 1998 elections for the five states that used the new electronic voting machines exclusively were compared to those in 1994 (paper ballots). This comparison clearly showed the impact of these machines. As seen in Table 7-1, the proportion of null and blank ballots was reduced considerably and as a result the valid vote and the election quotients were much larger.

The increase in the total valid vote varied between 21.87% in Alagoas to 53.20% in Roraima. The latter was a federal territory transformed into a state by the 1988 Constitution and received considerable migration in the 1990s. The more typical states—Rio de Janeiro and Brasília—had increases of 32.95% and 37.49%, respectively. As a result, the election quotients in all of the five states (with the same number of seats in 1994 and 1998) increased, instead of decreasing, as predicted by party analysts in 1997. The total null and blank votes in these five states was 3,950,199 in 1994, but was reduced to 1,061,832 in 1998. With the electronic voting machines in 1998, it became easier to vote for candidates rather than to vote null or blank—because the voter received no instructions regarding null or blank votes. In 1994, with paper ballots it was "easy" to scribble the ballot (null), or just deposit it in the ballot box (blank).

Each electronic voting machine was outfitted with a small color TV screen and a keyboard based on a touch-tone phone. Once the voter's ID was verified by the poll workers, the system was opened for him/her to vote, office by

TABLE 7-1. Impact of Electronic Voting on Elections, 1994 versus 1998

Year	Amapá	Roraima	Alagoas	Rio	Brasília
1994					
Electorate	197,171	119,888	1,156,990	9,129,373	1,064,247
Abstention	54,790	26,554	177,923	1,674,130	147,504
Votes Cast	142,281	93,334	979067	7,455,243	916,743
Nulls	22, 829	10,913	274,862	2,106,195	190,140
Blanks	20,599	7,641	206,617	1,009,518	100,885
Valid Vote*	119, 552	82,421	704,205	5,349,048	726,603
Seats	08	08	09	46	08
PR Quotient	14,944	10,302.6	78,245	116,283.7	90,825.4
1998					
Electorate	213,289	170,620	1,383,600	9,971,830	1,267,925
Abstention	28,941	36,897	390,465	2,017,061	196,417
Votes Cast	184,348	133,723	993,135	7,954,769	1,071,508
Nulls	3,844	4,097	65,099	420,245	31,078
Blanks	3,102	3,345	69,792	423,225	41,447
Valid Vote#	177,402	126,272	858,244	7,11,298	998,983
Seats	08	08	09	46	08
PR Quotient	22,175	15,784	95,350.4	154,593.3	124,872.9
*Valid vote in 1994= Votes cast minus Nulls					
# Valid Vote in 1998= Votes cast minus Nulls minus Blanks					
Differences 1994/1998					
Electorate	+08.17%	+42.32%	+16.38%	+09.23%	+19.14%
Abstention	-47.18%	+38.95%	+119.46%	+20.48%	+33.16
Votes Cast	+29.48%	+43.27%	+01.44%	+06.70%	+16.88
Nulls	-83.16%	-62.46%	-76.32%	-80.05%	-83.66%
Blanks	-84.94%	-56.11%	-66.22%	-58.08%	-58.92%
Valid Vote	+48.39%	+53.20%	+21.87%	+32.95%	+37.49%
PR Quotient	+7,231	+5,481.4	+17,115.4	+38,309.6	+34,047.5
1994: Total Nulls + Blanks = 3,950,199			1998: Total Nulls + Blanks = 1,061,832		
Nationwide: 61,111,922 (57.6%) voters used electronic voting machines in 1998.					

Source: Fleischer, 2006.

office. Once the voter keyed in the four- or five-digit code for a candidate, his/her photo popped up on the screen together with the candidate's name and party label, and the machine asked "Do you wish to vote for this candidate?" If this candidate was the voter's choice, he/she would push the green "Confirm" button and then proceed to the next office. Usually, voters take a "crib sheet" along with the code numbers for their pre-selected candidates.

These electronic voting machines were used exclusively in the 2000 municipal elections which were the first immediate reelection opportunity for Mayors. Of the 3,448 Mayors who ran for reelection, 2,006 were returned to office (58.2%). In 1998, 22 of the 27 governors ran for reelection and 15

(68.2%) were successful. Three of the latter who were victorious on the second round runoff reversed the first round result (Fleischer, 1998).

POLITICAL REFORMS, 2002-09

Several publications have focused on "political reform" during the Lula period, since 2003 (Avelar and Cintra, 2007; Avritzer and Anastásia, 2006; Benevides, Vannuchi, and Kerche, 2003; Rennó, 2007; Soares and Rennó, 2006; Teixeira, 2009; Viana and Nascimento, 2008).

Judicialization

This period witnessed several "reforms" in the rules regarding Brazil's elections that were determined [decided] by the Judiciary—changes not enacted by Congress—and thus are called the "Judicialization of Politics" (Ferraz Junior, 2008; Taylor and da Ros, 2008; Vianna, 1999; Vianna, Baumann, and Salles, 2007).

Verticalization

The first of these measures imposed by the Judiciary, was TSE Resolution 21002 in February 26, 2002 that verticalized election coalitions. The Supreme Electoral Court decided that coalitions among political parties in Brazil were *exdrúxulas* [odd, extravagant, unusual]—or "incongruent" comparing the composition of presidential and state-level party coalitions. That is to say, parties in a certain presidential coalition might oppose each other in some states, while parties in opposite presidential coalitions might be united in the same state-level coalition. This TSE Resolution obliged the presidential coalitions to be replicated in each of the 27 states, with no "incongruent" party alliances.

Although Congress attempted to approve a Constitutional Amendment reversing this decision, this was only possible in 2006 and so will only take effect for the 2010 general elections. Thus, this rule applied to both the 2002 and 2006 elections.

As seen in Table 7-2, the most visible effect of this verticalization was that the number of coalitions at the state level doubled—from 72 and 79 in 1994 and 1998 to 140 in 2002 and 2006 (Fleischer, 2006). However, this "new rule" did not inhibit Lula's victory in the presidential election nor the PT (Worker's Party) electing the largest number of federal deputies (91 versus 59

TABLE 7-2. Profile of State-Level Coalitions in 1994, 1998, 2002, and 2006

	1994	1998	2002	2006
Coalitions	72	79	140	140
Coalitions per state				
2	15	11*	0	0
3	8	11	0	1
4	2	3	8	7
5	2	1	11	10
More than 5	0	1	8**	9**
Average	2.97	2.93	5.19	5.19

Notes:*In 1998, Acre had only one coalition, and the PFL, PPB, and PMDB ran separate slates. **The Rio de Janeiro had eight coalitions in 2002, and nine in 2006.
Source: Fleischer, 2006.

in 1998). On the other hand, the PSDB (Brazilian Social Democratic Party) was reduced from 99 to 65 deputies and the PFL (Partido da Frente Liberal, Liberal Front Party) from 105 to 76 (Fleischer, 2007a: 310-11).

The PFL had been allied with the PSDB in the victorious Cardoso coalitions in 1994 and 1998, but broke with the PSDB in 2002 and did not participate in any presidential coalition, and thus was free to join the most advantageous coalitions at the state level. However, in 2006, the PSDB and PFL again formed a presidential coalition and were subject to the verticalization rules. In 2006, several political parties that had participated in presidential coalitions in 2002, decided to abstain in order to enhance their results at the state level—PMDB (Brazilian Democratic Movement Party), PSB (Brazilian Socialist Party), PTB (Labor Party), PL (Liberal Party), PP (Progressive Party), and PPS (Socialist People's Party). The smaller and medium sized parties were fearful of falling below the 5% threshold barrier that was in effect in 2006 (Castro, 2006; Fleischer, 2007a: 334-36).

Table 7-3 below shows how some of these parties maintained their state level alliances without participating in presidential coalitions. In 2006, the PSDB-PFL presidential coalition was replicated in only 13 states, while the PT (Worker's Party)-PCdoB (Communist Party) presidential coalition was replicated in all but two states. The traditional Lula coalition partner (PSB) did not participate in any presidential coalition, but joined in 15 PT-PCdoB coalitions at the state level. The former PCB (Brazilian Communist Party) changed its name to PPS as well as its political posture in 1991 and formed coalitions on the Right with the PSDB-PFL in 11 states, but did not join its former "comrades" (PT-PCdoB) in any states. Finally, the PMDB "went alone" in 2006, and was thus "free" to join any coalition at the state level in 2006—PSDB-PFL in 7 states, PT-PCdoB in 5 states, and "alone" in the other 15 states.

TABLE 7-3. Configuration of Presidential and State-Level Coalitions in 2006

Presidential Coalitions	State-Level Coalitions
PSDB + PFL	in 13 states
PT + PCdoB	in 25 states
"Independent" Parties	
PSB + PT + PCdoB	in 15 states
PPS + PT +PCdoB	in zero states
PMDB + PSDB +PFL	in 7 states
PMDB + PT + PCdoB	in 5 states
PMDB "alone"	in 15 states

Source: Fleischer, 2006.

Party Loyalty

A second exercise in "Judicialization of Politics" was imposed by the Judiciary in March 2007 regarding "party loyalty." Brazil has used the worst variant of proportional representation since 1945—the open list. The parties (and coalitions) organize their lists of candidates for deputy state by state in no predetermined order. The voters have two alternatives, either vote for the party or vote for one name on one of these lists—and usually some 95% choose to vote for a name. This system produces some aberrations and is very conducive to bloc voting by segments—religions, ethnic groups, labor unions, and other corporative groups that instruct "their" voters to concentrate their votes on one or two names in each state. The open-list PR system produces a weak party system (Nicolau, 2006b; A.M. Santos, 2006a; Viana and Coelho, 2008).

Traditionally, this system has been subject to frequent party switching by deputies as the President attracts politicians into his government support bloc in Congress (Melo, 2004; Reis, 2007; A.M. Santos, 2006b; F. Santos, 2006; Santos Filho and Miguel, 2008). This "party migration" following both the October 2002 and 2006 elections deprived the PFL of a simple majority over the PMDB in the Senate resulting from the elections—and also deprived it of the prerogative of electing the president of the Upper House.

As seen in Table 7-4, following the October 6, 2002 election, the PMDB declined from 23 to 19 senators, while the PFL delegation expanded from 18 to 20. However, as of February 1, 2003, the PMDB gained one senator and the PFL lost two. Thus, the PMDB elected Senator José Sarney (PMDB-Amapá) President of the Senate for a second time.

TABLE 7-4. Senate and Chamber "Party Migration," 2002-03 and 2006-07

Party	Sequence 2002->2003			Sequence 2006 -> 2007		
	August	Elected in October	Sworn in February	August	Elected in October	Sworn in February
Senate						
PMDB	23	19	20	20	15	20
PFL	18	20	18	16	18	17
PSDB	14	11	12	16	15	13
PT	8	14	14	12	11	11
PTB	4	3	4	4	4	5
PDT	5	5	4	4	5	4
PSB	3	3	3	2	3	3
PPB/PP*	2	1	0	0	1	1
Other	3	5	6	7	9	7
TOTAL	81	81	81	81	81	81
Chamber						
PMDB	87	74	69	78	89	91
PFL	97	84	76	64	65	62
PSDB	95	71	65	59	66	63
PT	58	91	91	81	83	82
PTB	33	26	45	53	22	20
PDT	16	21	17	20	24	23
PPB/PP*	53	49	44	50	41	42
PL/PR**	27	27	29	37	23	34
PSB	17	22	19	27	27	27
PPS	12	15	18	15	22	16
PCdoB	10	12	12	12	13	13
Other	8	21	18	27	38	40
TOTAL	513	513	513	513	513	513

Notes: *At the end of 2006, the PPB changed its name to PP. **At the end of 2006, the PL incorporated Prona and changed its name to PR.
Source: Fleischer, 2007a.

After the October 1, 2006 election, the PMDB was reduced from 20 to 15 senators, while the PFL increased from 16 to 18. Thus, in theory, the PFL should have elected the Senate President on February 1, 2007. However, in the interim between the election and the seating of the new senators, the PFL lost one senator and was reduced to 17, while the PMDB gained five "migrants," and its delegation again reached 20 senators and was able to reelect the Senate President—Sen. Renan Calheiros (PMDB-Alagoas).

Greatly dissatisfied at having "lost" the presidency of the Upper House twice (in 2003 and 2007) due to "party migrations," in late February 2007, the PFL filed a brief at the TSE regarding the problem of party switching—if the mandate of those elected "belonged" to the party that elected them, or whether the mandate was "personal"—the deputy or senator would be free to migrate and take their respective mandate with them to the new party.

The TSE responded quite quickly (by a 6-to-1 decision) to the PFL "complaint" on March 27, 2007 via Resolution 22610/2007—that, "yes" the mandate belonged to the party that had elected the deputy or senator and that those who switched parties after they were elected would lose their respective mandate. This new jurisprudence "regulating" the problem of "party infidelity" would be adjudicated by the TSE.

It took six months for this TSE decision to be confirmed by the Supreme Court (STF) on October 25, 2007. In the meantime, Congress could have approved legislation regulating the question of "party loyalty," but was unwilling or unable to do so. The only modification imposed by the STF was that the TSE resolution could not be retroactive, i.e. this decision would only apply for those who changed parties after March 27, 2007, and should not be applied for those who switched after the October 2006 elections and before that date. In the suits filed by parties who lost mandates through party "migration," as of October 2009, only one deputy lost his mandate via TSE decision.

However, the election law deadline stated that any person planning to run for office in the October 3, 2010 elections must confirm his/her party membership one year prior to the election—or by October 3, 2009. Because many politicians planning to run for reelection (or other offices) in 2010 traditionally seek a new party that offers more "advantages" just prior to this deadline—in September 2009, four senators and 32 federal deputies changed parties, and in the process "demoralized" this TSE attempt at "judicialization of politics" to regulate the question of "party loyalty" (Bragon and Cabral, 2009).

Reform Attempts in the Chamber

During the Lula government (2003-2010), three attempts were made to approve changes in Brazil's election laws—in 2003, 2007, and 2009 (Barreto and Fleischer, 2008; Caiado, 2007; Câmara dos Deputados, 2007; Fleischer, 2004b and 2004c; Klein, 2007; Teixeira, 2009).

In 1995, the Senate took the lead and established a temporary committee to study the question of "political reform" and produce concrete suggestions to this end. This committee produced several bills and proposed several constitutional amendments, some of which were actually approved by the Senate. The committee report organized by its reporter, Senator Sérgio Machado (PSDB-Ceará), was released in 1998 (Machado, S., 1998).

In early 2003, it was the Chamber of Deputies' turn to initiate a reform proposal and a special committee was constituted, with Deputy Alexandre Cardoso (PSB-Rio de Janeiro) as Chair and Deputy Ronaldo Caiado (PFL-Goiás) as Reporter. After many sessions and hearings—plus an international seminar organized by the Brazilian Political Science Association and the Chamber of Deputies on June 3-5, 2003—this committee finally voted out its report on December 3, 2003 in the form of *Projeto de Lei* (PL, legislative bill) 2679/03.

This PL was perhaps the best of the three proposals produced in the Chamber (Santos, E.C., 2004a), and had five components:

Election System. Brazil's election system would continue to use proportional representation, but with a closed list. Each party or coalition of parties would have to elaborate its list of candidates state-by-state in a predetermined rank order, and the voter would then vote for a party list, and no longer be able to select an individual candidate. The manner by which each party would elaborate its respective list was not detailed in this proposal—party executive committee, state party convention, or by a primary among its registered voters (Nicolau, 2006b and 2007). However, the proposal detailed the "preference order" (by individual vote totals in 2002) for inclusion on this pre-ordered list: first, candidates who had been elected in 2002; second, alternates who had become permanent deputies; third, alternates who served at least six months; and fourth, candidates who were elected in 2002 but switched parties. This fourth criterion was rejected by both the PTB and the PL; they had received the largest number of "migrants" after the 2002 elections.

Party "Federations." This quite "novel" idea would have replaced party election coalitions that were always dissolved immediately after each election. A "federation of parties" would be formed to elect deputies, but after the election, the federation would be required to remain together for three years (after the 2006 elections) and only be dissolved in September 2009, one year prior to the next (2010) election. This measure would have resolved three "problems:" it (a) would not have required the prohibition of coalitions in the PR elections; (b) would have preserved the identity of the small and micro parties within each federation; and (c) would have eliminated the problem of "migration" of deputies after each election.

Party Loyalty, as a result of the proposed reform, party loyalty would not be as rigid as during the military regime, but "migration" of deputies would be limited by the effects of the closed-list and party federations.

Exclusion Clause. This proposal set the "exclusion barrier" at 2% of the valid vote and the election of at least one deputy in five states. This would not have been a "rigid" barrier (as the 5% barrier in Germany), but parties not surpassing this barrier would not be allowed to "function" within the Chamber (could not have a leadership position, nor assign deputies to committees). The intent was to force mergers of these excluded parties with larger parties. In 2006, nine parties were not able to surpass this 2% barrier.

Campaign Finance. The proposed reform would have made campaign finance exclusively "public" and private campaign contributions would have been prohibited, both by persons and firms (Fleischer, 2004c). The total amount to be distributed among the parties would have been R$966 million (US$322 million)—R$7.00 (US$2.33) for each of the 138 million registered voters. The distribution would have been as follows:

1. 1% divided equally among all parties registered at the TSE
1% of R$966 million = R$9.66 million

2. 14% divided equally among the parties represented in the Chamber
14% of R$966 million = R$135.14 million

3. 85% proportionate to the size of each party delegation of deputies elected in October 2002
85% of R$966 million = R$821.1 million

This mechanism would have penalized the "small" and micro parties, and especially the middle sized parties, such as the PTB and the PL that had benefited from the "migration" of deputies after the October 2002 elections.

As an example, this calculation is applied to a "micro" party (PSD) and the largest party (PT) in the 2002 elections—considering that 30 parties might exist in 2006 and that by then 15 parties might be represented in the Chamber.

PSD (elected 4 federal deputies in 2002)
1/30 of R$9.66 million = R$322,000.00
1/15 of R$135.24 million = R$9,016,000.00
4/513 of R$821.10 million = R$6,402,000.00
TOTAL = R$15,740,000.00

PT (elected 91 federal deputies in 2002)
1/30 of R$9.66 million = R$322,000.00
1/15 of R$135.24 million = R$9,016,000.00
91/513 of R$821.10 million = R$145,653,000.00

TOTAL = R$154,911,000.00

The total for each party would be allocated as follows:

- 30% for the national administration of the party if it were in a presidential coalition,
- 20% for the national administration of the party if it were not involved in a presidential coalition,
- The rest (70% or 80%) would go to the state sections of each party, with 50% proportionate to the number of voters (in each state) and 50% proportionate to the size of the party's delegation in the respective state legislature.

This distribution would have funded the party's campaign in each of the 27 states (governor, senator, and state/federal deputies).

The vote by this 38-member committee that approved PL 2679/03 was 26 favorable, 11 against, and one abstaining. One PFL and one PMDB deputy voted against this proposal as well as the three deputies (each) representing the PTB, PP, and PL. The single PPS deputy abstained. The PSDB, PT, PMDB, and PFL deputies were cohesive in favor of this reform—but those from the PTB, PP, and PL felt "threatened." In 2004, the leaders of these three government bloc parties plus the PDT (Democratic Labor Party) refused to sign the "urgency" request for the deliberation of this proposal and threatened to adopt obstruction tactics if the PT leadership insisted on its deliberation. Because these three parties had 151 deputies in the government bloc, PL 2679/03 was never brought to the floor of the Chamber for deliberation. In July 2003, there were "signs" that the bloc of evangelical deputies was not favorable to this reform (Braga, 2003; Cruvinel, 2003).

Jairo Nicolau (2004) remembered that "public campaign finance with fiscal monitoring and penalties is the best way to reduce scandals" and misuse of campaign funds. On the other hand, Wanderley Guilherme dos Santos assumed a radical position against this reform, especially the "closed list" that he felt would limit the freedom of the voter to choose his/her [individual] candidate:

> The closed list imprisons the voter, who today—with the open list system—can vote for the party list (the party or individual candidate). This proposal does not allow the voter to choose his/her representative, allowing the usurpers to decide the candidates that this vote will elect. They say that this will elevate the moral paragon of Brazil's democracy (W. G. Santos, 2004).

Following the municipal elections in 2004, discussions regarding political reforms should have returned to the agenda of the Chamber. However the Lower House became preoccupied with its own internal scandals—the so-called mensalão involving a "monthly allowance" in return for deputies' votes, and the scandal that forced the resignation of the then Chamber President, Deputy Severino Cavalcanti (PP-Pernambuco) in September 2007.

Threshold Barrier. Because the Chamber was "distracted" in 2005, the "threshold barrier" that had been part of the election legislation since 1995 was not postponed [again] and went into effect for the 2006 elections. This added to the "anxiety" of some middle sized political parties that had already decided not to join any presidential coalition in 2006, in order to have more freedom to join diverse state-level coalitions—with the objective of surpassing the "stiff" 5% barrier.

Of the 21 parties that elected at least one deputy in 2006, only seven parties were able to surpass the 5% threshold barrier, twelve parties polled more than 2% of the valid vote, and seven had less than 1%. Had the "rigid" German threshold barrier been applied to these election results, the seven parties that surpassed the barrier could elect 395 deputies and the other 118 seats, "elected" by the other 14 parties, would have been redistributed among the seven parties (Fleischer, 2007b). Thus, many analysts thought that with seven parties in the Chamber, the governability of the Lula government in 2007 would have been enhanced.

In a desperate effort to surpass the 5% barrier ex post facto in October-November 2006, the PL merged with Prona (Party of the Reconstruction of the National Order) to form the new PR (Republican Party) and the PTB incorporated PAN (National Agrarian Party). Two other mergers were being contemplated: (1) PV (Green Party) + PSoL (Socialism and Freedom Party); and (2) PPS + PMN (National Mobilization Party) + PHS (Humanistic Solidarity Party) to form MD (Democratic Movement).

In December 2006, the STF ruled that this "make believe" barrier was unconstitutional, because it created first class and second class deputies. The "second class" deputies elected by the 14 parties that had not surpassed the 5% barrier would have been prohibited from having a leadership office in the Chamber and their 118 deputies would not have received committee assignments. The "intent" of this barrier was to force these deputies to "migrate" to the "first class" parties. With good reason, the Supreme Court decided that this was not constitutional. Probably, if the barrier had been "rigid" and just simply excluded those 14 parties from the Chamber altogether, the STF would have upheld this measure as constitutional.

In the "new" Chamber in 2007, after nearly a 50% turnover in the 2006 elections, another proposal (quite similar to PL 2679/03) was voted on in June. All the proposals were roundly defeated.

Two years later, in early 2009, the Lula government decided that, different from 2003 and 2007, the Executive Branch would get into the act to propose a political reform package and pressure for its approval by Congress. This "package" with seven proposals was elaborated by SAL/MJ (Secretariat for Legislative Affairs/Ministry of Justice) and delivered to Congress on February 10, 2009 (Guerreiro, 2009).The seven items that repeated some of the items in PL 2679/03 included in this "package" were:

1. A "rigid" threshold barrier of 1% of the valid vote and at least 0.5% in nine states. In 2006, this would have seated 14 parties and eliminated 7. Only 12 seats would have been redistributed.
2. A "closed list" in PR to "strengthen and institutionalize Brazil's political parties."
3. Establishment of exclusive public campaign finance, to reduce the dependence of parties and candidates on private campaign finance and make campaign spending more "transparent."
4. Prohibition of coalitions for PR elections, but allowing them for majority elections (President, Senator, Governor, and Mayor). The 2003 idea of "party federations" was not resuscitated.
5. Extension of ineligibility for running for office to include persons convicted of crimes at the first level of the Judiciary (by a federal or state judge). These persons would be ineligible for three years after their conviction. Those deputies and candidates with criminal records are nicknamed *fichas sujas* (dirty records).
6. Criminalization of vote buying, to reinforce the 1999 law in terms of ineligibility.
7. Reinforcement of party loyalty by establishing regulations to administer the 2007 TSE/STF decision that a deputy or senator who leaves or is expelled from the party that elected him/her would lose their mandate and be replaced by their respective alternate (*suplente*).

This package was defeated *in toto* in the Chamber of Deputies in June 2009. The main obstacles to its adoption were: (1) some 200 deputies have already been convicted of crimes at the first level of the Judiciary; and (2) many groups, corporative segments, evangelical church groups and the private sector use the open list PR system to elect "their" deputies.

Finally, regarding the *fichas sujas*, in September 2009 a massive, grassroots petition campaign—popular initiative—delivered petitions with over one and a half million signatures of registered voters proposing that Congress approve legislation making all persons with "dirty" criminal records [convicted at the first level] ineligible forever. This is similar to the prohibitions placed on felons by many states in the US. Congress approved this popular initiative on June 4, 2010 and the TSE confirmed that it would operate retroactively for the 2010 elections. However, the final version of this law prohibited candidacies of those convicted of crimes (election law violations, corruption, etc.) by second level court (a state supreme court or a regional federal court). Also, those who resigned their mandates to escape expulsion were also considered ineligible. In August 2010, the TSE received 1,253 cases from the state election courts requesting the ineligibility of *fichas sujas*.

In July 2006, the TRE-RJ (Tribunal Regional Eleitoral - Rio de Janeiro Regional Electoral Court) took the "novel" initiative to cancel the candidacies of all *fichas sujas* and it took the TSE some 30 days to overturn this decision. In the meantime, the TV networks in Rio de Janeiro aired this list of fichas sujas every day on their news programs with photos, names, and party affiliation of these "purged" candidates. After the October 2006 election, the TRE-RJ president had the satisfaction of announcing that none of these fichas sujas had been elected or reelected.

CONCLUSIONS

This "never-ending" story probably will continue in 2011 with the new Congress elected in October 2010. Traditionally, large reform packages are deliberated in odd years (as seen above) because of a more complete legislative calendar. In even years, Brazil has either municipal or general elections that occasion long "recess" periods, usually from late June to early November during the campaign period, when deputies and senators "disappear" to work on their own campaigns or those of their municipal allies.

In order to accommodate the heavy pressures to retain the open list PR system, it is possible that a mixed election system might be proposed in 2011 that would combine a single-member district system with the open-list PR system on a 50% /50% division of seats (Cintra, 2008).

Probably the topics from the 2003, 2007, and 2009 reform attempts would reemerge, such as: prohibition of coalitions in PR elections, campaign finance, a relatively "low" (rigid) threshold barrier, and party loyalty.

On the other hand, other topics might be deliberated, such as the elimination of the obligatory vote, but retaining the obligation of voter registration (Ribeiro, 2003; Santos, E.C., 2004b; P.H. Soares, 2004a).

8

Civil Society Discourses and Practices in Porto Alegre

J. Ricardo Tranjan

Abstract: An influential thesis put forward by Evelina Dagnino suggests that in Brazil those advocating participatory democracy and those holding neo-liberal views of the state use the terms civil society, democracy, and citizenship in sharply different ways. In Dagnino's view, this is a "perverse confluence" that has detrimental impact on democratization. In this chapter I test this argument in Porto Alegre, a city wherein two participatory programs and civil society discourse coexist. Participatory Budgeting (OP) is grounded on a discourse of radical democratization of the state and allows for popular participation in public administration. The Local Solidarity Governance (GSL) uses liberal terms such as social capital and social responsibility and encourages civil society to participate in public-private partnerships. I argue that this seemingly archetypical case of perverse confluence is not in fact perverse.

The various models of the state espoused by different political groups intrinsically include an ideal of civil society. In Brazil, those advocating participatory democracy and those holding neoliberal views of the state held sharply contrasting opinions about the meaning of civil society, democracy, and citizenship.[1] When these views lead to concerted political actions grounded in "a set of beliefs, interests, worldviews, and representations of what ought to be societal life," these views and actions are called "a political project." In the past two

1. Political projects here refer to concerted political actions grounded in "a set of beliefs, interests, worldviews, and representations of what ought to be societal life" (Dagnino, Olvera, and Panfichi, 2006: 38).

decades, however, the neo-liberal and participatory democracy views were modified and the differences between them decreased, providing an example of "perverse confluence" of political projects. Evelina Dagnino (2004: 96) argues that a democratizing and participatory political project emerged in the early 1980s, found expression in the debates leading to the adoption of the 1988 Constitution, and then continued to work for the deepening of democracy, the expansion of citizenship, and the "creation of spaces where the power of the State can be shared with society." In the 1990s, a neo-liberal political project promoted civil society and participation as part of a strategy to reduce the state's regulatory role. Since civil society, citizenship, and participation were notions already established in political discourse, the task of the neo-liberal project is to make their meanings more congruent with an international ideology that imposes severe restrictions on the social responsibility of the state. Dagnino (2007: 550) argues that the "perverse nature of the confluence between the participatory and the neo-liberal projects lies in the fact that both not only require a vibrant and proactive civil society, but also share several core notions, such as citizenship, participation, and civil society, albeit used with very different meanings."[2]

In this paper I test Dagninos' hypothesis of "perverse confluence" in Porto Alegre, a Brazilian city known for its active citizenry and participatory programs. Porto Alegre is one of the first state capitals to elect a mayor from the *Partido dos Trabalhadores* (PT, Workers Party) and in 1989, the city became known as the world-capital of participatory democracy. Porto Alegre's now-famous *Orçamento Participativo* (OP, Participatory Budgeting) was widely documented and influenced similar experiments in numerous cities in Brazil, Latin America, and the world.[3] In 2004, the PT lost the first municipal election in 16 years to a heterogeneous political coalition. The opposition had learned that in order to defeat PT it had to promise to keep the participatory budgeting (Pujol). The anti-PT coalition kept its promise but also launched a new participatory initiative called *Governança Solidária Local* (GSL, Local Solidarity Governance). While the first initiative allows for direct citizen par-

---

2. The "two civil societies" thesis has been also formulated in other studies: Jenny Pearce uses the terms civil society "builders" and "critics;" Burgos refers to "gransciams" and "liberals" *(Da Democratização)*; and Medeiros draws the line between organizations under the umbrella of the *Associação Brasileira de Organizações não Governamentais* (ABONG, Brazilian Association of Non-Governmental Organizations) and organizations registered as Organizações da Sociedade Civil de Interesse Público (OSCIP, Civil Society Organization of Public Interest).

3. In 2001-2004, 69 of 223 large Brazilian cities, i.e. cities with more than 100 thousand inhabitants, had some variation of participatory budgeting, as did Argentina, Uruguay, Peru, Chile, Bolivia, Mexico, Canada, Italy, Spain, Germany, France, Poland, and England (Marquetti, 2007: 77).

ticipation in the public administration, the latter encourages civil society groups to participate in public-private partnerships.

This chapter argues that this seemingly archetypical case of perverse confluence is not in fact perverse. A historical examination of the political projects behind these initiatives shows that they were attempts to surmount antiquated statist models whilst avoiding the free-market option. The actions taken by the *Orçamento Participativo* and the *Governança Solidária Local* reflect their respective notions of civil society as the alternative to distrust of the political models predominant in the second half of the twentieth century. These programs used different concepts and practices to support initiatives that enhance civil society's participation in public matters. Moreover, a study of their functioning demonstrates that, contrary to political rhetoric fuelled by PT militants, the operation of the GSL is not detrimental to the OP. Indeed, interviews with activists demonstrate that Porto Alegre's civil society is diverse and experienced enough to take advantage of both participatory channels.[4] In the case of Porto Alegre, the confluence of civil society discourses and participatory practices is augmenting the democratization of the state and creating new spaces for citizens' participation. I call this a "constructive confluence." Political projects inspired in certain theoretical traditions may successfully further a particular understanding of civil society, but they are not likely to impose a homogenous behavior on social activists. The opposite is more likely to take place: political projects and political theory will have to adapt to the various practices of civil society.

The next section of this paper examines the political and theoretical developments that led to the establishment of the Participatory Budgeting, describes how the program operates, and discusses its main current challenges. The third section does the same for the Local Solidarity Governance. The fourth section discusses the experiences of citizens active in both participatory initiatives. The conclusion summarizes the main findings and returns to the perverse confluence argument.

4. The field research for this study was carried in the period of May to July, 2008. In these four months I attended the weekly meetings of the OP Committee; visited all the major GSL projects; interviewed various members of the team responsible for implementing the GSL, including an independent UNESCO consultant; discussed OP recent developments with members of the independent monitoring non-governmental organization CIDADE; and carried 23 in-depth open interviews with OP and GSL participants, some more than once. It was an intentional sample and the selection criterion was diversity: during OP meetings and GSL visits I selected activists with a different political discourses; most interviewees have been involved in the programs for at least five years, three were in their first year; the sample was roughly equally distributed between male and female participants.

TO CIVIL SOCIETY, FROM THE LEFT

Gramscian Civil Society

The history of the Latin American Left is commonly divided into four periods (Löwy, 1999). The first period began in the 1920s, when the October Revolution in Russia (1917), the Leninist Comintern, and the writings of José Carlos Mariátegui spurred the creation of communist parties with revolutionary character throughout the region. In the mid-1930s these parties adopted the Stalinist doctrine promoted by the Comintern. The "national-democratic" strategy required the expansion of capitalism and the strengthening of a national bourgeoisie. In this second period, democracy was part of Marxists' discourse; however, the adjective "bourgeois" disfigured the concept and prevented reflections on it (Garcia, 1996: 121). In the third period, the Cuban Revolution inspired a new wave of revolutionary movements. This trend was centered on the Organización Latinoamerica de Solidariedad (1967: 313), according to which "the revolutionary armed struggles constitute the fundamental line of revolution for Latin America." Overall, in these three periods democracy and civil society did not constitute a substantial part of the political program of the Latin American Left.

The fourth period was incited by a number of theoretical and political developments that lead to the abandonment of traditional Marxist strategies and the construction of a political project that valued democracy and popular participation. On the theoretical side, a new alternative emerged as the ideas of Antonio Gramsci spread through the continent. Gramsci offered a conceptualization of civil society that allowed Marxists to come to terms with the concept (Cohen and Arato, 1992: 77-82). In his *Prison Notebooks,* Gramsci argues that a dominant group must exert control of both political and civil society in order to become a hegemonic force (Hoare and Smith, 1971: 245). The political society is the sphere of legal, overt control while civil society is the arena of cultural dominance where subaltern classes "spontaneously" give consent to the hegemonic group. Civil society is also the arena where a counter-hegemonic bloc is able to challenge the established order (Howell and Pearce, 2001: 33-34).

According to Raúl Burgos (2002), Gramsci began to play a major role in Latin American academia in the end of the 1960s. The Left had failed to seize control of the state using tactics learnt from Lenin and the Cuban Revolution. At the same time, democracy had become the demand around which resistance was organized and therefore new strategies had to endorse democracy in order to gain popular support. Gramsci allowed Latin American scholars to put forward the idea that revolution is not a single explosive act but a process in which political democracy is a necessary terrain where revolutionary forces gain strength. This idea permitted a more sophisticated understanding of the conditions of the continent, the preservation of a revolutionary ideal, and the galvanizing of the latent popular support for democracy.

PT's Political Project

Founded in 1979, the Brazilian Workers' Party (PT) did not embrace a particular Marxist doctrine or a clear socialist program. Instead, it allowed the coalescence of various unions, social movements, ecclesiastic community-based groups, student associations, and intellectuals in an internally democratic party (Cesar, 2002: 214-30). In spite of an amicable heterogeneity, two dominant factions argued over the party's political program. One faction saw the party as a popular, mass party, and emphasized democracy over socialism, while a more statist faction clung to Leninist ideals, envisioned the PT as a proletariat party, and placed less emphasis on democracy. A general trend marked the PT's discourse in the 1980s: from 1979 to the middle of the eighties, the democratic faction was paramount; in 1986-87 the country's economic and political crisis, allegedly a revolutionary opportunity, backed the raise of the statist faction; finally, the defeat of the PT in the 1989 presidential elections, the crumble of socialist role models, and a new analysis of capitalism brought the democratic faction back to the forefront in 1990-91. An analysis of official documents reveals the party's deliberations over matters of socialism, democracy, and civil society, and the consolidation of a radical democratic program.

The PT gradually modified its statement about the groups it viewed as forming its constituency. In its founding manifesto the PT declares itself to be a "mass party, ample and open, based on urban and rural workers" (Cesar, 2002: 248). Moreover, the document points out that in Brazil, "the rights of all workers are neglected, from peasants to doctors, from industrial workers to engineers to teachers." In 1980, notably breaking away from Leninist thought, the party stated, "there should be a clear *interest identity* (and not simply an 'alliance') between urban and rural workers." When the statist faction led PT more traditional statements appeared, as in, "industrial workers [are] the vanguard of all the exploited population" (Cesar, 2002: 248). In the 1990 VII National Congress, the party renounced the revolutionary vanguard attitude and civil society gained a privileged role:

> The relationship between the PT and Brazilian civil society is important not only because of the latter's growing influence, but also because the dispute for hegemony and political power by the workers and other popular social groups takes place much more intensely in the civil society sphere (Cesar, 2002: 262).

A year later, the First National Congress of the PT discussed how technological advances have changed the structure of capitalism and fragmented the contemporary working class, and the following statement was issued, "We want a Party that dialogues with other democratic and socialist forces, favoring the construction of a program and a historic bloc necessary in the promotion of an alternative development to the country" (Cesar, 2002: 265). In sum, the party goes through a discernible transition from a party that sees itself as the representation of the diverse sectors of civil society, at times the leader of these lesser groups, to a party aware of its location within it.

The party also reflected intensively on the role of democracy and the nature of socialism. In its first years the party reluctantly asserted itself as a socialist party, often making use of indirect statements, "the PT struggles so that economic and political power may be exerted directly by the workers" (Cesar, 2002: 273). In this period, the term socialism was almost unequivocally accompanied by the term democracy since, "there is no socialism without democracy, and no democracy without socialism" (Cesar, 2002: 272). In the 1987 Congress, wherein the Leninist segment was prominent, the objective of PT was clearly stated as socialism, though the term continued to be attached to the word democracy. In the 1990 Congress, the democratic faction was again strong, and the party issued statements explicitly rejecting the Soviet model; for example, "the communist parties in power drove their economies to a dead end because they failed to incorporate the concept of democracy [in their political program]" (Cesar, 2002: 286); and the PT "rejects any kind of dictatorship, and that includes the dictatorship of the proletariat" (Cesar, 2002: 288).

The concluding document of the 1990 VII National Congress of the PT posited that, "[democracy] is for us, at once a means and an end, an instrument of transformation and a goal to be achieved" (Partido dos Trabalhadores, 1990: 496-97). Later in the same document we find, "[s]ocialism, for the PT, is either radically democratic or it is not socialism" (Partido dos Trabalhadores, 1990: 500). The PT was particularly interested in the notion of participatory democracy with broad-based civic participation. The second-to-last paragraph calls for the expansion of instruments for direct democracy, "to guarantee the participation of the masses in the varied levels of organization of the political process and management of the economy" (Partido dos Trabalhadores, 1990: 503). These ideas were put into practice in one of the PT's first experiences in public administration: Porto Alegre.

The Participatory Budgeting

In 1988, the PT's Olivio Dutra became mayor after defeating the traditional *Partido Democrático Trabalhista* (PDT, Democratic Labor Party). In Dutra's first year the city had a large deficit, the party had a minority in the municipal assembly, the new public servants had little or no experience in public administration, and the organized popular sectors were highly frustrated with unfulfilled promises of participation. Dutra's team used a 1989 federal law to rearrange the city taxation system, increasing the city budget by 40%. Next, Dutra created the Planning Office, which decided to respond to civil society's demand for participation in the formulation of the city's budget (Abers, 2000). In 1990 the Participatory Budgeting of Porto Alegre began to be implemented.

The Participatory Budgeting is comprised of three levels. (1) At the local level groups organized in various forms work all year on their issues and participate in the regional preparatory meetings in March/April. At these meetings they discuss the execution of the previous year's demands and the priorities for the next year. In April/May each of the 17 regions of the city holds a Regional Assembly. In these Assemblies the government—often represented by the mayor—accounts for the investments in the region and the overall city finances. All attendees then vote on two items: they pick four priority investment areas, out of 16 options,[5] and they choose a group of four representatives who will serve as the region's counselors at the municipal level. (2) A thematic structure functions in a way similar to the process described above. The procedure is the same except that citizens gather around six broad themes instead of geographical areas.[6] These forums tend to attract the middle-class and representatives of specific segments of the population, e.g. sports

5. Basic sanitation, housing, paving, education, social assistance, health, accessibility, and urban mobility, youth, transport, leisure areas, sport and leisure, public illumination, economic development and taxation, tourism, culture, and environment.

6. Transport; culture; economic development and tourism; education, sports, and leisure; city organization, urban and environment development; and health and social assistance.

and culture (Fedozzi, 1999: 142-46). (3) The Participatory Budgeting Committee (COP) is the highest-level forum and it is comprised of two counselors and two alternates from each regional forum; two counselors and two alternates from each thematic forum; one counselor and one alternate from the municipal public workers union; one counselor and one alternate from the União das Associações de Moradores de Porto Alegre (UAMPA, Union of Neighborhood Associations of Porto Alegre); and two representatives, and their alternates, from the government's executive office (appointed by the mayor, these representatives participate in the deliberations but do not have voting power). The main function of the COP is to transform the demands made at the local and thematic levels into an official municipal budget that adheres to the technical criteria negotiated with the various city departments and the city's budgetary limitations. The other two important roles of the COP are to monitor the implementation of the previous year's budget and to conduct a review of the Participatory Budgeting structure in December/January (Orçamento Participativo, 2008).

Neither the people directly involved in the OP nor researchers suggest the process is flawless. In fact the opposite is true. As a live and continuingly adapting process its deficiencies are constantly debated. In the first five years of OP, for example, technical discussions were absent. The population demanded whatever they deemed necessary. The result was upset engineers, unfinished projects, and wasted resources. In 1995 the administration asked the city agencies to define "technical criteria" and present them to participants before the conclusion of the year's budget (Abers, 2000: 203-10). Since then the Participatory Budgeting Committee discusses the technical criteria every year. Participants' ability to effectively participate in the meetings, given their educational level, has also been widely discussed (Abers, 2000: 115-33; Gret and Sintomer, 2005: 73-96). On this front the government tries to educate the population through various publications, and the non-governmental organization CIDADE offers important courses to new participants.

Another issue is whether the Orçamento Participativo should become law. So far the process has been based on a constitutional article that encourages the participation of citizens in municipal administration.[7] The final budget still requires the approval of the legislative assembly. On one hand, it is argued that the non-legalization of the OP is what allows for flexibility and inclusiveness.[8] On the other hand, in a Committee meeting of June 2008, because of the coming elections, a counselor argued that "the

7. Article 29 of the 1988 Constitution.

OP ought to be law, otherwise it is a concession and stays in the hands of politicians."[9] These questions do not constitute a challenge to the process: continuous evaluation and debate strengthens the program.

However, two issues defy the effectiveness of this democratizing tool. The first regards the "trivialization" of the process and the emergence of "specialist participants" responsible for mediating participation (Beras, 2008). In other words, a small group of delegates and councilors learned how to control and manipulate the process. Instead of a process of popular participation and democratic exercise, this mechanism sometimes becomes simply an instrument for the attainment of material demands, with an unwritten restrictive code that hinders the participation of inexperienced members. According to Beras (2008: 241), "the Porto Alegre OP experiment initially produces a new understanding of democracy in the Brazilian society." In a second moment, however, "this new understanding is progressively incorporated and systematized under traditional forms of political engagement," i.e. clientelism. As a consequence, he argues, "the differentiation between civil society and state is weakened, and, once again, civil society is incapable of invigorating itself, the state lapses back into an arena for the pursuit of interests, and, in short, participation gains a merely pragmatic character." In the words of a new OP counselor, "the old guys push us aside and do not teach us how things work; they want to control the process." Prior to 2004, the Participatory Budgeting Internal Statute imposed a maximum two-year term for COP councilors; recently this clause was voted out, by the councilors themselves. As a result, the turnover rate of councilors, which declined from 75% in 2000 to 34% in 2008, is likely to continue to decrease; CIDADE (2007) has alerted to the "need to reflect on leadership renovation" or risk to negate the democratic history built by the OP process.

The second relevant concern regards the proportion of the city's total budget made available to the Orçamento Participativo. Only a portion of the budget that is destined to new investments is open for discussion: between 6% and 8% of the total budget in the last eight years (CIDADE, 2008). Furthermore, once the annual investment plan has been formulated, the government still has to actually disburse the funds. It is not possible to find consistent figures for government expenditure; figures vary according to the source. The fact is that a large number of approved demands are delayed, i.e., demands entered the City's Plan of Investment, following the OP procedure,

8. For comparative studies of participatory budgets and legally-institutionalized popular health councils, see Cunha and Avritzer.
9. Field notes, COP Meeting (June 10, 2008).

but the administration did not execute them. As of 2008, estimates range from 801 to 1,561 delayed demands (CIDADE, 2008). The delays began in the PT's last administration but worsened in the last six years.[10] The current administration argues that the PT left a large fiscal deficit; the opposition points to R$15 million spent in government publicity in 2007 alone (the equivalent to US$8.4 million in December of that year). In either case, lack of confidence in the mechanism threatens to reduce civil society's participation in the budgeting process: the poor sacrifice valuable time and resource to participate, sometimes even a bus fare is a forbidding cost. As one interviewee noted, "the community does not attend meetings anymore because they do not see results." Moreover, with so many delayed demands, how and who decides what demands are carried out? These setbacks point to the need to improve, not abandon, the Participatory Budgeting.

To Civil Society, from the Right

Neo-Tocquevillian Constructs

In the late 1970s, critiques of the welfare state advocated the adoption of neo-liberal economics, known as "the Washington Consensus." In this consensus, civil society is split into two parts: commercial society, commonly referred to as "the market," and "civil society," usually meaning non-governmental and charitable organizations. The main engine of growth and development is the market, the state has a regulatory role, and civil society has the responsibility to care for the destitute. The most important characteristic of this view is the belief in a benevolent and self-correcting market. Since the market is not harmful and the state is—as allegedly made evident by the malfunctioning of welfare programs—the best option is to replace government institutions by market mechanisms (Cohen and Arato, 1992; Howell and Pearce, 2001).

In the 1980s and 1990s, the two main proponents of the Washington Consensus, the World Bank and the International Monetary Fund, imposed Structural Adjustment Programs on developing countries that borrowed from them. The failures of these programs and the booming of East Asian economies reliant on state intervention drew attention to studies of

10. According to CIDADE (2008), 70% of the demands were executed in 2002-2004, and only 33% in 2004-2007.

market imperfections (Fine, 1999; Howell and Pearce, 2001). At the end of the 1990s, a number of orthodox economists began to accept the existence of market imperfections and admitted the need for state intervention.

In this context, civil society returned to the forefront of mainstream political analysis. In 1993, drawing on the work of Edward Banfield and James Coleman, Robert Putnam published a book in which he argued strong associational life and networks of civil engagement were distinctive features between more prosperous and democratic Northern Italy and less affluent and clientelistic Southern Italy (Howell and Pierce, 2001: 26). He used the term "social capital" to refer to the positive impact of associational cultural networks in the functioning of democracy. This theoretical development provided a non-market explanation for market imperfections and brought the notion of civil society to the center of neo-liberal discourse, although it would be a mistake to assume that the notions of "social capital" and "third sector" are used only by neo-liberals.

Luciana Tatagiba proposed the notion of "managerial democracy" to describe post-liberal reform governments that use civil society's participation as a mechanism to increase administrative efficiency. According to Tatagiba, governments seek partnership with the private sector and civil society in order to galvanize its limited resources. The "highly confrontational tone that used to constitute the participatory rhetoric is dissolved into the supposedly neutral, technical discourse of modern management" (Tatagiba, 2006: 142). In managerial democracy, discussions regarding what is of public interest are absent; the state retains the power to decide on this manner unilaterally. Instead, partners are asked how they can "do their part" in a specific action that aims at addressing a particular issue that "can only be solved with the contribution and solidarity of all" (Tagatiba, 2006: 146). Although associated with neo-liberal governments, this practice is not restricted to them.

PPS's Managerial Democracy

At a first glance, the Local Solidarity Governance (GSL) seems an expression of the neo-liberal political project: the proponents of the program endorse privatization, condemn state centralism, defend fiscal responsibility, and use terms such as "social capital" and "third sector." The program is an example of the managerial democracy approach described in the previous section. In Porto Alegre, the adoption of managerial democracy combines a defeatist attitude towards the hard-nosed economic globalization with an attempt to surmount anachronistic statist models associated with Marxist ideals and nationalist-developmentalist programs.

This section offers an analysis of texts and policies put forward by the political-intellectual group behind the GSL. Central to this analysis is Cézar Busatto.[11] Although most of the texts examined were authored by Busatto, he represents a group of less-visible intellectuals and politicians that actively participated in the conceptual development and implementation of the GSL, some of whom are also referenced here.

In 1991, Busatto attacked President Collor's reckless liberalizations that set in motion the Brazilian neo-liberal program with the following words,

> the development trajectory taken will do nothing other than exacerbate the social and regional imbalances. . . this development project confronts the interests of the destitute majority of the population. . . Evidently, the forces of an oligopoly market will not incorporate millions of men and women living in absolute poverty (Busatto, 1991: 143).

Later in the same text Busatto argued the need to install a new kind of state, distinct from the outsized state of the import substitution period and the liberal minimum state. He endorsed a developmental state: small and robust with a strategic role of formulating and facilitating a development program in collaboration with the private sector and society at large.

As the Secretary of Finance, Busatto implemented a program that counted on citizens' inspection of businesses to reduce tax evasion in small commercial transactions. As a reward, the population could choose institutions, e.g. orphanages and hospitals, to receive a portion of the incremental tax revenue. The program included a series of more traditional state policies as, "it wouldn't have been enough if society did its part and the state neglected its, and vice-versa . . . Synergy is fundamental" (Busatto, 1998: 55). Still commenting on PMDB's state administration, Busatto noted, "this is the vision I have of the role of governments in whatever level: they have to be partners among themselves and with society, in order to make the world a bit better to live in" (Busatto, 1998: 88).[12] Finally, Busatto (1999b: 97-98) argued that the fiscal incentives given to multinational corporations

---

11. Busatto is a political economist trained in the Universidad Autónoma de Mexico. He is a pro-democracy militant with a brief passage in the Castroist MR-8, who served two times as state representative for the PMDB; was Secretary of Finance of PMDB's state administration (1994-1998); and was the founding secretary of the Porto Alegre's Secretariat for Political Coordination and Local Solidarity Governance.

and the privatizations in the Brazilian economy "responded to the historical necessity of spurring a dynamic regional economy."

Busatto (1999a: 21) summarized much of this thought when affirming that one of the characteristics of the turning of the century is,

> the hegemony of the economy over politics, of the internationalized markets over states, and the transformation of citizens into consumers. The consequences are dramatic; especially in the social sphere. . . There are no longer possibilities for a nation—and much less a state within this nation—to not be involved in the process. Thus, there is an increasing consensus regarding the necessity of creation of a mechanism at the global level to counter the forces of the international market. While these mechanisms are not adopted, there is a search for national policies that at least attenuate the perverse effects of globalization.

This discontented and disillusioned political group led by Busatto sought a new political project in the turbulent 1990s. The past pointed to the inefficiency of statism models, the present made evident states' lack of muscle vis-à-vis international capital. Neither past nor present offered viable alternatives. In the words of Jandira Feijó (2008: 117), a journalist in the group, "to expect that the humongous state institutions are capable of being modernized, one needs much more than hope and political will power. To believe that the market is willing to include more people is almost like believing in fairy tales." The solution found was a dynamic and competent state trying to rally civil society and "build a new mindset in our business class" (Busatto, 1998: 107). It is in this context that concepts such as social capital and social responsibility entered the group's political project.

In *Democracy, Prosperity and Social Responsibility*, Busatto draws heavily on studies of the John Hopkins Institute in order to explain the notions of third sector, social responsibility, social entrepreneur, and social capital. In *Social Responsibility: The Revolution of our Times*, he further elaborates the idea of a political program resting on citizen participation, businesses ethics, and cooperation between state, civil society, and the private sector. In a later publication, Plínio Zalewski and Busatto established the groundwork for the Local Solidarity Governance and pointed out social capital, sustainable development, local power, and social responsibility as some of the main concepts shaping the initiative. Finally, Bussato and Feijó summarized much of the group's thought in *The Fireflies' Era. The Emergence of a New Political*

12. The inability to work together is a fault usually attributed to PT (Plínio Zalewski, 1999: 90). A journalist member of this political group stated that, "PT is the averse of plurality, [it] is intolerant, the heir of a totalitarian socialist tradition, de-linked from the main modernizing movements taking place in the globe."

Culture where in fireflies are the millions of isolated citizens doing their bit in the construction of a better world. While publishing these works, Busatto's team pushed a series of social responsibility projects in the municipal and state assemblies.[13]

My own interview with Busatto confirmed the conceptual developments traced above. Busatto said that his formal education and first years of political activism fostered a conviction in statist alternatives to a more just society, "Marxism and Keynesian influenced my thought a lot; the older my texts, the more clear this influence is." In 1980, the rise of the Washington Consensus and the subsequent fall of socialist models "baffled us" and "made us start seeking a new form of state." The Soviet Union had fallen, "neo-liberalism did not convince us," and "we did not want just to keep the system rolling, we wanted to promote an alternative." Social responsibility appeared as a new paradigm, "it animated me, gave me energy to try to improve things again." This concept "allowed us to move away from a stiff and fragmented understanding of society to a more harmonious, holistic view." Terms such as governance and networks helped them to articulate this horizontal, cooperative understanding of state-society relationship. The idea of the "local" also supports the move beyond grand meta-narratives since it "permits us to focus on life where it happens." Finally, Busatto acknowledged that it was Augusto de Franco who helped to give their ideas form.

Franco is the last piece in this puzzle. In 1993, Franco left the PT after 13 years of militancy and became involved in two mid-1990s national initiatives against poverty and hunger created by President Cardoso's administration. Since then he has been an enthusiastic proponent of what has been described here as managerial democracy. A marked characteristic of his writing is the vision of a fundamentally new political culture, in which "acting here and now in networks of solidarity" is the historical synthesis between the traditional societal forms and the unrealizable modern project.[14] Thus, a "change in the political culture" is an aim of and condition for the GSL. Franco (2008: 100) disentangles for us the thorny question of whether theory informed practice or vice-versa:

> It should be mentioned that the basic idea of [Local Solidarity Governance]. . . was conceived by the team long before this idea was developed and shaped as a

13. The Social Responsibility Award; the Solidarity Law; the Solidarity Day, and the Special Commission in Public Social Responsibility.

14. "Acting here and now" dissolves the dialectics between traditional monastic-mythical and the modern prophetic-utopia, and "networks of solidarity" solves the hierarchical-autocracy versus autonomous-democracy tension (Franco, 2008).

> program. But it should also be recognized that the more elaborate theoretical justification—which was created after the fact—for the later development of this basic idea was enthusiastically adopted by the team.

Thus, after a long decade of intense debate, this political group arrives at a participatory democracy, involving all sectors of society, as the best alternative to the 1990s' challenges. Contrary to the PT, this group did not have a distinct theoretical body in which to draw upon. Instead, they adopted terms in vogue in the international scenario and used them according to their ideals and needs.

Local Solidarity Governance

In 2002, Busatto and a number of PMDB (Brazilian Democratic Movement Party) members broke with the party and joined the *Partido Popular Socialista* (PPS, Socialist People's Party). The PPS was created in 1992 as a renovation of the Brazilian Communist Party (PCB) and was later joined by a number of former members of the PMDB and the PT. PMDB members joined PPS alleging their party lost sight of the democratic and social justice values in which it was founded (Busatto, 2001: 166-90). According to Dacanal, the PT's radical faction became dominant within the party in the mid-to-late 1990s[15]; as a result, a number of PT members from the moderate faction abandoned the party and some, like Zalewski, joined the PPS. In the 2004 election, PPS formed a twelve-party coalition and defeated PT: José Fogaça became mayor; Bussato the head of the newly created Secretariat for Political Coordination and Local Solidarity Governance (SMCPGL); Feijó and Zalewski, received coordinating positions within the Secretariat. In 2005, Fogaça called public meetings in each of the 17 Participatory Budgeting regions, wherein he inaugurated the *Comitê Gestor Local* (CGL, Local Managing Committee) and explained the new participatory initiative. Next, governance agents were hired to spur regional networks and initiate the eight steps that constitute the Local Solidarity Governance. This section describes the CGL, explains the eight-step process, and then discuses their implementation.[16]

According to the Secretariat, Comitê Gestor Local is a public network that integrates all sectors of municipal administration" and seeks to foment

15. Dacanal explains that this *tendência* was weak in early 1980s, but progressively gained the support of a "new class" of a low-educated proletariat massively admitted into the party's public offices.
16. This brief description overlooks intermediary implementation steps found in Perusso et al. (2008).

endo-governance actions and facilitate society's governance programs (SMCPGL, 2005). They operate from the Centros Administrativos Regionais (CAR, Regional Administrative Centers) which are responsible for solving citizens' day-to-day problems; they serve as a link between people and the various municipal departments. At the Regional Administrative Centers, clientelism happens at its best. CAR coordinators are directly appointed by the mayor; municipal departments' personnel are permanent public workers with their own political affiliations; and the community leaders who walk in to report issues often represent a number of voters. In order to change this traditional way of doing local politics, CGLs started to bring together once a month representatives from various municipal departments, the coordinator of the Regional Administrative Centers, the Participatory Budgeting regional coordinators, and the SMCPGL person in-charge of CGS. In these meetings municipal staff from various departments meet to discuss citizens' requests, draw on each other's knowledge, plan combined action, and demand cooperation. Meetings' records are posted online and the SMCPGL person follows-up on resolutions.

The backbone of the Local Solidarity Governance is an eight-step process, in which governance agents and community members: 1) receive training; 2) form a network team in their respective regions; 3) organize this team; 4) hold a "vision for the future" seminar; 5) diagnose the region's assets and needs; 6) define the participatory plans and goals; 7) set priorities; and 8) sign an agreement with all parties involved, committing themselves to the agenda. The GSL's website and materials teach the population the meaning of the concepts used above. In line with Tatagiba's definition of managerial democracy, these materials explain that actors (i.e. citizens, civil society organizations, businesses, and government agencies) ought to create local (i.e. territorially based, regional) networks that allow the flow of social and human capital; moreover, actors ought to see each other as partners whose ideological differences shall not interfere in the accomplishment of common goals; working teams are organized transversely, surpassing hierarchical structures; and decision-making is based on dialogue and consensus, moving beyond argumentative and voting methods.

In the period of August of 2006 and May of 2007, an estimate of 450 people from some 186 NGOs and social institutions attended a training course in project management, the CapacitaPOA. Augusto de Franco's consultancy group led the workshops with the support of the United Nations Education, Scientific, and Cultural Organization (UNESCO) and the

Lutheran University of Brazil (Perusso et al., 2008). The main objective of this course was to increase the administrative capacity of civil society organizations. As of November of 2008, the GSL consisted of eight large "demonstrative actions," a number of small actions, Solidarity Events, and two information portals.

The small actions function on the idea of *contrapartida* (pay back), and transversal partnerships. A circus wants an authorization to use a city's park for a month, the Regional Administrative Center coordinator gives the authorization, as *contrapartida* the circus lends their large tent for a public event, e.g. a Citizenship Day where people from poor areas can issue and renew documents, close to their homes on a weekend. An example of a "transversal partnership" is when the administration provides land (use license) and technical support (engineers) to a non-governmental organization (NGO) wanting to use private funds to build a day care. In one instance, the administration transformed an abandoned small bus terminal into a community kitchen and passed it on to a religious group who served soup to the homeless from a small house.

The Solidarity Actions are events organized with the collaboration of civil society groups, businesses, and different municipal departments. For example, a middle school wanted to bring together the rival neighborhoods in the region and decided to organize a Christmas party in the park in the area. The local YMCA bought the idea and helped to organize the event. Local businesses made donations in kind. The governance agent contacted the police, the firefighters, and the Secretariat of Culture to support the event. The party was "a success at zero cost," according to the school's principal.

Finally, the GSL has a communication structure. The *Blog da Governança* (Governance Blog) is the main engine of the regional networks. The main page shows a map of the city, the user clicks on a particular region and gains access to GSL news, Managing Committee reports, and developments of the eight-step process. The SMGL has installed a number of *TeleCentros* (Public Computer Labs) across the city to facilitate citizens' access to public information. A number of *TeleCentros* were themselves the result of partnership with businesses. The *Observatório de Porto Alegre* (ObservaPOA, Porto Alegre Observatory) "makes available a large geo-referenced data bank about Porto Alegre, contributing to the consolidation of citizen participation in the city's management."[17] According to one of its staff members, the initial idea was to create a "non-governmental public institution," in which the state

17. See www2.portoalegre.rs.gov.br/observatorio.

would contribute as much as the academia, the private sector, and civil society. The idea did not blossom as wished and the ObservaPOA remains a government project. In the interviewee's opinion, in Brazil a truly participatory culture is very weak; organizations' main motivation to partner with the government is to access public resources, not to contribute to society. He defends, however, that it is the state's responsibility to continuously promote a truly participatory culture. Unfortunately, ObservaPOA and the NGO CIDADE do not collaborate; both provide vital services to enhance the city's democratic cultural but political lines set them apart.

The proponents and managers of the Local Solidarity Governance offer four explanations to the slow implementation process. First, the GSL versus OP attitude prevented a more enthusiastic adoption of the program in the communities. The new administration kept its promise of maintaining the Participatory Budgeting. However, skeptical activists and the PT opposition continually incite the OP versus GSL antagonism, notably visible in OP meetings. Moreover, the GSL is referred to as a neo-liberal process attempting to release the government from its responsibilities. The administration defends the Local Solidarity Governance by arguing that the program is complementary to the Participatory Budgeting. While the latter discusses the best allocation of public funds, the former assists communities to recognize and utilize other resources (Perusso et al., 2008).

The second issue hampering the GSL is lack of capacity. Governance agents were few and unprepared. The total number of agents never passed ten, there was a high turnover, and among the current agents most do not have any experience in public administration. Both Augusto de Franco and the UNESCO consultant have expressed their frustration with this team (Franco, 2008; interview with Andréa Martins, August 10, 2008). Within the communities there is also an educational barrier that prevents people from engaging with complicated strategic plans and financial diagnosis. I asked the UNESCO consultant whether people were having a difficult time with the more intricate administrative tools; she replied that "often the problem is illiteracy." The third fact slowing this initiative is the lack of involvement of the private sector. This fact is linked to a broader phenomenon: the "lack of a truly participatory culture," the fourth and most common explanation offered to explain the slow-moving Local Solidarity Governance program. Proponents of the program often assert that the GSL involves the solidification of a new political culture, which takes time.

In my analysis, two other important factors obstruct the running of the GSL. First, responding to the political demand for new alternatives in the 2004 elections, the GSL was designed by the Socialist People's Party, as part of the electoral campaign. By contrast, in 1990-91, Participatory Budgeting proposals were drafted in consultation with the population (Abers, 2000; Fedozzi, 1999). Activists reminded me innumerable times that "It was we who created the OP!" The GSL affronted activists' understanding of participation by launching a program drafted behind closed doors. The second problem is the knotty language used by the GSL. A number of activists humbly admitted they never understood its content. In the wish to be innovative and overcome outdated models, planners overused conceptual jargons.[18] The GSL is a positive attempt to broaden participatory channels in the city. Nevertheless, in order to be effective the program needs to depart from what the city understands as legitimate forms of participation and from there build new participatory mechanisms. In order to make the Local Solidarity Governance politically accepted and functional, the administration needs to invite civil society to revise and rewrite the process. The most serious risk facing the GSL is the circular and disingenuous argument that the program does not work yet because it requires a "change in culture."

CITIZENS' EXPERIENCES

The field research for this study included interviews with citizens active in at least one of the initiatives. The material collected does not suggest the two programs are incompatible; in fact, the opposite is true. Citizens participating in the Local Solidarity Governance tend to see it as more suitable to them than the Participatory Budgeting. A regatta coordinator who used GSL support to start a sailing school for low-income children affirmed that, "I never liked this OP stuff, I always thought this is for people to demand paving and sewage, important, but not for me." According to the president of the São Guilherme Neighborhood Association, a former OP counselor and now head of a GSL initiative, "adding the GSL to the OP was very important. . . We know there are too many demands, there is no way you can address all of them, doesn't matter whose government it is." In an interview with five

18. For example, one document written by the creators of the GSL defines the initiative as following: "Local Solidarity Governance is a multidisciplinary network that is territorially organized in order to promote the culture of solidarity and cooperation between government and local society. Its aim is to stimulate partnerships based on the principles of participation, autonomy, multidisciplinary, and co-responsibility in favor of social inclusion" (SMCPGL, 2008).

women leaders in the Cruzeiro neighborhood, the GSL was seen as empowering civic leaders, "With the GSL the government challenges us to go further. We don't just say what we want, but how we want it as well." One would make a tremendous error in assuming these women are co-opted, "In these 16 years of OP the government trained us politically to discuss and argue with them. Today we discuss with any government, face-to-face." Overall, GSL participants endorse the OP, but welcome the new initiative.

OP counselors are divided about the GSL; some view it with askance, others seem open to the new initiative. In an interview with two 80-year-old OP counselors with a long history of activism, one stated, "the GSL is just clientelism;" the other said she is willing to give it a chance, but admitted she cannot understand the program, though she attended many meetings and read all the material. Another OP old-timer, a chess instructor, thinks the two programs are not incongruous; he argues that "if the GSL had been implemented through the OP, it would've been a success, but the administration opted for creating a parallel, confronting structure, it was a strategic mistake, they played chess poorly." The president of one of the street vendors unions in the city declared that he attended two GSL meetings and did not like what he witnessed, "it appeared to me as if the government was trying to wash its hands on things I consider its responsibility." In September of 2008, four years after the election of Fogaça, one could still sense in OP cycles the fear for the termination of the process, and its replacement for the GSL. The government response is that the two programs are complementary: public funding is still open for public debate in the OP, while the GSL tries to facilitate partnerships and resource allocation among various non-public actors.

Finally, there is a third group of activists whose view is succinctly summarized in the words of a neighborhood leader in the north side, "We did partnerships with everyone; what is important for us is to get things." A public health care worker expressed a similar opinion in a more elaborated manner, "I think there are no intrinsic values. You can't just think, 'Is it good, is it bad?' I think it is the result that counts, the sort of door it opens." In a more confrontational tone, another OP old-timer stated that, "I will always be in opposition [to the government]; our party is the community." With the exception of some OP old-timers with a zealous attitude towards the initiative,[19] activists' allegiance rest with the "community" not with a particular program or ideal of civil society.

19. Fedozzi (1999) called this "the pioneer syndrome;" old-timers resent the label.

Despite their prominence and political importance, these two participatory initiatives are only part of the activists' history and repertoire of action. A number of interviewees made references to struggles against the military government; the public health care worker was active in the student movement that helped to bring down President Collor; two interviewees are committed primarily to their labor unions; some are active in party politics; two OP councilors head social movements for urban housing that occupies abandoned buildings and often have to confront the police; the list of examples goes on. A truly proactive civil society—as allegedly advocated by leftists and neo-liberals—does not limit its actions to space created by government institutions and political discourses.

CONCLUSION

In electoral periods, PT and PMDB supporters in Porto Alegre stand in clearly demarcated sides of the Redenção Park, waving their flags and provoking each other. Likewise, Participatory Budgeting and Local Solidarity Governance supporters often stand on different sides, cheering for one program and booing the other. A hasty examination may further the antagonism created by party politics, setting one program as "radical democratic" and the other as "neo-liberal." However, a historical examination shows that the groups behind these initiatives faced essentially the same challenge: how to avoid statist models without surrendering to free-market ruling. In the PT's theoretical tradition, Gramsci's writings allowed a new understanding of the worth of civil society and democracy, and backed a proposition for the radical democratization of the state. In turn, the PPS adopted terms in vogue in the international political scenario and used them according to the group's ideal.

This study also examined the operation and current challenges of each program. The OP allows citizens, directly and through their representatives, to discuss the utilization of a small but significant portion of the public budget. This program breaks with traditional clientelism by opening public administration to popular scrutiny. Moreover, it teaches citizens about their rights and fosters reflection on collective issues. The process is now vulnerable to small groups of individuals who try to control it and limit the access of new community members. Furthermore, the large number of unattended demands threatens the program as citizens' participation is dependent on the delivery of services. In turn, the GSL attempts to facilitate partnerships among the various sectors of society, galvanizing non-public resources towards collective concerns. However, the programs still lacks a more clear language and a more transparent process that respects the city's participatory culture.

Finally, the third section of this paper drew on field interviews to show that Porto Alegre's activists are diverse and experienced enough to take advantage of both participatory initiatives. Neighborhood leaders, regatta coordinators, chess instructors, public health care workers, union leaders, housewives, students, homeless urban-dwellers, and other groups, will participate in public matters distinctively; each according to its need, ability, interest, resource, and geographic location. The OP has been a useful tool for many years and activists almost unanimously endorse it. The GSL now offers a new alternative: some groups have learned how to benefit from it; others are studying it, trying to get through its complicated language; still others remain skeptical and prefer to work with the more familiar OP. Thus, from an activist perspective the issue seems to be how to make these programs function better, not what ideal of civil society should be advanced.

The present study supports the first part of Dagnino's argument by providing a historical account of the development of two political projects with distinct understandings of civil society and participation. However, the study challenges the second part of Dagnino's argument by suggesting that in Porto Alegre, the meaning and practice of civil society and participation has been expanded by the creation of a new participatory initiative. In practice, neither program directly challenged market forces, although both increased the state apparatus as new agencies were created to manage the programs. Overall, participation in public matters increased as two programs gave citizens more choice on how to participate. Finally, the existence of two distinct programs fueled a discussion on democracy, participation, and the role of civil society—a very democratic exercise. For these reasons, in the Porto Alegre case, the confluence of civil society discourses seems constructive, not perverse.

Brazil has *one*, diverse and active civil society. The language and practices that pushed the democratizing period are now complemented by terms such public-private partnerships, social capital, and social responsibility. Initiatives based on this language ought to be welcomed as new efforts to deepen democracy, increase citizen participation, government transparency, and public awareness. To dismiss these initiatives based on *a priori* theoretical arguments is a regrettable mistake. In democratic Brazil, citizens themselves will determine the usefulness and value of participatory mechanisms. Political projects and state models can influence but not determine what civil society is or is not.

Part II
Social and Cultural Dimensions

9

PENSION REFORM IN BRAZIL: ADDRESSING A SOCIAL PACT

José Roberto Ferreira Savoia

Abstract: The following study highlights the key features that define today's social security scenario in Brazil. One of the most important issues raised is the striking lack of balance between revenue and expenditure within the social security sector against a backdrop of worrying trends such as unequal benefits rights and a large contingent of casual workers. This article proposes a number of ways toward improving the nation's pension laws and system.[1]

Social Security reforms in Latin American countries have some peculiar characteristics that have changed the role of the State. In short, the welfare state is in decline as the importance of the private sector has increased. In Brazil, before the Constitutional Amendments of 1998, the State was viewed as the only provider of pensions. This has been slowly abandoned and individuals are being encouraged to set up their own pension savings accounts. Complementary pensions are increasing owing to new measures such as new regulation, enforcement by supervising authorities and adoption of tax incentives. Consequently, the number of participants and private

1. I would like to thank Albert Fishlow and Carmelo Mesa-Lago for their comments. Liliana Reyes and Shawn Pearce from ILAS-Columbia University, Bruno Buscariolli, Daniel Bergman, Ana Paula Alcântara, and Anthony de Faria Dovkants assisted me with comments and data collection.

pension plans has increased, creating a positive impact for the long-term savings culture (Savoia et al, 2007).

Nowadays, Brazil's pension system is made up of various inequalities allowing some groups to benefit while the majority of those retired end up worse off. This distortion occurs because of an old institutional arrangement, molded during the seventies, and not completely reformed. This is just one example. But overall, Brazil has the same problems observed in other countries, such as fiscal deficits, a low level of affiliation to the official system, an aggravating aging problem, differences in eligibility criteria between the sexes and an imbalance between the number of public- and private- sector workers. The government must increase affiliation levels and incorporate informal workers into the formal labor sector in order to bring balance to the social security system.

After President Luiz Inácio Lula da Silva came to power in 2003, many expected his key Social Security reform to change the imbalances created over many decades, but like any bill certain elements were watered down and compromise was reached to ensure it was passed. During the reform process, the most important parameters that were targeted for change included limiting the amount paid to pensioners, retirement criteria for public-sector workers and for the next generation of public servants an end to their full pensions involving a parity between the value of active workers' wages and their pensions. Tax measures to promote higher affiliation and institutional changes to reduce informality, however, are showing some good results on the fiscal side, and the number of self-employed people increased to 4.1 million in 2008 from 3.3 million in 2007.

This text is organized as follows: after this introduction, a background section provides a description of the Brazilian social security system. The next sections analyze the main issues to be addressed, review measures adopted by Lula's reform, indicate the bill's financial impacts and analyze the role of a social pact aimed at promoting reform.

Background

Historical causes explain the distortions in the Brazilian pension system. A good historical perspective is provided by Oliveira, Beltrão, and Ferreira (1997). Path dependency and the role of collective action help to clarify the current situation and the emergence of so many deep problems.

A 1998 reform cleared up some distortions such as the absence of age limits on retirement for the public servants and produced conditions to help control the Social Security deficit. However, its results were partial since an imbalance between account and benefit values continue. At that time, studies were made to calculate the cost of changing the Brazilian social security system into a capitalized system, which proved to be impracticable ranging between 188% (General Regime) and 255% of GDP (General Regime and Special Regime), depending on the transition's form. As mentioned by Nakahodo and Savoia (2008) the transition from a defined benefit to a defined contribution scheme entails high transition costs because, with creation of individual accounts, not only would the government stop collecting mandatory contributions from current workers, but it would also need to fund new individual accounts until the system became self-sustainable. Consequently, government was left with the option of stimulating complementary pensions and making a parametric reform.[2]

The pensions system in Brazil comprises:

1. The General Regime for private-sector workers and the Special Regime for employees of the public sector. The General Regime is a pay-as-you-go (PAYG) system in which contributions from both employers and employees are used to pay defined benefits to pensioners. The National Institute for Social Security, or INSS, is responsible for managing the social security of around 26.7 million active workers (in a nation of more than 190 million people). In 2008 INSS collected R$180.4 billion in contributions and paid R$242.6 billion in benefits to 26 million people, representing an average benefit of R$777.56 per month. The observed deficit of R$62.4 billion was equivalent to 2.32 percent of GDP.
2. The Special Regime, which gathers Union, State, and Municipality Civil Servants, pays high benefits and charges very low contributions, generating severe deficits. The last official Federal report from 2008 presented total expenses of R$63.2 billion whilst contributions were R$8.2 billion, which generated a deficit of R$55 billion (2.06 percent of GDP). There were around 5.3 million contributors and 1 million pensioners. The public-sector civil servants have pensions readjusted in the same way as the active workers' salaries.

   There is also a Complementary Pension Regime for the future employees of the public sector still regulated but not yet implemented. It is a mandatory Pension Fund only for the next generation of public servants.
3. A Complementary Pension Regime (RPC), working on a voluntary basis, is comprised of Closed Pensions (Pension Funds and Multi-employer Funds) and

2. A reform that changes parameters, or requirements for eligibility, like: years of contribution instead of years worked; the abolition of early retirement for new insured; and the adoption of minimum age criteria for civil servant retirement; total contributions and age are used for the calculation of social security payments.

Open Funds provided by financial institutions. Similar to the US, Pension Funds are voluntary and can be organized as Sponsored Funds by the businesses or in Multi-employer Form. In 2008 there were 371 pension funds, with R$442.9 billion of assets and 2.6 million participants. The value of benefits paid was R$2.2 billion. Pension Funds play a significant role in the Brazilian economy, providing a stable basis of long-term resources to finance productive investments and also are major buyers of Brazilian treasuries.

The Open Funds are managed by the financial system and offer plans to individuals and corporations. These plans are capitalized, optional, and most of them have defined contributions. In 2008, they comprised of R$147.5 billion in assets and approximately 96,000 beneficiaries who receive some type of income (ANAPP, 2008).

4. There is also a "zero" pillar that provides poverty relief to the elderly. It is financed by the Treasury and managed by the INSS. Since the passage of the 1988 Constitution, the community and casual workers have benefitted thanks to an enhancement and extension of retirement rights. These programs were implemented in the beginning of the 1990s, and have achieved important results in poverty reduction among the deprived.[3] The most important ones under the pensions regime are the Rural Pensions (Previdência Rural) and the Organic Social Security Law (Lei Orgânica de Assistência Social—LOAS). Rural Pensions started in 1991 and pay a minimum wage to approximately 7.2 million rural workers. The social assistance program (LOAS) reaches 2.9 million people. It pays one minimum wage to those who have 65 years or some kind of disability. In 2008 expenses were R$15.6 billion paid to 3.2 million beneficiaries.

THE SOCIAL SECURITY DIAGNOSIS

The Brazilian Social Security System has some crucial issues that should be addressed as part of a process of continuous institutional change and political negotiation, addressing: the aging problem, the differences in retirement criteria between gender, the low affiliation level, the disparity between benefits of public and private employees, actions focused on reducing poverty, and the growth of the General Regime deficit.

3. Brazil has a great number of poor people, even though in 2008 its income per capita was around US$8,400 (63rd position in the World).

The Aging Problem

PAYG models are sensitive to the number of beneficiaries, to the level of benefits and to the number of contributors. To establish equilibrium, it is necessary to balance the actual value of all contributions paid and the actual value of the future benefits. In this sense, averting the problems of increasing life expectancy becomes fundamental to sustain the system. Since people are living longer, the system should aim for sketching plans that deal with this new situation.

In the last few years, the problems of early retirement have been partially offset by adopting age parameters that promote an adjustment between the number of years of contributions and the value of the pension. Early retirees receive an adjusted benefit that is lowered due to the application of a formula, referred to as the Social Security Factor, an actuarial approach that adjusts the benefits value versus the period of contributions and age of retirement.

In 2008, around 10.2 percent of Brazil's total population was older than 60 years old. The average age of retired Brazilian men was close to 56 years old. This figure is considered one of the most worrisome characteristics of the social security system since it triggers serious intergenerational costs, posing a high taxation on future generations. Besides that, in the last two decades, the child mortality rate has dropped dramatically and the living conditions for the elderly have improved. In 1991 Brazilians had an average life expectancy of about 66 years of age. In 2005 this figure changed to 71.9 years of age, a growth of 6 years in 14, an impressive evolution of more than 5 months per year. Based on Brazilian historical data and numbers from some more developed economies—in which the growth rate is smaller—it is possible to affirm that the Brazilian population's average life expectancy will reach 74 by 2010, being 70 for men and 78 for women.

It is remarkable that the elderly are increasing their life expectancy, and for instance, by 2010 life expectancy at 60 years old is calculated by IBGE as 83 years for women and 80 years for men. But this will put more pressure on the expenses. One way under consideration to help resolve this issue would be to adopt a minimum retirement age—something that has been done in several countries. However, such a move would have a significant impact on the number of opportunities for young people trying to enter the workplace.

On the other hand, the Brazilian birth rate has been reduced to around 1.4 percent during the last decade amid expectations it will drop to 1.2 percent between 2040 and 2050. As a result, the net population growth rate was 2.89 in 1991, 2.39 in 2000, and 1.89 in 2008, and it is estimated that it will be by 1.50 by 2028. A smaller working force will have to support the increasing expenditures of the social security. Brazil is facing a "demographic transition," which occurs when high natality and high mortality rates are changed. In the first phase there is a sudden increase of the population, because mortality rates declines faster than natality, but it will tend to stabilize in the second step. During this period the country faces a "demographic bonus" that is characterized by a still large amount of people in working age (14-64 years) in relation to the elderly (over 65).

The Gender Issue: Age and Contribution Time Differences

The latest pension reform runs contrary, however, to the latest demographic findings, making the retirement age for women 5 years earlier than for men. On average, in Brazil, men will live at least 3 years less than women, so there is an implicit 8-year benefit discrepancy for women. Although there are differences in the retirement age in other countries, we can identify three tendencies in the world scenario (Giambiagi and Castro, 2003). In the United States, Ireland, Iceland, Denmark, and Norway, there is no legal difference between men and women when it comes to retirement age. In Germany, Holland, Spain, United Kingdom, Finland, Sweden, Luxembourg, and Canada there is a difference that is lower than five years between men and women. Even when there is a five-year difference between men and women, in general, the women cannot retire before they are 60 years of age. This criterion is adopted in Japan, Austria, Italy, Portugal, France, Belgium, Switzerland, and Greece.

About half of the Latin America's nations do not differentiate between the retirement ages of men and women. In those countries where there is a difference, women tend to retire 2 to 5 years before men. However, some Latin America countries are reducing this minimum age differential between the sexes to the average of two years. Table 9-1 reveals the minimum retirement age and estimated period of benefits in various regions and countries.

In the European Community and North America, the minimum retirement age is being raised from 65 to 67 or 68 years of age. In the next decade, France will count on an age limit of 69 years of age and 41 years of contributions. Similar measures of age versus contribution period increases must be adopted in Brazil. Currently, the system charges future generations with the

TABLE 9-1. Minimum Age of Retirement and Estimated Period of Benefits, 2005 and 2007

	Minimum Age of Retirement (years)		Expected Length of Retirement (years)	
Countries	Men	Women	Men	Women
OECD (29 countries)	64	63	16	21
Latin America (7 countries)	62	60	17	21
Others (66 countries)	62	60	16	21
Brazil				
Pensions by Contribution Period	54[a]	51[a]	23	29
Special Rural Pensions	60	55	19	26

Notes: [a]Average retirement age. 2007 figures for Brazilian data and 2005 for all others.

Source: Rocha e Caetano (2008).

costs of current policies. In the near future, the country will not be able to adopt such generous policies if it aims to bring balance.[4]

Brazil needs to set an age limit for retirement as the population evolves. To do this, the age limit could be adjusted by using a two-stage approach. In the first stage, the minimum retirement age would be established at 65 years for men and 62 for women. In a second stage the limit is set to 65 years of age for both genders. This gradual increase of the age limit for retirement creates a natural transition and reduces conflicts.

The inclusion of a longer contribution period is crucial for dealing with the growth of a longer-lived population. The contribution time has to be slowly increased to 35 years for women and 37 years for men.

The Disparity Between Public and Private Workers Issues

The system comprised by the General Regime and the Special Regime generates a deficit of 5.7–5.9 percent of GDP. The Special Regime accounts for 75 percent of the total deficit, and the General Regime is responsible for the other 25 percent.

In 2008, for the Public Sector (Union, States, and Municipalities) estimates are that total expenses reached R$121.25 billion and contributions R$70 bil-

4. According to OECD (2002), in 2001, only 8.4 percent of Brazil's total population was over 60 years of age; nevertheless, its social security expense corresponded to 11.5% of GDP. Proportionally, these expenses were greater than the ones of the richest countries, with a higher number of elderly people, for instance Sweden and the United States. These two countries had for the same period annual expenses of 9.2 percent and 6.3 percent of GDP, respectively, with 22 percent and 16.1 percent of the population being older than 60 years.

lion, generating a deficit of R$60.9 billion (2.16 percent of GDP). There are around 4.9 million contributors, 1.6 million retired, and also another 0.6 million pensioners. There are high disparities in the values of pensions as shown in Table 9-2. In the Special Regime, pensions can be up to 22 times greater in terms of value than the average pension value for the General Regime.

Inequality between General and Special Regimes benefits can be explained mostly by a public-sector worker's capacity to negotiate and keep benefits and the institutional difficulties inherent when trying to change the law.

In order to accommodate people who will soon be granted benefits, it is preferable to make progressive changes in age limits, or in the contribution period, avoiding sudden measures. Usually, the political reactions tend to be lower when the loss imposed to the beneficiary does not materialize immediately, and the perspective of its realization is in the medium to long term.

TABLE 9-2. Comparison of the Average Value of Pensions for Federal Public Servants, 2003

Categories		Average Value of Pensions	Ratio
General Regime		US$259	1
Special Regime	Executive (Civilians)	US$1,360	5.2
Union	Military	US$2,400	9.3
	Legislative	US$5,900	22.8
	Judiciary	US$5,550	21.4

Source: Pensions and Social Security Ministries—a diagnostic of the Brazilian pensions system presented March 18 2003, and Social Pensions statistics bulletin Vol. 9 No 3.

The Poverty Issue

In the last decade poverty in Latin America has been falling, especially among people in the base of the income pyramid. Nonetheless, the permanence of high poverty levels in the region challenges the pension model, especially because the poor are unable to contribute to the pension system. The situation in Brazil shows that social security is distributed widely although it could be much improved. Analyzing a decomposition of the "Gini Index," Ferreira (2003) noticed that the return on pensions is uneven between the elderly poor and those better off but also elderly. This happens because many elderly poor do not receive any social security benefit creating an inverted redistribution of income in which those who make less money are financing those who retire earlier and get paid more.

In this context, pensions are badly distributed when considering that social expenses are intended for poverty alleviation. Amsberg (2000) performed analysis in the Northeast and Southeast, which together have 73% of the population and 80% of the poor in Brazil. Amsberg observed only 13% of such pensions went to the poorest people. Neri (2001) noticed that the top 10% of benefits, including INSS and public-sector inactive worker benefits, consume almost half of all the benefits distributed.

Poverty Reduction

One positive aspect is that poverty has decreased since 1998, but it is clear that there is still much to do to improve the distribution of wealth in Brazil, however, improvements in salaries and wealth distribution can be seen in economic data and the amount the government pays to those who have retired. This is demonstrated in an increase in the amount of formal contributions made and an increase in the value of the contributions, helping improve the balance between INSS revenue and expenses.

Brazil is reducing inequality and will achieve the lowest level since the inception of these measures in the sixties. Nevertheless inequality within the country is considered one of the ten largest in the world, and despite the improvement and maintaining the observed track it would take another thirty years to reach the level of developed countries, like the US.

The combination of high growth and the shortage of inequality during the period of 2003-2008, the proportion of Brazilian people living in poverty was reduced by 43%, and 19 million people went out of poverty levels. Another 32 million people became middle-class citizens in the same period.

The Gini index has constantly fallen since 1997 from 0.60 to 0.54, highlighting a drop in the inequality of the distribution of wealth. This improvement in wealth distribution is good news for the pensions sector as the number of formal workers, fiscal and pension contribution revenues, and quality of life increase.

FIGURE 9-1. Percentage of Extremely Poor People in the Total Population, 2008

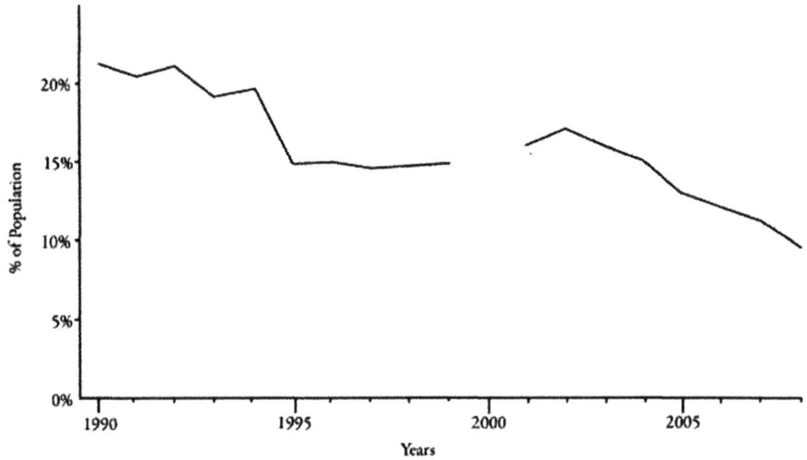

Source: IBGE and PNAD.

The Revenue Issue

The main consequence of an imbalance in the social security system is that the Government is forced to make a decision. To use public resources to pay social security benefits is one option, which leads to a reduction of investments in other areas such as infrastructure, social assistance, and health. Essentially, it is a perverse transference of the society's income to a small portion of people who already have the retirement benefits and that in general have a per capita income much higher than the average population.

Analyses about the factors that broaden the Brazilian social security deficit were extensively explored by Cechin (2002), Giambiagi and Castro (2003). They are summarized here:

1. Since 1988 minimum wage payments are made to rural workers who had never contributed to social security.
2. Some 500,000 public-sector workers, who contributed more than the stated General Regime ceiling and moved to the private-sector, were able to retire since 1988 receiving generous benefits.
3. An increase in the number of retirement by contribution period, without a minimum age requirement, and during 2002 to 2005 its participation reached almost 40% of total expenses.
4. A real increase in the minimum wage, which serves as an index for Social Security benefits.

5.Fraud and tax evasion.

Figure 9-2 shows the evolution of the INSS benefits' expenses during the years following the approval of the 1988 Constitution. The total value went from 2.5% of GDP in 1988 to 6.6% of GDP in 2008. This growth tendency is worrisome because it is directly linked to the real minimum wages gains, which indexes social security benefits. This should be changed so that social security benefits are readjusted by a price index related to the cost of living, while the minimum wage would have the freedom to produce real income gains for workers according to economic productivity gains.

FIGURE 9-2. Expenditure on INSS Benefits, 1980-2008

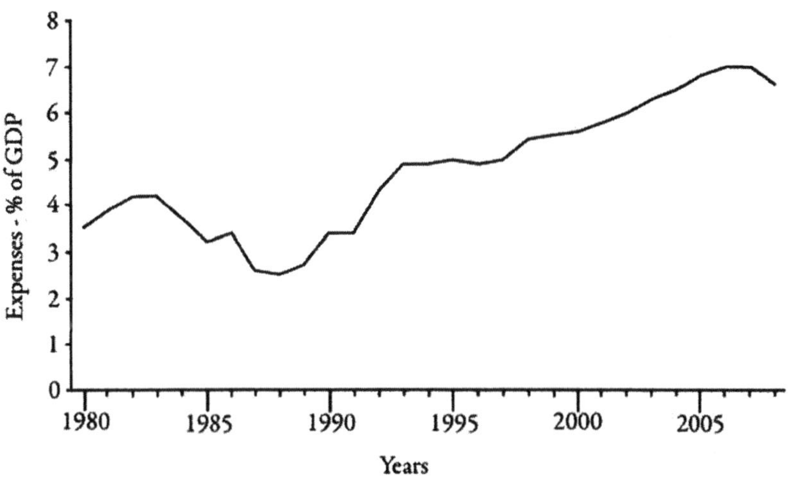

Source: Giambiagi and Além, 1999, p. 229; Social Security Statistics Bulletin (Boletim Estatístico Da Previdência Social)—vol.5, n°12, vol.6, n° 10 e vol.7, n°6, and Ministry of Planning's Budget Data 2005-2007.

The increase in INSS benefits payments is not just in absolute value terms but also in relative value terms between 1988 and 2007, increasing to 7% from nearly 3% of GDP (see Figure 9-2). This growth is extremely dangerous for Brazil given there is a clear absence of fail-safes aimed at controlling increasing expenses. This level will just keep rising until the government is no longer able to meet benefits payments. Another factor preventing a balancing out between revenue versus social security payments is that two thirds of all benefits are linked to the minimum wage, or rather by law no benefit payment can be inferior to the minimum monthly wage. Between 1995 to 2009 the minimum wage rose to R$465 (US$258 at US$1/R$1.85) from R$100, which was then approximately worth US$95. This represents a more than 100% increase in the minimum wage's real buying value since 1995, and this increase was automatically passed to those who are retired. In turn pension payments rose too.

The Low Affiliation Issue

In Latin America, statistics show that social security has not been adequately extended to the entire population and the coverage level is typically low. The reforms that happened in the region did not emphasize the low coverage level issue, although this has been pointed out by Murro (2001) as the main problem because the excluded population is almost two thirds the total (Mesa-Lago, 2000), and two countries with large public systems—Brazil and Panama—have levels of coverage much higher than the other seven that implemented some form of structural reform (Mesa-Lago, 2004).

As mentioned by Schmidt-Hebbel (1997: 10) "Coverage of affiliates—that comprise both active contributors, and non-active members—is very different from coverage of contributors." So, it is important to address the reasons for this difference and to increase compliance levels.

The Role of Informality

Informality is a concept with different meanings, but in this paper it is the lack of a formal working relationship that can provide individuals with workers' rights. In this situation, there are no benefits, but there are some kinds of tax evasion, including non-payment of pension contributions. In the macro level this will lead to an increase in tax burden on formal corporations and on individuals, constraining investments and reducing productivity, in such a combination that affects economic growth.

In 2008 the average unemployment rate was 7.9%, declining from the previous levels between 9%-10% prevailing since 1999. There was an increase in the number of top educated workers within the workforce losing jobs—those with more than eleven years of schooling were 11.9 million in 1992 before reaching 30.4 million in 2005—meanwhile less skilled workers lost 6.5 million jobs during the same period (Ramos, 2007:27).

According to IBGE the casual workforce represented 48.2% of the total labor force in 2007. Casual work is more intense in intensive labor sectors and less intense in sectors with medium to high levels of technology. Formal companies totaled 5 million, and informal ones came to 10.3 million. The great majority of firms in the informal sector are micro and small companies where 60% of the entrepreneurs are women and 40% are men, and whose average age is 42 years. Eighty-five percent of the entrepreneurs have no partners, and 78% do not hire employees. Fifty-six percent of them work at home and 33% do not have a fixed place to work.

Younger workers are the most affected by casual informal work. Informal workers' salaries are 20% less than ones earned by formal workers but this difference varies according to the number of years of schooling and age.

At higher ages, 50 to 54 years, formal workers make twice the income of informal ones. Approximately 41 million workers are not covered by the social security system and only 30 million contribute. Figure 9-3 shows a drop in the total number of informal workers between 1992 and 2007 but the number still remains at a very high 48.5%. This has led to a drop in the relative number of social security contributors, impacting revenues and reducing the capacity to pay benefits to pensioners. Nowadays, the ratio is 1.2 contributors to each retired person. When analyzing the composition of the non-contributors group, families earning an average per capita income of one and a half of minimum wages make up almost 50% of that group. In other words, the group that does not contribute to the system is the very group that needs social security the most.

FIGURE 9-3. Informality: A Historical Evolution, 1992-2007

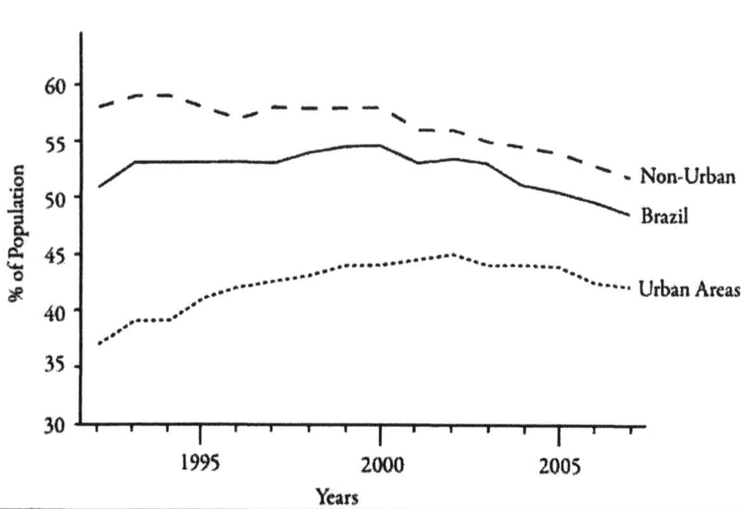

Source: IPEA.

Reforming Social Security in Lula's Government

President Lula's Government came to power in the beginning of 2003. It was charged with widely reforming the social security system. A strong reform was expected to promote equity between private and public-sector pensions as well as parametric changes already diagnosed as necessary. What has been seen, however, is the proposition of very restricted measures essentially when it came to the Special Regimes without making any relevant changes to the workers in the General Regime. The reform oriented to the public sector, specially the future civil servants, was an option to avoid a confrontation with the current servants, facing a typical collective action problem and those reform policies contribute to lower resistance from labor unions and leftist parties (Nakahodo and Savoia, 2008).

Analysis of the Last Reform's Measures (2003)

The most important measures,[5] approved in December 2003, were:

Creation of a New Benefits Ceiling: The pension ceiling was raised around 28.4% to US$1,333. This same amount was also applied to private-sector workers and to the next generation of public-sector staff. They are able to contribute to pension funds. This pension ceiling was the only general measure of the reform while all the others were related to the characteristics of the civilian workers.

Fixing the ceiling of payments to retirees at R$1,333 in the General Regime brings in income to the government and postpones benefits payments. The employees are responsible for one-third of contributions to their Social Security while the employer is responsible for the other two thirds. With the increase in the ceiling, the employee can raise his or her contribution to up to 53%. On the other hand, payments made by the employer cannot be increased. In the future, benefits will be raised without the corresponding financing by the employer. In praxis, it will be a partial subsidy of the State, there is no change or benefit with this measure for those currently retired.

Age Limit and Contribution Length Time: Employees who are in the public service receive a whole pension if women are 55 years of age and have 30 years of contribution; men are 60 years of age and have 35 years of contribu-

5. A detailed discussion is provided by Giambiagi et al. (2007, 2010).

tion; or for both it is necessary to have 20 years of public service and the last 5 in the post in which they retire. The possibility of early retirement has been maintained, beginning at the age of 48 for women and 53 for men. Nevertheless, a reduction of 5% a year is applied relating to the age reference—60 years of age for men and 55 years of age for women. For public-sector workers who previously worked in the private sector, the calculation of their benefits is being done considering the average contributions to the General Regime.

The minimum retirement age for public workers causes a 5-year delay in starting benefits and adds a valuable additional contribution period. In addition, this measure postpones the staffer's departure from his or her activities, thus postponing the necessity of hiring a substitute.

The new formula for calculating a pension's value adjusts wages and contribution period in both public and private sectors. For instance, a person who contributed for 35 years to the Social Security System is about 60 years old, has worked 30 years in Public Service and 5 years in the Private Sector, and receives a retirement pension value equivalent to his or her wage as a public servant that has been reduced by between 10% and 13%. But, in a situation in which the person decided to join the Public Sector after working 20 years for the Private Sector, the reduction applied to the wage is higher—starting at 39.3% and reaching up to 52%.

Benefits Limit: Active workers' remuneration and also the pensions have a maximum ceiling ranging around US$8,300 per year, as of 2008. The reduction of the pension value from its original amount is based on the argument that there are fewer people being sustained after the death of the original beneficiary.

Pensioners' Contribution: Retired public-sector workers and pensioners pay 11% of the pension's package that exceeds the US$1,300 ceiling. Between 1995 and 2002, the federal expense on personnel was only 2.1% per year, while the expenses on retired workers grew 2.4%. Based on these facts, it is possible to affirm that charging inactive workers was an indispensable measure. It is also important to lower the deficit of states and municipalities.

End of Parity between Wages and Pensions: Before the 2003 reform, a public-sector worker's pension was the same value as that of his or her last month's salary. According to the reform, the benefits are in line with the average contribution made during a person's working life—the same benefit provided in the General Regime. The end of parity between wages of active workers applies the same criteria of pension calculus to both public servants and civilian workers linked to the General Regime.

Creation of Pension Funds to Future Public Servers: The reform in 2003 established that every person who enters the public administration has their pension calculated by an average of contributions made with a ceiling of ten times the minimum wage. There is also a Complementary Pension Fund available to public-sector workers. The fund provides a defined contribution plan but joining the fund is optional. Although the regulation is ready and because there is much opposition to the starting of the fund, in practice the situation did not change and it must be improved only in a new legislature, after Lula da Silva.

Analysis of the Reform's Impact

Pension expenditures are one of the two most important fiscal issues that President Lula addressed. The establishment of equal ceilings for the General Regime and the Special Regimes undoubtedly represented a first step for better social equality. Table 9-3 presents a comparison of social security contributions before and after the Government's reform. When analyzing the contributions brackets to the General Regime, it is easy to see that this has not changed, that is, it has collected more than it needs to offer the benefits level to a retired person.

In the current situation, to cover all the INSS benefits, without taking special situations into account, a contribution bracket of 17% is enough to bring the pension system into balance. Nevertheless, the current bracket is about 21%. It is possible to introduce a lower contribution bracket without changing the current benefit level. To do so, better transparency is necessary in the accounts related to assistance benefits by separating them from the General Regime budget since it is the Treasury's responsibility to finance them.

In public civil service, the percentage collected increased and the necessary contribution diminished with the reform. The necessary contribution to cover such a worker's benefit level would have been between 45 percent and 50 percent of his or her wages—very different from today's levels of between 85 percent and 16 percent of the wages. The reform produced an increase of those contributions and a reduction in benefits. Nonetheless even with such changes, the necessary contributions to provide such benefits would be from 19 to 27 percent of wages, while collecting would be between 18 and 21 percent.

TABLE 9-3. Comparison of Social Security Contributions Before and After Lula

	Prior Situation		Lula's Government	
	Contribution Needed (%)	Contribution Collected (%)	Contribution Needed (%)	Contribution Collected (%)
INSS	17	21	17	21
Public Servers	49	16	27	18
Judiciary	48	15	25	18
Legislative	47	15	25	18
Executive	50	16	27	19
Military	47	9	19	12

Source: Zylbersztajn, Souza, Stancioli, Milan 2003.

The effects of leveling the benefits for future public-sector staff and workers from private companies will be observed only in the long run but it is necessary to observe an entire generation[6] for this measure to show full effects.

In 2005 the government started administrative measures to increase revenues and cut expenses. Some of them are related to a more severe control on fraud and tax evasion. Other measures included a management turnaround at the INSS and investments in technology.

A Social Pact to Reform Pensions in Brazil

In a great number of countries social security systems are not funded where active workers contribute to their respective programs to guarantee the payment of benefits to current retirees. This pay-as-you-go model is sustained by the existence of a "pact between generations" in which the current taxpayers will receive their pensions in the future thanks to payments of the next generation.

What happens when the benefit to current retirees is disproportionate to their previous contributions? Should the benefits be reduced in the future by allocating a loss to the current generation of workers? To avoid problems of this nature and ensure more solid institutions, reforms are being made

6. Under Brazilian law, regulation changes cannot modify acquired rights, that is, for those who already receive pensions. However, there are theses of Economic Law that guarantee State constitutional changes that alter the law's expectations, that is, the conditions for those workers who have not completed all the requirements necessary to achieve retirement status. Such changes would produce countless questions in the courts and have been avoided in practice.

with the objective of ensuring equity between contributions and promises made to each generation to create a balance between generations.

Another set of problems appears when workers, who are not affiliated to the system or who are not entitled to certain benefits, begin to pressure law-makers to ensure they are supported in some way. At this moment, wide-spread benefits can be created that are not based on contributions but are instead generated by taxing the rest of the population, usually impacting the middle class the most.

However, the middle class cannot choose how its tax money is used and if there had ever existed such an opportunity to voice opinion on the use of such resources they probably would have chosen to allocate them differently into areas such as education, health, or housing for example. In this way, the problem of creating public benefits is that of finding coherent means to cover costs without imposing on less politically organized sectors to attend to organized special interest groups.

The 1998 reform cleared up some distortions such as retirement vis-à-vis service time and produced some measures aimed at controlling the Social Security deficit. However, its results were only partly successful given that the imbalance between contributions and deficit continues. Reform by President Lula's government consequently did not meet expectations because it did not alter a series of imperfections that have historically been present in the Social Security System. The government suffered various limitations throughout the reform process. Despite the political power shown in the negotiations there were no conditions, or willingness to implement all the necessary changes.

The impossibility of changing age limits and contribution time for private workers is a demonstration of political opportunism clearly brought on by a lack of interest in making the essential transformations toward better systems—a process that is happening in most countries. As mentioned before, an alternative toward diminishing the imbalance at the INSS is by progressively raising the age limit to between 60-65 years for both men and women over the next decade. To the same effect, gradual additions to the contribution time in an evolutionary course for 37 years would be a must.

In Brazil, the democratic debate prevails over the search of what Brazilian society desires and considers fair. In this sense, reforming pensions is not a consensual matter. In fact, some institutional changes have been set out, although the role of those with the power of a veto continues to stop major social changes. Brazil goes through drastic changes in its priorities and perceptions. Setting and keeping the privileges by groups is part of a culture whose roots are founded on the origin of a bureaucratic and conservative state. The array of benefits offered to public-sector workers date back to the last century when they were consolidated under a military dictatorship and are clearly rooted in Brazilian tradition.

Lula's pension reform set the limits on pension payments and allowed for private pensions for public-sector workers; however the latter is yet to be fully realized. The resistance to implement the measures voted and approved by Congress shows the lack of commitment by various groups of society.

An assessment of the main problems of the Brazilian social security system can be found in Giambiagi et al. (2007), Savoia (2007), and Brooks (2009); and can be consequently summarized in five points:

1. In the last two decades the country saw an increase in the population's life expectancy, which is explained by the strong reduction of the child mortality rate, and also by better living conditions among the elderly;
2. Early Retirement, at an average of 55 years, with no minimum age for most workers, makes spending on pensions in Brazil disproportionately high and comparable to that made by developed countries;
3. There are more than 16.4 million people receiving assistance benefits from the social security system because they were not entitled to regular pensions due to lack of contributions. In the future this figure must increase much more, reflecting informal labor markets that comprise 41% of the economically active population;
4. The low growth in gross domestic product (GDP), on average 3.0% per annum since stabilization in 1994, reduces the level of revenue, which makes it difficult to finance social security expenditures because benefits grow at higher rates than GDP growth. Benefits whose values are indexed to the minimum wage doubled over the past 15 years; and there has been an increase in pension and healthcare costs not linked to contributions;
5. There are different opinions about the changes to be adopted in Brazilian social security. However, there is a consensus that the following measures should be adopted. These measures are (i) the gradual adjustment of the minimum retirement age to 62 years for women and 65 for men, (ii) the gradual adjustment of the contribution period from 35 to 37 years, (iii) the indexing of benefits to the Index of Consumer Prices for higher pension values and the Minimum Wage Index for the lowest values, and (iv) the elimination of all exemptions for contributions.

Key issues that should be taken into consideration when making changes include respect for existing rights and care when adopting rules that lead to transition. New legislation should not undo the positive effects of existing reforms. Attention should also be paid to the combination of private and public-sector mechanisms whether they be optional or mandatory when it comes to providing pensions coverage for the population.

Another crucial point is the consolidation of the way the pension system is handled by uniting the supervising organs that take care of it and of the rules that enforce the system. Today, it is handled between two different ministries. And finally, an evaluation should be made of best practices abroad and whether there could be possible convergence with local mechanisms.

Why a Social Pact

According to Dion and Roberts (2008) pensions are the "third rail" of politics. Politicians cannot cut benefits without suffering electoral retribution. Reform of social security is made difficult as people above 50 vote in greater proportion than those bellow 30 and therefore insist that any changes do not affect current recipients. In this way, most countries reform their system gradually.

Pierson (1998) states that the contemporary politics of the welfare state centers on renegotiation, restructuring, and modernization rather than on dismantling the current situation. This is difficult because the simple mention of the possibility of reform creates feelings of insecurity among those who benefit from the status quo. Thus, many proposals for serious and well-intentioned social security reforms have been repeatedly destroyed (Nakahodo and Savoia, 2008).

Social pacts were negotiated in many European countries in the 1980s and 1990s and have become a major issue in comparative research on industrial relations, corporatist policy-making, and welfare state reform (Siegel, 2005). According to Baccaro (2002, 413-414), the experiences of pension reforms in Italy (1995), Spain (1997), France (1993), Austria (1997), and Finland (1999), took the form of "centralized agreements between government and the 'social partners' (business and labor) or even, as in the case of Italy and Spain, between governments and the labor unions."

One of our main analyses will be how much validity there is in using a social pact for this process. Siegel (2005) affirms that they may provide an advantage for initiating pensions reforms in comparison to other techniques of promoting consultation and consensus building.

On the flip side, it can be said that there is little use for social pacts when it comes to reforms. Indeed, reforms have occurred without social pacts or other concerted efforts exerting a major role on such a process in countries such as Germany, Austria, Sweden, and the Netherlands. In contrast to macroeconomic coordination and reforms of wage bargaining systems, the findings reported by Jochem and Siegel (2003) imply that the impact of tripartite social pacts on welfare state reforms do vary. In many countries they were restricted, in some cases at least disputable and in others not observable at all.

A broad reform of the Brazilian Social Security System by the creation of a social pact that aligns the interests of various sectors of society within the same document would generate greater credibility and less political friction than a multilateral process of negotiation between the government and the unions.

Such a Social Pact document should be expressed as a plan, which would become a Constitutional Amendment, voted and approved by a majority of Congress without suffering opportunistic change or restrictions on scope and content. Evaluation of the program would be done in five years, with new actuarial studies, which would allow for refiguring of effects of previous measures for the correction of distortions.

10

FEMINISM, THE STATE, AND GENDER EQUALITY

Lia Zanotta Machado

Abstract: The paper argues that from a dynamic confrontation against dictatorship in the early seventies, the Brazilian feminist movement has changed towards logic of negotiation in the 21st century. My main point is that, despite these important changes, the logic of addressing the state has always been present. Lula's Government (2003-2010) set up an original and very innovative coalition to sustain political strategies with feminist movements. The building up of the National Council of Women's Rights and the proposal of National Conferences for Women's Policies led the government to approach the positions of feminist movements and vice-versa. However, when pressures became strong against key proposals of the movement, resistances, and contradictions came about within the governmental arena, stressing contradictions and setting apart political positions between government and feminist proposals concerning women's rights.

One singular trait brought about by the Brazilian feminist movement is its strong connection with the defense of women's rights interwoven with the social rights issue, rather than the insulated notion of women's freedom or liberation. While, in the early moments, the feminist movement in the US and France claimed the right to choose and freedom in the realms of love, sex, and household issues leading to a complete freedom and autonomy in labor relations and in the political sphere, the Brazilian feminist movement stressed, since its inception in the second half of the seventies and the first half of the eighties, a demand for the rights of the women and their fight for democratization (Goldberg, 1991).

WOMEN'S RIGHTS AND DICTATORSHIP IN THE SEVENTIES

The feminist movement for women's liberation in the US in the sixties and in France in seventies placed emphasis on sexual freedom, condemning the fact that the female body and sex were controlled by men. The battle for sexual freedom was congruent with the denouncing of sexual violation and oppressive sexual relations, at large. It consisted of politicizing the private life.

In Brazil, the feminist movement, since its beginnings in the seventies, has the presence of an international exchange of ideas and proposals with women in exile in Paris, Berkeley, and Santiago (Chile). Discussion groups were built around exiled women, writers, young university students, and left-wing party women who rapidly joined together with women such as Romi Medeiros, a lawyer from Brazilian elite who attained the approval of the Married Woman's Act in 1962. This Act was responsible for releasing the woman from a "relatively incapable condition" in relation to her husband. Before the passage of this act, a woman's right to work and to choose a place to live was dependent on her husband's decision. These discussion groups introduced proposals similar to those proposed by the American and French women's movements, but were also featured as something "good for Brazil" in the words of Goldberg (1987 and 1991). That is to say, they had been effective in bringing together the feminist struggle and the defense of citizenship rights and democracy.

To a large extent, the strength of the feminist movement's repercussion depended upon its participation in the general struggle for democracy, against dictatorship and social inequalities.

The movement's specific issues gained ground, especially in the discussion groups which got together to talk about their daily experiences, and the very same women proposed the holding of encounters and congresses, searching for visibility and political repercussion. Starting in Rio de Janeiro and São Paulo, these encounters aimed at stressing both their own struggle and the struggle for democracy, fighting the authoritarian regime, and getting heard. Male control over female bodies was strongly denounced.

The first public demonstration (1975, Rio de Janeiro) came about with the Seminar on the Role and Behavior of Woman in Brazilian Society. The main issues of the Seminar were dedicated to the daily conditions involving

Brazilian women, such as labor relations, physical and mental health conditions, racial discrimination, and female homosexuality.

As Leila Barsted (2007: 4) wrote, "still in the decade of 1970, we can record perhaps the first media manifestation in favor of abortion through *Jornal Opinião* (1973), an alternative newspaper that in 1973 published some stories on feminism, one of them about voluntary abortion, explaining new and safe abortion techniques." And further ahead: "In 1978, the Ceres group, within a funding program for research about woman from Fundação Carlos Chagas, has carried out a research about social and sexual identity from Brazilian women, also approaching life experiences and perceptions on the abortion through witnesses from many interviewees in this research" (Barsted, 2007: 5).[1]

And yet, denouncing of "the extreme case of men's power over their women's life and death" was the key point that was able to spread across the vast majority of feminists and reach public opinion and elites at that time. The specific issue of the movement with larger visibility is the murder of women, with the first watchwords relating to violence coming up in 1979. These were the denouncing of homicides committed by husbands against their wives and the fact these men were absolved or were released from prison (Sorj and Montero, 1985; Cavalcanti and Heilborn, 1985; Gregori, 1993). The critique of daily and permanent violence against women was not the key point that was able to reverberate in the political elites at that time.[2] The key was the denouncing of women's murder. In fact, women's movements concentrated on the right to survive. Public opinion had great repercussions in the press regarding the cases involving upper and middle classes homicides. Broader than the demand for sexual freedom, the voice that managed to be heard was the denouncing of misogynist and discriminating cultural values in the Penal and Civil Codes and in the jurisprudential interpretations. The repercussion of spouses' homicides from men against their partners gave rise to feminist mobilization with the creation of

1. See Alves, Branca Moreira, Barsted, Leila Linhares, Boschi, Sandra Azeredo, Pitanguy, Jacqueline and Ribeiro, Mariska (1981), members of the Grupo Ceres and authors from this book.

2. A well known case was the murder of Ângela Diniz by her partner, Doca Street, both from the social elite. Soon after in 1980, there were the homicides of Maria Regina Rocha and Heloisa Ballesteros. The first trial of Doca Street was in 1979. With a large audience, the trial showed the judicial practice of considering such guilty persons innocent in the category of "defense of honor." Stanciolli, murderer of Heloisa, was condemned in 1982 to two years in prison. The defense accused the victim of being more interested in her entrepreneurial activity than in her role of a mother and wife. Christel Johnston was threatened, pursued, and murdered by her husband who did not accept divorce and, despite looking for help in the police station and courts, she was not protected. See Sorj and Montero (1985) and Cavalcanti and Heilborn, (1985).

centers and of the Committee on Violence Against Women. The public sensitivity about daily violence against women was not equivalent to the debate about female homicides. Some feminist groups, depending on their voluntary work, started to build up help groups offering services targeting women who were victims of violence.

ADDRESSING THE STATE

In the next moment, the demand from feminist movement (action) was the attempt to place their policies in the agenda of the state public policies. This demand had to do with the proposal for the creation of councils joined by feminists, legitimized by the public authorities, and serving as a consulting and proposal making at local and regional levels. The first State Council of The Feminine Condition (Conselho Estadual da Condição Feminina) was created in São Paulo in 1983. This first Council was the pioneer in suggesting the creation of the first specialized police station[3] providing service for women in 1985.

It is in this context that the idea of specialized police stations to serve women or in the defense of women became relevant. It then possible to build up a certain consensus about two assertions: the prevalence of social values and customs where the importance of violence against women tended to be minimized, and the existence of differences between the male and female approach about violence.

Without a special attention towards violence against women, it would continue invisible, unpunished, and almost legitimized by state power and ruling common sense, as if it were not a social problem. There was an understanding that the specialized police stations were the place where the female voice and denunciations could be heard as well as the place to address properly the male violent acts as crimes. In the majority, these specialized units should be run by female police inspectors. The rationale and claim for this rested upon the idea that their cultural background and identification with the issue would make women more able to give credibility to denouncements made by women.

An important result was the "stop" given by feminists to the alleging of the defense of honor as an argument leading to crime exemption or milder punishment. Under the aegis of the impact of the political voice from femi-

3. The specialized police stations were being created beginning in 1985 and in 2010 are still being created (Machado, L., 2001 and 2002; Silva, 2001; SPM, 2008).

nists and from repercussion in the press, it was possible to build up a comprehensive category of "violence against women" that included the "sexual violence" and the inflicting of "light and severe daily body lesions" by partners against their women.

I stress here the fact that, in common-place thought, the idea of murder reminds us of a very severe fact, but it resembles the idea of a single and extraordinary event. When this idea is brought into the field of marital violence, it can reinforce the sense that murder is unbearable, but small eventual and circumstantial violent acts are not. Murder is thought of as inadmissible, but does not point out, in its own turn, its possible inclusion into a permanent and systematic scenario of "severe and small" violence. The systematic and daily "habit" of "beating the women" or of "being beaten by men" is disguised under the curtain of silence and in the assumption of the light injuries towards the eventual and very severe happening of homicide.

And yet, the wrathful indignation towards homicides has created a context able to emerge and "spring up" the cases of systematic and permanent body lesions, more or less often. Whether or not medical symptomatology would call these lesions "severe" or "light," almost always, one and the other are the ground for enormous losses in the women's health and integrity.

The peculiar fact is that female homicide, the landmark in the creation of specialized police stations, has not been defined as pertaining to the jurisdiction of such stations. Specialized police stations being responsible for the investigation of homicide crimes against women are exceptions. It is important to stress that those police stations mostly specialized in the investigation of crimes where interpersonal relationship between victims and witnesses is intense are set apart from the carrying out of such investigation when it comes to homicides.

The slogan "our body belongs to us" gained ground in the beginning of eighties. Feminists criticized proposals for birth control, that, however, were not implemented by federal governments stimulated by international agencies such as the World Bank (Alvarez, 1990; Knudsen, 2006). Birth control turned into facts, by the sterilization provided by two nongovernmental organizations in Brazil linked to and financed by two international nongovernmental organizations. Their activities were allowed by federal and state governments (Costa, 1996). These organizations did not give women complete information either about the consequences of sterilization or about alternative forms of contraception.[4]

The feminist movement was against imposing birth control on the population, but claimed the right to family planning, the right of women to control their fertility, and the public duty to offer contraceptives alongside with information. They were understood as women's rights to autonomy and decision-making. Women's movements and Brazilian health professionals, especially sanitarians, (a term that includes all physicians and health professionals that identify themselves with the international and national movement struggling to introduce sanitary regulations and public policies in order to achieve improvement in environmental conditions and public health)[5] suggested a "Complete Assistance Health Program for Women" (Programa de Assistência Integral à Saúde da Mulher/PAISM) and managed to get an approval from the Ministry of Health in 1983 for a public health system allowing a complete service for female health. It was in opposition to the almost exclusive health service for women as mothers in child and mother's hospitals; therefore, including the right to conception and contraception.

In 1983 in Rio de Janeiro, several feminist groups organized the Encounter About Health Sexuality, Contraception and Abortion.[6] This Encounter "became a landmark for the public debate on abortion due to its national dimension. During three days, it gathered around three hundred representatives from 57 women's groups from all over the country besides parliament members (senators, congressmen, state congressmen, and town councilors) (*Jornal Mulherio*, 1983)... In this Encounter, September 28 was established as the national Day of Fight for the Right of Abortion that became the cornerstone of mobilization in the decades to follow" (Barsted, 2007: 13)

4. BEMFAM, Sociedade Civil do Bem-Estar Familiar (Civil Society for Familiar Welfare) was created in 1965 and was linked to the International Planned Parenthood Federation (IPPF), created in 1952. Centro de Pesquisa de Assistência Integrada à Mulher e à Criança (CPAIMC) (Center for Research and Integral Assistance to Women and Children) was linked and financed by Family Planning International Assistance. Paradoxically these two institutions, although they offered Surgical Sterilization to poor women without all the information needed, were the only institutions offering contraceptive pills. See Costa (1996).

5. In Brazil, the international Sanitarians' questions strongly influenced public health policy makers, scholars, and physicians, since the Sanitarians' inception in 1901, and especially, in the seventies and eighties, after the end of dictatorship's period. It was the need to disseminate information, in fact, that led to the establishment of the Pan American Sanitary Bureau. As the American governments became increasingly concerned about the need to collaborate on a wide range of social, economic, and political issues, the First International Conference of American States, held in Washington, D.C., in 1890, established the agency known today as the Organization of American States. That body, at its Second Conference in Mexico City in 1901, called for a "general convention of representatives of the health organizations of the different American republics" to formulate "sanitary agreements and regulations" and to "designate a permanent executive board" to be known as the International Sanitary Bureau—the precursor of the Pan American Sanitary Bureau (Pan American Health Organization, 1998: 1)

6. Grupo Ceres (Ceres Group), Casa da Mulher do Rio de Janeiro (Woman's Home in Rio de Janeiro), Coletivo de Mulheres do Rio de Janeiro, Projeto Mulher do IDAC (Instituto de Ação Cultural) (Woman Project from Cultural Action Institute), and Grupo Mulherando (Womanhood Group).

In 1985, the National Council of Women Rights (Conselho Nacional dos Direitos das Mulheres, CNDM) was created in response to the "Women's Movement for Direct Elections." Violence, since then, continues to be an issue constantly renewed in the national, state, and municipal Councils for Women's Rights. Although the equal rights to work and health are also present, the exposure of violence tends to be essential in these councils and in the feminist movements.

In 1988, the National Council of Women Rights formed an interest group, the "lipstick lobby." It presented to Congressmen of the Constituent Assembly the "Letter From Women" (CNDM, 1986), elaborated by a great number of feminists (see Pinto, 2003). Here the singularity of the Brazilian women's movement is reinforced by presenting its first agenda in the name of democracy and social issues: social justice, creation of a Unified Health System, public and free education in all levels, unions' autonomy, agrarian reform, tax reform, and negotiation of foreign debt. In the second part, the Letter referred to women's rights: labor, health, property rights, sharing in marital relations, defense of physical and psychic integrity of women as a strong point to fight violence, redefinition of penal classification of rape, and creation of specialized police stations to serve women in all towns. The Letter is more contained in relation to the proposal of legalization of abortion. A constitutional principle was suggested in the following terms: "The right to know and decide about her own body will be assured to woman."

The pressure of diversified emergent social movements for democracy in the eighties brought about new possibilities for the interlocution between the state and civil society (Paoli and Telles, 1998) that I call "informal public spaces." Different demands circulate: demands coming from distinct groups in name of different constructions of the "politics of identity" as feminist and women's movements, black people and gays, the so called "new social movements" (Alvarez, 1998; Jelin, 1998); demands for public policies as health, housing and water, and union demands for increase of salaries. (Paoli and Telles, 1998). Fraser would call these "informal public spaces" as "subaltern counter publics" or "parallel discursive arenas where members of subordinated social groups invented and circulated counter discourses, so as to formulate oppositional interpretations of their identities, interests, and needs" (Fraser, 1993: 14).

"A consciousness of the right to have rights was elaborated in this public space, an unprecedented experience in Brazilian history," as Brazilian authors Paoli and Telles (1998: 65) say referring to the eighties. This was the period of eruption of new social movements anchored in groups demanding in name of their identities access to civil rights and recognition.

In the nineties, the trend of feminist movements was to organize in non-governmental organizations (NGOs) in the search for resources to carry out projects related to the elaboration, follow-up, and "social control" of public policies, as well as participating in the international feminist movement. In response to the need of a greater effectiveness from action proposals within public policies, from social accountability and from representation in international meetings and conferences on the women rights, there was the formation of huge networks[7] to connect local groups in a nationwide network such as the "National Feminist Network of Health and Sexual and Reproductive Rights" (Rede Nacional Feminista de Saúde e Direitos Sexuais e Reprodutivos) created in 1991 and the "Brazilian Women's National Articulation" (Articulação das Mulheres Brasileiras) created in the previous years of the preparation of the Conference of Women's Rights in Beijing in 1995. In 2000, there was the creation of the "Black Brazilian Women NGOs' Articulation" (Articulatio de ONGs de Mulheres Negras Brasileiras), and, soon after, the "Brazilian Lesbian League" (Liga Brasileira de Lésbicas).

Organized in this new way, the feminist movements focused in the nineties and in the first decade of the 2000s on the search for support in the National Congress and in the national and state-level executive institutions for the implementation of a broad range of rights: black women's rights, decriminalization of abortion, and the right to health service in the Unified Health System (Sistema Único de Saúde, SUS) for women who had an unsafe abortion, implementation in the public health system service for abortion cases allowed in the Penal Code from 1940, but not assured as rights, as in the case of interruption of pregnancy in the situation of rape and in situations in which woman's health is in danger.

From 1995 on, in the Government of Fernando Henrique Cardoso, the CNDM was linked to the Ministry of Justice. In 2002, at the end of his second term, the "Special Secretariat for Women's Rights" (Secretaria Especial para os Direitos das Mulheres) was created attached to the Ministry of Justice. The priorities set by the Secretariat were to aid women in the combat against violence against women, in their participation in the political scenario of the country, and in their entrance into the labor market (Bandeira, 2005).

7. See Alvarez (1998) for the "boom" of Latin American feminism.

On the other hand, the feminists were called by the Ministry of Health to look after the continuity of the Woman's Health Committee, (achieved in 1983), with a new design of a Legal Abortion Service policy to undertake public service in the case of abortions allowed in the Law so that the public health service for women would provide treatment to women who had an abortion in unsafe conditions.

THE FEMINIST NETWORKS AND THE NEW PUBLIC SPACES

The new Constitution and the informal public spaces opened up by the social movements in eighties and nineties have turned possible the institutionalization of "formal public spaces" within the State. Formal public spaces within the State have been constructed to negotiate conflicts and social demands, such as the diverse consultative or deliberative councils established at federal, state, and municipal levels. Focusing on creation and empowerment of all kinds of Councils, the very notion of liberal citizenship has been partially transformed into "collective participation in dialogue and negotiation" as Paoli and Telles argued since 1998, much before the expansions and empowerment of these councils.

The empowerment of the councils has especially increased by the decision of Lula's Government. However, against the expectations of the nineties, its scope has been restricted, from my point of view, to fields and issues demanded by the "new social movements," not including the generalization of decisions about public budget, or social and economic policies, as proposed by Labor Party (Partido dos Trabalhadores, PT) in the eighties and nineties.

In 2003, on the first day of Lula's government, the "Special Secretariat for Women's Policies" was created (Secretaria Especial para Políticas para Mulheres, SPM), directly attached to the President's Cabinet and with the status of a Ministry. The difference in the name of the secretariat from that established by Fernando Henrique Cardoso (the State Secretariat for the Rights of Women) reflects the fact that Lula wanted to emphasize that his government was making policies for women.

The government, through the creation of this Secretariat with such status, gave it more budget autonomy than had been given to the precedent Secretariat of Women's Rights. The new government recognized the need to design specific public policies, coordinating and stimulating action on other government bodies, aiming at "transversal gender issues," meaning interconnected gender priorities in public policies that should be implemented by different Ministries, under a common initiative.

Its immediate political strategies were: (1) to establish a new form of relationship with feminist movements, women's movements, and unionized women's movements; and (2) to establish a new form of relationship with and management of state-level and municipal-level bodies.

As an upshot of the first strategy, the SPM started to include the totally restructured National Council of Women's Rights (Conselho Nacional dos Direitos das Mulheres, CNDM). Until then, the members were indicated and nominated by the governments, nevertheless they were recognized by the movement. Since 2003, the new government has introduced the possibility of participation in the Council of representatives of feminist organizations and brokering in the national women networks. One condition is that they are national networks, or exceptionally regional networks attached to diverse specific conditions, for example, such as Women living in Amazonia, as many live in forest and rural areas. The second condition is that they are demanding participation, by their own initiative, justifying and proving their existence and indicating a representative and a surrogate. Heterogeneous organizations comprised the first Council (2003-2005), and the second Council (2005-2008). They included national feminist organizations; feminist women's organizations traditionally bound to political parties, but as autonomous organizations; professional women's organizations; and union organizations that promote women's rights being represented by their women's sections. It is only in the third Council (2008-2010) that special quotas are set for two groups: a first group classified as "feminist networks and movements in the defense of women's rights" (redes feministas e de movimentos de mulheres em defesa dos direitos das mulheres) gets 14 seats and a surrogate entity as an alternate to replace one of the seats, when one of these entities are unable to attend. The second group was classified as "union organizations, associative, professional or category acting in the promotion of women rights, represented by their women's bodies' sections," (organizações sindicais, associativas e profissionais que atuam na promoção de direitos das mulheres, representadas pelas seções de mulheres) with seven seats and a surrogate. The entities present themselves as candidates and indicate their representatives. The representatives chosen by these entities are those with the right to vote and be voted.

The properly recognized feminist networks are present in all three councils: they are the Brazilian Women's Articulation (Articulação de Mulheres

Brasileiras), Black Brazilian Women NGOs' Articulation (Articulação de ONGs de Mulheres Negras Brasileiras), National Feminist Network on Health (Rede Nacional Feminista de Saúde), World Women's March (Marcha Mundial das Mulheres), Women's Forum in Mercosur (Fórum de Mulheres do Mercosul), and Articulated Amazonian Women's Movement (Movimento Articulado de Mulheres da Amazônia). Two other feminist party-leaning organizations, but which are autonomous, are the Brazil's Women's Confederation (Confederação das Mulheres Brasileiras) and Brazilian Union of Women (União Brasileira de Mulheres), that also have been present since the beginning of Lula's government. It is important to point out that in the third Council the recently created Brazilian Lesbian League, the National Forum of Black Women, and the Peasant Women's Movement, strengthened the trend to organize the feminist movements in networks accounting for the diversity of their representation. A new thematic feminist network has a place in the Council: the Economy and Feminism Network.

Differently from the First and Second Councils with a representative from the National Council of Indigenous Women (Conselho Nacional das Mulheres Indígenas) (an exclusively female organization), the native Indigenous representation in the Third Council is the Committee of Indigenous Organizations from Brazilian Amazon, (Coordenação das Organizações Indígenas da Amazônia Brasileira), a more general organization represented by its women's section.

With exclusively or mostly female members, the first group of 14 seats includes the Household Workers Federation (Federação Nacional dos Trabalhadores Domésticos) and as surrogate the Federation of Business Women Associations (Federação das Associações de Mulheres de Negócios e Profissionais do Brasil).

In the second group of the Third Council, since the beginning of Lula's Government, there is the presence of the Labor Trade Union (Central Única dos Trabalhadores), the National Confederation of Agricultural Workers (Confederação Nacional dos Trabalhadores da Agricultura), the National Teachers Union (Confederação Nacional dos Trabalhadores em Educação), and the Brazilian Association of Lawyers (Ordem dos Advogados do Brasil).[8] If in the first and second Councils, the proportion of civil society's representatives and federal government representatives is 20 to 13, without accounting for the three seats for "women with expertise on gender issues," in the third Council, this proportion is 21 civil society's representatives to 14 government representatives.

The second strategy implicated in new forms of relationship with states and municipalities. There were various political gestures to change federal relationship with states and municipalities: the proposal of the National Conferences on Women's Policies, preceded by state and municipal conferences; the support to the formation of Women's Rights Committees in the states and in towns; the signing by municipal and state bodies of the National Pacts concerning each program such as Combating Violence Against Women and Reduction of Maternal Mortality, and the incentives given to the elaboration of State and Municipal Plans.[9] I argue that the national, state, and municipalities conferences for Women's Policies proposals provided the foundation of and legitimized all the new federal relationships with states and municipalities, as well with feminist and women's movements at national, state, and municipal levels.

In its turn, the Conferences for Women's Policies were legitimized by the joint proposal of the National Council of Women's Rights and the Secretariat for Women's Policies to organize the Conference on Women's Policies. Its approval will depend, however, on the appraisal by the government and civil society representatives as well as those from municipalities and states. Although the numerical relation between civil society and government representation in the Conference will be favorable to civil society, the government has greater political weight, given its initiative being prioritizing in the political deals so far.

The initial theme proposals for the First National Conference, preceded by State and Municipal Conferences, were the initiative of the Secretariat for Women's Policies (SPM) in a discussion with National Council of Women's Rights (CNDM) through the representatives' members of the council who elected some of them, to organize the Conference. In this consulting and election process, there was a tacit allowance in the priority to nominate feminists. In relation to the elaboration of the themes, they were

8. Important workers confederations are not present anymore such as Labor General Confederation (Confederação Geral dos Trabalhadores) and Union Strength (Força Sindical). Both are general unions from Brazilian workers. Similarly, the National Articulation of Worker Rural Women (Articulação Nacional de Mulheres Trabalhadoras Rurais) is no longer present. For the first time at the Council, there are present the National Gathering Family Farm Workers (Federação dos Trabalhadores na Agricultura Familiar) and the Association of Graduate Courses in Public Health (Associação Brasileira de Pós-graduação em Saúde Coletiva), an association of those university centers and research centers that provide Graduate courses in Public Health. The continuities and the changes between the entities represented in the Council of Women's Rights indicates the great diversity of women's autonomous organizations as well as their diversity in specific sectors within more broad organizations and unions.

9. Federal transfers were delivered conditional on formally committing to the targets of the Federal Plan.

proposed by the Secretariat and its technical staff, with the support of feminist academics specialized in the topics in agreement with the Council. The themes for the first Conference were: "Autonomy and Equality in the Labor World;" "Inclusive and Non-racist, Non-homophobian, and Non-lesbophobian Education," "Women's Health, Sexual, and Reproduction Rights," "Combat Against all Forms of Violence Against women" and "Plan Management and Monitoring."

The same topics are reinforced in the second Conference and are expanded with two more areas suggested by the Secretariat: "Participation in the Power Spaces" and "Sustainable Development;" and four more areas suggested by civil society in the Conference: "Right to Land and Decent Living in the Rural and Urban Areas, Considering the Traditional Communities"; "Culture, Communication and Democratic and Non-discriminating Egalitarian Media"; "Combat of Racism, Sexism, and Lesbophobia"; and "Combat of Generational Inequalities Affecting Women, Especially the Youngest and the Oldest." The new topics indicate the strength of the idea of presenting claims referring to interest. They demand diversity from women according to age, race, and lifestyle. Diversity of claims coming from differences of class, race, sexuality, age, and conditions of life, between women, have been included successfully in Feminist and Women's Movements and in the "new public spaces."

PUBLIC POLICIES FOR GENDER EQUALITY

Since the first National Conference held in 2004 and from the second National Conference held in 2007, it was possible to design policies elaborated as The National Plan for Women's Policies: I and II. These Plans covered not only proposals and activities to be carried out by the Secretariat for Women's Policies itself, but by the many ministries. For this, a Juncture and Plan Monitoring Committee with members from all Ministries was created in March, 8, 2005 by Presidential Ordinance. For the first time, a structure with such a broad scope was outlined in the Brazilian Government. However, the differentiated participation in the support of the proposals of the conferences from each Ministry is evident. The difference in participation to a large extent depends on the stronger or weaker acquaintance and tradition with topics related to women's rights, such as the cases of the Ministry of Health and the Ministry of Agrarian Development. In the same way, the many proposals do not correspond to an activity with a budget, but to a qualitative way of acting that it may not be possible to evaluate.

Still more difficult to evaluate is the impact of support and implementation from state-level and municipal-level policies.

The symbolic effectiveness, however, produces reciprocal effects between feminist movements, union movements, state and municipal committees devoted to women rights, as well as between social movements and the Special Secretariat for Women's Policies. In terms of a coordinated political maneuvering, there is a strong novelty in Lula's Government. And yet, when seen from the global scale of public policies, the budget of the Special Secretariat is pretty tiny, as well are insufficient the budgets supporting the National Plans for Women's Policies encompassing goals and resources from other Ministries.

General data concerning work, education, and health can signal achievements directly linked to new policies and new forms designed to revolutionize our understanding of gender equalities. These measurements of gender equalities can show the effects of the feminist movement and of legitimating feminist goals by the State and can also signal resistance to gender equality which is not yet possible to remove.

Among the data[10] that allow seeing issues relative to gender (in-) equality, I point out the significant rise of women's participation in the active population and labor market. While in 1996, 52.2% of women over 16 years old were active; such a figure reached 59% in 2006. However, if women's participation in the labor market reached 17.8% in 2006, male activity in that year was still responsible for 82.2% of labor market participation. The unemployment rate was smaller for men (6.4%) in comparison to 11% for women, revealing their greater difficulty in obtaining access to the labor market. While white men accounted for an unemployment rate of 5.7%, black women accounted for a rate of 12.5%. Women to a larger extent are housemaids, self-employed workers for their own consumption and without any pay, and the men are often employees, self-employed workers, and employers.

Data from the Brazilian Geographical and Statistics Institute (Instituto Brasileiro de Geografia e Estatística, IBGE) for 2006 indicate[11] that while

10. See *II Plano Nacional de Políticas Públicas para as Mulheres* (SPM, 2008). Also see for specific data:*Pesquisa por Amostra de Domicílios* (PNAD) from Instituto Brasileiro de Geografia e Estatística (IBGE), in IBGE. *Pesquisa Nacional por Amostra de Domicílios (PNAD) 2006.* http://www.ibge.gov.br/home/estatistica/populacao/trabalhoerendimento/pnad2006/default.shtm. Also see *Banco de Dados do Sistema Único de Saúde (DATASUS)* from Ministério da Saúde. http://tabnet.datasus.gov.br/cgi/deftohtm.exe?sim/cnv/matuf.def.

90.2% of occupied women dedicate themselves to household tasks, only 51.4% of men say they do them, although this data is probably something new. While women say they spend 25 hours looking after household tasks, men spend less than ten hours. A significant inequality is the continuity of greater income for men than for women, despite the relevance of a smaller difference with a 2% drop between 2001 and 2006. Women earned an average 65% of men's earnings. The racial issue has a strong presence. Black people earn less than the half of white people's earnings.

In education, women are stronger in comparison with men; women have higher educational levels: high school (54.06%), professional education (50.87%), and higher education teaching (62.8%) compared with men whose compared educational levels are 45.94%, 49.13%, and 37,02%.[12] Even so, they earn less in the labor market. On the other hand, there is strong inequality concerning the gender segmentation in the matter involving distribution of careers. The areas in higher education with more women are Teacher's College [pedagogy] (91.3%), Languages (80%), and Nursing (82.9%). The larger male percentages are in the careers of Computing Science (81.2%) and Engineering (79.7%).

In Brazil, the ratio of maternal mortality has been falling over the years, reaching a rate in 2005 with the adjusted figure of 74.6 maternal deaths for each 100,000 live births.[13] Even so the rate is elevated if compared with developed countries where these ratios move around 6 and 20 maternal deaths for each 100,000 live births. In the Unified Public Health System, 222,840 post-abortion curettages were made, with 37 maternal deaths. There may be an underestimation of all kinds of maternal deaths, stemming from child-bearing, from post-child-bearing and from abortion; the underestimation is still larger for maternal death result of unsafe and clandestine abortions. Maternal death is the most probable avoidable death in 95% of the cases and death by abortion is estimated as the fourth cause of maternal mortality. Estimates for abortion done according to reckoning from international organizations for Brazil, considering the figure of 222,840 post-abortion curettages, the number would be around 800,000 or 1,000,000 abortions done every year in clandestine conditions.

11. IBGE. *Pesquisa Nacional por Amostra de Domicílios (PNAD)* 2006. In http://www.ibge.gov.br/home/estatistica/populacao/trabalhoerendimento/pnad2006/default.shtm. See also SPM (2008).

12. Instituto Nacional de Estudos e Pesquisas Educacionais Anísio Teixeira (INEP) Ministério de Educação 2006. In http://www.inep.gov.br/superior/enade/default.asp. Also see SPM (2008).

13. Secretaria de Vigilância da Saúde. Ministério de Saúde http://tabnet.datasus.gov.br/cgi/deftohtm.exe?sim/cnv/matuf.def and SPM (2008).

According to data from the Ministry of Health for the year 2000, there were 26.7 homicides per 100,000 inhabitants. The growth of violence in the last decades in Brazil is clear if we compare the period from 1980 to 2003. It was 14 homicides per 100,000 inhabitants in 1980, reaching a peak of 28.9 for each 100,000 in 2003.[14]

Between 2004 and 2006, there was a drop in the rate of homicides to 23.9 per 100,000 inhabitants in 2006. An analytical document produced by the Ministry of Health and the Secretariat of Health Surveillance (SVS, 2006: 12) mentions as probable causes of the drop in violent deaths: "[the] disarmament act, the gathering of firearms by government authorities, and the investments in security by the Federal Government and by the states and towns which played the role of stimulating the development of structures of public security and local projects for the combat of violence."[15]

Even taking into account the impact of public policies, it is necessary to expand the international comparison to see the remarkable amount of homicides in Brazil. Data from the US in 2000 showed there were around 6 homicides per each 100,000 inhabitants, in France; the number was 4, in England, Canada, and Australia from 2 to 3. (SENASP, 2001; Souza, 2003)

Comparing homicides and female murdering and focusing on Brazilian capital cities (Souza and Carvalho, 2006), mortality data in 2003 register a difference in the victimization of men and women. Female mortality due to homicide in the Brazilian capital cities in the Northeast ranges from 1.8 per 100,000 inhabitants (João Pessoa) to 8.4 per 100,000 (Cuiabá), and male mortality ranges from 37.2 (Natal) to 134.6 (Recife).

These rates of murdering females evens out or overcomes the total rate of homicides, including men and women, from Western European countries (3 to 4), in North American countries (2 to 6), and in Australia (2 to 3). This comparison reveals the high incidence of homicides of women in Brazil, without mentioning the recognized amount of male homicides.

Such murdering of females is mainly done by former partners, ex-husbands, relatives, and acquaintances. So are the body lesions and daily threats in the

14. All Brazilian data about homicides are collected and informed by Ministry of Health's database (DATASUS) (http://www2.datasus.gov.br/DATASUS/index.php). The specific data from 1980 and 2000 are included in the report made by Secretaria Nacional de Segurança Pública (SENASP, 2001). The specific data from 2000 to 2003 are included in the analytical text written by Filho and Gazal-Carvalho (2007).

15. In Brazil, the "Disarmament Statute" is a federal law of December 22, 2003 that prohibits civilians from carrying, with exception for the cases where there is threat to the person's life. In those cases, there will be permission for limited duration. See Estatuto do Desarmamento Comentado. Lei nº 10.826, de 22 de Dezembro de 2003 (http://www.deolhonoestatuto.org.br/downloads/biblioteca/002.pdf).

family, marital, and domestic environments. While young men are particularly the guilty and victims of murder in the case of male homicides, women are the victims of daily violence (see Machado, L., 1998 and Bandeira, 1998). The combination of forms of violence from organized crime together with the high incidence of interpersonal violence between men and women enable us to understand that the issue of "violence against women" is the most visible form of a violent sociability lived as something unimportant.

These data give us both the confirmation of gender inequality and possibly positive results stemming from public policies and forms of feminist movement and from human rights producing its effects upon the State, but also in the forms of sociability.

However, perhaps the achievements and challenges from feminist movement can be better scrutinized when there is a focus on the two main political projects of feminist movement (action) over the last eight years and the strategic position performed by the Special Secretariat for Women's Policies towards the Federal Government in the decision to introduce the project into the political scene.

FEMINIST DRAFT BILLS UNDER LULA'S GOVERNMENT

In Lula's Government (2003-2010) there were two ongoing projects due to the initiative from the feminist movement. There were two draft bills arising from the mobilization from feminist organizations that depended, however, on taking the leading role from the official initiative of the Special Secretariat for Women's Policies. Feminist intellectuals working in NGOs and universities, as well as their knowledge of Law, Social Sciences, Health Sciences, and other disciplines were crucial to the design of these projects.

The first draft bill is about domestic violence against women. The negotiations between a consortium of feminist nongovernmental organizations and the Special Secretariat for Women's Policies began in 2003 and a new law was presented by Lula's Government and approved by the Parliament in August 2006.[16]

The second draft provides the right to halt pregnancy during the first twelve weeks, decriminalization of the termination of pregnancy during this period, and the guarantees its coverage by the national health care sys-

16. Act n 11,340, August 7, 2006 (http://www.planalto.gov.br/CCIVIL/_Ato2004-2006/2006/Lei/L11340.htm).

tem and by private health insurance plans. The need to change the law that criminalizes abortion was a decision of the First National Conference on Women's Policies en 2004. A new Draft Bill was written in 2005, but has not been approved or presented and directed by Lula's Government to Parliament as of March, 2010.

The first draft presented by the Government to Parliament, the one related to violence against women, went through a broad discussion, always with the presence of feminist organizations. It was presented to Parliament as a governmental draft act akin to the initiative from the Special Secretariat for Women's Policies. It was approved by Parliament on August 7, 2006, becoming the Act 11,340, known as the Maria da Penha[17] Act. The Act is being enforced although it encounters resistance because of conservative values held by many judges, in contrast to the values expressed by public opinion and the majority of lawmakers. The idea "the women do not want to suffer violence" was legitimized. In other words, they are not embedded in symbolic violence, without any help... They do not allow it...

The juridical resistance towards the Act reveals how much the former understanding of the Penal Code hindered any measure of protection of women and of combat against violence. Today, in the places where the Act is being enforced, protection measures are being applied and force anyone convicted of violence against a woman to move from the home and not approach the woman.

Before the new Act, crimes of violence against women were under two different systems: one before 1995 and the last, between 1995 and 2006. Until 1995, under the rules of Penal Code, only about 6% of accused were condemned and very few were convicted.[18] From 1995 to 2006 there was the Act 9099/95 ("court of small causes") that included the majority of cases of violence against women (Campos, 2001). This act only demanded that the accused pay the value of a package of essential goods, representing one fifth of minimum wage, to the community when he injured his wife. As a member of the couple, the victim, in some way, had to lose some of the

17. The *Act: "Lei nº 11,340" (2006)* has been called the "Lei (law) Maria da Penha," in honor of Maria da Penha, a woman severely injured as the victim of her husband's violence. A document on behalf of this woman was sent by the feminist movement to the International Court, and Brazil received the recommendation to change the impunity situation of the perpetrators of violence against women. This situation has improved the favorable conditions for the government to propose this law.

18. See research on judicial sentences on Violence against Women in Rio de Janeiro in Carrara, Vianna and Enne (2000).

family's income. Besides, she wasn't even listened to by the Judge or didn't receive any protection measure...

There are at least two challenges posed by marital violence as presented in the new Act Maria da Penha to the Justice System, to specialized police stations, and to traditional and specialized courts. The first is to deal with crimes or violations inscribed in cultural hegemonic values and disseminated across all social classes and traditionally inscribed in jurisprudence:[19] the trend to tolerate daily marital violence, in the name of legitimating male control over sexual loyalty from wives and partners. The allegation of honor in Brazilian jurisprudence, accounted for the absolution of a confessed murderer, have effects even today, alleviating acts of violence against women. The allegation of the need to keep up the family currently stands out as a justification for non-punishment. The "jurisprudential tolerance" towards domestic violence against women is in favor of the strong idea of "family harmony," considered as juridical good.

Owing to his traditional role as a provider, a man can prevent, control, and demand sexual fidelity from his partner and control the role performance of "mother" and "housewife." Once more, the old legal power through which husbands could allow or not allow their wives access to paid jobs is only a cue to the strength of these assumptions in the social order (CFEMEA, 1994). Despite a great number of legal and social changes, these values are far from being eradicated and continue to guide social behavior and jurisprudential interpretations. These values are what "New History" historians call "long standing values."

The second challenge for the Justice System is the fact these crimes and infractions are in the realm of the so-called private and interpersonal, strongly loaded with emotion and affection without the traditional distancing between the accused and the victim that is very common in crimes against property.[20] The investigation, reconciling, arbitration, and judging are carried out in a context interweaving shared values and interests of a greater complexity and peculiarity that are very different from relations between accused and victim in most of crimes against property or crimes motivated by instrumental interests.

---

19. Carrara, Vianna, and Enne (2000), by researching two inquiry centers in Rio de Janeiro, point out how, in the name of the family, the petitions against domestic violence against women are systematically shelved or the guilty absolved. This is done with the agreement of prosecutors, attorneys, and judges. From the total of petitions only 6% ended up in condemnation. See also Baratta (1999) and Campos (2001).

20. For different conceptual typologies and crimes, see Machado, L. (1998 and 2004); Ratton Jr. and Luiz (1996); Suarez and Bandeira (1999); Soares, L., (1996).

The second draft act that is very worthwhile for the feminist movement is the one that legalizes the cessation of pregnancy. At the end of 2009, abortion was considered to be a crime. The present Brazilian Penal Code says, according to article 124 and 128 written in1940: To provoke abortion in herself or to consent that somebody else provokes it, has a detention of one to three years. There are two circumstances where there is no punishment: (1) if there is no other means of saving the pregnant woman's life; and (2) in the case of pregnancy resulting from rape (Codigo Penal Atualizado, 1940). In the new shape of national networks, the Brazilian feminist movement (action) for legalization of abortion has been brought back from the nineties over the last years with growing intensity. A great visibility was obtained with the proposal to legalize abortion undertaken by the decision of women during the first twelve weeks of pregnancy, elaborated and presented to a Three-party Committee (Comissão Tripartite) named by the President of the country, to the Social Security and Family Committee of the National Congress in 2005. The Ministry of Women's Policies presented the draft to the National Congress' Social Security and Family Committee. This is a draft act in the political scene that "establishes the right to voluntary termination of pregnancy, assuring the procedure is included in the Unified Health System, and determining its coverage by private health plans to provide assistance to health among other provisions" (SPM, 2005b).

The Three-party Committee joined by members of the Federal Government, from civil society and from the National Congress of Brazil and run by the Special Secretariat for Women Policies (SPM/PR) was set up with the purpose of discussing, elaborating, and furthering the proposal to review punishing legislation concerning voluntary termination of pregnancy, according to the Regulation N° 4 of April 6, 2005. The Three-party Committee was made up of 18 members, equally distributed between Government, Parliament (National Congress), and Civil Society.[21] A Committee, run by Special Secretariat for Women's Policies, finished its job on time

21. Representatives from Government: Maria Laura Pinheiro (SPM), Maria José Araújo (Ministério da Saúde), Pedro Abramovay (Ministério da Justiça), Denise Figueira (Casa Civil da Presidência da República), Paulo Sérgio Muçouçah (Secretaria Geral da Presidência da República), Carolina Melo (Secretaria Especial dos Direitos Humanos da Presidência da República). Representatives from Legislative Power: Câmara dos Deputados: Maria Suely Campos (PP-RR), Angela Moraes Guadagnin (PT-SP) e Elaine Carvalho Costa (PTB/RJ); Senado Federal: Serys Slhessarenko (PT/MT), João Capiberibe (PSB-AP) e Eduardo Suplicy (PT-SP). Representatives from Civil Society: Shuma Schumaher (Articulação de Mulheres Brasileiras, AMB), Maria Ednalva Lima (Central Única dos Trabalhadores, CUT), Maria Elvira Ferreira (Fórum de Mulheres do Mercosul), Lia Zanotta Machado (Rede Nacional Feminista de Saúde, Direitos Sexuais e Direitos Reprodutivos), Edmund Chada Baracat, represented by Jorge Andalaf (Federação Brasileira das Associações de Ginecologia e Obstetrícia) and Thomaz Rafael Gollop (Sociedade Brasileira para o Progresso da Ciência, SPBC).

and presented the product of this assignment in the form of a proposal of "Punishing legislation review concerning the Voluntary Termination of Pregnancy (SPM, 2005a and 2005b)."

There were two political events that played essential roles for the creation of the necessary conditions for the building of a Committee appointed by the President Cabinet to review the abortion legislation.

The first was the creation and constitution, by the initiative of the National Feminist Network from Reproduction and Health Rights from a network of feminist NGOs, of actions to bring back the proposal of legalizing abortion: the organization of "Brazilian Journeys for Legal and Safe Abortion" (Jornadas Brasileiras para o aborto legal e seguro) in February 2004 (*Jornadas*, 2005). The second was the holding of municipal, state, and national conferences by the Special Secretariat for Women's Policies and by the CNDM. Its organization started in 2003, and the holding of municipal and state conferences took place in the first semester of 2004, leading to the National Conference held in July in 2004, with more than 2,000 women and mobilizing around 120,000 women.

The message below from "Journeys" (Jornadas) reveals the importance given to debates held in the Conferences;

> Fighting against contempt and disrespect to the right of decision by women, feminism created Brazilian Journeys for Legal and Safe Abortion and called for women and men to be united and participate in the struggle to force the Federal Government to send recommendations from the First National Conference on the Policies for Women (July, 2004) supporting decriminalization and legalization of abortion (*Jornadas*, 2005: 1).

Certainly, the campaigns made by *Jornadas*[22] also were responsible for assuring the attention to and the vote on this controversial issue inside the broader women's movement, for feminism, in strict terms, is far from being the point of view of the majority of women. Among the 2,000 women or more present in the National Conference in 2004, only 200 opposed this resolution. From the State Conferences, with more than 20,000 women, only one Conference on the policies for woman from Minas Gerais did not approve the demand for the review of the legislation punishing abortion. Once the assignments from Three-party Committee were finished, the Special Secretariat for Women's Policies handed a draft of the project to Jandira

22. Two representatives from civil society in the Three-party Committee took part in the campaigns for the right of legal and safe abortion: representatives from "Articulação das Mulheres Brasileiras" (Brazilian Women's Articulation) and "Rede Nacional Feminista de Saúde e Direitos Sexuais e Reprodutivos" (Feminist Network for Health and Sexual and reproductive Rights).

Feghali of the Health, Security, and Family Committee (Comissão de Seguridade Social e Familia, CSSF). In that moment, Jandira Feghali was asked to give a statement about a precedent draft legalizing abortion presented many years before. She adopted the draft presented by the Three-party Committee as a replacement for the draft she was considering.

Her statement was in favor of the draft bill made by Three-party Comm ision. The resistance was huge in the Health, Security, and Family Committee (CSSF), made more difficult by the absence in that meeting of congressmen, members of (CSSF) expected to be favorable. With the proximity of elections, and the uncertainty of the results, it was not sent out for a vote (Machado, L., 2008; A.L. Cunha, 2007). The contrary positions in the Congress grew stronger with the setting up of a Congressional Front against abortion. With new Congress members elected in 2007, the Draft Bill has been tabled.

The ongoing negotiations for the agreements between the Vatican, Congress, and Lula's Government (Vaticano, 2008) as well as the pressure from the National Bishop's Conference of Brazil against the draft act of legalization of abortion forced the government to retreat from its earlier position regarding the voluntary termination of pregnancy. Still in the II Conference for Women's Policies, the Conference approved the official resending of the same draft bill on the Voluntary Termination of Pregnancy to the Congress, but this proposal is not included in the II National Plan for Women's Policies, nor has it been accepted by the Government as a draft bill to again be presented to Congress.

In international feminist movements in the 1960s and 70s, women's rights were placed in a field of discourse in which women's emancipation was placed in polar opposition to conservative, masculine, religious, and traditional family values. The pro-life arguments were incipient as a social movement.

In Brazil today, the center of the debate is increasingly polarized between "the defense of women's rights and women's dignity" by feminist and progressive movements, and the "pro-life" arguments, particularly defense, as an absolute value, without any balance, of the life of the embryo or fetus. The new approach of conservative thought is internationally organized as a movement. Against conservative movements, the "defense of women's life" has to be advocated using the techniques employed in the seventies and eighties to modify public opinion towards violence against women that only was changed with the murder of women. Female reproductive and sexual rights will only be heard by public opinion, and not always understood, if women's lives are in danger or lost.

Public opinion, despite being encouraged by the fundamentalist movement, seems to be anchored to an illusory notion of a large distance between guiding "private" behavior (in which mandatory and justifiable reasons appear in the intention of aborting in a specific situation) and guiding based upon a "collective morality." There is an idea of opposition between a notion of "us" who can decide privately with responsibility, justifying the termination of pregnancy in name of a specific and constrained situation, and a notion of "them" (all others) who are incapable of making a responsible decision, for whom, therefore, there is a need to criminalize abortion.

Despite all encompassing political difficulties and the failure to obtain government support for the legalization of abortion, the feminist movement is continuing to fight for the lives of nearly one million Brazilian women per year who abort in response to various constraints, according to national and international estimates, and are in danger of dying as a result of procedures performed in conditions that are unsafe, because they are illegal.

CONCLUSION

Beyond the fact that building new forms for the composition of National Council of Women's Rights and the proposal of the National Conferences for Women's Policies yielded a visible by the government towards the positions of feminist movements and vice-versa, "Lula's" political strategies have helped to combine diverse approaches formulated by feminist movements and union and professional movements, and have contributed to the absorption of government mechanisms in the implementation of women's rights at the state and municipal levels.

Formal public spaces within the State have been constructed by Lula's government to negotiate conflicts and social demands. The very notion of liberal citizenship has been partially extended and transformed into "collective participation in dialogue and negotiation." The strength of the feminist movement on maintaining its goals limits the possibility of cooptation. The search for social rights for all women and the need for public policies always has been taken up as a goal by the Brazilian feminist movement. The majority of the feminist women, since the beginnings, were leftist and politically articulated against dictatorship. They assumed they could speak both in their own names and in the name of all women workers, middle and lower class women.

In 2009, the most important feminist networks included women of different classes, races, and sexual choices (or sexual identities). At same time, feminist black women and feminist lesbian women are organized in their own networks. All these feminist movements give priority to the establishment of common targets and reciprocally support their specific goals, as well as supporting the organization of indigenous women, unionized women, and rural women. Constructing NGOs and strong networks, despite the differences of power and access to financial resources between feminist groups, has made it possible to advocate gender equality to the government and to amalgamate alliances between widely differing segments of the feminist movement.

The Lula government has accepted the possibility of introducing and consolidating "public spaces" as Councils and new government bodies, as well as enacting and enforcing "public policies" against gender inequalities, and has approved the First and the Second Plan for Women's Policies. The first and the second Conferences called by the Special Secretariat for Women's Policies, for listening to and being accepted by the social movements has produced the effect of amalgamating the diverse claims of all these different segments of women's movements. The challenge will be the real implementation of all these claims, especially when resistances and contradictions come about within the government, setting apart political positions between government and feminist proposals for the rights of women.

Public opinion differs about how to accept all these new policies. In its mainstream, it has been very receptive to the idea of ending discrimination based on gender, sexual choice, and race. The most varied education policies of inclusion, as teaching ways of combating sexism, homophobia, lesbophobia, and racism as well as gender discrimination have been accepted and been legitimized as social values. They have been internalized as modern moral values. This does mean that discrimination cannot be, anymore, realized as legitimate and "natural" values. This does not mean that gender, race, and sexual discrimination have ended in the daily social relationships within the System of Public Health or the System of Public Education. It also does not mean that a new bill legalizing civil union or establishing racial quotas for entering at Universities has been accepted by the mainstream of public opinion.

Public Opinion surveys (Instituto Patricia Galvão, 2004) on violence against women show that Brazilians believe the woman should not put up with aggressions by her companion (86%). Statistics reflect the high incidence of violent social practices. Nonetheless, the generalized acceptance of the idea of ending violence against women probably is one of the results of the multiple campaigns made by the NGOs feminists and by the government.

I have argued here that the feminist movement's seeking the government as one allied and prior partner is due to the fact that portions of public opinion and parts of public institutions in Brazil are still very conservative concerning sexual and reproductive rights and women's rights for a life without violence. By the same token, the juridical institutions continue to be predominantly conservative in regard to violence against women. Moreover, conservative ideas have been reinforced by a new fundamentalism, namely by such components as "Prolife" and "Profamily Movement." These groups are strongly organized around some religious political representatives, mainly Catholics and Evangelicals. Fundamentalism is also supported by the most important organization of the Catholic Church in Brazil, the Conference of Bishops in Brazil, and by the new Juridical Catholic Association.

I also argue that addressing the government in these late years, the Brazilian feminist movement achieved some important goals: introducing and reinforcing public policies for women and public policies for gender equality, and contributing to some changes in public opinion. My point of view is that the institutionalization and partial professionalization of the feminist movement has increased the possibilities of achievements. We cannot forget the fact that, at the same time, the interconnections between feminism, black feminism, lesbian feminism, and all women's movements as unionized women and neighborhood women's association has been reinforced by the creation of "public spaces" for dialogue and negotiation.

The challenges are huge. From now on, the goals should continue to be addressed to the state, as well as interconnected with international feminism, but also addressed to civil society on the search of new alliances, while the new conservative and fundamentalist movements are also organized on national and international levels.

11

Nation-State Consolidation and Cultural Patrimony

John F. Collins

Abstract: In Brazil cultural heritage has played a key role in nationalism even as Brazilian definitions of patrimony have shifted across the 20th century. In this discussion of the history of Brazil's federal cultural heritage institution, IPHAN, I analyze how heritage planning has tacked in different historical periods between a concern with monuments and buildings, on one hand, and people's everyday habits, on the other. I argue that at a moment when a new class of patrimony, usually called "intangible heritage," has become salient in both Brazil and the United Nations, people's everyday habits have come to be commodified as part of a patrimonialization process that is no longer based on demonstrating national sovereignty, but on producing value through the packaging of national culture.

On November 10, 1937, shortly after President Getúlio Vargas announced the establishment of an *Estado Novo* intended to counter the "Universal suffrage...[that] has become the instrument of the astute, the mask which thinly disguises the connivings of personal ambition and greed" (Lacerda, 1938: 103), Francisco Campos, Minister of Education from 1930 to 1934 and the drafter of the new 1937 constitution, burned each of Brazil's twenty states' flags in a ceremony in Rio de Janeiro. As is well-known, and as these pyrotechnics by one of the Estado Novo's ideologues suggest, Vargas' ascension represented a restructuring of Brazilian society. This involved an "expansion within its own territory, conquering itself and the integration of the State, making its dimensions as vast as the country" (Vargas, 1938, vol. 5: 163). A crucial aspect of this "interior colonization" (Vargas, 1938, vol. 6: 88) lay in the creation of institutions that would foster "a hierarchization of activities, a coordination of means, and a continuity of action" (Martins dos Santos, 1941: 69).

The Estado Novo's expansion represented a marked increase in the production of data and the encouragement of nationalist pride around activities like mapmaking, record-keeping, and statistics. For bureaucrats, these were not simply representations of what Brazil already was, but rather important tools in nation-state consolidation since, for example, statistics is "more than a matter of representation. . . [it] is a tool of political intervention" (Asad, 2002: 82). Yet numbers and textual description were not the only tools open to experts focused on molding Brazil's population, geography, and culture.

On November 30, 1937, twenty days after the flag burning, Getúlio Vargas issued Presidential Decree Number 25 which outlined the responsibilities and organization of a new federal institution, the National Artistic and Historical Patrimony Service, (SPHAN). It defined the cultural manifestations around which SPHAN was organized as "patrimony," or the "set of mobile and immobile goods that exist in the nation whose conservation is of public interest, whether because of their ties to memorable facts of Brazilian history or because of their exceptional archaeological, ethnographic, bibliographic or artistic value."[1] In this way, at the outset of the Estado Novo and as a part of the project of national consolidation underway since Vargas gained power in 1930, the regime moved to outfit Brazil with a bureaucracy that would define, protect, and foment cultural expressions deemed representative of the nation.

SPHAN's establishment was an important step in terms of sovereignty, as it indicated that Brazil was prepared to protect and showcase its cultural treasures, an impetus gaining momentum at mid-century in Europe and North America, and which would increase markedly after World War II with the establishment of UNESCO. However, in spite of Decree 25's importance to sovereignty, there is something more important about the concern with cultural patrimony under Vargas than the establishment of a state office that might take the lead in, for example, recuperating stolen treasures. This involves the role of culture in the creation of a patriotic citizenry,

1. The full text, in Portuguese, of Getúlio Vargas' Decreto-Lei 25 of 1937 is available at http://www.planalto.gov.br/ccivil/Decreto-Lei/Del0025.htm (last accessed 7/13/10). All translations from Portuguese to English in this chapter, unless otherwise noted, are the author's.

and thus in the nation-building project developed during the 1937-1945 Estado Novo.

The term "cultural patrimony," or "cultural heritage" in the Anglophone world, describes sets of actions as well as the collections of objects produced by those actions that play decisive roles in the state-citizen interfaces so important to modern nation-states. This is because patrimony, in its noun form, is a collection of cultural objects, or a type of ideally shared property held by the nation for the future benefit of citizens. This heritage—I will use "patrimony" and "heritage" interchangeably in what follows—is usually produced by state governments which specify, protect, and inscribe in national or supranational ledgers the sets of relations, everyday habits, and artistic or architectural expressions deemed worth saving or celebrating as symbolic of a community's most important qualities. In other words, almost anything can be heritage, but in order to take on this special state it must be transferred symbolically from its everyday context and enshrined through research and state-directed ritual. Such collectively held goods that allow citizens to identify themselves in relation to a particular community, or what some analysts refer to as a "secular sacred" (MacCannell, 1999) in recognition of their inalienable, protected qualities, are essential to the pilgrimages to landmarks, the commemorations, and the museums so basic to nationalist fervor.

Analysts of the Estado Novo's role in the forging of a modern Brazil have emphasized, among many other themes, the state's involvement in education (Dávila, 2003), trade unions and shop floors (Erickson, 1977; French, 1992; Wolfe, 1993), social reproduction (Guzzo Decca, 1987), gendered forms of work (Besse, 1996; Weinstein, 1997), and music and radio industries that would have enduring effects on Brazilian society (McCann, 2004). Additionally, a number of works in Portuguese as well as English have examined cultural heritage during the Estado Novo (Cavalcanti, 1999; Fonseca, 1997; Williams, 2001) and the extent to which important aspects of the Estado Novo initiatives for heritage were continued across the second half of the twentieth century (Bomeny, 1995). Yet, as I will discuss below, cultural heritage management in Brazil today functions somewhat differently than it did during the mid-twentieth century, having undergone important breaks in the late 1970s and then again in the first years of the twenty-first century. In fact, heritage planning went through a shift in the first decade of the new millennium as UNESCO planners, conscious of the fact that a folkloric dance and a cathedral are quite different entities, complemented the world's existing supranational heritage ledgers of "natural" and "cultural" patrimony with a new listing called "immaterial" or "intangible" heritage.[2]

Intangible patrimony, established officially at the international level by UNESCO in 2003, is understood as,

> practices, representations, expressions, knowledge, skills—as well as the instruments, objects, artifacts, and cultural spaces associated therewith—that communities, groups and, in some cases, individuals recognize as part of their cultural heritage . . . transmitted from generation to generation, [it] is constantly recreated by communities . . . and provides them with a sense of identity and continuity (UNESCO, 2008: 7).

This newest class of patrimony has generated enormous interest in Brazil, a nation whose planners had already envisioned, but not necessarily implemented, initiatives that looked much like intangible heritage long before the end of the twentieth century. Thus the form of heritage planning being developed in the Lusophone Americas today in light of shifts in United Nations' conceptualization appears to owe much to earlier moments in Brazilian history, and not simply UNESCO edicts. This does not suggest that intangible heritage was invented in Brazil. Rather, today's immaterial heritage initiatives must be contextualized historically and understood not simply as Brazilian reactions to international programs, but as part of a long history of give-and-take between Brazil and the world.

In this essay I survey the history of Brazil's engagement with cultural heritage planning, and with associated trends in capitalist development and democratic governance, in order to situate in relation to nation-state consolidation processes some of the ways of relating to culture and the past discussed in my recent ethnography of heritage planning in Salvador, Bahia (Collins, 2008a; Collins, forthcoming). Put simply, both Lula and his predecessor Fernando Henrique Cardoso have sought in distinct as well as complementary ways to "chart a new path" (Cardoso, 2001) that might combine capitalist development with social justice in a nation long portrayed as formed on capitalism's periphery (Schwarz, 1992; Viotti da Costa, 2000). Within these recent efforts to reposition the state, Brazilian culture has come to be seen as an important source of development funds and foreign exchange earnings in manners that go beyond the export of archetypical figures like Carmen Miranda or the marketing of samba, carnival, and

---

2. UNESCO, which supervises heritage programs at the international level, is responsible for the transnational advising and registration processes that officially recognize "natural," "cultural," and "intangible" heritage. See UNESCO 2008 for an overview.

sexuality in places such as Rio de Janeiro. In the process, cultural heritage, which for most of the post-World War II period was configured as more of a symbol of national sovereignty than an economic resource, has leapt to the fore as an important component of the nation's political economy and culture industry, which is perhaps best-known today for the export of television dramas, or *telenovelas* (Kottak, 2009).

The history below suggests that culture's growing fungibility in contemporary Brazil is not simply a novel response to shifting economic conditions, but rather a complex resuscitation of earlier models of cultural management. While Brazilian approaches to national culture are constantly evolving, they do so in a manner indebted to experiences in cultural heritage management which have marked the federal institutions in charge of culture and which, in turn, provide Brazil's planners with sophisticated resources and perspectives in the creation of new cultural goods and the mobilization of vernacular culture in spurring greater democratic participation.

In exploring contemporary conceptions of political belonging produced in a historical relationship to cultural heritage planning, I look first at the origins of Brazilian cultural heritage programs in modernist circles and the Estado Novo. I then move to the post-World War II development of SPHAN into one of the world's most technically competent, but somewhat iconoclastic in terms of its relationship to other strands in Brazilian nationalism, cultural patrimony institutions. Next, I follow as the institution takes on a more politicized direction in relation to the challenges to the 1964-1985 military dictatorship. This pushes the essay toward its conclusion by forcing a consideration of the ways that a late 20th century fomentation of cultural heritage as a tool for political economic development has blurred the boundaries between culture and economy in ways that have transformed culture and identity into increasingly important economic resources. I then conclude with suggestions for further research on how recent reformulations of the Brazilian tradition of cultural heritage management that support efforts to turn a populace's everyday habits into a more marketable entity have impacted state-citizen interactions, and thus the nature of democratic participation today.

A Blueprint for a Cultural Institution

Histories of cultural heritage planning in Brazil typically trace the federal institution dedicated to monuments and national culture to a planning document presented in 1936 to the Minister of Health and Education, Gustavo Capanema, by Mário de Andrade, the folklorist, novelist, and leader of Brazil's modernist movement of the 1920s (Ministério da Cultura, 1980: 22). In his proposal, Andrade defined cultural patrimony, "as all pure or applied artworks, popular or erudite, national or foreign, that belong to public powers, social organisms, individual citizens, and foreign citizens resident in Brazil" (Andrade, 1993: 40). He divided conceptually such "pure or applied artworks" into eight basic categories: (1)Archaeological Art; (2) Amerindian Art; (3) Popular Art; (4) Historical Art; (5) National Erudite Art; (6) Foreign Erudite Art; (7) National Applied Arts; (8) Foreign Applied Arts (Andrade, 1993: 41).

Andrade then argued that these categories could be collapsed, and thus mobilized to begin the transformation from quotidian object into a possession of the collectivity, so as to generate four registries of the nation's patrimony. These encyclopedic, state-managed volumes, similar to those which serve around the world as the archival tools through which governments inscribe their citizens' habits as patrimony today, were:

> Archaeological and Ethnographic Registry, corresponding to the first three categories of arts: archaeology, Amerindian and popular.
>
> Historical Registry, corresponding to the fourth category, historical art
>
> Fine Arts Registry—National Gallery of Fine Arts, corresponding to the fifth and sixth categories: national and foreign erudite arts
>
> Applied Arts Registry and the Museum of Applied Arts and Industrial Technologies, corresponding to the seventh and eight categories: national and foreign applied arts (Andrade, 1993: 45).

Andrade's catalogue of cultural possessions—a method of imagining the nation that stands in importance and, given the emphasis on the gathering of information under the Estado Novo, alongside the legislation that regulated industrial trade unions or radio broadcasting or the public health initiatives directed at mothers and infants, for example—separates and defines the popular, erudite, and applied arts.[3] The divisions revolve around objects' valorization in three areas. These include an association with a Brazilian people being defined under Vargas; aesthetic or "fine" arts criteria as mobilized by Andrade and his team in tense relation to European definitions; and industry, an area of great interest during the mid-century push for mod-

3. Andrade also proposed that each *livro de tombo*, or patrimonial registry, be complemented by a separate museum dedicated to one of the four categories of national possessions.

ernization. This is significant in terms of an understanding, from the perspective of the cultural elite of the Estado Novo, of the future of a modernizing Brazil in which the nation is understood as composed of its "popular," "erudite," and applied or industrial sectors.

Two concerns were salient in Andrade's attempts to give substance to Brazil. The first was an interest in participant observation and concerns with the everyday life of common people that led him to a fascination with creative process, and thus with the techniques, types of knowledge, care, and creativity with which common Brazilians produced material culture. The second was an event-based theory of history in which culture stood as a mark of development. Both approaches reflect Andrade's historical moment, his prior experiences managing São Paulo's cultural office, and, as emphasized in subsequent histories of Brazil's patrimony movement, his particular genius (Gonçalves, 1996; Nogueira, 2005).

In Andrade's suggestion for listing objects to be protected, the "popular" arts came to include the Amerindian and the archaeological, thus illustrating the temporal and ethnic bases of a national popular substantially dependent on a relationship between the cultural production of Native Brazilians in the present (Amerindians) and Native Brazilians in the past (the producers of "Archaeological Arts"). Here, at a critical moment in the development of ideas about racial mixture in Brazil, and a juncture roughly contemporaneous with Gilberto Freyre's influential argument about miscegenation in the 1933 *Masters and the Slaves*, the organization of the nation's patrimony locates Amerindian and popular culture in a historical time linked to archeological investigation, and thus the past.

Andrade's contradictory attempt to unify the nation follows fairly standard moves within mid-century social scientific and museological movements. But this congruence with international norms suggests that within an ideology of supposedly egalitarian and exemplarily Brazilian culture there exist a range of distinctions and evolutionary evaluations that undermines a dominant discourse on the coeval, forward movement of a single national race. In other words, within the version of citizenship being supported in its cultural facets by the SPHAN institution that would be in charge of cataloguing, protecting, and exhibiting the nation's artistic and historical possessions, the forward-thinking folklorist Mário de Andrade created a series of social hierarchies that implicitly located rural and nonwhite peoples in the nation's past, but not necessarily its future.

To make the point that SPHAN's documents relegated certain people and their cultural manifestations to history indicates that the nation is not constructed via a homogeneous time that avoids racisms. Rather, Brazil's federal heritage institution took form in the late 1930s in relation to a national consolidation dependent, at least in part, on separations between high and low art; past, present, and future; and a particularly Brazilian configuration of the relationship between Europeans, Africans, and Native Brazilians. This means of charting the future around heritage seems to have drawn on tendencies established in the previous decade within the Brazilian modernist movement.

Modernism and the Birth of Cultural Heritage Planning

Brazilian modernism, which gained attention in relation to the arts festival held from February 11 to February 18, 1922, or what is usually referred to as São Paulo's "modern art week," was a transformative impulse for most of Latin America. It gave form to a differentiated movement whose emphases, personnel, and politics and aesthetics shifted across the 1920s and, as many of its proponents took on posts in the Estado Novo in institutions like SPHAN, across the twentieth century. It is thus difficult to equate modernism to a discrete set of ideas. Yet there are two tendencies that are widely accepted as integral to its coherence as well as important to the development of cultural heritage institutions. First, modernists valued tradition and associated it with the activities of minority and rural populations like São Paulo's rural cowboys (Andrade, 1968). Thus tradition is central to Brazilian modernity: the nation's march into the future was grounded by a past celebrated in research and writings about citizens' everyday lives. Second, in seeking to valorize such lifeways, the modernists set out also to challenge European cultural dominance and scientific denigrations of Brazil's mixed race people.[4]

Research was essential to the modernist attempt to redeem the non-European populace and chart an independent course for Brazil. Andrade and his

4. This movement to counter European racisms and to valorize Brazilian nationhood on the basis of the cultural traits of its mixed race populace was not limited to the intellectuals surrounding modern art week, or even those commonly accepted as modernists. For example, the enormously influential public intellectual from Brazil's Northeast, Gilberto Freyre, is typically understood, and often presented himself, as what was known as a "regionalist" even as he is closely associated with the movement to celebrate Brazilian racial ideology and cultural independence. For discussions of these dynamics see especially Chacon (2001), as well as Gilberto Freyre's own definition of his "regionalist" focus in his 1926 Regionalist Manifesto (Freyre, 1996).

associates delved into music, art, Brazilian Portuguese, and domestic habits in an ethnographic manner which stressed the careful surveying of what people actually did, rather than the collection of objects for museums or the publication of unresearched impressions about working classes. This is apparent in Andrade's conception of SPHAN. He makes room for objects with historical or aesthetic value, but the first category of patrimony he proposed was the "Archaeological and Ethnographic Registry."

Andrade's empirical focus on vernacular culture is notable in light of the proposals for a patrimony service that preceded his 1936 outline for SPHAN. During the first three decades of the 20th century an effort to establish a national institution that would oversee monuments and historical sites had been gaining support. For example, in 1923 the State of Pernambuco's delegate, in a speech to the national congress, reported that,

> I have been able to overcome my embarrassment and natural hesitation in order to occupy myself with an issue that has not previously required our care. Nonetheless, this is an issue that is essentially Brazilian, and which holds great interest for the civic education of our people. The State should not remain indifferent to this cause. It involves the defense of our historical monuments and to this end I have just proposed a project that intends to place under State protection all buildings which present historical or aesthetic merits.[5]

Pernambuco's delegate was not alone in his interest in buildings and monuments. In 1925 the president of Minas Gerais, Mello Vianna, created a commission to study historical monuments. Minas Gerais had also been the site of early cultural heritage work in Brazil when in 1924 the Swiss poet Blaise Cendrars, after a voyage there with Mário de Andrade and other Brazilian modernists like Oswald de Andrade and the renowned painter Tarsila de Amaral, put together a draft document that suggested not only that buildings and monuments be protected, but that their surroundings also be considered patrimony (Telles, 2009: 7). Then in 1930 Bahia's representative, José Wanderley de Araújo Pinho, proposed to congress a law that synthesized important aspects of previous plans and brought together wide-ranging concerns with personal and collective property as well as historical, ethnographic, and aesthetic considerations. But Pinho's bill was interrupted as Getúlio Vargas gained power in 1930 (Fonseca, 1997). Federal heritage initiatives languished during the first years of Vargas' rule and portions of Pinho's attempt to regulate Brazil's patrimony would be retaken only in 1934 with the creation of an Inspectorship of National Monuments under the aegis of Brazil's National Historical Museum. However, this initiative

5. This speech is reproduced in Telles (2009: 3).

ran counter to the efforts to protect and foment national culture by the federal bureaucrats who had emerged from the modernist movement.

The National Historical Museum was run by Gustavo Barroso, well-known for his anti-Semitism, sympathies to the fascist and nativist movement known as *integralismo* which accompanied the Estado Novo's rise, and who competed with the group recruited by Gustavo Capanema for control of federal cultural policy (Fonseca, 1997). Nonetheless, Pinho's attempt is significant in that it did not focus simply on buildings.[6] He supplemented a concern with monuments with cultural goods that had ethnographic or archaeological value. In other words, a concern with the creation of a state institution that would protect and regulate Brazilian buildings and everyday practices as something conceived of as national culture, or patrimony, was an important part or result of modernist debates by the end of the 1920s.

Andrade's collaboration with a variety of modernist figures and involvement in debates about folklore and ethnography is important in two somewhat different manners. First, his approach provides a contrast to that developed within SPHAN across most of the second half of the twentieth century by another Andrade, the lawyer and administrator who would direct the institution from 1938 until 1967, Rodrigo M.F. de Andrade. Second, Mario de Andrade's insistence on a cultural heritage that moves between monuments, buildings, and more ephemeral or personal and quotidian practices raises the issue of how culture is to be defined within Brazilian nationalism, something to which I will return at the end of this essay as I consider how culture and democratic inclusion intersect in the first decade of the new millennium.

Exceptional Brazilianness: Buildings and Monuments

Despite his influence on the modernists and role in establishing SPHAN, Mário de Andrade never served as the institution's director. Instead, Minister Capanema chose Rodrigo M.F. de Andrade to direct the new cultural heritage institution. This Andrade seemed to enjoy bureaucratic process as much as Mário de Andrade valorized the ethnographic celebration of Brazilian creativity. Under Rodrigo's guidance, SPHAN exhibited an elitist class orientation and a south and central-Brazilian geographic bias (Rubim, 1997). The institution largely ignored the discussions of miscegenation and

6. Getúlio Vargas took power in 1930 and remained Brazil's leader until 1945. While he was forced from power at the end of the Estado Novo, he returned to Brazil's presidency in 1951 until his suicide in 1954.

popular culture that have come to define images of Brazil, and which are a staple of analyses of mid-twentieth century Brazilian nationalism.

Instead, in the decades following World War II, SPHAN became one of the world's most technically adept heritage institutions. It concentrated not on popular culture or on Mário de Andrade's directives, but surveyed monuments and buildings in constructing a canon of Brazilianness linked tightly to ideas about Portuguese baroque contributions to the nation (Williams, 2001). This quasi-European, high cultural version did not become hegemonic in representations at home or abroad, in no small part because of cultural initiatives under Vargas, the florescence in cultural production prior to the 1964 coup that was nonetheless not linked directly to state institutions in the 1950s and 1960s, and the subsequent impact of the military's 1964-1985 authoritarian fomentation of national integration and a culture industry based on television and radio (Chaui, 2000; Cohn, 1984).

SPHAN's activities during and after the Estado Novo suggest the extent to which representations of the nation and its salient imaginaries vacillated between visions of harmonious racial mixture, on one hand, and a valorizations of enduring attachment to Portuguese traditions on the other (Cunha, 2000). This seems at least in part a reaction to an elite and southern-Brazilian based aversion to discussions of African and northeastern regional influences in the internal development of the nation as a whole. It is also emblematic of a certain class-related disjuncture between Brazil's federal cultural heritage bureaucracy and the activities, the everyday cultural manifestations, and interests of the majority of its citizenry and artists in the post-World War II period.[7] Thus, despite the interest in folklore Mário de Andrade enunciated over the course of his career and within his SPHAN blueprint, for most of the mid-to late 20th century the federal heritage bureaucracy that today champions minority rights and multicultural initiatives stood as a purveyor of Brazilian ideas about European culture (Fonseca, 1997).

Under Rodrigo M.F. de Andrade's direction, SPHAN focused on the Iberian baroque heritage of Minas Gerais and Rio de Janeiro. The states of Pernambuco and Bahia—Brazil's first capital and hence a major site of colonial architecture—dominated the attention paid to regions outside of the south-central region that concentrated political and economic power. In choosing buildings and monuments, SPHAN focused on criteria related to aesthetic and historical value that were somehow iconic of what made Brazil

7. In an example of the history of art, rather than social historical or archaeological, focus of SPHAN, the institution did not have an archaeologist on staff until 1979. For a discussion of IPHAN, archaeology, and national education, see Najjar and Najjar (2007).

special, or particular, among nations. The result was mainly scattered, individual interventions that restored edifices understood as exceptionally Brazilian, often because of their relationship to the Portuguese baroque which the modernists had come to valorize in their mid-1920s excursions through the state of Minas Gerais. Yet the physical areas or the social processes surrounding monuments chosen for registry attracted little SPHAN attention. Nor did the dances, ways of cooking and worshipping, music, or religious practices that interested Mário de Andrade and which were included implicitly in Bahian congressman Wanderley Araujo Pinho's 1930 proposal become an important part of SPHAN policy.

The three decades during which Rodrigo M.F. de Andrade ran SPHAN showcased the enduring existence of a section of Brazil's federal bureaucracy which was in no small degree cut off from the everyday worries or the political concerns of a majority of Brazil's citizenry. Heritage planning in this environment responded to technical criteria imposed by architects and advocated within closed planning circles by an international and Brazilian community of experts. This rarified discourse set off architectural gems as collective representations that were in reality marks of the tastes and desires of a small segment of society. The extent to which SPHAN's architectural orientation continued to predominate after the 1945 demise of the Estado Novo suggests not only a class bias within Brazilian cultural heritage, but the extent to which the corporatist reordering continued to impact the memory work and commemorations critical to the "invention of tradition" (Hobsbawm, 1983) that produced the attachments to community so important to the smooth functioning of a national community.

SPHAN's importance to the objects to which nationalist "structures of feeling" (Williams, 1977) bonded is important to understanding the reconstitution of the state undertaken in the late 1990s by Fernando Henrique Cardoso's government and retaken by the Lula government after 2002. SPHAN, unlike, for example, Brazil's health or retirement or electrical energy system, was never identified as in need of renewal due to cost overruns or a lack of efficiency. On the contrary, it was one of the world's most technically competent state heritage institutions and it balanced local and federal interests while interacting effectively with UNESCO.

The Brazilian federal heritage institution's trajectory means that the continuing influence of an orientation that arose during Vargas' corporatist restructuring is difficult to portray, in the SPHAN case and thus in relation to national culture, as an issue of an oversized bureaucracy or a heavy-handed state presence in areas supposedly more adequately served or run by private industry. The management of the nation's cultural possessions is instead a realm in which the interfaces between a citizenry and a collection of national objects that supposedly belong to all citizens have been overseen for most of the second half of the twentieth century by a well-oiled, technocratic institution. SPHAN under Rodrigo M.F. de Andrade, then, was not conceived of as a site for the production of value, but rather as a space for the development of Brazilian modernity, and thus sovereignty. SPHAN continued the modernist goal of cultural autonomy, or transnational parity among nation-states conceived of as culture-bearing entities, even as it expunged the modernist project's more democratic components. Yet this would change, due in no small part to Brazil's 1964-1985 military dictatorship.

Patrimony, the Military, and Democratic Openings

After the Estado Novo's demise in 1945, Brazilian cultural life gained momentum even as state policies seem to have played little direct role in this effervescence. Nor did SPHAN, which continued to espouse a high cultural orientation around buildings and monuments that contributed little to the explosion in film, theatre, and the plastic arts that would be dampened only by the military's 1964 incursion into civil society. Nonetheless, during this period SPHAN did begin to work, for example, with the Cuban government to establish museums described as intended to educate the two nation's populaces. This led to meetings in Havana in 1957 and 1958, and Rio de Janeiro in 1956, overseen by UNESCO, SPHAN, and the Cuban National Committee for Museums (Trigueiros, 1958: 45).

Such cooperation was part of an expanding transnational investment in culture after World War II, a movement led within the United Nations by technicians from France, England, and the United States, and on a wider stage by U.S. post-war development efforts that sought to encourage hemispheric tourism (Schwartz, 1999). The attempts in the 1950s to establish transnational networks serve as evidence of SPHAN's continuing engagement with currents in cultural heritage management around the world, if not with Brazil's vernacular culture. This took place in an environment in which, despite the florescence of student culture and civil society more generally, "cultural policies put forth by the Brazilian state . . . are practically inexistent with the exception of SPHAN interventions [into the built environment]" (Rubim, 2007: 18).

SPHAN, reorganized as the Department of Historical and Artistic Patrimony (DPHAN) in 1946 with the fall of the Estado Novo and the Institute of Historical and Artistic Patrimony (IPHAN) in 1970, was so detached from the core of the nation's intellectual life that the 1964 coup led to little change in its orientation (Fonseca, 1997). Instead, as military planners sought to convert the relatively independent cultural initiatives of the 1950s and early 1960s into a culture industry that might produce vast fortunes and integrate the nation around its authoritarian versions of society via television and radio, SPHAN continued to focus on monuments and baroque architecture as a symbol of European influence.

The welter of programs through which military planners sought to colonize the nation's pre-1964 cultural life seem to have had little bearing on cultural heritage policy at a national level even as the sorts of popular literacy and handicrafts programs established under the military—but not supervised by SPHAN—did help residents of cultural heritage sites in the state of Bahia begin to recognize themselves as special populations who gained a certain identity from what they perceived as their close relationship to the practices identified by their state as national culture (Collins, forthcoming; Moreira, 2007). In other words, even as SPHAN cared mainly for buildings and monuments, shifts at the national level through which the military sought legitimacy came to impact residents of at least the Bahian historical center in ways that would come to alter how citizens interacted with patrimony in Brazil.

Yet SPHAN's policies were not altered significantly, even with the retirement of Rodrigo M.F. de Andrade in 1967, until the graphic designer born in the northeastern state of Pernambuco, Aloisio Magalhães, was appointed director in 1979. At this time, what had become IPHAN became joined administratively to an institution concerned with national memory, the Fundação Nacional Pró-Memória. During this late 1970s and early 1980s period of opposition to the military regime, planners working with the municipality of São Paulo like the social historian Silvia Lara and Bahian intellectuals like the anthropologist Ordep Serra, director of the Bahian Institute of Cultural and Artistic Patrimony ("IPAC"), sought to move patrimonialization policies at local, federal, and state levels toward a greater engagement with the citizenry's everyday lives. IPHAN under Magalhães supported such initiatives: In an environment of Brazilian redemocratization and United Nations' challenges to the industrialized world's stranglehold on patents in the 1970s and 1980s, IPHAN re-instated a more processual understanding of culture akin to Mário de Andrade's view of a Brazilian folklore. This was influenced by Aloisio Magalhães' more anthropological approach which emphasized not monuments, but everyday practices.

Magalhães had come to IPHAN after founding the National Center of Cultural Reference (CNRC) in Brasília. This CNRC, which he headed from 1975-1979, was a think tank and design studio concerned with popular culture. Supported by an array of state institutions like the Bank of Brazil and the University of Brasília and financed by the Ministry of Industry and Commerce, the CNRC sought to map a form of "know-how" that might somehow be translated into national business policy. In other words, the CNRC came about not simply as an attempt to define Brazil, but to mobilize its labor power in relation to something called national culture. As its name suggested, the CNRC was concerned with cultural *reference*, rather than a collection of cultural objects (Anastassakis, 2008). Yet how reference was defined is a matter of contention.

Magalhães, somewhat like Mário de Andrade, approached culture as a compendium of interactions and thus relatively ephemeral practices and representations. He linked this culture to tradition, suggesting that traditional knowledge and values were disappearing in the context of industrialization. Hence Brazil needed to document its practices before they disappeared (Magalhães, 1997). Such an emphasis on saving threatened culture permeated IPHAN at the end of the 1970s (Gonçalves, 1996) and filtered into regional heritage institutions like Bahia's IPAC by the early 1980s (Collins, forthcoming).

Brazilian popular culture came to be understood, even by a number of bureaucrats working within the state, as an arena that might open more democratic futures.[8] By politicizing culture in the service of Brazil's return to democracy by including working class people's everyday practices and Afro-Brazilian historical sites as components of the nation's heritage, planners associated with Magalhães further synthesized an understanding of vernacular culture as something special that belonged to the nation due to its origins in an authentically Brazilian people. In other words, even as popular culture was invoked in an attempt to foment a democracy rather than an authoritarian, corporate Brazil, intellectuals continued a tendency central to Mário de Andrade's approach to national culture. This involved a valorization of folklore as a redemptive and harmonious voice of the people.

8. For a discussion of how a variety of actors agitated for a democratic opening from within state institutions, see Cardoso (1992).

The late 1970s also saw a multiplication of municipal, state-level, federal, and quasi-governmental agencies concerned with patrimony. Intellectuals sought to reverse what they considered racist and Eurocentric criteria. This rethinking of the cultural goods imagined as evocative of Brazil's true essence led to the 1982 registry of Salvador's oldest continually functioning Candomblé temple and Palmares, the site of a sixteenth century maroon community in the state of Alagoas. These efforts to include social struggle and Afro-Brazilian and working class heritage as patrimony arose in part from the fact that from the late 1970s onward intellectuals committed to democracy looked increasingly at culture as a force that might be mobilized to open the political system. Article 216 of Brazil's new 1988 constitution made this orientation into law, defining "cultural patrimony as goods of a material and immaterial nature, taken individually or as a group, which are significant to the identity, action, or memory of the different groups that make up Brazilian society."

The constitutional article, written as indigenous rights were becoming a major issue in Amazonia and internationally, points to an incipient multiculturalism in its reference to social groups increasingly distinguished and painted as making up Brazilian society. It thus mitigates against the sort of high cultural orientation common under Rodrigo M.F. de Andrade's SPHAN by avoiding a language of monuments or simplistic exceptionality tied to a putative national essence. Instead, it defined patrimony in relation to cultural manifestations' significance to particular communities, which in turn make up the nation. The dissemination of ideas about diversity from the CNRC and IPHAN alongside Brazil's adoption of a new national constitution also created room for individual states to move to protect and foment practices that could be defined under the mantle of Brazilian culture.

Article 270 of the 1989 state constitution of Bahia specified that cultural policy should "facilitate the population's access to the production, distribution, and consumption of cultural goods" and "guarantee . . . communities' own abilities to direct popular, traditional, and contemporary cultural manifestations." But despite the beauty of the new Bahian constitution's legal language, the state's largest 20th century cultural initiative, the US$100 million transformation of its capital city's colonial center, the Pelourinho neighborhood, has taken form as a top-down packaging of culture for the benefit of elites and outsiders (Collins, 2008a). The project, begun in earnest in 1992, bears little resemblance to a grass-roots fomentation of the community's involvement with its own cultural practices and is instead directed in large part at the fabrication of representations of Afro-Bahian lifeways that might attract tourists.

The Pelourinho's reconstruction as a cash cow intended to permit local elites to dominate politics and disseminate representations of Afro-Bahiannness in manners that enrich them has lessened since the 2002-2005 demise of the political coalition run by the feared Bahian populist leader, Antônio Carlos Magalhães. In Bahia's new environment, and in spite of the continuing pressure by the federal and local states and development organizations to commodify culture, Workers Party (PT) politicians have challenged the patron-client relations developed by Antônio Carlos Magalhães around a discourse of traditional, rooted Bahiannness, or what is known as *baianidade* in Brazil. Nonetheless, the Pelourinho, now largely devoid of its pre-1992 populace forced out by state edicts, is not a place where an Afro-Bahian community of the sort usually credited by policymakers with generating popular culture has been able to remain or control what passes as its cultural production.

Instead, in a process repeated around the world during the 1990s, a constriction of possibilities that enriches a few at the expense of the majority has benefitted a small number of residents able to present themselves as community leaders or supposedly authentic avatars of Bahian tradition. These successful cultural entrepreneurs, who include members of neighborhood social movements active in redemocratization, have been enshrined as a species of symbolic ancestor to the nation represented by the restored Pelourinho. At the same time, many of their former neighbors have been exiled to peripheral neighborhoods where, in the eyes of the state, they belong. In this way selected Afro-Bahians have been permitted to gain a toehold in a neighborhood once infamous as Salvador's red light zone and celebrated as a core of Afro-Brazil but now reserved mainly for tourists, the bourgeoisie, and the money-making activities of investors from around the world (Collins, 2008a). The entwined Brazilian and transnational mechanisms for packaging culture through which this has taken place are critical technologies for understanding shifts in patrimony, and in Brazilian cultural policy, since the early 1990s.

Marketing the Everyday as Cultural Property: "Intangible" Patrimony

As should be clear from the history recounted so far, definitions of culture and thus cultural heritage policies change over time. The renaissance in heritage planning associated with the return to democracy and Aloisio Magalhães' stewardship of IPHAN came to an end by the final years of the 1980s as President Fernando Collor de Mello sought to balance the national budget by doing away with the Ministry of Culture. Yet after Collor de Mello's impeachment and Itamar Franco's interim presidency, the election of Fernando Henrique Cardoso in 1997 led to the re-establishment of the Ministry and pragmatic attempts by the federal government to support cultural initiatives in the face of calls for fiscal restraint and shifting international development paradigms. By the late 1990s, the Ministry of Culture came to approach buildings, cultural production, and even working class, indigenous, and Afro-Brazilian lifeways as national properties that might be bundled as alienable goods to generate income and help alleviate Brazil's fiscal challenges. One of the more intriguing aspects of this way of mobilizing culture for national development, something presaged by Aloisio Magalhães' tenure at IPHAN, involved the role of cultural heritage professionals' social scientific research in the Cardoso administration's interest in cultural heritage. Rather than employing ethnography to define Brazil as a modernist project in formation, such research helped bureaucrats package something called culture that held a critical economic role in a changing Brazil. This was not an entirely novel development in world history, since visits to ruins or orientalist fascination with non-European cultural production have long been a motor for exploration and tourism in many areas of the world, especially former colonies.

But Brazil of the mid- to late 1990s represents a shift in the tenor of initiatives through which people's everyday habits were collected and exhibited by institutions that configured them as collective possessions valuable to capitalist development. In this environment culture came to stand as more than a set of traditional activities that distinguished nations or impede western-style development and market economies (Weffort, 2000). As Minister of Culture Weffort stated in a World Bank meeting in New Orleans' restored French Quarter in 2000, "We must turn history around to combine development and heritage preservation" ("IDB President," 2000).[9]

The shift away from culture as a source of independence and pride and toward culture as an economic resource—a move that mirrored developments around the world whereby the "information economy" led to an emphasis on "intangible" assets and alienation of areas of social life previously excluded from the market—came at a moment in which worldwide approaches to and definitions of patrimony underwent significant alteration (Yúdice, 2004). The engagements between institutions like UNESCO and the World Bank and national-level planners have given rise to the welter of instruments now available for the management of culture. For example, by the mid-1990s UNESCO planners found themselves responding to critiques of the anthropological conceptions of culture that focused on everyday life rather than on exceptional historical or artistic icons, and to the increasing momentum of worldwide attempts to transform social and cultural relations into social or cultural capital. UNESCO's experts thus came to recognize a need to augment "cultural patrimony" and "natural patrimony," the two existing categories available for listing national treasures under the institution's auspices. In 2003, with the "Convention for the Safeguarding of the Intangible Cultural Heritage," UNESCO officially added another, third, realm of patrimony to its supranational ledgers that, in a manner akin to Mário de Andrade's ethnographic registry proposed for SPAHN in 1936, define the epistemological and archival categories that turn into patrimony formerly unmarked or everyday practices like dancing the samba, playing the Afro-Brazilian dance/martial art *capoeira*, or cooking the fish stew known in Brazil as *moqueca*.

While statecrafting efforts of the 1930s and 1940s rested prominently on efficient statistical, public relations, and policing tools for managing everyday life, the rolling back of the Estado Novo's corporatist labor, industrial, and pension systems in the 1990s occurred in relation to a different, yet nonetheless related, alteration in the state's knowledge or research-based treatment of social relations (Mattar, 2003). Aspects of everyday life celebrated for political ends during redemocratization in the 1980s as the cultural possessions of particular social groups came to be treated in the 1990s as properties that might be bought, sold or even help the national state produce rents through the re-occupation of territories like the Pelourinho, a neighborhood left to Afro-Bahian invaders during an earlier period of "order and progress."

9. This document no longer appears on the IDB website even as it was available until 2004 at http://www.iadb.org/exr/am2000/release/7100.htm.

The state, in reconstructing and then overseeing spaces like Salvador's formerly abandoned Pelourinho through the regulation of residents' activities and the fomentation of folklore, came to use attention to the health and well-being of residents as a way of sanitizing their cultural practices. The goal was to exhibit folkloric manifestations in the reconstructed UNESCO center for the enjoyment of visitors. Such expansion of state activity during a period usually characterized as neoliberal and thus supposedly involving a rollback of government involvement in the economy took place in Bahia as a citizenry's everyday habits on which important democratic initiatives during redemocratization had rested, came to be configured as alienable economic goods (Collins, 2008b).

The 1988 constitution makes clear that so-called immaterial culture and its preservation had by the mid-to late 1980s become an important part of Brazilian democracy. But as something called culture has come to be conceptualized as a marketable resource by organizations like Brazil's Ministry of Culture and IPHAN of the 1990s, citizenship has come to mean something quite special to a number of Brazilians with whom I have conducted fieldwork in Salvador's Pelourinho. More than simply indicating that political subjects participate in a shared medium called culture, today's citizenship around culture in places like the Pelourinho often means that people conceptualize this culture as a thing with value that they might possess. Many Pelourinho residents argue that culture accrues to particular groups and that members of those groups may deploy it in interactions with tourists and bureaucrats so as to generate cash (Collins, 2008b). This means that culture often becomes configured as an interiorized essence, rather than as something available to all.

The extent to which residents of Salvador's Pelourinho are reinterpreting the relationship between culture and citizenship in a rather unexpected manner today is one function of an emphasis on everyday habits and identities that became a part of federal policy when, in August of 2000 and in advance of UNESCO's 2003 legal and bureaucratic definition of its new category of "intangible" patrimony, Brazil's Federal Decree number 3,551 augmented the cultural ledgers envisioned by Mario de Andrade. It specified that the nation's immaterial cultural heritage should be inscribed in four volumes:

1] The Book of Knowledges [*Livro dos Saberes*]

2] The Book of Celebrations [*Livro das Celebrações*]

3] The Book of Expressive Forms [*Registro das Formas de Expressão*]

4] The Book of Places [*Registro dos Lugares*]

The innovations promulgated by IPHAN and institutions like Bahia's IPAC are impressive in terms of their potential for supporting democratic reform. In their wake, municipal administrations like Porto Alegre's mayor's office have permitted common citizens, as opposed to experts like architects or museum staff, to draw up documents and propose the registry of aspects of a community's culture as cultural heritage (Meira, 2004). Additionally, in Brasilia planners have put together a revolutionary concept of patrimonial merit around a notion of scale whereby the relationships between plazas, buildings, and streets might be registered, and thus preserved (Ribeiro, 2005; Sinoti, 2005).

As these revolutions in heritage planning have been going on, Brazil, once described as a nation "of the future" and characterized by foreign social scientists as lacking an intense engagement with memory or history, has been undergoing a veritable memory boom (Collins, 2008a). Thus it seems that heritage legislation and practice both piggyback upon, and reveal, the existence of shifting temporal conceptualizations of the national community. Heritage also seems to have permitted citizens to gain a diverse toolkit that encourages them to perceive, and attach themselves to, the polity on the basis of cultural manifestations.

Nonetheless, the more recent innovations in heritage practice have taken place during a period characterized by a marketization of the social. Such a shifting economic picture suggests that culture and identity have come to mean something new to bureaucrats, policymakers, and citizens at the turn of the millennium (Comaroff and Comaroff, 2009; Collins, 2008b). Cultural practices' and social identities' bundling as economic goods around the world in the late 20th century have helped lead to, and make visible, a situation in which attachment to the community has come to signify something more than sovereignty or democratic participation, at least in places like the Pelourinho where visitors and residents encounter their habits as highly reified things called cultural heritage. Seemingly as a result, those residents of the Pelourinho configured by their state as valued cultural producers and able to resist IPAC attempts to dislodge them from the restored heritage center, increasingly view culture as a resource through which they may profit and demand inclusion in a Brazil, and a world, where consumption has come increasingly to stand as a mark of political belonging.

Similar shifts in emphasis in the relationship between politics and economics have been repeated to various degrees in many sites around the world over the last two decades (Yúdice, 2004). Yet given Latin America's largest democracy's position as a creator of cultural products for global export, its economic and social vitality, its return to democratic governance, the reach of its early 20th century modernist project, and its enduring class divisions, it appears that the contradictions so much a part of the marketing of social relations as a thing called culture are especially visible, or important, in Brazil.

A key facet of the growing importance of cultural heritage in Brazil's economy involves international loan programs. In the 1990s institutions like the World Bank and the Inter-American Development Bank (IDB) decided that culture was good business. In 1999 Brazil gained a US$125 million IDB program designed to support the restoration of cultural heritage centers. But this *Projeto Monumenta*, administered by IPHAN and the Ministry of Culture, is not only about monuments. Instead, the loan program, which may be transferred between different sites according to needs as put forth by Brazilian authorities, focuses on restoring buildings, the internal workings of IPHAN, and the patrimony-based education of local people. As the IDB makes explicit on its website, Monumenta supports

> the training of instructors and artisans in restoration techniques, including carpenters, stone masons, blacksmiths, stone cutters, stucco workers and painters. The training of local cultural and training agents will also be financed. The fifth component finances educational programs to inform Brazilians of their historic and artistic heritage, its care, and its use.[10]

Here the IDB made loans not for highways or dams, but for cultural heritage as culture began at the turn of the millennium to take its place alongside such industries as a major source of earnings and investment. But what interests me most in the above statement from the IDB is its hybrid nature and its focus not only on buildings, but on quotidian activities that come close to anthropological definitions of culture: The masons, carpenters, and blacksmiths will restore buildings and the IDB proposal includes these people's training as a focus of its lending. Of course, their skills involve restoring a monument—after all, workforces in any industry need to be trained and Monumenta thus continues an IDB interest in producing qualified workforces. Yet educational programs designed to "inform Brazilians of their his-

10. See the International Development Bank's documents for the Monumenta Project at http://www.bid.org.uy/projects/project.cfm?id=BR0261&lang=en, (site last consulted 7/15/10).

toric and artistic heritage" present an apparently trickier situation. Are these Brazilians who will be schooled in the value of heritage the ultimate consumers of national culture? Is the IDB, in an echo of mid-century development efforts to expand internal markets, fostering a public for cultural heritage products made in Brazil? Or, in a model well-known in ecotourism and sustainable conservation efforts, can governments simply do a better job of protecting their treasures if a populace is informed as to those objects' value and their roles in citizens' and their communities' identities?

The situation in Salvador, Bahia's Pelourinho during the period in which the Monumenta funding was announced suggests that the above explanations are inadequate. First, even as Salvador's Pelourinho was initially contemplated by the IDB and Ministry of Culture for financing, the Bahian historical center failed to qualify for the monies. This was due to the state's 1992-1998 removal of the overwhelming majority of residents and a lack of private investment in the area.[11] Also, IDB consultants I interviewed stated that until the Bahian government put together a more just policy towards residents, no monies would be disbursed in Bahia. To this end, the IDB sent personnel to Salvador in early 2000 to educate Bahian planners as to its cultural heritage policies and goals, but met substantial resistance (Collins, 2008a).

A concern with an overbearing, rapacious state and with the residents of historical centers underscores the IDB's suspicion of state inefficiency and the extent to which development efforts today take into greater account the well-being of populations impacted by their projects. But this does not mean the IDB is interested only in bureaucratic efficiencies, or the management of some ostensibly discrete sphere that might be called "the economy." Instead, the Monumenta Program reveals a double-sided IDB concern with IPHAN's ability to manage Brazilian culture and the people involved with that heritage, whether workers restoring antiquities or a public expected to care for these treasures and come to know themselves as a community on the basis of their appreciation of this supposedly shared cultural heritage. As emphasized in the Monumenta documentation,

> The preservation, promotion, and knowledge of national culture are essential to social development. Common understanding and appreciation of the different aspects of history and culture are important to social consensus and political cooperation. Cultural knowledge of shared symbols is essential to

11. Members of Antônio Carlos Magalhães' coalition sought to use the state, which they dominated throughout the 1990s and employed as a mechanism for personal gain, to further their profits extracted in the Pelourinho. For an analysis of the Magalhães' clan's enrichment in the context of a broad critique of global development and corruption, see especially Henry (2003).

> communication among citizens. Many of these shared symbols are historical references preserved materially in built heritage.[12]

The claim above helps explain why Monumenta is structured around buildings, the training of people in architectural restoration, and the fomentation of a public who might consume or participate in the development of national culture. All three foci revolve around specifying the proper shape and role of the state in fostering community, a philosophical and practical discussion at the core of Getúlio Vargas' Estado Novo whereby an authoritarian, corporatist state was portrayed as something that might rectify the vicissitudes of a supposedly corrupt liberal democracy.

In an early twenty-first century light, national symbols become an issue not only of economic advances as the IDB makes clear that culture can be mobilized for development, but also of the nature of governance and the acquiescence of communities to state power. Yet as the IDB invests in culture, "social development" becomes an end in itself, rather than a necessary correlate to an industrial development tied to the market, democratization, and consumers and well-behaved workers. In its focus on culture, the IDB works instead to spur such "social development" and well-being through communication among citizens. This is supposed to lead to "social consensus and political cooperation" as an essential aspect, and goal, of its programs. Such harmony is not portrayed as emanating from just wages or full bellies, but rather "historical references preserved materially in built heritage" which might take on the dual role of producing value and encouraging social harmony by configuring as central to a nation's economy those so-called "immaterial" relations between, for example, people and monuments and craft producers and students.

Conclusion

This essay has focused on a tension, and a historical oscillation, between two sides of the Brazilian and the international cultural heritage movements. In doing so, it has put forth a history of the institution now called IPHAN that focuses on the borders, and overlaps, between cultural policies directed at what might be dubbed monuments, on one hand, and everyday life, on the other. This orientation brings out the shifting nature of Brazil's federal cultural heritage bureaucracy and links Brazilian changes to cultural

12. See the International Development Bank's executive summary for Monumenta at http://idbdocs.iadb.org/wsdocs/getdocument.aspx?docnum=437363, (site last consulted 7/15/10).

heritage initiatives at the supranational level and in the Brazilian city of Salvador, well known as a center of Afro-Brazilian culture. This effort reveals how, for most of the latter half of the twentieth century, people's habits as well as architectural wonders were subsumed within the same category of cultural patrimony in Brazil and the rest of the world. But by the end of the twentieth century, and thus at the moment of Brazil's redemocratization, the gap between quotidian activities and monumentalized stones and mortar came to be codified in heritage registries split by both UNESCO and the Brazilian state between cultural heritage and intangible, or immaterial, heritage. Thus the case of the rise of a Brazilian federal heritage bureaucracy, when supplemented with ethnographic data from the implementation of such policies used to restore Brazil's first capital city, the Pelourinho UNESCO World Heritage Site in Salvador, Bahia, reveals some of the ways culture and social development have come to play changing roles in modern governance, nationalism, and the global production of value.

My argument has charted not only a back and forth between buildings and everyday practices, but also a more linear movement toward a commodification of the cultural heritage that has become so important to fomenting nationalism and recognizing cultural and ethnic groups' contributions to nations around the world. In the hands of Aloisio Magalhães' patrons in the Ministry of Industry and Commerce, culture appeared a way to get at the mythic, traditional core of the nation which also promised to unlock that nation's potential in terms of its people's creativity. But this was understood mainly in relation to production, or goods that offered an alternative to modern manufacturing. However, by the late 1990s when Minister of Culture Weffort and the intellectuals associated with Fernando Henrique Cardoso put together their cultural policy, concerns with so-called immaterial labor and social capital had come to the fore. In this context, everyday cultural practices were treated as valuable in terms of their performance. This version of culture promised also to attract lending, rather than simply fostering the production of goods of the sort envisioned in Aloisio Magalhães' time. Thus culture came to be seen in the late twentieth century as not simply a correlate to economic development and an aspect of democracy, but rather a core component of the both.

The perambulations of the concept of cultural heritage suggest the importance of attending to the ways that today's emphasis on reconstructing Brazil's heritage may be altering the nature of democratic participation and national belonging.[13] This is not to say that something resolutely new has taken place—after all, SPHAN/IPHAN history demonstrates the extent to which institutions have drawn on and reinterpreted enduring concerns and problems in Brazilian national life. But it is to suggest that at a moment when people's quotidian practices come to be valued and defined in new ways, so too might their politics. The issue is best addressed empirically, and via research that tacks between everyday life and government initiatives and includes collaboration among different social sciences. Such cooperation underscores in turn the prescience of the Estado Novo bureaucrats who sought to define a nation through the development of ever sharper, and powerful, social scientific instruments. After all, how else might one turn a dance or a recipe into a collective possession of the nation that attracts outside funding? And, finally, how else might one convince an international organization to dedicate US$125 million to training masons and restoring crumbling baroque ruins in a move that suggests culture may be a motor for, and not just the effect of, development policies directed at one of the world's most dynamic economies?

13. These early descriptions of intangible heritage and "living human treasures" may be found at http://www.unesco.org/culture/heritage/intangible/html_eng/index_en.shtml, (site last consulted on 1/20/07).

Part III
Financial Crisis and Response

12

THE FINANCIAL SERVICES INDUSTRY

Fernando Sotelino

Abstract: One characteristic of the Brazilian banking industry as it stands today is the balance of power between private and public sector banks; another is the balance of power within the private sector between domestic and foreign banks; a third is that it ranks among the world's best capitalized and supervised; and a fourth is that most of the financing of investment is shouldered by public sector banks. This paper examines how this unique industry profile came to be and explores the prospects for the consolidation of a strong domestic long term credit market in Brazil.

It is now the aftermath of the global financial crisis triggered by the US subprime meltdown in 2008. Most analysts are back to projecting GDP growth for Brazil for 2010 and beyond in the 5 percent plus range. They also rejoice with a gradual return to normality of domestic credit markets and a renewed flow of global equity offerings by Brazilian companies. Plus, the leading Brazilian banks have come out not only unscathed from the crisis but in an even stronger relative position in terms of market value vis-à-vis peers around the world.

One characteristic of the Brazilian banking industry—as it stood prior to the subprime meltdown and stands today—is the balance of power (in terms of shares of deposits and loans) between private and public sector banks; another is the balance of power within the private sector between domestic and foreign banks. This is a unique profile when compared not only to OECD countries—where domestic private sector banks are dominant and the role of public sector banks is modest—but also to other large emerging economies such as Mexico, where foreign banks are dominant and the presence of public sector banks is relatively modest, or India, where the public sector banks are dominant and the market share of foreign banks is modest.

The Brazilian banking industry is also perceived to be among the world's best capitalized and supervised. On the other hand, long term lending by Brazilian private sector banks is very small by any standards when matched against private or public sector banks of both the OECD and other leading emerging economies; public sector banks provide most of the financing of investment by businesses (industries and infrastructure) and families (housing).

How did this unique profile come to be? Is it likely to change? How was it indeed affected by this last global financial crisis? Is the Brazilian financial sector finally becoming capable of transforming short-term savings into long term availability of credit at costs competitive with important economies in the world?

Section 2 provides a historical perspective of Brazilian banking from its origin in 1808 to the eve of the *Plano Real* (Real Plan) in 1993. Particular attention is given to exploring how private sector banks came to be and managed to develop a firm foundation so that the they never ceased to exist, and to examining the evolving roles of public and private sector banks in the financing of consumption and investment in Brazil from the late 1830s to the early 1990s.

Section 3 begins with an assessment of the effects of *Plano Real* (the stabilization plan put in motion in December 1993 to finally, with a strong fiscal adjustment and no element of surprise, extinguish hyperinflation in Brazil) and the late 1994 Mexican crisis on bank behavior and systemic risk, and proceeds to examine in some detail what the author characterizes as three quite distinct stages of industry consolidation that followed: government assisted (1995–1998), market driven (1999–2007), and subprime meltdown induced (2008–2009).

Section 4, concluding remarks, revisits the strengths and weaknesses of the Brazilian financial system as it stands today and highlights the obstacles to be overcome for the consolidation of a strong domestic fixed income securities market.

BANKING IN BRAZIL, FROM 1808 TO *PLANO REAL*

Early Banking, 1808–1889

Commercial banking in Brazil began with the foundation of Banco do Brasil in 1808, when the King of Portugal, Dom João VI and his court, in flight from the imminent invasion of Lisbon by the Napoleonic troops, arrived in Rio de Janeiro (Smith, 2002: 39).

The Banco do Brasil was conceived as both a commercial bank for takings deposits and discounting commercial paper, and a central bank for issuing paper money. It could also engage in trading commodities and foreign exchange. Its intended minimum capital upon foundation was 1,200 contos.[1] But after four years of operation, paid-in capital was only 126 contos. Additional incentives were put in place, allowing the original minimum capital to be reached in 1818.[2] But, by 1821, as a result of year-after-year printing of money to finance the Crown, over 70 percent of Banco do Brasil's assets were government bonds and only less than 15 percent of its notes in circulation were backed by metallic reserves.

Upon Independence in 1822, withdrawals by the Portuguese royal suite returning to Lisbon exposed the bank's delicate liquidity situation. Additional remedial rounds of capitalization approved by the new Brazilian Emperor, Dom Pedro I, were not sufficient to avoid continued deterioration. By mid-1829 gold coins commanded a 200 percent premium over Banco do Brasil's paper money. On September 23, the bank's liquidation was declared. The Banco do Brasil's notes in circulation were gradually replaced by new Treasury notes explicitly backed by the Nation. Brazil's first commercial banking venture, characterized by a hybrid (public-private) ownership, dangerously conflicting objectives (bank of issue of paper money and commercial bank), and poor governance (favored treatment of related parties and high dividend distributions on accounting profits) had ended.[3]

1. 1 conto equals 1,000 "mil réis." Réis is the plural of Real, the standard unit of account for the Brazilian currency. So 1 conto equals 1 million "réis." In August 1808 one thousand réis (or the "mil réis") was equivalent to 67.5 British pence. The "mil réis" appreciated to 96 pence in May 1814 and, then, devalued continuously to 54 pence in January 1821, and 21 pence in January 1831 (see Cavalcanti, 1999: 523-25).

2. Incentives included knightly honors to capital subscribers to a Government commitment to subscribe 100 shares per annum from tax collections with the dividends on these shares for the first 5 years being paid to the private shareholders.

3. For more details on the sequence of events between the foundation of Banco do Brasil and the end of the Empire see Ribeiro and Guimarães (1967: 37-117).

When Brazil's Emperor, Dom Pedro I, returned to Lisbon in 1831 to become King of Portugal, he abdicated in favor of his five year old son. Brazil's government was temporarily entrusted to the Regency.[4] The Regency government (1831-1840) had to face several regional revolts (including the Farrapos War in Rio Grande do Sul, 1835), but managed to keep the country whole and to restore financial order. Coffee exports grew significantly and the occupation of the country's interior by industrial and agricultural enterprises accelerated. As a result, the demand by society for banking services—payments and collections, deposit taking and credit—increased substantially.

The creation of a new government sponsored Banco do Brasil was again attempted in 1833. Proposed bank's by-laws established that bank notes issued would be exchangeable on demand for gold or silver and prohibited the bank from lending to the government without approval by Congress. But not enough public trust had yet been built to allow for the initiative to materialize. So, private sector banking began to flourish in Brazil.

Private sector banks were born in Ceará (1836), Rio de Janeiro (1838), Bahia (1845), Maranhão (1846), Pará (1847), and Pernambuco (1851). Brazil's first multi-state banking enterprise was private. It was named "Banco do Brasil." It was established in 1851 by the Barão de Mauá, and had headquarters in Rio de Janeiro and branches in São Paulo and Rio Grande do Sul.[5]

Notes issued by private sector banks began to be accepted as means of payment in their own geographic vicinity. But lack of a paper medium with countrywide acceptance remained an obstacle to economic development. In July 1853 a major new arrangement was announced: a new Banco do Brasil would be formed through the merger between the country's two largest private sector banks (Mauá's Banco do Brasil and Banco Comercial do Rio de Janeiro) plus new capital subscriptions by the provinces interested in having Banco do Brasil's commercial branches and by investors at large. The resulting ownership structure was 11/15 private (1/3 Maua's Banco do Brasil, 1/5 Banco Comercial, 3/15 other investors) and 4/15 public. Representation on the board of directors was proportional to shareholdings; but the bank's President and Treasurer had to be appointed by the Emperor.

The new Banco do Brasil was, again, authorized to operate as a commercial bank (deposit taking, payments and collections, credit, and foreign exchange and commodities trading) and had the mandate of a central bank

4. Initially a triumvirate, after 1834, one single Regent was chosen every four years by the General Assembly (Smith, 2002: 48).
5. For more details on Maua's Banco do Brasil see Caldeira (1995), chapter 18.

(the country's monopoly issuer of paper money). This time the bank's by-laws established clear liquidity and leverage guidelines[6]: paper emissions should not exceed two times metallic reserves and total loans should not exceed two times net worth.

Unfortunately, however, this was another short-lived attempt. In 1857, Banco do Brasil, weakened by higher leverage and lower levels of metallic reserves than specified by its by-laws, refused to borrow abroad to lend to the government. The government then broke the Banco do Brasil's monopoly of issuing currency (Ribeiro and Guimarães, 1967: 80). In 1866, with notes outstanding in excess of 5 times its metallic reserves, it lost (together with the other banks also granted the right to issue currency in 1857) the right to issue paper money.[7] Another two decades would go by before the Brazilian government would again entrust any financial institution with the right to issue paper money.[8] But private sector banks had begun to learn when to expand or contract their balance sheets in response to external conditions and perceived risks, and would never cease to exist in Brazil.

From "Encilhamento" to the Great Depression, 1889–1930

The winds of liberalization towards the last days of the Empire had not been limited to the end of slavery. In May 1888, the government had already granted three private sector banks the right to issue paper money. Proclamation of the Republic (on November 15, 1889) reinforced the trend. With the goal of stimulating credit and economic growth, the new government decided to allow a plurality of paper money emissions. Commercial banks could be formed with the right to issue notes that were legal tender backed by bonds deposited with Treasury. No restriction on bank leverage was imposed and shareholders' liability was limited to the invested capital. The free market should be capable of self-restraint.

6. Bank liquidity is defined as the bank's ability to meet its financial obligations as they come due without incurring losses of a magnitude that could threaten its solvency. Bank solvency is defined as the bank's capacity to meet all financial obligations to third parties in full and on time. Bank leverage is the ratio between the bank's total financial obligations to third parties and its shareholder's capital.

7. The debate on who should be entrusted with the right to issue money (paper notes with legal tender) was also in debate in the US in the late 1800's. For a detailed discussion see Knox (1969).

8. Law 401 of September 1846 debased the gold standard from 2.5 *mil réis*/ounce to 4 *mil réis*/ounce. The following amount of metallic money was minted in Brazil (assuming the 4 *mil réis*/ounce standard) until 1888: 45.7 contos de réis in gold coins, 21.0 contos in silver, 3.9 contos in bronze, and 2.7 contos in nickel. Old Portuguese coins also circulated as metallic money. In addition, in 1849 the government gave legal tender status to English money. For more details on money in Brazil during the Second Empire (1831-1889) see Ribeiro and Guimarães (1967: 100-02).

The response was phenomenal (Ribeiro and Guimarães, 1967: 117). Registered capital by the (private) banking industry increased forty-fold, from 18.5 thousand contos in May 1888 to 828 thousand contos in October 1890. Private sector joint stock corporations were created throughout the country, with banks taking the lead. In Rio de Janeiro alone, 57 banks of issue were in operation. It was what historians would call the "Encilhamento," the saddling-up and frenetic betting which precedes a horse race.

Not all banks issued paper money and/or pursued unsecured optimistic lending. Several chose to simply ride the wave of other people's money and engage in basic commercial banking activities. But, as a result of the extraordinary monetary expansion, inflation permeated the economy, causing Brazil's currency to devalue by more than 100 percent between 1889 and 1892. Uncertainty regarding the soundness of banks began to mount. The Treasury eventually had to intervene to rescue the financial system. It cancelled all banks' licenses to issue paper money, liquidated many weaker banks, and pressured the shareholders of the private sector Banco República dos Estados Unidos do Brasil and the public-private Banco do Brasil to merge the two banks to form Banco República do Brasil. Banco República do Brasil's registered capital was 190 thousand contos. But initial paid-in capital was only 25.5 thousand contos and loan losses between 1893 and 1900 were more than 60,000 contos. By the end of 1900, the Treasury had begun the liquidation of the bank.

A period of fiscal and monetary orthodoxy ensued.[9] Finally, by legislation of December 30, 1905, a new (the fourth to operate) Banco do Brasil was formed to absorb the now smaller and cleaner balance sheet and the banking operations of Banco República do Brasil. Paid-in capital was 70,000 contos, 1/3 each approximately provided by the Banco da República's shareholders, the federal government, and the public. Born to be the country's leading commercial bank, the new Banco do Brasil would not be granted the right to issue paper money this time around. The bank's management was formed by five directors, two (the president and the director for foreign exchange) appointed by the government and three elected proportionately by the stockholders. As a result, the government obtained the effective control of the enterprise. By 1921, Banco do Brasil had 40 branches (from Manaus, in the Amazon Region, to Porto Alegre, in Rio Grande do Sul)

9. M1, currency plus demand deposits, stayed constant at 670,000 contos from 1900 to 1905 (Onody, 1960: 28).

and operated a clearing house for checks and a rediscount window for liquidity support to other banks.

The post–World War I economic euphoria lasted until 1920.[10] In the second semester of 1920 Brazil was dragged into a global, brief but severe, recession. This triggered increasing complaints throughout the economy against the scarcity of credit (Neuhaus, 1975: 60). Inspired by prevailing economic models in more developed economies,[11] Minister of Finance Homero Baptista proposed the establishment of an independent central bank to control the supply of money and credit, therefore freeing the economy from the negative influences of Treasury (fundamentally concerned with the financing of government deficits) in this area. Concerns regarding potential abuse of the power to issue paper money by a new central bank led to the approval of Law 4182 (1920) creating the Carteira de Emissão e Redesconto within Banco do Brasil but to be run by a director appointed by the President and having an initial authorized ceiling of 200,000 contos for future emissions. Decree-Law 4635 of January 8, 1923 (under President Artur Bernardes) gave Banco do Brasil absolute central banking powers, as it abolished the ceiling on emissions which had been set in 1920. But Decree-Law 5108 of December 18, 1926 (under President Washington Luiz) determined a return to the gold standard[12] suspending, for all practical purposes, the paper money issuing powers of Banco do Brasil (Neuhaus, 1975: 86) leading to a contraction of the monetary base[13] and suspending the central banking powers of Banco do Brasil.

Brazil's economic stability and growth potential had stimulated in the 1910's the entry of foreign banks (e.g. Banco Francês e Italiano para a América do Sul, later Sudameris, 1910; First National City Bank, later Citibank, 1915; Banco Holandês Unido, later ABN, 1917). Restored tranquility to the banking system as a result of the establishment of the Carteira de Emissão e Redesconto had given rise to new private sector Brazilian banks (e.g. Banco Moreira Salles, later Unibanco, 1924 and Banco da Lavoura de Minas Gerais, later Banco Real, 1925). But, perhaps as a result of the monetary tightening of the late 1920's, provinces around the country

10. GDP growth was 5.9 percent in 1919 and 10.1 percent in 1920 (Neuhaus, 1975: 58).

11. The U.S. Federal Reserve System (FED) had been established in 1913.

12. This would be a short lived attempt. Decree-Law 19423 (November 22, 1930) would determine the end of the gold standard and Decree-Law 19525 (December 24, 1930) would re-establish the Carteira de Redesconto do Banco do Brasil (Neuhaus, 1975: 105).

13. The monetary base (defined as the stock of paper money issued) expanded from 1,748 thousand contos in 1920 to 2,649 thousand contos in 1923; and remained stable at around 2,600 thousand contos through mid-1927 (Neuhaus, 1975: 158).

felt that insufficient support was available from the Banco do Brasil and the private sector for financing agricultural and manufacturing initiatives in their regions. So, government controlled state banks (e.g.: Piauí, 1926; São Paulo, 1927; Paraná and Rio Grande do Sul, 1928) (Baer and Nazmi, 2000: 5) were formed. This may have been well intended, but the clean-up of state banks was quite costly to society at large seven decades later.

From Great Depression to "Fifty Years in Five," 1930–1961

The 1930's were particularly tumultuous, both politically and economically in Brazil. On the political front, President Washington Luís decided to break an alliance between São Paulo and Minas Gerais for rotation in power. He backed Julio Prestes, governor of São Paulo for President. Antônio Carlos Ribeiro de Andrada, the governor of Minas Gerais, reacted by throwing his support behind Getúlio Vargas, the governor of Rio Grande do Sul, for the presidency, and João Pessoa, the governor of Paraíba, for the vice-presidency. Júlio Prestes defeated Getúlio Vargas in the March elections. But, in July, still prior to his taking office, João Pessoa was assassinated in his home state of Paraíba. This added fuel to flames of country-wide dissatisfaction with what was perceived as excessive dominance by São Paulo on all relevant national affairs. In early October, Julio Prestes was arrested by the country's military command and told to resign, and the presidency was handed to Getúlio Vargas.

President Vargas dissolved Congress and replaced state governors with individuals of his personal choice. This generated further political dissent. A bloody revolt erupted in July 1932 in São Paulo, the richest state and by far the largest contributor to the federal coffers. The paulistas' revolution lasted three months and ended with their defeat, but with Vargas' commitment to call for congressional elections in 1933 and enact a new constitution in 1934 (Calógeras, 1939: 340). The political situation would, however, deteriorate further. Following a communist leaning mobilization in 1935, Vargas shut down Congress and suspended individual rights protected under the 1934 Constitution, making it clear that his regime, which lasted until 1945, was a dictatorship.

On the economic front, as previously indicated, Brazil had entered the 1930's highly dependent on coffee exports. With the advent of the Great Depression, coffee prices dropped from 22 cents per pound in 1929 to 9 cents in 1931. Every aspect of the Brazilian economic life was affected. Private sector banks, "known for a tradition of prudent lending" (Neuhaus, 1975: 115), adjusted their deposit taking and lending activities to the extremely volatile environment surrounding them. As a result, Banco do Brasil reinforced its central role in the provision of credit in domestic currency.

The economic odds for Brazil began to turn as the world gradually stepped out of depression and would substantially improve with the advent of World War II. Devaluation of the Brazilian mil réis (from 44.4 mil réis per British pound in 1930 to 65.7 in 1931) (Ribeiro and Guimarães, 1967: 149) and import taxes (imposed by the government to diminish the outflow of foreign exchange) had already triggered an initial process of imports substitution[14] and industrialization. Brazil's cotton production, for example, had increased six fold from 1932 to 1939 with a growing share being absorbed by a rapidly expanding domestic textile industry. World War II would make textiles Brazil's main export earner (Smith, 2002: 171-173). Coffee prices also rebounded back to 20 cents per pound, further reinforcing export surpluses. Brazil had regained the ability to invest and put it to use: installed production capacity of energy, cement, and steel more than doubled between 1938 and 1945.

This new wave of economic growth stimulated the demand for banking services. Private sector banks formed during this period include Banco Mercantil de Minas Gerais (1941), Banco Bradesco (1943), Banco Nacional (1944), and Banco Itaú (1945). The movement initiated in the late 1920's by a handful of provincial governments of establishing their own banks also gained force. By year-end 1945, the country's banking network had expanded from 860 to 2,035 branches, the number of processed checks had increased from 1.9 million to 4.8 million, the monetary base had grown from 4.8 million to 20.5 million cruzeiros;[15] and every state of the federation owned a commercial bank.

This expansion posed enormous challenges of systemic coordination and risk. In the words of José Whitaker (Ribeiro and Guimarães, 1967: 166) (former Vargas' Minister of Finance) in 1944: "We live, in reality, in the illogical situation of having banks but not a banking system; we live in a regime of sudden and frequent alarms, without tranquility, without confidence, with insufficient credit not so much because of lack of money but

14. Imports substitution: development policy characterized by the imposition of trade barriers to increase the competitiveness of local firms for faster domestic industrialization. For a detailed discussion see Södersten (1970: 375-80).

15. The Cruzeiro "(1 CR$= 1,000 réis) became the Brazilian monetary standard in October 1942.

because of its slow and defective circulation." An old debate[16] about the creation of an independent central bank was revived.

Contemporary to this domestic debate was Brazil's participation in the United Nations International Monetary Conference in Bretton Woods in 1944—which resulted in the adoption of a new international fixed exchange rates regime and the establishment of the IMF. It served as lender of last resort to sovereign nations to help ease temporary balance of payments disturbances, and of the World Bank, to assist governments with the financing of investments in reconstruction and development.

In this historical context, Brazil's Superintendência de Moeda e Crédito (SUMOC) was created (Decree-Law 7293 of February 2, 1945)[17] with the objectives of coordination of monetary policy and preparation of the basis for the establishment of an independent central bank. SUMOC's managing board was chaired by the Minister of Finance and had as directors the President of Banco do Brasil and its directors for Foreign Exchange and International Trade, and SUMOC's Executive Director.

In 1946, under democratically elected President Eurico Dutra (1946-1950), a proposal for a major banking reform was put forward by Minister of Finance Corrêa e Castro. It called for the creation of a 100 percent government owned Central Bank (under the direct supervision of an independent Monetary Council) to act as the sole issuer of paper money and the controller of foreign exchange flows in and out of the country. The new Central Bank would have to maintain gold (or hard currency) reserves of at least 25 percent of the total value of notes in circulation. The Banco do Brasil would become purely a commercial bank and five new specialized banks of joint public-private ownership—Rural, Mortgage, Export-Import, Industry, and Investment—would be formed to provide and stimulate the availability of credit to key areas of economic activity. Corrêa e Castro's proposal was not implemented but many traces would later be found in the major banking reform finally carried out twenty years later.

An initial post-war movement in the direction of free trade and economic liberalism was reversed in 1947, as massive imports of consumer goods caused

16. In the context of the successful negotiation of Brazil's foreign debt in the early 1930's he conducted, Minister of Finance José Whitaker himself had presented to Sir Otto Niemeyer, Director of the Bank of England, a program calling for a balanced fiscal budget and the creation of an autonomous central bank (Ribeiro and Guimarães, 1967: 151).

17. SUMOC's main functions were to decide upon the need of paper money emissions and request Treasury authorization to execute them, be the depositary bank for the reserve requirements of commercial banks, monitor interest rates, act as the primary dealer in government securities, monitor the exposure to other banks of Banco do Brasil's Carteira de Redesconto, and bank supervision (Neuhaus, 1975: 141).

rapid depletion of foreign exchange reserves accumulated during the war. By the end of Dutra's term in office, Brazil enjoyed a significant trade surplus (US$425 million, up from US$130 million in 1947) and had averaged real GDP growth close to 8 percent per annum for the previous 4 years.[18]

When Getúlio Vargas took office as president in 1951—this time through direct elections—the benign external economic environment of the previous years had begun to sour. Lower export revenues from coffee (due to new entrants to this market) added to stockpiling of basic materials (to protect the Brazilian industry from potential shortages as a result of the Korean War), causing a major reversal in the balance of trade (from a US$425 million surplus in 1950 to a US$277 million deficit in 1952).

On the political front, a climate of unrest brewing since the elections deteriorated rapidly in 1954 as a consequence of an attempt against the life of a journalist by Vargas' chief of security. Under the demand of senior military commanders to resign, "Vargas shot himself in the heart on August 24 (1954)"(Smith, 2002: 160). With Vargas' death his vice-president, Café Filho, took office and conducted the country without major policy changes until the orderly elections of 1955, won by Juscelino Kubitschek, then governor of Minas Gerais.

Still, Brazil's industrialization had marched on. In the three years from 1951 to 1954, electric power generation capacity had increased by 47 percent (from 1.9 to 2.8 million kilowatts); steel production, by 43 percent (from 840 thousand to 1.2 million tons); and cement production, by 66 percent (from 1.5 to 2.5 million tons) (Ribeiro and Guimarães, 1967: 157). GDP growth had still averaged over 6 percent per annum; but the monetary base had more than doubled (from 31.2 billion cruzeiros in 1950 to 65 billion cruzeiros in 1954)(Ribeiro and Guimarães, 1967: 158), bringing the annual inflation rate to approximately 30 percent in 1954.

The most important banking event of this period was the foundation in 1952 of the 100 percent government-owned Banco Nacional do Desenvolvimento Econômico (BNDE).[19] Embodying, in essence, the missions outlined for two of Corrêa e Castro's proposed banks in 1944 (the Industry Bank and the Investment Bank), BNDE was formed to provide, and to stimulate the availability—in cooperation with the private sector—of long term credit for investment in industrialization and infrastructure. For pri-

18. Instituto de Pesquisa Econômica e Aplicada (IPEA), www.ipeadata.gov.br.

19. BNDE, the Brazilian government owned development bank, was renamed BNDES (Banco Nacional do Desenvolvimento Econômico e Social) in 1982.

vate sector banks, this was a time for consolidation and gains in efficiency: the total number of banks dropped from 444 in 1946 to 357 in 1957 and the total number of branches increased from 1,783 in 1946 to 4,628 in 1957 (Bouzan, 1975 and Toledo, 1994: 137).

President Kubitschek (1956-1960) sought to deliver on his campaign promise of "fifty years in five." Import substitution policies were further reinforced and greater emphasis placed on central economic planning to stimulate domestic and foreign investment. There was rapid development of the automobile industry (130,000 vehicles produced in 1960, up from 30,000 in 1957) and other core industries such as shipyards, chemical, capital goods, and agricultural equipment. There was also massive public sector investment in transportation (primarily highways), hydroelectric plants and, last but not least, the construction and inauguration of the country's new capital, Brasília. As Kubitschek left office, Brazil was a fast growing (7 percent on average during his term) and significantly more industrialized country; but it was also one facing increasing balance of payments challenges and escalating inflation.[20]

Extreme political instability was to follow Kubitschek's relatively calm period in office. His immediate successor, Jânio Quadros, introduced austerity measures and managed to temporarily mitigate balance of payments pressures. He negotiated an important loan with his successor President João Goulart (1962-1964) and took an expansionist path under deteriorating financial conditions. Paper money emissions escalated (M1 up from 206 billion cruzeiros in 1956 to 890 billion in 1963 (Ribeiro and Guimarães, 1967: 162), and annual inflation reached almost 100 percent (annualized) during the first quarter of 1964. A growing sense of economic disorder created the political conditions for the March 31, 1964 military coup, and marked the beginning of two decades of authoritarian rule in Brazil.

For the banking sector, the 1956-1964 period was, again, a time for further consolidation (328 banks in 1964, down from 351 in 1957) and expansion of branch networks (6,424 branches in 1964, up from 4,628 in 1957). The economic optimism of the Kubitschek years had been tempered by the financial reality of monetary uncertainty. Higher inflation made it also harder for banks to perform their function of transforming short-term savings into medium-term loans at acceptable risks.[21]

---

20. Trade balance reversal, from US$194 million surplus in 1956 to US$430 million deficit in 1960; inflation approaching 40 percent for 1960, as a result of expansion of the monetary base from 80 billion cruzeiros in 1956 to 206 billion cruzeiros in 1960 (Ribeiro and Guimarães, 1967: 161).

From Economic Miracle to Monetary Chaos, 1964–1993

The military junta (formed by the heads of the Army, Navy, and Air Force) was quick to instruct Congress to choose a new president and vice-president. On April 11, 1964, General Castelo Branco was elected by a large majority and took over the government under the motto "economic development and national security." While political liberties were severely restricted, a highly qualified team (under the leadership of Octávio Bulhões, Minister of Finance, and Roberto Campos, Minister of Planning) undertook the mission of reshaping public policies to attack Brazil's chronic inflation and balance of payments problems. It was in this context that perhaps the most important set of economic reforms in Brazilian history, with major consequences for the workings and organization to-date of the financial system, was put in place.

First, the concept of monetary correction was born. Law 4357 (July, 1964) imposed adjustment for inflation on overdue taxes and introduced the first inflation indexed financial asset, the ORTN (monthly adjusted treasury bill); and Law 4380 (which also created the Banco Nacional da Habitação, BNH) authorized financial institutions to monetarily correct both installments on mortgage financing and interest paid on savings deposits.[22]

Second, an autonomous central bank—operating under the supervision of a Monetary Council chaired by the Minister of Finance and formed by the Minister of Planning, the Minister of Industry and Commerce, the President of the Central Bank,[23] the President of Banco do Brasil, the President of BNDE, three Central Bank directors and two representatives of the private sector appointed by the President of the Republic—was finally created. Law 4595 (Lei da Reforma Bancária, December 1964), created the Banco Central do Brasil (through conversion of SUMOC), for managing the money supply, for controlling foreign exchange flows into and out of the country, and for supervising banks.[24]

21. The spread (the margin added to the cost of funds a bank charges a borrower) incorporates a charge for credit risk (the risk of default by the borrower) and a charge for market risk (the risk of loss resulting from an interest rate and/or a currency mismatch); the higher and more volatile the inflation rate, the higher (to the limit of becoming prohibitive) the charge for market (or mismatch) risk.

22. These measures restored banks' ability to manage interest rate risk, therefore increasing their willingness to lend.

23. The President and the directors of the Central Bank are appointed by the President of the Republic and have to be confirmed by Congress; but differently from the US, their terms do not cross presidential electoral terms.

Third, a major push towards the rapid development of the domestic securities market was undertaken. Law 4728 (July, 1965) imposed new rules for securities underwriting and trading; it introduced a wide range of new tradable instruments, and established that dedicated companies, also subject to Central Bank supervision, should be formed to pursue specific financial services activities (e.g. investment banking, asset management, consumer finance, mortgage lending).[25]

Fourth, a 100 percent government owned federal housing bank (Banco Nacional da Habitação—BNH, Law 4380, 1964) was created and new guidelines for mortgage lending (including a minimum required allocation by banks of savings deposits to mortgage loans) were imposed.

And last but not least, the compulsory savings mechanisms of FGTS (Fundo de Garantia de Tempo de Serviço, Law 5107, 1966) and PIS (Programa de Integração Social, Lei Complementar 07/70) were created.[26] FGTS and PIS are funds constituted by contributions made by employers on behalf of workers managed by the government. The below market remuneration (monetary correction plus a small spread) would make them the key sources of long term funding in domestic currency for investment in Brazil, a situation which persists to our days.

These measures fell under the umbrella of PAEG (the program for government action, 1964-1968) which also included more effective tax collection, reduction of government expenses, restrictions to the automatic transmission passing of inflation to labor costs (there was an estimated purchasing power loss of 30 percent for the minimum wage between 1964 and 1967), export incentives, and the introduction of the mini-devaluations system to continue the competitiveness of Brazilian exports, by making the exchange rate more realistic.

---

24. Decree-Law 4635 of January 8, 1923 (under President Artur Bernardes) gave Banco do Brasil the monopoly right to issue paper money, as it abolished the ceiling on emissions which had been set for the Carteira de Emissão e Redesconto in 1920 (200,000 contos). Decree-Law 5108 of December 18, 1926 (under President Washington Luís) determined a return to the gold standard suspending, for all practical purposes, the central bank authority of Banco do Brasil.

25. Differently from the US market (then under the restrictions of the 1933 Glass-Steagall Act), these specialized companies could be part of a financial group that also controlled a commercial bank.

26. The FGTS fund is constituted by monthly deposits made by all employers in the amount of 8 percent of every worker's salary in an account kept for this employee at Caixa Econômica Federal. PIS is similarly constituted but as a percentage of gross revenues, with deposits being made at Caixa Econômica Federal for private sector workers, at Banco do Brasil for public sector workers. Caixa Econômica Federal and Banco do Brasil act as fiduciary agents for the funds. Withdrawals by workers of their FGTS savings are restricted to certain specific events (purchase of a home in value not to exceed R$300,000, dismissal without just cause, and upon retirement). PIS benefits can only be paid in situations of temporary unemployment, major disease, and old age. For further details on origin and uses of FGTS and PIS-PASEP/FAT refer to the IPEA website, www.IPEA.gov.br.

The seeds had been planted for the Brazilian economic miracle. Inflation went down from 100 percent in 1964 to 25 percent in 1967 and to 12 percent in 1970. GDP growth averaged 11 percent per annum between 1968 and 1973.

For the financial sector, greater monetary stability and economic growth stimulated expansion and structural changes. Bank loans grew over 20 percent per annum in real terms between 1965 and 1974, and private sector banks more than doubled their share of total loans, from 17 percent 1963 to 46 percent in 1974.[27] Government incentives to industry consolidation combined with market driven pursuit of scale economies to increase private sector mergers and acquisitions.[28] Also, the Brazilian domestic securities market received a major boost. Larger financial groups established their investment banking arms (in some cases in partnership with foreign interests).[29] Independent broker-dealers were formed.[30] And the legal framework for capital markets activities was refined further through enactment of Lei das Sociedades Anônimas (1972) and establishment of the Comissão de Valores Mobiliários (CVM, the Brazilian equivalent to the SEC).

Unfortunately, however, Brazil's economic miracle had become too dependent on oil imports and foreign borrowings. In November 1973, OPEC imposed its first oil embargo. Oil prices more than tripled (from US$3 to US$10/barrel), Brazil's import bill doubled (from US$6.2 billion in 1973 to US$12.6 billion in 1974), and the current account deficit quadrupled (from US$1.7 billion to US$7.1 billion[31]). Relatively cheap external funding available from the Eurodollar market[32] would still permit the newly empowered Ernesto Geisel government (1974-1978) to postpone a major fiscal adjustment. PND II (Plano Nacional de Desenvolvimento II, an ambitious government sponsored investment program in infrastructure—primarily transportation and basic industries—to last the entire presidential term) launched in December 1974, was maintained through the end of President Geisel's term, as well as the trend of gains in real wages were maintained. By year-end 1978, GDP growth had dropped by more than half but still stood at 4.8 percent for the year. Inflation, however, was back

27. Source: Banco Central do Brasil.
28. The number of banks dropped from 152 in 1970 to 80 in 1978 while the total number of branches increased from 5,576 in 1970 to 6,583 in 1978 (Baer and Nazmi, 2000: 7).
29. e.g. Banco de Investimentos do Brasil (BIB), 1966.
30. e.g. Corretora Garantia, 1971.
31. Baer, 2008, chapter 6.
32. Petrodollars accumulated by oil exporters with leading international money center banks.

to 40 percent (up from 16 percent in 1974) and foreign indebtedness had more than tripled to reach US$43 billion.

General Figueiredo (empowered in March 1979 to be the last military president and prepare the country's transition back to democracy) was almost immediately confronted with the dramatic consequences for Brazil of the Iran-Iraq war. Oil prices went from US$12/barrel in 1979 to US$36/barrel in 1981 and the US FED raised its federal funds target rate[33] from 7 percent to 13 percent in 1979—and, subsequently, in additional increments to almost 20 percent in 1982 (with immediate pass through to the LIBOR[34] market).

Brazil's path to growth and development had suffered a most severe double hit: a (second) tripling of the price of its major and critical import plus the doubling of the interest cost on its fast growing foreign indebtedness. By early 1981 it was clear that strong medicine was required. Monetary tightening, reduction in government expenditures, and acceleration of the minidevaluations mechanism followed. The economy contracted 6 percent between 1980 and 1983, to grow back 5.5 percent in 1984 and 8 percent in 1985. But, by then, inflation was over 200 percent per annum and high frequency indexation had spread throughout the economy. Five economic stabilization plans (Cruzado, Bresser, Verão, Collor I, and Collor II) would be put forward between 1986 and 1991 and fail. Brazil would be eventually forced to impose a moratorium on its non-trade related foreign debt service (1987), to only reestablish normal relations with the international banking community in the early 1990s upon implementation of Plano Brady.[35]

It should be no surprise that this fifteen year period (1978-1993) of high uncertainty would cause private sector banks to make fewer high risk loans. Still, private sector banks managed to remain profitable and continue to develop their asset-liability management, credit, and client servicing skills by limiting themselves to very short-term (and often collateralized) lending in domestic currency; foreign currency match-funded international trade

33. The federal funds rate is the rate of interest at which depository institutions lend money to one another overnight. By trading government securities, the FED can affect the federal funds rate. The Federal Open Market Committee establishes the target for trading in the federal funds market.

34. The London Interbank Offered Rate (LIBOR) is a daily reference rate based on the interest rates at which banks lend to one another in the London wholesale for certain tenors. The most common base interest rate for international sovereign borrowings is the LIBOR for 6 months.

35. Brady Plan stands for the framework for restructuring of the sovereign debt of most Latin American countries in the aftermath of the late 1980s. Named after the US Treasury Secretary Nicholas Brady, it offered banks a menu of choices to swap their exposures with some debt reduction (either through a discount on face value for LIBOR based bonds or through fixed below market rate bonds without a discount on face value). Specific Brady plans were reached by Mexico and Costa Rica (1989), Venezuela (1990), Uruguay (1991), and Argentina and Brazil (1992). For further details see Vásquez (1996).

finance activities; match-funded floating rate medium term lending to industry; and growing exploitation of inflation revenues (spread between the daily yield on Treasury bills and the cost of third party funds parked in the bank) through expansion of their branch networks.

From an organizational standpoint, private sector banks were quick to capitalize on the benefits of pooling of capital and managerial synergies arising from Central Bank Resolution 1254, enacted in 1988. Resolution 1254 authorized financial groups to consolidate into a single balance sheet (the multiple bank)[36] their different specialized financial companies (commercial banks, broker-dealers, investment banks, asset managers, consumer finance companies, Savings and Loans). Between 1988 and 1993 (Studart, 2000: 30), 206 multiple banks were formed and the number of single-purpose financial institutions reduced dramatically (commercial banks, 106 to 36; investment banks, 56 to 17; finance companies, 107 to 40). Universal banking—later to become the dominant form of organization for most of the large publicly traded financial institutions globally—had arrived in Brazil.

BANKING IN BRAZIL POST *PLANO REAL*

Fast Start and Sudden Stop

Brazilian society's exhaustion with life under hyperinflation (approaching 1,000 percent in 1993) brought about the political conditions for the *Plano Real* (Baer, 2008, chapter 7), proposed to Congress by Finance Minister Fernando Henrique Cardoso in December 1993. Differently from previous stabilization attempts, the *Plano Real* did not carry any element of surprise or impose any sort of price controls. A full indexation system was put in place to remain until a certain moment in the future, to be known by all in advance, when society's confidence on the fiscal adjustment being made would allow the introduction of the new currency, the Real. This general sense of credibility was built through a major initial fiscal adjustment[37] and a commitment by the executive branch to work with Congress to pursue

36. There is, actually, a great similarity between the scope of Brazil's Lei do Banco Múltiplo (Resolution 1254) and the US Bank Holding Act (1999) which revoked the forced separation between commercial banking and any type of securities underwriting activities that had been imposed by the 1933 Glass-Steagall Act.

37. A 5 percent tax increase across the board plus the establishment of the Social Emergency Fund comprising 15 percent of all tax revenues for discretionary use by the Federal Government.

constitutional amendments to reduce the amount of fiscal transfers from the Federal to state governments.

The new indexing system created a shadow currency (the Unit of Real Value, URV) tied to the US dollar on a one-to-one basis, therefore adjusting daily to a higher equivalent in the circulating currency, the Cruzeiro Real (Cr$). From paychecks to products on the shelves of retailers, every transaction was denominated in both, the official currency (Cruzeiro Real) and the shadow currency (the URV). Full indexation lasted for five months. On July 1, 1994, the Real (BRL) was finally introduced (equal to 1 URV and CR$2,750). A quite restrictive monetary policy (high real interest rates and 100 percent compulsory reserve requirement on new demand deposits) was put in place to curb excessive expansion of aggregate demand and minimize the chances of an early return of inflationary pressures.

The initial achievements of *Plano Real* were highly impressive. The monthly inflation rate fell from 46.6 percent in June to 2.5 percent in October, and 0.6 percent in December (Baer, 2008: 132); aggregate consumption increased over 20 percent in real terms between July and December; and GDP growth reached 5.9 percent for the full year. Fueling the rapid growth in consumption was the substantial increase in the purchasing power of the population as a result of the sharp drop in inflation as well as the willingness of banks to expand credit. Eager to compensate for the loss of float revenues,[38] banks—some more aggressively than others—increased lending. Bank loans grew by over 25 percent between June and December, leading to a total bank debt to GDP ratio of 36.6 percent in December 1994, up from 28.9 percent in December 1993.

Unfortunately, trouble brewed elsewhere in Latin America. A delicate political transition in Mexico was further complicated by the assassination of a presidential candidate, triggering massive capital flight. Between October and December, Mexico's foreign exchange reserves fell 75 percent (from US$17.6 billion to US$4.4 billion) and the Mexican peso devalued by 50 percent (from 3.4 to 5 Mexican pesos/US dollar). The crisis would be eventually resolved with financial assistance from the US Treasury and the IMF, but it would also cause the Mexican banking industry, highly exposed to the Mexican peso to US dollar currency mismatch, to come close to collapse. This time around no banking industry wide nationalization would take place in Mexico, as it had happened in the early 1980s. But the Mexican

38. Estimated at 35 percent to 40 percent of total revenues for most banks (Baer and Nazmi, 2000: 8).

banking sector would eventually re-emerge largely dominated by foreign banks (Tschoegl, 2006).

Serious threats were posed to balance of payments equilibrium and exchange rate stability throughout Latin America where countries had just begun to reengage with the international financial community after the implementation of their Brady plans. Seeking to avoid a major devaluation of the BRL[39]—which could result in significant inflationary pressures—the Brazilian Central Bank reacted swiftly. The Central Bank's target base rate, the SELIC,[40] was raised sharply (from 50 percent in January to 70 percent in March) and new reserve requirements and lending restrictions (e.g. strict limitations on credit card borrowings) imposed. This abrupt pulling on the monetary breaks after such a fast start of lending had to cause damage to banks' balance sheets. Past due loans for the system increased from under 6 percent of total loans in mid-1994 to over 17 percent by mid-1995.[41] The survival of a number of private sector banks and of most public sector banks was under question. By November 1995 it was clear that a major government intervention was necessary to rescue the financial system.

Government Assisted Consolidation, 1995–1998

By year end 1995 three government programs had been put in place to support the reorganization and recapitalization of the financial sector: the Programa de Estímulo à Reestruturação e ao Fortalecimento do Sistema Financeiro Nacional (PROER), to facilitate the transfer of the banking operations of endangered financial institutions to healthier private sector banks; the Programa de Incentivo à Redução do Estado na_Atividade Bancária (PROES), for the restructuring and subsequent privatization of state banks; and the Programa de Fortalecimento dos Bancos Federais, to recapitalize federal banks. In addition, foreign banks were permitted to acquire Brazilian banks.

39. BRL is the International Organization for Standardization code for Brazil's currency, the Real.

40. The SELIC (Sistema Especial de Liquidação e Custódia) rate is Banco Central do Brasil's equivalent to the FED's federal funds rates.

41. Central Bank statistics on past due loans excluded FCVS (Fundo de Cobertura de Variação Salarial) exposure, a substantial portfolio of federal government obligations held by banks resulting from the difference accumulated since the mid 1980s between the monetary correction on mortgage contracts under SFH (the National Housing System) and the nominal increase in minimum wages. By mid-1995 some banks had 100 percent provisions against their FCVS exposure; but others carried it at face value. As it turned out, FCVS obligations ended up being swapped for Treasury bonds at a present value for banks' FCVS obligations at an estimated at 1/3 of their face value. For a complete discussion see Barbosa (2008).

The largest transactions under PROER were the absorptions of the banking operations of Banco Nacional by Unibanco,[42] Banco Bamerindus by HSBC (UK), and Banco Econômico by Banco Excel (shortly thereafter acquired by BBVA, Spain).[43] The largest privatizations under PROES were of BANERJ (Rio de Janeiro), BEMGE (Minas Gerais) and BANESTADO (Paraná), acquired by Banco Itaú; and of BANESPA (São Paulo), acquired by Banco Santander (Spain). The most important transaction under PROEF was the R$8 billion recapitalization of Banco do Brasil in 1996. It is estimated that the combined fiscal cost of the three financial rescue programs reached approximately 9 percent of GDP (0.9 percent for PROER, 2.1 percent for PROES, 5.7 percent for PROEF) (Goldfajn, 2003: 16).

Specific measures to help prevent future systemic banking crises included the creation of the FGC (Fundo Garantidor de Crédito)[44] in 1995 and the enactment between 1997 and 1999 of a series of Central Bank resolutions imposing strict and closely monitored credit rating and provisioning rules for loans as well as capital charges for currency and interest rate mismatches. In addition, the minimum capital adequacy ratio for banks operating in Brazil was set by the Central Bank at 11 percent, significantly above Basel's minimum of 8 percent.[45]

The extraordinary expansion in bank credit after the introduction of the Real on July 1, 1994 had caused total bank debt-to-GDP to increase from

---

42. The first good bank/bad bank transaction under PROER was the absorption, in November 1995, of Banco Nacional, the fourth largest private sector Brazilian bank, by Unibanco, the fifth largest. Bad loans absorbed by the government exceeded R$5 billion; in exchange for the good bank being transferred to Unibanco, the government was able to retain a 1/3 equity stake in the new Unibanco (now the third largest private sector bank). This equity stake was sold in May 1997, in the first major global public offering by a Brazilian bank, for US$1.2 billion.

43. Bamerindus, Nacional, and Econômico were the sixth, seventh, and thirteenth largest commercial banks in Brazil on June 30, 1994. Their total assets in BRL equivalent (1BRL = Cr$2,750) were R$12.0 billion, R$9.8 billion, and R$5.0 billion respectively. Source: Banco Central do Brasil, Informações Contábeis, Ranking dos Bancos, www.bcb.gov.br.

44. FGC, formed on August 31, 1995, is funded by contributions from all banks; it currently guarantees individual deposits up to R$60,000.

45. Per the Basel I accord of 1988, the Bank of International Settlements (BIS) declared that banks had to maintain a minimum capital ratio of 8 percent of maximum expected losses (weighted risk assets, WRA), where WRA was defined as the sum of each of a bank's loans multiplied by a weight which differentiated between sovereign risks (OECD versus non-OECD country) (Apostolik et.al., 2009). Per the 1996 Market Amendment to the Capital Accord to Incorporate Market Risks, the minimum capital ratio became 8 percent of maximum expected losses not only for credit risk (as per Basel I) but also market risk (Apostolik et.al., 2009); per Basel II in 2004, the minimum capital ratio became 8 percent of maximum expected losses from credit risk (now with WRA methodology making use of either external or internal ratings for credit exposure), market risk, and operating risk (BIS, 2004). As of 1997, Banco Central do Brasil not only imposed a higher minimum capital ratio than per Basel accord (11 vs. 8 percent) but also more specific and stringent requirements, and capital charges for credit risk and market risk. For further details on the Basel accords see BIS (2004).

29 percent in year-end 1993 to 36.6 percent in 1994; the sudden stop, as a result of the Mexican crisis, brought this ratio back to 28 percent in December 1998. But PROER, PROES, PROEF had not only reinvigorated the Brazilian financial system but also contributed to fundamental changes in the structure of the industry.

In July 1998 ABN-Amro (Holland) announced the conclusion of negotiations for the acquisition of Banco Real. This was a purely market driven (non-PROER) transaction in which ABN-Amro managed to outbid the competition to acquire the country's fourth largest private sector banking franchise, an early sign of a new stage of consolidation to come.

The number of public sector banks among the top 21 had dropped from 9 in 1995 to 6 in 1998; the number of foreign banks had increased from 3 to 7 (2 among the top 10);[46] private sector banks had expanded much faster than public sector banks; but, by year-end 1998, the two largest public sector banks (Banco do Brasil and CEF) still had over twice the total assets of the largest private sector bank (Bradesco).

Market Driven Consolidation, 1999–2007

Brazil's *Plano Real* was once again threatened, this time by the eruption of the Russian economic crisis in the second half of 1998 following the 1997 financial market upheaval in Asia. Capital flight caused Brazil's foreign exchange reserves to drop abruptly, from US$75 billion in August to US$35 billion in January. An emergency line of credit was put in place in November with IMF and US Treasury support (US$41.5 billion in total). But open political dissent regarding the scope of the fiscal adjustment necessary to maintain the recently acquired relative monetary stability continued to feed uncertainty. In January 1999 the BRL was finally allowed to float, devaluing over 70 percent in a few weeks. The inflation rate shot up from close to zero during the last quarter of 1998 to 4.5 percent per month in February.

From then on Brazil's macroeconomic policy took a major shift: from dependence for monetary stability on an exchange rate anchor (defended via very high real interest rates) and only secondary attention to fiscal discipline, to adherence to pre-established targets for the inflation rate and the primary fiscal surplus, and a floating exchange rate regime.

46. ABN-Amro (#14) was soon to join the also foreign Santander (#6) and HSBC (#10) among the top 10 as a result of its acquisition of Real (#8).

Tight monetary policy (SELIC in excess of 1.5 percent per month in real terms) combined with fiscal austerity measures kept inflation in check (11.3 percent for the year 1999) and the exchange rate relatively stable (R$1.7 per U.S. dollar in March to R$1.85 per U.S. dollar in December[47]). Tax increases (Goldfajn, 2003: 16) plus cuts in government expenditures produced a 3.9 percent primary fiscal surplus[48] in 1999 (well above the 3.1 percent target promised to the IMF in 1998). In addition, to enhance fiscal sustainability going forward, three important sets of initiatives were put in place: restructuring of the debt of each individual state with the federal government; enactment of the Fiscal Responsibility Law, comprising a legally binding framework for budgeting, execution, and reporting for all levels of government (federal, state, and local); and setting of the stage for discussion of the so-called structural reforms (labor, fiscal, and social security).

The first two sets of initiatives were implemented during President Cardoso's second term in office (1998-2002). Regarding the third set, some modest progress has been made on social security by President Lula's administration; fiscal and labor reforms remain a work-in-progress.

Brazil's GDP would remain flat for 1998 and 1999, and grow 4.5 percent in 2000. But a severe drought, with resulting major disruption to energy generation and distribution, caused the economy to slow to 1.3 percent growth in 2001. First quarter 2002 annualized projections were for GDP growth to again reach the 4 percent to 5 percent range. But, this time, an entirely domestic event—coming of the elections for President and the consequent uncertainty regarding future economic policy and the treatment of holders of Brazilian domestic and foreign debt by an increasingly likely to win opposition—caused a new and major reversal of capital flows. This time even short-term trade finance lines (on which Brazil had never defaulted) from international banks to their Brazilian correspondents (including the leading Brazilian banks) were cut, causing the BRL to devalue 70 percent (from R$2.3/US dollar in March to R$3.9/US dollar in September). Consistent with its inflation targeting policy, the Central Bank was forced to sharply raise the SELIC rate. The yield on the one-year fixed rate Treasury note jumped from 19 percent in March to 29 percent in July and 34 percent in November, to finally come back to below 20 percent only eighteen months later (September, 2003), after the dissipation of market fears. As a result, GDP growth slowed

47. IPEA, Taxa de Câmbio Comercial, www.ipea.data.gov.br.
48. Primary fiscal surplus equals total federal government revenues minus total federal government expenses excluding the interest cost of the federal government's debt.

(2.6 percent in 2002, 1.1 percent in 2003)[49] and credit expansion remained subdued (9.2 percent in 2002, 5.6 percent in 2003).[50]

The extraordinary exchange rate and interest rate movements brought about by such a succession of financial crises (Asia, Russia, and Brazil[51]) could have caused a serious weakening of the Brazilian financial sector. But, actually, the opposite occurred. Private sector banks did retract from expanding credit (private sector bank debt- to-GDP dropped from 15.4 percent 1998 to 14.8 percent in 2003[52]) but, well capitalized; confident on a just tested (under PROER and PROES) capacity to implement acquisitions; and motivated to pursue further gains of scale and/or scope (Davis, 2000, chapter 3), they went shopping, acquiring smaller commercial banking franchises[53] and the larger independent consumer finance companies in the market.[54]

By early 2004 private sector Brazilian banks had already begun to see the benefits of their strategic repositioning over the previous ten years reflected in their market values. The yield on the one-year Treasury note would still go up from 15.5 percent in January 2004 to 19.5 percent in April 2005 (due to another round of monetary tightening by the Central Bank in response to inflation fears), causing a slowdown of GDP growth from 5.7 percent in 2004 to 3.1 percent in 2005. But it would then drop continuously for the following 32 months, from 19.5 percent in April 2005 to under 12 percent in December 2007. Monetary stability had been re-conquered, bringing with it robust economic growth (average GDP growth of 4.7 percent per annum for 2004-2007) and substantial credit expansion (25 percent per annum growth in total loans for 2004-2007, compared to 7.5 percent per annum for 2001-2003).

Two pieces of legislation further contributed to the willingness and ability of banks to lend: specific payroll lending legislation, enacted in 2004, allowing a bank to deduct interest and principal on personal loans from the paychecks of individuals; and a new bankruptcy law, approved by Congress in February 2005, significantly strengthening creditor rights (Queiroz and Anselmo, 2005). Higher margins in consumer lending, combined with a

49. IPEA, PIB (preços 2009), www.ipea.data.gov.br.

50. Banco Central do Brasil, Sistema Financeiro Nacional, 50 Maiores Bancos e Consolidado do Sistema, Relatório de Ativos, www.bcb.gov.br.

51. Argentina's foreign debt default in late 2001 had not caused significant foreign exchange volatility for Brazil; but its disastrous consequences for investors and banks (domestic and foreign) certainly contributed to the market panic regarding the potential implications of the political transition in Brazil.

52. Banco Central do Brasil, Sistema Financeiro Nacional, Relatório de Ativos, www.bcb.gov.br.

53. e.g. Bandeirantes, by Unibanco; Noroeste by Santander; BBVA by Bradesco; Bank Boston, by Itaú.

54. e.g. Fininvest, by Unibanco; Finasa and Zogbi, by Bradesco; Losango, by HSBC.

gradual return of larger corporate borrowers to the capital markets, also led to a change in the structure of banks' balance sheets: loans to businesses dropped from over 65 percent of total in 2002 to under 50 percent in 2007. In addition, as shown in Table 12–1 below, private sector banks gained share on public sector banks.

TABLE 12-1. Loans by Private and Public Banks, 2003–2007

Year	Private Sector (% of GDP)	Public Sector (% of GDP)	Total (% of GDP)
2003	14.8	9.8	24.6
2004	15.8	9.9	25.7
2005	17.8	10.4	28.3
2006	19.6	11.3	30.9
2007	23.2	12.0	35.2

Source: Banco Central do Brasil, "Sistema Financeiro Nacional, Operações de Crédito do Sistema Financeiro."

In the capital markets arena, greater confidence in the direction of the country's economic policy had also helped revive expectations for fast growth of brokerage, underwriting, and asset management businesses. Some of the leading universal banks since 1998 had begun to revisit segmentation strategies and organizational structures to better compete with the investment banks in capital market activities. By 2002, most large private sector banks had formed strong wholesale banking divisions by combining renovated in-house corporate and investment banking platforms and by acquiring independent wholesale banks (e.g. Bozano Simonsen by Santander, Credibanco by Unibanco, BBA by Itaú). International banks also expanded their Brazil dedicated teams (at headquarters and in the field) and increased capital commitments to participate in the Brazilian primary and secondary securities markets; and some of them pursued acquisitions, the most visible having been the purchases of Garantia by Credit Suisse (1998) and of Pactual by UBS (2006).

The last and major event of this market driven period of consolidation was the acquisition in September 2007 in Europe of ABN-Amro by a consortium formed by Banco Santander, Royal Bank of Scotland, and Fortis Bank. Banco Santander's targets were ABN's Italian franchise (Banco Antonveneta, sold shortly thereafter to Banca Monte dei Paschi de Siena) and ABN-Real in Brazil (valued at US$17 billion) (Babington and Barrett, 2007). Consolidation between the banking operations of Santander-Banespa and ABN-Real in Brazil only took place the following year. But, for all practical purposes,

Santander ended 2007 ranked among the top three private sector banks in Brazil, with a scale comparable to those of Bradesco and Itaú.

Table 12-2 portrays the structural changes the Brazilian banking industry went through over this 1995-2007 period of fundamentally market driven consolidation. The Brazilian banking industry experienced large structural

TABLE 12-2. Industry Ranking, Top 10 plus BNDES, 1995, 1998, and 2007

December 30, 1995		December 30, 1998		December 30, 2007	
Bank	Total Assets in R$bn	Bank	Total Assets in R$bn	Bank	Total Assets in R$bn
1. CEF	80.0	1. Banco do Brazil	121.4	1. Banco do Brasil	316.4
2. Banco do Brasil	79.1	2. CEF	114.3	2. Itaú	267.0
3. BNDES	43.6	3. BNDES	76.7	3. Bradesco	254.9
4. BANESPA	37.0	4. Bradesco	57.5	4. Santander -ABN	253.5
5. Bradesco	25.1	5. Itaú	44.8	5. CEF	239.0
6. Unibanco	20.7	6. Santander	35.8	6. BNDES	198.7
7.Itaú	18.7	7. Unibanco	26.7	7. Unibanco	132.8
8. Bamerindus	14.3	8. ABN-Real	24.1	8. HSBC	69.4
9. Real	10.9	9. Banrisul	15.0	9. Safra	65.8
10. Nossa Caixa	8.7	10. HSBC	13.9	10. Votorantim	60.6
11. BANRISUL	7.6	11. Nossa Caixa	13.6	11. Citibank	54.7
Sub-total (Top 11)	345.7		543.8		1,912.8
Top 11 - BNDES	302.1		467.1		1,714.1
System Total	532.0		753.4		2,382.5
Total - BNDES	488.4		676.7		2,183.8
Public in Top 11	256.0		341.0		754.1
Priv. Br. in Top 11	89.7		129.0		781.1
Foreign in Top 11	0		76.8		377.6
Top 11/System Total	65%		72.2%		80.3%
Top 10/System Total (w/o BNDES)	61.8%		69%		78.4%
Public in Top 11	48.1%		45.3%		31.6%
Private in Top 11	16.9%		17.1%		32.7%
Foreign in Top 11	0%		9.8%		16.8%
Bank debt - GDP	32.1%		28%		34%

Source: Banco Central do Brasil, Sistema Financeiro Nacional, Informações Contábeis, 50 Maiores Bancos, www.bcb.gov.br.

change over this 1995–2007 period of fundamentally market driven consolidation. Private sector banks among the top 11 had expanded by 5 to 6 times (compared to 2 to 3 times for the public sector banks). Brazilian private sector banks had almost doubled their share of total assets (from 17.1 percent to 32.7 percent); foreign banks among the top 11 had also gained (from 9.8 percent to 16.8 percent); and public sector banks had lost, (45.3 to 31.6 percent). Industry concentration had firmly marched on: the top 10 banks' (BNDES excluded) percent share of total assets having reached 78.4 in 2007, up from 69 in 1998 and 62 in 1995.

Subprime Meltdown–Induced Consolidation, 2008–2009

The world entered 2008 projecting another year of strong economic growth. For Brazil, the global boom had translated into consistently higher volumes of exports (primarily commodities) at continuously higher prices, and robust trade surpluses (4 percent of GDP in 2007). Most analysts' projections for the year pointed to a relatively stable exchange rate (around R$1.8 per US dollar) and a declining SELIC rate (then, 11 percent). Brazil had accumulated enough foreign exchange reserves to become a net creditor in US dollars and finally enjoyed investment grade status for its sovereign risk. But net public sector debt remained too high (over 40 percent of GDP) for its cost (a real interest rate of 7 percent per annum). And big trouble had been brewing up North.

Lax US monetary policy (particularly between December 2001 and November 2004) had not only stimulated high levels of consumption (in great part of products made in China at stable prices in US dollars) but also a real estate bubble (real estate prices rose on average around 10 percent per annum between 2002 and 2006 versus 3 percent between 1990 and 2000). Subprime lending (100 percent of home value mortgage financing at subsidized rates in the early years to be reset later) had become hugely popular. Capital markets' creativity, lax regulatory supervision, less than adequate credit ratings and generalized greed had conspired to bring about additional levels of poorly priced financial instruments. As real estate prices peaked in late 2006 (to start falling in 2007) the bubble began to crack. At its roots, the subprime meltdown crisis was not very different from other previous financial crises: first, generalized expectations of continued economic stability and growth leading to excessive optimism by lenders and borrowers; then, the surprise of an economic slowdown causing asset prices to stabilize and begin to fall; and, finally, severe balance sheet problems for banks. The trouble this time around was that the so-called subprime meltdown crisis had been nurtured over a long period of time in the world's largest and most globally interconnected economy, and the one home to both, the most creative financial market and the most widely accepted currency.

By mid 2008, early hopes that the US Federal Reserve Bank could continue to fight the battle alone, without major involvement by the US Treasury, began to dissipate.[55] In June, the US Congress authorized the Treasury to purchase shares of the government sponsored Fannie Mae and Freddie Mac.[56] In early September, Fannie Mae and Freddie Mac, as well as the country's largest insurance company, AIG, had to be put into conservatorship.[57] Congress approved TARP (the Troubled Assets Relief Program), committing up to US$700 billion for recapitalization of banks in October 2008, and President Obama's US$780 billion fiscal stimulus plan in March 2009. All combined, US$2.2 trillion (15 percent of GDP) had been committed by the Treasury alone to prevent the collapse of the financial system and to attenuate the social impact of a major recession.

The difficulties in the US financial markets had begun, since early 2008, to spill over internationally, with greater impact on the economies with banking systems more interconnected with the US financial markets. Central banks and treasuries around the world were gradually forced to act in accordance with their perceptions of—and ability to deal with—the problems faced by their own financial systems and the threat of the recession to come.

While claims of decoupling between the developed world and the emerging economies had continued to dominate the media and the sell side reports from Wall Street during the first semester of 2008, the global credit crunch ended up having a major impact on Brazil. In spite of the country's position as a net creditor in US dollars, investment grade status, and minimal interconnectedness with the US domestic financial markets, the BRL suffered in less than 4 months a 50 percent devaluation (from R$1.56 to R$2.32/US dollar between August and October). Opposite to what was being done in most countries around the world, the Brazilian Central Bank, consistent with its inflation targeting policy, was forced to raise the SELIC rate by 25 percent (from 0.9 percent/month in June to 1.2 percent/month

55. A lot had already been done by the US Federal Reserve including continued lowering of the FED funds rate to below 2 percent, acting as lender of last resort for liquidity support to banks with greater flexibility regarding collateral required, and liquidity assistance to induce absorption of large problem companies (such as the mortgage bank Countrywide by Bank of America and the investment bank Bear Stearns by JPMorgan Chase).

56. The Federal National Mortgage Association (Fannie Mae) was established as a federal agency in 1938 to make mortgages more available to low income families. In 1968 it was chartered by Congress as a private shareholder-owned company. Rather than making home loans directly to consumers, Fannie Mae acted in the secondary markets, acquiring mortgage portfolios, and financing itself in the domestic and international capital markets. The Federal Home Mortgage Corporation (Freddie Mac) was chartered by Congress in 1970 to compete with Fannie Mae. Because of their congressional charters, Fannie Mae and Freddie Mac are considered government-sponsored enterprises (GSEs), therefore being perceived by the market as (almost) US sovereign credit risk. For further details refer to www.fanniemae.com and www.freddiemac.com.

57. For all practical purposes (at least temporarily) nationalized through capital injections from Treasury in exchange for over 80 percent equity stakes.

in October), leading the yield on the one-year Treasury note to increase to 15.25 percent on October 30, up from 11.9 percent on January 1, 2008.

The consequences for the financial sector were severe. Small and medium sized banks, largely dependent on the institutional market for funding, were faced with tremendous liquidity challenges. The liquidity squeeze was also felt by the larger banks, in proportion to the market perception of their leverage and sustainability of their funding sources.

As it turned out, prompt action by the Central Bank—in the form of liquidity support against collateral to small banks and the use of foreign exchange reserves to provide US dollar lines of credit to banks for them to be able to meet immediate foreign currency needs of important corporate clients—was sufficient to shore-up the financial sector without the need for Treasury involvement. But the sequence of events since May, more significantly felt by those more dependent on market counterparts for their total funding, forced all banks to revisit their strategic plans.

On November 3, the merger of Itaú and Unibanco, the largest ever in Latin America, was announced. The transaction consisted in a share exchange by which Unibanco shareholders received one Itaú non-voting share for either 3.4782 Unibanco non-voting shares (reflecting the average relative price between the two stocks for the 45 days prior) or 1.1797 Unibanco voting share (implying in a 195 percent premium for voting over non-voting stock).[58] From Itaú's shareholders standpoint it meant paying 1.6 times book value for Unibanco non-voting stock, 4.8 times for voting stock, 2.3 times overall (approximately R$30 billion) for 100 percent of Unibanco. The new Itaú-Unibanco would close 2008 as Brazil's largest bank by equity and total loans, although still second to Banco do Brasil in number of branches.

On November 20, Banco do Brasil completed the acquisition of 71.25 percent of the São Paulo state bank Nossa Caixa for R$5.45 billion (100 percent ownership to be achieved later, in October 2009, via a share swap); and on January 9, 2010, Banco do Brasil announced the purchase of 50 percent of privately held Banco Votorantim, regaining the position of Brazil's (and Latin America's) largest bank by total assets. This was a cash transaction in the total amount of R$4.2 billion (Banco do Brasil S.A., 2009), R$3 billion paid to Votorantim's shareholders for 49.9 percent of the voting stock and R$1.2 billion as fresh capital in the form of non-voting shares. In July, Banco Santander (Spain), the controlling shareholder of Santander-

58. Itaú-Unibanco Banco Múltiplo S.A., 2009.

Brasil, announced that it would conduct a global public offering to raise capital to boost growth across the whole spectrum of its activities in Brazil. This public equity offering, the largest in the world in 2009 (and to mid-May, 2010 in Brazil), attracted R$13.2 billion in fresh capital (Banco Santander, 2009) (for approximately 1/6 of the bank) bringing Santander-Brasil's capital adequacy ratio to 33 percent, three times the minimum required by the Central Bank. These movements significantly impacted the structure of the industry.

First, banking industry concentration increased sharply: the shares of total assets of the country's top 6 banks (BNDES excluded) increased from 67 percent in 2007 to 76.5 percent in 2009, a variation of the same order of magnitude as the one observed for the nine year market driven stage of consolidation (from 59 percent in 1998 to 67 percent in 2007). Second, public sector banks increased their share of total assets (from 31.6 percent in 2007 to 39.4 percent in 2009), in a clear reversal of the trend observed during the market driven consolidation stage (1999-2007). Third, the balance of power remained relatively unchanged between private sector Brazilian and foreign banks, approximately 32 percent of total assets for the former, 16 percent for the latter. And fourth, BNDES had by far the largest organic growth, in great part due to the government's decision to have the Treasury provide an extra R$100 billion to enable the BNDES to lend for infrastructure and industry. As of December 30, 2009 BNDES had R$280 billion in loans, 20 percent of the countries total bank debt of R$1.4 trillion (45 percent of GDP).

CONCLUSION

The recent development of the Brazilian financial system has been impressive, particularly after 1999, as a result of the government assisted industry re-structuring stage described in section 3 and of the beginning of a decade long adherence to a macroeconomic policy characterized by firm compliance with inflation and primary fiscal targets, and a floating exchange rate.

As of year-end 2009, two Brazilian private sector banks (Itaú and Bradesco) ranked among the top 20 most valuable banks in the world. Santander-Brasil had conducted a most successful global offering and accounted for approximately one-third of Banco Santander's (Spain) total market capitalization. Total bank debt had expanded from 25 percent of GDP in 1999 to 45 percent of GDP in 2009. Medium term (typically 3 to 5 year) fixed rate automobile financing, inexistent a decade ago, had reached R$94.1 billion (approximately 3 percent of GDP). And banks ended 2009 showing very high capital adequacy levels by any world standards, therefore enjoying a quite comfortable position to engage in significant additional credit expansion without immediate pressure on capital base.

The equities market has also been another bright spot of financial activity in Brazil. Benefiting from the country's market size, continuous development of important companies across the different sectors of the economy, consistent progress in the legal and regulatory framework (from the creation of the Comissão de Valores Mobiliários[59] in the early 1970s through the New Market legislation in 2002), continuous investment in the quality of trading platforms and, last but not least, top notch standards of transparency and corporate governance by publicly traded companies, BOVESPA (Bolsa de Valores de São Paulo) ranks today among the most respected equity exchanges globally.[60] An increasing number of Brazilian companies have also been listed on other international stock exchanges (mainly the New York Stock Exchange) and Brazilian global equity offerings have made, particularly since 2004, the headlines of the business media around the world.

But equity capital should always be the smaller part of the capital required for investment, that part which is permanent and the basis for borrowings (from lenders or in the fixed income securities market) at a financial cost below the expected rate of return on investment. The Brazilian process of economic development is constrained by the limitations of its domestic long term credit markets, more specifically, by the availability of affordable long term credit in reais, the currency in which most businesses earn their revenues and individuals earn their salaries.

Mortgage loans outstanding have increased by almost 80 percent over the past ten years, in great part as a result of the Central Bank imposed minimum lending requirements of 65 percent on savings deposits. But, at year-end 2009, the total amount of mortgage loans outstanding was only 3 percent of GDP (R$91.9 billion),[61] versus 15 percent for Mexico (Investment Properties Mexico, 2010) and 20 percent for Chile (Global Property Guide,

59. CVM, the Brazilian securities and exchange commission.

60. Total market capitalization of the companies traded in the São Paulo Stock Exchange reached US$1.34 trillion in December 2009, approximately equal to those of the Deutsche Borse and the Bombay Stock Exchange, half those of the London and Shanghai stock exchanges (World Federation of Exchanges).

61. Banco Central do Brasil, "Operações de Crédito do Sistema Financeiro, Saldos com Recursos Livres e Direcionados," www.bcb.gov.br.

2010). Also, 85 percent of total mortgage lending in Brazil was still provided by the public sector (mainly, CEF).[62]

Long-term financing in reais for investments by businesses and in infrastructure continues to come, in almost its entirety, from BNDES. Benefiting from stable compulsory social contributions (remunerated at below market rates) for over 2/3 of its funding, BNDES has had a long history of praiseworthy support of important companies and projects, as well as an effective partnership with the private sector banks to whom it also lends at preferential rates in order for them to be able to finance—in domestic currency, on a matched basis, and at their own credit risk—their corporate clients. But how can BNDES continue to expand its balance sheet to support higher levels of investment in Brazil without resorting to the market? And if so, how can it do this without passing on to borrowers the higher free market financial cost? For the moment, Treasury has been the solution. In 2009, BNDES received an extra R$100 billion in transfers from Treasury (in what was, perhaps, the most important fiscal measure by the government) to help mitigate the impact on the economy of the credit crunch. As a result, BNDES' loan book reached R$283 billion,[63] corresponding to 20 percent of total bank credit in Brazil. What can we expect for 2010 and thereafter?

The evolution of the Brazilian fixed income securities market towards establishment and enforcement of high standards of transparency, corporate governance, and protection of lenders' rights has also been impressive when compared to any other emerging economy. But the capacity of the Brazilian debt securities market to provide long term credit for the financing of investment is still extraordinarily modest. As of September 2009, the total amount of medium-term corporate bond issues in reais outstanding stood at R$271 billion[64] (under 10 percent of GDP, 1/5 of total bank debt) and consisted entirely of floating (as opposed to fixed) rate instruments, for the most part issued by leasing subsidiaries of financial conglomerates, not by businesses tapping the market directly to finance their investments.

The Brazilian Treasury remains, fifteen years after the introduction of the Real, incapable of issuing long term notes in reais at a fixed interest rate competitive with other major emerging market economies in their domestic currencies.[65] This has prevented the development of a strong domestic long

62. Ibid.
63. Ibid.
64. CETIP - Initiating Coverage, Credit Suisse Equity Research, December 10, 2009.
65. Yields on 10 year treasury notes in domestic currency: 3.3 percent for U.S., 5.4 percent for Australia, 7.5 percent for India, 12.7 percent for Brazil (www.bloomberg.com, government bonds)

term credit market. And Brazil has become increasingly dependent on public sector banks' long term investment.[66]

Let us hope that the coming 2010 elections in Brazil can bring together the necessary degrees of conviction and political commitment to move forward with the structural reforms necessary for the conquest of a long term fiscal credibility that has been pursued for two centuries. Were that to happen, one of the world's most robust long term fixed income securities market would rapidly materialize, consolidating the pre-conditions for a much more vigorous and sustainable process of economic growth.

66. On May 20, 2010 the Brazilian newspaper *O Estado de São Paulo* reported an additional R$80 billion loan made in April by the Brazilian Treasury to BNDES at below market rates (Fernandes, A. e Veríssimo, R., "Tesouro aumenta subsídio a BNDES," *O Estado de São Paulo*, Economia, 20 de maio de 2010).

13

Regulation & Compliance: Anti-Money Laundering

Monica Arruda de Almeida

Abstract: As an active member of the Financial Action Task Force (FATF), an international agency that combats money laundering and financial terrorism, Brazil supports the global anti-money laundering (AML) regime as a means to improve the reputation of its financial institutions, and ultimately their capacity to attract foreign capital. This study finds that although Brazil's AML compliance is considered credible by international players, the recent improvement of its international reputation is attributable to other government initiatives such as the improved management of its debt portfolio and more effective monetary and fiscal policies.

The global effort to combat money laundering, promoted by the G-7 countries in the last twenty years, has stirred a great deal of criticism among skeptics who are suspicious of the motives of the leading economies that "name and shame" countries that do not adopt anti-money laundering (AML) practices.[1] As an active member of the Financial Action Task Force (FATF), an international agency whose sole mandate is to combat money laundering

1. Most non-adopting countries are offshore financial centers (OFCs). One reason for such wariness is the concern that the pressure on offshore tax havens to adopt anti-money laundering controls is being used by the G-7 members to diminish the competitiveness of the financial centers' tax schemes. According to the OECD's *Harmful Tax Competition* of 1998, tax havens jurisdictions are characterized by: (1) little or no tax on relevant income; (2) ineffective system of information sharing; (3) lack of transparency, and (4) the existence of activities claimed by a haven location that are unsubstantiated (Kudrle, 2008).

and financial terrorism, Brazil has regulated and monitored money laundering cases and other financial crimes since 1998.

The Brazilian government has endorsed the global AML effort on many occasions as a means of improving the international reputation of its financial institutions, and ultimately their capacity to attract foreign capital. As Antonio Gustavo Rodrigues, a Brazilian former president of the FATF stated, "an international financial center perceived to be open to dirty money will eventually lose trust—and investments."[2] This rationale for adhering to the G-7 countries' anti-money laundering agenda is, in many ways, novel. The question of whether to adopt the AML standards is generally seen by scholars as a prisoner's dilemma. Because states can gain from stricter financial regulations elsewhere, there are substantial benefits for free-rider countries (see for example, Hülsse and Kerwer, 2007). Hence, it is commonly assumed that countries will limit restrictions on foreign capital inflows to gain a competitive edge.

One of this study's goals is to examine Brazil's declared reasons for the support of international AML efforts. The literature on the political economy of financial flows is mostly silent about the economic benefits that countries derive from restricting the cross-border flow of illicit money or its flow within domestic boundaries.[3] With the passage of the Law No. 9,613 in 1998, Brazil's federal government attained the mandate to regulate, monitor, and prosecute illegal financial activities, particularly cases of money laundering. Two questions that arise from its AML initiative are whether its regulatory reforms are credible and whether they have tangibly improved the country's financial standing. This study finds that, contrary to the position maintained by Brazilian authorities, there is no evidence that adherence to the AML standards has yielded an economic benefit. I argue that although Brazil's AML compliance is considered credible among international players, the recent improvement of its international financial status is attributable to other governmental initiatives, such as the improved management of its debt portfolio and more effective monetary and fiscal policies. A significant side effect of Brazil's AML program is the strengthening of the law enforcement capabilities of the Executive branch in areas traditionally within the ambit of the judicial system. Hence, in the context of post-neoliberal reforms of the 1990s, Brazil's recent experience of federal

2. Keynote address delivered on November 24, 2008. Antonio Rodrigues was president of the FATF until early 2009. He is currently the president of Brazil's Council for Control of Financial Activities (COAF), the main Ministry of Finance agency responsible for combating financial crime.

3. Veiga and Andrade (2006) and Kudrle (2008) are exceptions, as reviewed later.

reregulation has allowed the executive government to exert greater control over the country's financial affairs.

The following is a brief description of the initial years of the global anti-money laundering effort and a review of the literature concerning the political economy of financial flows. My goal is to search for both scholarly and empirical justifications for the global anti-money laundering regime. Later, I review certain aspects of the AML policymaking process in Brazil and examine the reception that the effort has received internationally. I conclude this study by arguing that even though Brazil's current justification for combating money-laundering is unsubstantiated, the program might nevertheless be worthwhile because of its utility in combating corruption.

RATIONALE FOR AN AML REGIME

Money laundering is defined in legal terms as the concealment of funds and the illegality of their origin (Machado, M.R., 2008). Money laundering was first criminalized by the US in the mid-1980s as part of its war on drugs. The US later led other G-7 to promote a global effort against the activity and in 1989 they founded the Financial Action Task Force (FATF), whose exclusive mandate is to combat global money laundering. The FATF standards consist of forty financial practice recommendations that, although not binding on members, are enforced by sanctions that vary from warnings to outright expulsion from the organization (Hülsse and Kerwer, 2007).[4] After the 9/11 terrorist attack, nine special recommendations were added to the FATF regime to combat terrorism financing. In practice, countering the finance of terrorism (CFT) functions as a subset of the AML standards. A feature of the AML global effort is that it involves numerous international and regional organizations, including the United Nations, the OECD, the World Bank, and the IMF.[5]

4. The FATF began blacklisting non-participating countries in 2000 but that was abandoned six years later because it was perceived as being too confrontational in addition to raising concerns of double standards between member and non-member states (Sharman, 2006).

5. Sharman explains that the IMF and World Bank were "recruited" by the G-7 nations to offer financial expertise to members and surveillance of illegal financial activity. For that purpose, there has been a division of labor between these two institutions whereby the IMF works with developed countries and offshore centers, and the World Bank with developing countries. Sharman argues that the high number of institutions participating in the AML regime pays testimony to the priority placed by the G-7 countries on the issue, despite the challenges involving the coordination and overlapping of many initiatives (Sharman, 2006).

Currently there are thirty-five full member states and jurisdictions that observe the AML standards. The FATF's financial regime is not only expensive to implement but also technically challenging, particularly to countries lacking sophisticated financial sectors.[6] But if on one hand the widespread adoption of the FATF's recommendations is seen as a successful case of transnational policy convergence, on the other hand this outcome is puzzling, because of the lack of evidence regarding the regulations' efficacy. Due to the "naming and shaming" strategy pursued by the OECD and the FATF, for example, many authors have argued that states adopted the AML/CFT regime primarily because of reputational concerns (Helleiner, 2000; Simmons, 2000; Sharman, 2006; Hülsse and Kerwer, 2007).

One of the questions that this article raises is whether the reputational concerns are justified. Studies that have attempted to measure the effects of adhering or failing to adhere to the anti-money laundering standards on a country's investment level fail to convincingly establish a direct link. Veiga and Andrade (2006) analyze, among other questions, whether the existence of anti-money laundering institutions and regulations affects a country's economic performance. They find that Latin American and African countries' efforts to criminalize money-laundering for offenses that are not drug-related have a positive association with investment and economic growth. However, they observe an opposite result in the OECD countries, whose AML efforts do not translate into additional economic rewards. Unfortunately, one has to be skeptical of Veiga's and Andrade's results because they use data from 1991 to 2000, a period when the implementation of the AML standards had barely begun anywhere.

Kudrle (2008), on the other hand, examines whether the blacklisting program pursued by the OECD (2000–2007) and the FATF (2000–2006) negatively affected financial activities in tax haven jurisdictions.[7] Using data on financial flows to and from 38 jurisdictions, Kudrle finds no systematic evidence of a negative impact on the volume of their financial transactions due to blacklisting. However, this author recognizes that the reputational liability of a blacklisting might have prompted the tax havens to adhere to the AML/CFT standards given their current high level of compliance.

---

6. A survey by Celent Communications, a consultancy firm, finds that in order to adhere to the AML/CFT standards, the US and European financial firms spent over US$5 billion only in 2003 (*The Economist,* 16 October 2004). A different survey organized by KPMG, another consulting firm, shows that among Latin American banks alone spending with anti-money laundry controls rose by 73 percent from 2001 to 2004 (*Valor Econômico,* 21 June 2005).

7. The OECD and the FATF had separate blacklists. However, their lists overlapped considerably. Of the 45 jurisdictions ever to be blacklisted, 20 were the target of both organizations.

But if the literature on the economic impact of a country's adopting, or declining to adopt, an anti-money laundering program is still scarce and inconclusive, there is consensus among scholars about certain economic and political variables associated with changes in perceptions of a country's risk. Moreira et al. (2008) remark that scholarly understanding of emerging markets' vulnerability to external shocks has evolved rapidly, especially after the Asian (1997) and Russian (1998) currency crises. Since then, important economic and institutional determinants of financial risk have been identified. For example, investors tend to be watchful of (1) the scope of a country's financial liberalization, (2) the quality of its foreign debt management program (to assess a government's ability to repay its debt), (3) its fiscal and monetary policies (to assess the probability of nominal exchange rate devaluations), (4) its growth sustainability, and (5) its institutional guarantees of property rights, as measured by the quality of its laws and regulations as well as the effectiveness of their enforcement (Ibid.).

There is also a very interesting branch of scholarly work that studies the determinants of bond spreads in emerging countries, namely, the difference between interest rates paid on bonds issued by emerging countries and those offered on the US 10-year Treasury note. Most work in this area tends to focus on investors' response to changes in countries' macroeconomic fundamentals. A good example is Akitoby and Stratmann (2008), who examine the effect of policy changes on interest rates in the bond markets of 32 emerging countries. The authors contend that investors' reactions to a country's fiscal adjustment vary according to the makeup of the particular economic policy. For instance, they find that revenue-based adjustments (i.e., increases in tax collection) lower spreads more than spending-based adjustments (i.e., government spending cuts). In addition, the authors show that cuts in current spending are more effective in reducing spreads than cuts in investment, and that tax-financed current spending lowers spreads, as opposed to debt-financed current spending, which increases sovereign risk. Financial investors appear to be more nuanced in their assessment of a country's risk than previously believed.

A recent phenomenon related to bond markets in emerging economies is that since mid 2002 spreads have narrowed to record lows. Puzzled by this event, scholars noticed that the overall improvement in the countries' macroeconomic indicators was insufficient to explain the spread reduction. They found instead that lower spreads were also caused by a surge in international liquidity, which in turn is attributable to the overall reduction in interest rates in industrialized countries (IMF, 2004; Hartelius et al, 2008; Moreira et al., 2008).

Arguably, Brazil has taken advantage of the favorable international financial environment in recent years by considerably reducing its sovereign risk and, starting in 2008, by achieving an investment-grade debt rating.[8] One of the main benefits for a country whose debt is rated at investment grade, and is therefore considered more likely to meet its payment obligations, is that interest rates charged on foreign debt tend to be lower, which in turn makes capital cheaper for domestic borrowers.

In addition to the Lula administration's efforts to improve Brazil's macroeconomic indicators and debt portfolio (as detailed below), Moreira et al. (2008) cite various reforms that have raised Brazil from the 25th percentile to the 75th percentile in least vulnerability among emerging markets between 1998 and 2007. These reforms include, for example, the reduction of currency exchange transaction costs, greater incentives for foreign investors to participate in public ventures, and the standardization of accounting practices among companies traded in the open market. None of these reforms is related to the control of money laundering.

Nonetheless, there is evidence that political institutions, events, and scandals can affect the performance of a country's sovereign debt. Although comparatively new, the literature on this subject is rich, especially in relation to developing countries, which tend to have weaker institutions and present greater uncertainty in the sustainability of their economic policies when compared to developed societies. Financial investors' confidence in a country's economic performance (as measured, for example, by the volatility of the exchange rate, bond spreads, and stock earnings) is tested in particular during election seasons, when governments in both developed and developing countries are tempted to adopt expansionary (and inflationary) fiscal policies. Such policies often cause exchange rate depreciation, which many times can lead to increases in its foreign debt denominated in international currencies.[9]

Recent Brazilian history offers good evidence of the negative effect that political scandals and perceived uncertainties have on a country's financial market. A case in point is Brazil's 2002 presidential election when the "Lula

8. The Lula administration has indeed been very fortunate to experience an almost crisis-free international economic environment, with notable exception of the current major crisis that started in late 2008. That wasn't the case in the decade that preceded the Lula administration. Before then, Brazilian financial authorities had to cope with the Mexican crisis (1994-1995), the Asian crisis (1997-1998), the Russian crisis (1998), the September 11th 2001 attacks, the Argentine crisis (2001-2002), and finally the financial turmoil caused by the 2002 Brazilian presidential election.

9. For a review on related studies, see Parra and Santiso (2008).

effect" caused a substantial increase in the country's bond spreads. The crisis was also fed by prominent investment banks that one after another downgraded Brazil's credit ratings in a domino effect. There also have been other politically motivated financial crises that, although not as dramatic as the 2002 episode, have forced the Brazilian government to respond to international pressure by enacting legislation that addresses institutional vulnerability as it surfaces.[10] The events leading to Brazil's adoption of anti-money laundering legislation in 1998 seem to fit this pattern.

BOND MARKETS AND CREDIT RATINGS

International authorities encourage participation in the global effort to combat money laundering with promises of future financial market rewards. They preach that legitimate investors will lose confidence in, and decline to invest in, countries that provide safe havens for tainted funds. This paper challenges this doctrine by focusing on the Brazilian AML program. It contends, instead, that Brazil's money-laundering policy has had no effect on the country's financial reputation. Although Brazil's financial rating has risen significantly in the last decade or so, the improvement in its economic reputation is attributable to the better management of its macroeconomic indicators and debt portfolio. Two sets of data presented in this paper (qualitative and quantitative) substantiate this conclusion.

One measure of the markets recognition of Brazil's efforts to combat money-laundering is the favorability of the reports published by companies specializing in investment analysis and forecasting. One need not be a day trader to appreciate the massive amount of research put into financial forecasting and investment-risk assessment for companies and countries. I choose to track the Country Report and the Financial Report, both published by The Economist Intelligence Unit (EIU), a leading research and advisory firm that is part of The Economist Group, along with the weekly magazine *The Economist* and the American news outlet *Congressional Quarterly (CQ)*.[11] I examined 131 editions of the Country Report and 37 editions of the Financial Report published from 1996 to 2009.[12] I searched for "money laundering" using the search utility of Adobe's "PDF" (portable document format)

10. Martinez and Santiso (2003) present an excellent study of the Brazilian financial crises in the 2002 and other presidential elections.
11. The Economist Group is, in turn, half owned by the daily newspaper *Financial Times.*
12. Country Report is published more frequently than Country Finance.

TABLE 13-1. Brazil Country Report, August 1996 to September 2009

Date/Mentions	Content	Context
Sept. 2003 1 mention, 38 pages	1) Notes involvement of some members of the PFL (Partido da Frente Liberal) in a money laundering scandal associated with the Banestado Bank.	Political analysis. Assesses the clout of the PFL as opposition party.
Sept. 2004 1 mention, 33 pages	1) Highlights Brazil's efforts to police its borders with Colombia Paraguay, and Argentina, and the cooperation among those countries in the war against money laundering.	International relations. Analyzes whether the Lula administration is more likely to partner with the US or to align with other leftist governments with an anti-US stance.
Dec. 2004 1 mention, 37 pages	1) Calls attention to the resignation of president of the Banco do Brasil on November 16, 2004, who was accused of money laundering.	Description of the reshuffles taken place in government posts.
June 2005 1 mention, 33 pages	1) Appointment of Romero Jucá as minister of Social Security. Mentions the involvement with money laundering of one of his main finance contributors, a money changer from the state of Roraima. Jucá was governor of Roraima (1988-1990) and currently represents the state as senator. 2) Supreme Court decides to proceed with an investigation against the president of the Central Bank, Henrique Meirelles, who was accused of engaging in tax evasion and money laundering in the late 1990s.	Describes some of the corruption probes the government has faced.
Dec. 2005 2 mentions, 35 page	1) Describes the downfall of Severino Cavalcanti, who stepped down of the presidency of the Chamber of Deputies under accusations for receiving kickbacks on restaurant concessions in Congress.	A currency dealer convicted of conspiring to evade tax and money laundering helped law enforcement officials in the investigation against Cavalcanti.
Sept. 2007 1 mention, 36 pages	1) Mentions the expulsion from Congress of Roberto Jefferson, a deputy of the PTB (Partido Trabalhista Brasileiro), who was accused of money laundering.	Describes some of the indictments of the "mensalão," a major political scandal of vote-buying that took place in mid-2005.
August 2008 1 mention, 24 pages	1) Describes the arrests, and subsequently releases by habeas corpus, of banker Daniel Dantas, who was accused of tax evasion and money laundering.	Story exposes the constitutional crisis that was occurring between the minister of Justice, the federal tribunal, and lower courts, which publicly criticized each other's decisions.

Source: The Economist Intelligence Unit. Country Finance on Brazil.

reader in all 168 editions for coverage on the topic. Tables 13-1 and 13-2 show only the editions in which the term "money laundering" was found. The Country Reports tend to mention money laundering only as part of their political analysis, in the context of assessing the stability of the federal government. They look for political crises that can adversely affect the executive branch's capacity to push for reform or the ability of Congress to pass legislation. The September 2007 edition contains an edifying example of a country political risk analysis. It mentions the mensalão, a major scandal in 2005 involving President Lula's party, the PT (Workers' Party), which allegedly paid a number of Congress members around US$12,000 a month in exchange for votes on legislation favored by the PT. Despite the resignation of many executive officials and Congress members, President Lula was able to distance himself from the episode and was reelected in 2006. Although the reports abound with political scandals, there are relatively few mentions of money laundering and, when they do happen, they have little relevance to the country's AML program. The publishers of the Country Report do not appear to consider Brazil's anti-money laundering program a noteworthy effort for improving the government's international image.

My analysis of the Country Finance editions yields similar results. I found one mention of the creation of the COAF in 2003, which is repeated using the same language in subsequent years. The reports also cite the passage of Law No. 10,406, which, among other things, recognizes factoring firms as financial entities and therefore subject to government regulations. The same language is also repeated in subsequent editions.

Since Brazil's anti-money laundering efforts are barely mentioned by the EIU reports, two of the most prominent international publications in country-risk analysis, it appears that the Brazilian authorities have overestimated the impact of the policy on the country's reputation.

As already mentioned, certain economic policies adopted in recent years reduced Brazil's vulnerability to external economic shocks. One outcome of the country's improved performance was an upgrade in its investment status by Standard & Poor's, Fitch, and Moody's, three major credit rating agencies. This change has helped Brazil to reduce the interest paid on its internal and external debt to historically low levels.[13] For example, by the end of 2009, the difference in interest paid on Brazil's and the US's Treasury bonds was less than 5 percent (500 basis points), a far cry from the 2002 presidential election year, when interest on the Brazilian bonds reached almost 25% (2,500 basis points).

But if Brazil's AML program did not contribute to its recent economic recovery, what else can explain such a change? This study posits that a series of initiatives by the Cardoso and Lula administrations placed the country on a more stable financial footing. Brazil's pursuits of greater debt portfolio management efficiency, of higher accumulation of foreign reserves, and of

13. Note that in Brazil, as in most of the other Latin American countries, the capital market is still dominated by government bonds. For example, by 2007, the stock of Brazil's government bond was about 60 percent of the country's GDP, whereas bonds issued by corporate and financial companies make up only about 10 percent of the Brazilian GDP (Banco Central do Brasil, Financial Stability Report, 2008).

TABLE 13-2. Country Finance, Brazil, 1996–2009

Publication Date	Content	Context
February 2003 2 mentions, 22 pages	1) Mentions a new Civil Code (Law no. 10,406) that recognizes factoring firms as financial agents. Until then, factoring firms were not considered financial institutions and thus were not regulated. 2) In a paragraph cites that Brazil has met all international standards related to the control of money laundering. Also mentions the law that created the COAF. (Exact same words used in earlier editions)	1) Brazil's national association of factoring (Anfac) approved the change because it will help to improve the reputation of the sector, which was being damaged by some firms that have been involved with money-laundering schemes in the past.
February 2004 1 mention, 53 pages	1) In a paragraph cites that Brazil has met all international standards related to the control of money laundering. Also mentions the law that created the COAF. (Exact same words used in earlier editions)	
December 2004 2 mentions, 53 pages	1) Mentions a new Civil Code (Law no. 10,406) that recognizes factoring firms as financial agents. Until then, factoring firms were not considered financial institutions and thus were not regulated. 2) In a paragraph cites that Brazil has met all international standards related to the control of money laundering. Also mentions the law that created the COAF. (Exact same words used in earlier editions)	
February 2005 1 mention, 80 pages	1) Mentions a new Civil Code (Law no. 10,406) that recognizes factoring firms as financial agents. Until then, factoring firms were not considered financial institutions and thus were not regulated. (Exact same words used in earlier editions)	
February 2006 1 mention, 85 pages	1) Mentions a new Civil Code (Law no. 10,406) that recognizes factoring firms as financial agents. Until then, factoring firms were not considered financial institutions and thus were not regulated. (Exact same words used in earlier editions)	
April 2007 1 mention, 90 pages	1) Mentions a new Civil Code (Law no. 10,406) that recognizes factoring firms as financial agents. Until then, factoring firms were not considered financial institutions and thus were not regulated. (Exact same words used in earlier editions)	
April 2008 1 mention, 90 pages	1) Mentions a new Civil Code (Law no. 10,406) that recognizes factoring firms as financial agents. Until then, factoring firms were not considered financial institutions and thus were not regulated. (Exact same words used in earlier editions)	
April 2009 1 mention, 75 pages	1) Mentions a new Civil Code (Law no. 10,406) that recognizes factoring firms as financial agents. Until then, factoring firms were not considered financial institutions and thus were not regulated. (Exact same words used in earlier editions)	

Source: The Economist Intelligence Unit. Country Finance on Brazil.

more stable exchange rates were among the most important. For example, to reduce the country's debt exposure, the government started gradually buying back some of the highest yielding bonds and replacing them with new bonds with lower interest rates (therefore, making foreign capital cheaper at home) and longer maturities. As Table 13-3 shows, by February of 2008, 63% of the debt issued by the federal government consisted of fixed-rate and inflation-indexed securities, a portfolio mix that tends to do a better job

TABLE 13-3. Domestic Federal Debt Held by the Public

Financial return per bond type	2004 Dec	2005 Dec	2006 Jun	Dec	2007 Feb	Apr	Jun	Aug	Oct	Dec	2008 Feb
Fixed rate											
Value in R$bn	163	273	320	395	396	417	464	433	422	457	443
%	20	28	31	36	35	36	39	36	35	37	36
Selic rate											
Value in R$bn	425	522	470	440	456	454	451	463	464	449	466
%	52	53	46	40	41	39	38	39	39	37	37
Price index											
Value in R$bn	121	152	221	246	253	269	286	295	313	322	334
%	15	16	22	23	23	23	24	25	26	26	27
Exchange rate											
Value in R$bn	80	11	-15	-12	-12	-14	-30	-30	-27	-28	-27
%	10	1	-1	-1	-1	-1	-2	-3	-2	-2	-2
Others											
Value in R$bn	22	21	20	24	26	27	27	28	27	26	26
%	3	2	2	2	2	2	2	2	2	2	2
Total in R$bn	810	910	1016	1093	1120	1151	1199	1189	1199	1225	1242

Source: Ministry of Finance, Banco Central do Brasil. Financial Stability Report (May 2008).

of insulating the country from exchange-rate volatility and even possibly an international currency crisis. That was an important improvement over 2004, when these financial instruments made up just 35% of the country's portfolio. The government's goal is to phase out the offering of floating-rate and foreign exchange-indexed securities. In addition, Brazil became in 2006, for the first time ever, an international creditor and no longer owes debt in a foreign currency.[14] Still the government has not been very successful in extending the maturity of its bonds when compared to other 10-year government bonds issued by OECD countries, very popular among international investors. As Figure 13-1 shows, Brazil's average of bond maturity has stubbornly remained below eight years. Another highlight of Brazil's performance is the significant reduction in the size of its total external debt, which is currently just above 10 percent of the GDP, its lowest level since the 1970s.

Equally important in the effort to secure greater financial stability is the accumulation of foreign exchange reserves. Here, Brazil has also made significant progress over the years, especially considering that it does not adopt the economic strategy of trade-surplus-oriented nations, but relies instead on the bond and stock markets to attract foreign capital. Some important indicators of financial liquidity point to a favorable forecast for Brazil. The

14. Brazil repaid all its debt to the IMF in December 2005 (*Bloomberg News*, February 21, 2008).

FIGURE 13-1. Debt Characteristics, 1971–2008

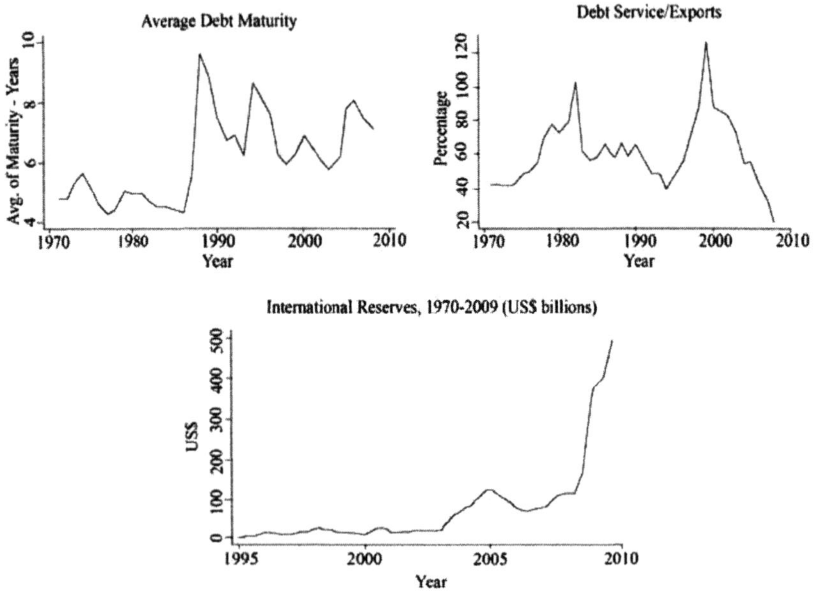

Source: Banco Central do Brazil: Sistema Gerenciador de Séries Temporais (SGS).

proportion of the country's debt service to exports, for example, is at the lowest level since the 1970s, just below 20 percent (Figure 13-1). Other indicators of financial liquidity also performed excellently in recent years, improving Brazil's ability to pay for its short-term external debt and to defend itself against speculative attacks on its currency (see Figure 13-2).

FIGURE 13-2. International Reserves

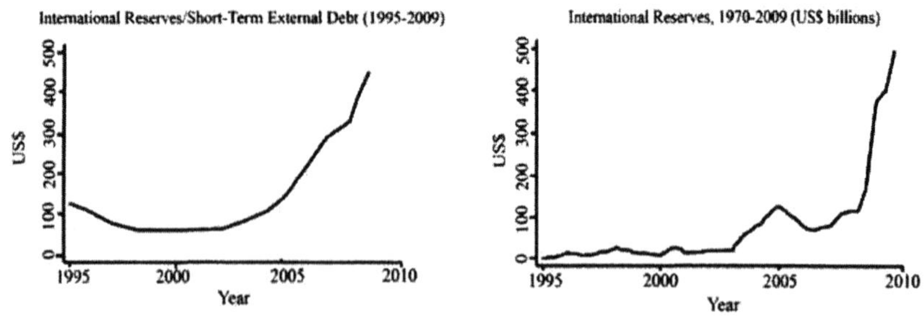

Source: Banco do Brasil, Sistema Gerenciador de Séries Temporais.

A third set of economic indicators that deserves attention relates to Brazil's exchange rate performance, which has been considerably stable in relation to other major international currencies. The anti-inflationary policies that started in 1994, year in which Brazil's Real was created, has allowed for greater stability of its exchange rate. One of the reasons for the Brazilian government's success in controlling inflation is that it has kept public debt in check. However, this objective is being accomplished by greater taxation of the productive sector rather than by cuts in government spending.

All in all, the economic indicators highlighted above were very positive for Brazil. The country's recent rise to an investment-grade level corroborates the findings of studies that were reviewed earlier in this chapter. With the exception of few areas that still display some economic vulnerability (e.g., Brazil's inability to cut public spending), the country's experience is almost a textbook for financial stability.

Next, I examine the Brazilian authorities' rationale for adopting the FATF's AML standards.

THE BRAZILIAN AML INITIATIVE

Despite the absence of empirical support for Brazil's economic rationale for adopting the AML standards, there seems to be a link between the country's increased vulnerability to external economic shocks and the push for an anti-money laundering program. Teixeira's (2005) account of the policy-making process that led to the signing of the 1998 money-laundering legislation suggests that the government used legislation as political cover for the lack of effective policies. She writes that whenever Brazil needed to improve its international reputation because of a domestic political scandal or to ward off the contagious effect of an economic crisis elsewhere, advances in the country's AML program were made. Teixeira contends that the government's goal was to reassure investors by signaling its commitment to curb financial misconduct and corruption. In the absence of such pressures, the governmental agencies in charge of drafting money-laundering legislation were unable to achieve consensus.[15]

After the first internal evaluation of Brazil's existing money-laundering controls, spearheaded by the central bank and the revenue service in 1993, it took 19 different drafts of the bill and the advocacy of Minister of Justice

15. Brazil's constitution allows the executive government to introduce legislative proposals to Congress.

Nelson Jobim before the government sent the bill to Congress for an "urgent" vote in late 1997.[16] The bill was part of a legislative package sent to Congress to improve the image of Brazil's financial institutions in the aftermath of the Asian currency crisis (Teixeira, 2005).

There are two important aspects of the decision-making process that led to the submission of the bill to Congress. One is the dominance of the executive branch in the drafting of Brazil's AML legislation. Among the offices that contributed to the AML bill were the President's cabinet, the ministries of Planning, Justice, and Foreign Relations, the central bank, the federal tax service, and the Department of Federal Police. The private sector also participated in government meetings, including representatives of the Brazilian Federation of Banks (FEBRABAN) and the stock exchange. The legislative and the judiciary branches had little or no involvement in the drafting (Teixeira, 2005; Machado, M.R., 2008). As a result, the creation of the Council for Control of Financial Activities (COAF), Brazil's financial intelligence unit (FIU), strengthened the executive branch's law enforcement capacity in areas traditionally under the jurisdiction of the judicial branch. According to Machado, countries such as China, Indonesia, and South Korea, for example, have in the past dealt with cases of financial regulatory reform by shifting power from executive agencies to legislatures and to the courts. Brazil is an outlier in this regard. Moreover, the pattern of Brazil's regulatory reform is inconsistent with the Cardoso administration's approach to governing, which emphasized deregulation as part of the administration's liberalization program.

Another fact worth noting is the relative absence of legislative debate on the executive bill. The document that was ultimately signed into law contained no material alterations. Teixeira argues that this reflects a lack of expertise in Congress about such a complex financial regulatory matter rather than an ideological endorsement of the President's proposal. Another significant feature of Brazil's AML law is that it incorporates, with little deviation, the financial practice standards promoted by the FATF. One may thus conclude that the Cardoso administration opted to closely comply with the AML guidelines promoted by international actors.

Brazil's compliance with international money-laundering protocols arguably enhanced its international credibility. Since becoming a full member of

16. As minister of Justice (1995-1997), Jobim gained praises for being an effective political articulator of the Fernando Henrique Cardoso administration (1995-2002) in Congress. Even after being nominated justice to Brazil's Supreme Court in April 2007, he continued to work on behalf of the executive until the passing of the AML legislation in March 1998.

the FATF in 2000, Brazil has been evaluated twice, in 2001 and 2005. On both occasions it was considered compliant with the organization's standards. Nonetheless, the international reviewers sometimes have found vulnerabilities in Brazil's AML program, including vulnerabilities related to financial secrecy: the reviewers believed that Brazil needed to improve its mechanisms for disclosure of data. Another common problem involves the "know your customer" practices, where greater government pressure on financial entities is required so that they properly identify users or issuers of all sorts of monetary instruments, such as pre-paid credit cards that are easily available at street vendors. On many occasions, the Cardoso and, later, the Lula administrations acted rapidly to address the shortcomings of the Brazilian program and, whenever called for, promptly requested Congress to pass additional legislation.[17] The FATF evaluations are performed with on-site visits and conducted in a system of mutual review by its members. Overall, Brazil's commitment to combat money laundering has been considered very credible by international actors. In fact, COAF's president Antônio Rodrigues was President of the FATF in the 2008–2009 term.

Following the Money Trail

In COAF's online statement in celebration of its twelfth anniversary, the council claimed to have frozen $2 billion Brazilian reais (US$1.1bn) in banking accounts involving over 63,000 people investigated for money laundering and other crimes. Subordinated to the Ministry of Planning, COAF has the authority to analyze financial data sent by the national banking system and other economic entities that are mandated by law to report monetary transactions that fit the category of "suspicious," such as accounts of R$100,000 (US$55,600) or more. Companies that fail to report the transactions to the COAF are subject to fines.[18]

It is important to note, however, that the COAF can only analyze the data it receives from the financial system, which by law need to be handled with confidentiality. Among the reports that are actually investigated by the council's intelligence officials, the ones that are confirmed as suspicious

17. Machado recounts some of the initiatives taken by the executive office to have Congress pass legislation either in response to, or in anticipation of, FATF's evaluations (Machado, M.R., 2008).

18. The COAF has received more than $4.1 million (US$2.3 million) in proceeds from such penalties. The guideline issued by Brazil's central bank also cites other lesser amounts that are subject to inspection by the COAF. For further information, see "Circular no. 3,461 (July 24, 2009)" at https://www.coaf.fazenda.gov.br/.

become subject of an intelligence financial report (RIF). The RIFs are then forwarded to other federal agencies that will perform the actual investigation, such as the federal police and prosecutors. However, law enforcement authorities will still need judicial authorization to freeze somebody's bank account or confiscate its property, for example.[19]

Among the almost 8,500 RIFs produced, there is a significant number of high profile cases of money laundering, embezzlement, and tax evasion that received wide coverage in the news media. In retrospect, if the decision-making process that led to the passage of the AML legislation lacked public debate, one cannot say the same about the financial intelligence work performed at the COAF. Arguably, the agency has become a household name among those who follow corruption scandals in Brazil. "Operação Furacão," for example, was a police operation that unveiled a scheme of illegal gambling that was being run thanks to the bribes paid to numerous police officers and highly placed public officials, including a judge from the Federal Appellate Court. According to COAF's 2008 report, 25 people went to prison for this crime. Another important case was "Operação Aquarela," when 19 people ended up in prison after law enforcement officials stopped a scheme involving private companies and non-governmental organizations that received payments from government agencies for services that they did not provide. The president of Bank of Brasília, a state bank, and public agencies from São Paulo, Goiás, Distrito Federal e Paraná were was also implicated in this crime, which had the involvement of around 300 individuals and cost R$20 million (US$11 million) of stolen money from the public sector.

Other police operations cited in the 2008 report include "Operação Kasper," where 22 people were sentenced to prison and 52 others received arrest warrants, and "Operação Exodus," resulting in seven prison sentences and 15 arrest warrants. Although the combat of corruption has been a central element of COAF's policy agenda, the agency has also the mandate to pursue cases against those who avoid paying tax in Brazil by sending their money abroad illegally. The report claims that the council's exchanges of financial intelligence with similar agencies in over 70 countries, including Portugal, Belgium, Switzerland, Uruguay, and the US, has helped on that front. Factor-

19. The sharing of confidential financial data among governmental agencies predicted in Brazil's AML legislation has caused some controversy. Justice Marco Aurélio Mello of the Supreme Federal Court, for example, has been quite vocal against the measure citing it as being unconstitutional (see for example, *Folha de São Paulo*, January 11, 2008).

ing firms, real estate, bingos (illegal in Brazil), and lotteries are the sectors with the highest number of reported irregularities in the country.

CONCLUSION

This study's primary goal is to examine Brazil's reasons for the adoption of money-laundering controls. According to Antônio Rodrigues, who was head of the FATF and is currently president of Brazil's COAF, a financial center whose image is blemished by the presence of tainted money will "eventually lose trust and investment." This study finds Rodrigues' claims to be empirically unsubstantiated. Instead, it contends that Brazil's AML program has had no effect on the country's economic standing. Although Brazil's financial rating has improved significantly in recent years, the advancement in its reputation is better explained by the more efficient management of the country's macroeconomic indicators and debt portfolio.

However, despite the legitimacy problems caused by the relative absence of legislative debate on Brazil's anti-money laundering policy, the program has shown a surprising utility in the fight against public corruption with the arrest of public officials involved in high profile criminal cases (e.g., "Operação Furacão"). This is an important accomplishment especially because the bulk of the money laundered in the country is stolen from the public sector. I believe this development should offer enough rationality in support of an anti-money laundering program that is better tailored to serve the needs of Brazil in its fight against financial crimes.

14

Financialization, Crisis, and a New Mania in Brazil

Elaine da Silveira Leite

Abstract: The Brazilian financial market has developed several institutions to create a stable environment and encourage savings and investment from the majority of the population who were previously unfamiliar with the financial system. This "financialization process" was unique in Brazil, because it involved the Brazilian state, corporate governance practices, democracy, and equality issues that appeared associated to self-help ideals, paving the way for the emergence of financial intermediaries that legitimize personal economic activities. This chapter presents the roots of personal finance, the principal institutions and intermediaries, and their roles in the development of financial issues. I argue that this cadre has grown and is becoming an important agent in the production and diffusion of social values as "moral entrepreneurs" of finance.

The Brazilian economic scenario at the beginning of the twenty first century presented a reasonable growth of the stock market. The Brazilian capital market reached impressive valuations; consequently, the market witnessed a large increase of its investor base, attracting individuals that earlier were unimaginable into the market.

In recent years, the São Paulo Stock Exchange (Bovespa)[1] has grown over 500 percent; this growth is related to the number of individual investors. In

1. São Paulo Stock Exchange (Bovespa) is the principal stock exchange of Brazil. The State of São Paulo has more individual investors in Bovespa than do other states; it contains 233,490 individual investors.

2002, there were 85,249 individual accounts in brokerages and banks. In 2005, the number rose to 155,183 accounts; an increase of 82 percent in three years ("Investidores individuais," 2008). In July 2008, this number went up to 516,000 and also recorded 555,768 individual investor accounts in October 2009, even after a period of uncertainty related to the economic crisis that shook the world ("Número de investidores," 2009).

In addition, many people participate in the market indirectly. They invest in long-term funds, private pension plans, mutual funds, and investment clubs that purchase stocks from companies listed on Bovespa.[2]

Recent economic growth confirms this positive outlook. The Brazilian media justifies this sudden interest in the financial market as a result of the country's recent economic growth. The decline in interest rates, along with other measures, stabilized the economy and increased GDP.[3]

An additional contributing factor in Brazil's economic growth is the well-publicized reconfiguration of its principal stock exchange. Bovespa adopted corporate governance ideals and implemented a transparent approach to reach ordinary people. In effect, Bovespa's major campaign focused on popularizing the stock market, which contributed to the capital market's increased competitiveness.

Other important policy initiatives were essential for the growth of the Brazilian financial market, including new laws for corporations offering strong protection for minority shareholders;[4] strengthening of the Securities and Exchange Commission of Brazil, whose activities were restructured to support financial market development;[5] establishing benefits for companies that adopt the corporate governance practices of the Brazilian Development Bank;[6] and Bovespa's guiding the creation of a capital market plan[7] that was to guarantee the sustainability of the stock market. These recent

2. Milton Gamez. "Os investidores estão voltando." *Revista Bovespa*, Janeiro/Março, 2006. Online.

3. From 2002 to 2007, real GDP in US dollars almost doubled, going from US$714 billion to US$1.313 trillion, with constant growth from 2004 onwards. Brazil is today the tenth-largest economy in the world, ahead of Russia and India, and the largest in Latin America. The country was classified by the United Nations Development Program (UNDP) as having a high Human Development Index (HDI), ahead of the other BRIC countries (Russia, India, and China). Data taken from "A favorable economic, political, and legal environment" Brasscom. Web 10 Oct. 2009.

4. Adriana Dias, "Impactos positivos da nova lei das Sociedades Anônimas." Empreendedor. 15 Fev. 2008. Online.

5. "FIDC: novas instruções da CVM devem trazer mais proteção ao investidor" in *Administradores* 12 December, 2006. Online.

6. Catherine Vieira. "Os pioneiros da governança corporativa." *Valor Econômico* 29 Jun. 2004.

7. "Plano Diretor do Mercado de Capitais, o que muda para o investidor?" in *Portal Acionista* 10 August, 2009. Online.

events increased security and ensured the creditability of the Brazilian financial market.[8]

Therefore, in April 2008, Brazil was classified as investment grade. It suggests that the country is regarded as having low risk of default and the nation is safe to receive investment. The news affected the stock market and the Bovespa index registered a new record score. It is important to mention that Brazil also received substantial foreign investment as a consequence of the world attention on the BRIC countries (Brazil, Russia, India, and China).[9]

Symbolically, at least, Brazil achieved a greater position in the international scenario and it is now seen as having a solid economic, political, and legal environment. In this context, the Brazilian financial market developed institutions to create a stable environment and encourage savings and investment from a sector of the population which was previously unfamiliar with or marginalized by the financial system.

In this scenario, new agents emerged; they are considered financial intermediaries that entice ordinary people to enter the finance field through different activities such as production of books, lectures, and coaching. I argue that it is attractive to map the financial market intermediates and their activities to understand how some actors are able to bring such a different pool of individuals into the same market for the first time.

This paper begins with a review of the bibliography to explain how the Brazilian state assimilated some market practices, providing autonomy to financial institutions to allow the growth of the capital market. These circumstances were unique in Brazil because they involved issues of corporate governance, democracy, and equality that appeared related to self-help ideals. In all, it paved the way for the emergence of financial intermediaries that legitimate personal economic activities.

As a second step, the paper presents the roots of personal finance, the principal institutions and intermediaries—commonly known as "gurus"—and their role in the development of finance issues. As a result, a huge cul-

8. It is important to mention Apolinário et al. (2002) who states that the Brazilian government has adopted new strategies to make the national stock market stronger. The "desestatização," which has been observed for the last years by selling government's stocks from the two biggest Brazilian companies, Petrobras and the Companhia Vale do Rio Doce, represents the last stage of privatization process, which was initiated in 1997. This process is called "Stock Market Democratization." The success in moving funds from FGTS (Time Service Warranty Funds) to Petrobras Privatization Mutual Funds (FMP) greatly increased Brazilians' interest in investing their money into the FMPCVRD, causing the biggest stock sale operation that has ever happened in Brazil.

9. Anne Warth and Francisco Carlos de Assis, "Brasil é o 10° em ranking mundial de investimento estrangeiro." *Agência Estado* 17 Sep. 2009. Web. 10 Nov. 2009.

ture of investment—emerging as a new mania—is blending concepts of success and happiness to the wealth in Brazilian society.

STATE, DEMOCRACY AND SELF-HELP

The debate about the role of the state and the economic model in Brazil led to a series of studies, mainly from the 1980s to the present, about the state's role and the debate between regulation and economic liberalization.

After the failure of welfare state principles, the economic position taken at first by England and then by the United States spread throughout the world. It was organized around the notion of a minimalist state that should not interfere in economic issues. Supporters of this perspective see the state as promoting delays, inefficiency, and economic irrationality. Thus, it is argued that this creates the need to reduce the duties performed by the state in promoting economic development (Evans, 1995).

Overall, the 1980s was characterized by a neo-conservative wave and its proposal of a minimal state. In the 1990s, the movement shifted toward reform. More specifically, state reconstruction began to be a dominant program, as Bresser-Pereira (2000b) sums up in the following extract:

> The great political task of the 1990s is to reform or to rebuild the state. Between the 1930s and 1960s, the state became a significant factor in fostering economic and social development. During that period, and particularly after World War II, we witnessed a time of economic prosperity and an increase in standards of living as never before in the history of mankind. Yet, since the 1970s, because of its distorted growth coupled with the globalization process, the state entered into a crisis and became the main cause for the drop in economic growth rates and the increase in unemployment and inflation rates that have taken place throughout the world. A neo-conservative wave and market oriented economic reforms were respectively the ideological and political responses to the crisis—reforms which neo-liberals or neo-conservative politicians and intellectuals hoped that would bring about the size of the state reduced to a minimum. But, in the 1990s, when the neoconservative proposal of a minimum state proved not to be feasible, the true nature of the reforms was disclosed: the rebuilding of the state was essential for it to undertake not just its classical tasks of assuring property rights and contracts, but also those required to ensure social rights and promote competitiveness in the country (Bresser-Pereira, 2000b: 176).

According to Bresser-Pereira and Grau (1999), the globalization process of the 1990s required new methods of more efficient public administration. Consequently, new actors for executing social services guaranteed by the state became increasingly important. At the same time, the state was seen as inefficient and corrupt. This dichotomy provided the rise of new agents and organizations such as non-governmental organization (NGOs) and self-help groups that were concerned with bringing social and economic development to the country (Bresser-Pereira and Grau, 1999).

This framework helps us understand not only the evolution of state reform but also the development of the Brazilian financial market and the emergence of corporate governance issues in Brazil (Grün, 2003). Corporate governance—shaped by the financial sphere—appeared as a requirement for transparency via society, emerging as a criticism of the Brazilian bureaucratic model.

The corporate governance movement is evidenced clearly during the Fernando Henrique Cardoso government (1995-2002). Transparency was key to warm up the capital market and attract investors in the context of privatization and reform during this period. Therefore, the government was required to adopt corporate governance strategies to increase transparency (Grün, 2003).

Carvalho (2002) argues that changes of institutional investors' attitudes are evident during the Cardoso government. As a result, very important facts emerge, such as the internationalization of the Brazilian capital market; the increasing number of companies accessing international markets through American Depositary Receipt (ADR);[10] the opening of the financial system for multinational institutions; and the increasing importance of foreign investors in the domestic stock market.

In 2002, then presidential candidate Luiz Inácio Lula da Silva of the Workers Party visited Bovespa. At that time, he wanted to demonstrate adherence to economic and corporate governance practices established in the financial market. At least from a symbolic approach, corporate governance has gained much attention in the nation (Grün, 2003).

After 2002, the pension funds grew and adopted the corporate governance practices as an instrument for their protection. The pension funds are essential to understand the advancement of corporate governance, since the corporate governance conflict is between institutional investors (the pension fund is considered a minority shareholder) and owners (the majority shareholders) in Brazil.

It is important to emphasize that the principal leaders of unionism control the major pension funds in Brazil (Jardim, 2009). From this perspec-

10. "International Investing: get the facts." *Securities and Exchange Commission*. Division of Corporation Finance. Online.

tive, Jardim (2009) states that the unions stopped answering simply "no" to the market, and began to consider the possibility of negotiation, discussing questions such as worker's savings.

The dialogue established between the left and the financial market, created a base for the "domestication" and/or "moralization" of capitalism in Brazil (Jardim, 2009). Jardim (2009) shows that certain social projects implemented by Lula's government go through the market—such as micro-credit projects—negating the idea of the quest for profit and redefining the concept of financial market. Through these projects the popular classes start to interact with the financial market.

Jardim (2009) also illustrates how the Lula government promotes active participation of some unions in the financial market through corporate governance. For example, at the micro level, the unions begin to discuss democracy and transparency as workers gain access to their employer's shares becoming "owners" and gaining the new title of shareholders. Consequently, this also introduces social, ethical, and worker perception in the financial market field resulting in a social and financial integration never before seen in Brazilian society.

It is important to highlight, according to Sá (2003), that the corporate governance discourse is associated with economic progress. The financial actors claim that it is through the economic growth that Brazilian nation will achieve social development. Symbolically, this discourse forms a "mix" in the common sense about what is social and economic development. In general, social and economic development came to be seen as part of the same political approach.

For these reasons, corporate governance is becoming the great solution for Brazilian society. It is recognized not only as a neoliberal prescription to solve the problem of companies' capitalization, but also as a means to enlarge not only the financial markets and economy but also the social field (Grün, 2004).[11]

11. At the same time, it is important to examine some research that focus on the entrepreneurial changes and their effects on the Brazilian enterprise structure. Diniz and Boschi (2003) state that crisis of the national development model and the transition to a market model provided the keynote of the 1990s. In addition, reforms and their impacts have influenced the composition of plans and business elites' collective action. Filho and Silva (2001) state that some enterprises decided to move to a new control (from the traditional and family control to a professional management); as a result, there was a redefinition of the family enterprises' priorities. On one hand, family businesses (which represent the majority of Brazilian enterprises) have found themselves under strong pressure, such as difficulties in establishing their own capital structure and inability to open their capital to foreign and other investors. On the other hand, institutional investors begin to gain significance in the control of large national companies. As a result, corporate governance practices that institutional investors are supposed to follow began to shape the national economy.

Also important to the development of corporate governance is the "New Market" (2002), created by Bovespa. This segment of the stock market is dedicated to shares issued by companies that voluntarily adopt governance rules and implement strong corporate governance practices. The capital of listed companies in the "New Market" is composed only of shares with voting rights; an important factor in Brazil where most of the market's liquidity is concentrated in non-voting shares.

The "New Market" has inaugurated a new phase of the capital market in Brazil. It is supported by corporate governance practices of transparency, accountability and social responsibility that are designed to reduce uncertainties in the financial market. According to Bovespa, the value and liquidity of listed shares are positively influenced by levels of security rights to shareholders and by quality of information disclosed by companies. Bovespa also has companies qualified as Level 1; these are required to provide improvement in the provision of information, including requirements for consolidated financial reports. They must also maintain 25 percent of their shares on the market. On the other hand, companies qualified as Level 2—in addition to the practices of Level 1—have to adopt strong practices related to minority shareholders rights such as extending 70 percent tag-along rights to non-voting shares.[12]

In 2001, Bovespa also initiated a campaign focused on educating the general population about the stock market. The principal program, which is called "Bovespa Goes to You," aims to bring the capital market closer to civil society. The key point is to make the stock market more popular. In order to spread this campaign, Bovespa focuses on the idea that the market is transparent and democratic. As part of this project, other initiatives have been developed such as "Bovespa at the Beach," "Bovespa at the Factory/Company," "Bovespa at the University."

This new dynamic created by the market gave rise to new economic actors that appeared as a solution to change the "uncertainty" of the economic and political scenarios. At the same time, there is also a boom of the self-help literature. McGee (2005) explains that in a period of declining security there is no surprise if one finds a marked increase in the number of self-help titles. In this way, McGee emphasizes how the promise of self-help can lead indi-

12. "Tag along" is a mechanism to protect a minority shareholder. For example, if a majority investor buys the control of the company, then the minority shareholder has the right to join the transaction or sell his or her minority part in the company.

viduals into a new sort of enslavement and into a cycle where the self is not improved but endlessly belabored.

As the financial market is being reshaped, there is an increase of personal finance literature that it is linked to self-help schemes in Brazil. Bookstores' shelves are filled with books and releases that deal with money and financial education. These books focus on the idea of getting rich, that is, they establish the "steps" to reach the "first million."

Thus, the pathway of corporate governance in Brazil—ranging from economic and political issues to the capital market—opens a new way to understand how actors try to change the traditional perception of the market through their symbolic strategies (Grün, 2007). Moreover, regarding the popularization of financial market issues, the Brazilian state is watching its expansion, but to some extent, without control over the situation.

THEORETICAL BACKGROUND

In this part of the chapter, I review the literature that reports on current economic processes through studies about financialization in order to provide theoretical elements offering some connections between the current bibliography and the empirical data that will be presented.

Financialization is a relatively new term that refers to the increasing importance of financial markets, financial tools, and financial actors in the economy's operation. According to Martin (2002), financialization, like other recently coined concepts of postmodernism and globalization, gets stretched and drives us in numerous directions. "Part of the complexity of these terms is that they stand simultaneously as subject and object of analysis—something to be explained and a way of making sense out of what is going on around us" (Martin, 2002: 08).

Brazil, like other emerging nations, is experiencing rapid financialization. This process is shaped by financial changes in the global financial market and involves restructuring of the country's financial organization through privatization, fiscal and monetary reform, and the creation of new programs and institutions that encourage economic growth and popular investment (Grün, 2009). Financialization includes not only financial intermediaries but also self-help ideals. The country's financialization processes are formed by an interesting dynamic in which corporate governance practices gain significance in the context of the critique of the inefficient state.

Nowadays, the economic changes and increases in market tools are discussed as part of a new context. According to Thrift (2008), they are considered a "new economy" perspective. Thrift argues that the "new economy" is spread by investors who seek protection and information; and as a result creates a "cultural circuit of capital." Mainly business schools, advisors, and gurus—intermediaries who increasingly gain space in this new financial expansion—create and participate in this cultural circuit.

However, the "new economy" is different from other periods of economic change because the principal agents are intermediaries who try to motivate the masses (ordinary people) to create and establish a new market culture. "The growth in the number of shareholders and in shareholder choice was buttressed by the increasing mediation of finance, which meant that narratives like the new economy could travel further" (Thrift, 2008: 264).

In this context, discussions about financialization have increased and have had increasing importance among academics, media, and the business world (Erturk et al. 2008). For Erturk et al. (2007), there are several differences among researchers about their emphases in analyzing the financialization processes. The cultural economy analysis, which is the main mode of financialization studies nowadays, includes terms such as "corporate culture," "market culture," and the "knowledge economy." Crotty (2003) emphasizes the non-financial corporation. On the other hand, some researchers such as Martin (2002) focus on the individual analysis and identity that is changed with the implementation of financial tools.

In general, Erturk et al. (2008) highlight that the actual financialization process is different from other forms that previously existed. This new format is particular in some points, such as: structure, where there is a creation of mass markets in the domestic economy (for example, in the United States); the growth of financial intermediaries; and in the popular reaction to certain facts released by companies. Thus, it is possible to argue that Brazil is currently going through the financialization process. Moreover the Brazilian case has been regarded as an extreme example of "financialization" because interest rates and bank spreads between borrowing and lending rates are considered the highest in the world, and, more recently, because of the apparent submission of Lula's government to the financial markets (Jardim, 2009). It is also important to stress that the markets are international and it is through them that most of globalizing pressures are internalized in the Brazilian society (Grün, 2009). Within this context, international economic events impact Brazil's economy and add to uncertainty about Brazil's economic future.

In a dramatic period of social change, the general promise of self-help is increasingly important, because the self-help offers "comfort and consoles us, suggesting that vast material, social, and personal success are available to anyone who is willing to work long and hard enough to improve the self" (McGee, 2005: 13).

This evidence shows a great "combination" that is the onset of financialization, at least beginning with Fernando Henrique Cardoso's government. It was further developed by Lula's government (2003-2010) and now by Bovespa and private sector financial advisors and nonfinancial intermediaries. The latter were incorporated by self-help ideals that employ concepts of democracy shaped by corporate governance.

So economic development has become embedded into the ideals of democracy (corporate governance) and self-help schemes; simultaneously, it allocates to individuals the need to rely on private financing rather than on the government. It formed the basis for the development of a new way of thinking in Brazil in which individual ideals of self-help stimulate economic growth. "The fantasy has maintained considerable appeal, despite its troubling corollary: if success is solely the result of one's own efforts, then the responsibility for any failure must necessarily be individual shortcomings or weaknesses" (McGee, 2005:13).

Based on McGee's arguments about the self-help industry in the United States, where this phenomenon has a long tradition, one can argue that at the moment when self-help in Brazil emerges, the country is focused on issues of democracy, equality and the financial market's embeddedness in society.

Beginning in 1990, according to Bresser-Pereira and Grau (1999), there was an incredible growth of private and non-private organizations (such as NGOs) that developed together with self-help practices. At this time, the national discourse was about equal positions both in the economic and in the political sphere.

However, the varieties of the financialization processes present some similarities among different nations. These include the broadening of their activities to include a mass audience and the spread of financial literature for ordinary people. Erturk et al. (2008), based on a survey, found that among Anglo-Saxons, the finance literature was responsible for bringing financial education to Americans, which enabled and taught the public about investments and the varieties of financial products.

Therefore, based on these studies, I argue that the personal finance literature supported by self-help is an important point of convergence in the theoretical financialization debate, both in the international and national spheres. The market euphoria boosted the personal finance industry related to self-help schemes in Brazil. This literature seeks to reach the general population; it is not restricted to a portion of society able to save and invest in the markets.

Again, I reinforce the importance of mapping financial market mediators and their activities because it provides sound evidence about the emergence of new actors. It also offers some analytical elements for discussing the role of the state related to the growth of the financial market in Brazil.

The next part of this article presents some empirical data about the roots of personal finance; its principal institutions and agents (commonly known as "gurus"); and their role in the expansion of personal finance. These created a stable environment to encourage savings and investment by the majority of the population who were unfamiliar with or had been marginalized by the financial system.

ROOTS OF PERSONAL FINANCE

The onset of financial speculation has been attributed to medieval Europe, where the carnivals caused by Lent and other cultural events were amongst the few social spaces in which economic activity for profit was sanctioned. More importantly, investments in stocks of companies could be sold in such events, along with municipal bonds and lottery tickets. At this time, according to Harrington (2008), financial bubbles were caused by two factors: innovation, like fashion in the Netherlands by the Turkish tulip; and necessity, such as the plan to nationalize the debt of the British government through the issuance of South Sea Company's shares. The boom of populist investment in the 1990s could be described as a combination of innovation and necessity, driven in part by technological innovation (World Wide Web and e-commerce, in particular) and by the requirement for many Americans to meet the needs of private funding instead of relying on the government or the employer's safety net (Harrington, 2008).

In the same way—through the great results brought by corporate governance that was motivated by the democratic ideal (Grün, 2003)—the view that popular investment in the stock market would lead to economic development was popularized in the press beginning in the year 2000 in Brazil.

As indicated above, there were about 85,000 individual investors in 2002 in Brazil while in 2009, the number of investors exceeded 550,000, even with the effects of the global economic crisis.

Meanwhile, the number of female investors increased by more than seven times (647.74 percent), from 15,030 in 2002 to 112,386 at the end of 2007, and the growth of the male audience in this period was 390.14 percent. In 2009, Bovespa had 136,062 women investors.[13]

In an interview with a shareholder at Bovespa, I was asked if I had read the book *Rich Dad, Poor Dad. Rich Dad, Poor Dad: What the Rich Teach Their Kids About Money—That the Poor and Middle Class Do Not!* was first published in 2000, by Robert T. Kiyosaki and Sharon L. Lechter. This narrative, largely based on Kiyosaki's own upbringing and education in Hawaii, focuses on the idea that the poor and middle classes work for money and the rich men have money work for them. The Poor Dad is based on Kiyosaki's real father—a PhD holder and graduate of Stanford University, University of Chicago, and Northwestern University—who was the head of the Department of Education of the Hawaii. In the book, he is greatly respected until he decides, late in his career, to go against the governor of Hawaii. As a consequence, Poor Dad loses his job, and is unable to find comparable work. Since he never learned how to handle money, and instead depended on the government (his employer) for support, he dies in severe debt.

In contrast to this character is Rich Dad, his best friend Michael's father, and Kiyosaki father's partner. Rich Dad dropped out of school in eighth grade, but became a self-made multi-millionaire regardless. He taught Kiyosaki's son and Michael a variety of financial lessons, and emphasized that the boys need to learn how to make money work for them to avoid spending their whole life working for money.

In Brazil, Paula and Wood Jr. (2002) highlighted that the first signs of demand for personal finance issues were noted after the release of the books *Seu Futuro Financeiro* by Louis Frankenberg[14] and *Rich Dad, Poor Dad.*

Yet another empirical landmark of personal finance in Brazil was the publication of the Personal Investments Guide in 2006 by an important Brazil-

13. "Número de mulheres na Bolsa cresce nove vezes em sete anos." *Infomoney* 11 Jan. 2010. Online.
14. Louis Frankenberg is considered to be the first financial planner in Brazil.

ian economic journal. It offered a list of books to help readers make their money increase without much effort.[15] The guide presents some best-selling books in Brazil, such as *Casais Inteligentes Enriquecem Juntos* (Gustavo Cerbasi); *Rich Dad, Poor Dad for Teens*; *Rich Dad in Comics* (these two books were written by the same authors of *Rich Dad, Poor Dad*); and *Nice Girls Don't Get Rich* (Lois P. Frankel). The only Brazilian book is *Young Couple Be Rich Together*, by Gustavo Cerbasi. Today, he is the main author of personal finance books in Brazil. The segment of personal finance became one of the most significant of the Brazilian publishing market and each month, there are several new titles related to finance.

The recent expansion of publications related to personal finance—and classified as self-help—is evidence of the popularization of finance in Brazil representing a new mania. Since its release, *Rich Dad, Poor Dad* has been classified as a best-seller.[16]

ACTORS, ACTIONS AND MOTIVATIONS[17]

The personal finance phenomenon has spread to television programs, courses, magazines, web sites, communities, and events such as Expo Money. Expo Money is considered the most important event on financial education in Brazil.[18] Each month, it takes place in a different Brazilian state, but the principal one happens in São Paulo. In 2008, the three-day gathering received more than 20,000 visitors.[19]

Expo Money produces a collection of books with the main purpose to educate children, explaining how to escape from consumerism, help with the budget, and be financially independent. For example, there are titles such as *The Tree of Money*; *The Traps of Consumption*; *Investing in Options*; *How to Increase Your Money*; *Financial Education*; *500 Questions (and*

15. "Investimentos pessoais." *Guia Exame*. Editora Abril, 2006. Print.

16. Ibid.

17. I have analyzed the literature about self-help and finance in Brazil to map the "moral entrepreneurs" of personal finance. The number of books related to personal finance phenomenon is "amazing," so I selected the books that are considered best-sellers in the vehicles of information about finance, business, and careers in Brazil. I also participated in courses, attended lectures, and interviewed some gurus of finance.

18. Expo Money is produced by the World Money Show, the traditional event about investments in the United States. It also happens in Japan, China, Russia, United Kingdom, Australia, Germany, Canada, South Africa, and Vietnam.

19. Expo Money 2009. http://www.expomoney.com.br.

Answers) about Finance; and *The Pocket Diet*. The collection is written by financial advisors.[20]

The Expo Money collection is organized by Gustavo Cerbasi, the principal financial advisor and author of personal finance in Brazil. Cerbasi was considered by Revista Época to be one of the 100 most influential Brazilian personalities in 2009.[21] After 500,000 copies sold since the release of his book *Young Couples Be Rich Together* in 2004, a special edition was issued in which the author's preface emphasized the importance that the book had reached in Brazilian society.

In this field, there is also a segment that works to introduce financial education for children; the goal is encouraging the culture of savings and introducing concepts of credit in schools and universities (Savóia, 2006). In this sense, many institutions have worked to introduce financial education in their curriculum including The Financial Education Institute that offers courses to guide people on investment and money.[22] This segment also applies "steps" to teach how to achieve wealth following the same script used by Expo Money and its advisors. Bovespa also maintains an educational program focused on assisting students of public and private schools with information about capital markets. Its focus is to explain basic economic and finance concepts that are used in daily life.

In general, the personal finance segment that is directed to women shows how the financial sector reached important segments of society. There are a lot of books for women, such as, *Rich Woman* by Kim Kiyosaki. The formula she uses is her husband's idea—he is the author of *Rich Dad, Poor Dad*. Kim Kiyosaki employs her own history to teach how to be financially independent.

Meninas Normais Vão ao Shopping—Meninas Iradas Vão à Bolsa by Andréia Assef and Mara Luquet stresses the concept that "you do not know, but you were made to invest" focusing on how women are educated to hate money.

In general, advice for women emphasize the idea that they do not enrich themselves because they focus on needs of others rather than their own, preventing women from becoming truly independent. The literature highlights that women always hear messages such as "don't be greedy" or "learn

20. "Coleção Expo Money." *Expo Money.* 2009. Online at http://www.expomoney.com.br/2009/colec.asp.
21. "Os 100 brasileiros mais influentes de 2009." *Revista Época* 05 Dec. 2009.
22. *Instituto de Educaçao Financeira*. Online at http://www.edufinanceira.org.br.

to be happy with what you have." Furthermore they explain how these messages are forms of interference that keep women from having a prosperous future. The following extracts are from the book *Normal Girls Go Shopping; Expert Girls go to the Stock Market:*

> You do not get married waiting to divorce. You do not start to work on a new job waiting to be dismissed. But these things happen and, now, increasingly often. I have already said, but it is important to repeat: If you're dependent on someone—husband, boss or anyone else—about your financial future—you must think twice. Sometimes, we don't perceive how we are dependent, until the moment that we have to take control of our lives.
>
> "Don't be greedy" or "Learn to be happy with what you have." These messages are forms of interference that avoid your seeing a great future. To accumulate wealth, no matter how much, requires a clear vision that could show you surrounded with money on all your sides.

Normal Girls Go Shopping; Expert Girls Go to the Stock Market reached a great importance, so much so that the "*Geração Futuro*" brokerage created the first investment club for women. The club is called "Girl Experts" and it is based on precepts of sustainability. In this context, Bovespa also created the "Women in Action," which is a project about financial education for women. The program focuses on approaching women and teaching them stock market concepts.[23]

In general, the contents of books, lectures, and fieldwork already examined are advice that aims to guide individuals. The advice is more or less practical, for example, "Do Something!" or "Where and Why to Invest." But, it also gives advice, such as "you need to be self-confident, think positively." In general, these kinds of advice are combined, and the general public does not distinguish them and they understand them as a coherent actions and values.

Behind these exhortations, there are "gurus" who are mediators that explain, instruct, educate, and illustrate the advice with case studies. Gurus' performances help to instill in the public a new perception about the financial world. According to Becker (1977), social norms are created by groups or individuals that are called "moral entrepreneurs." So these gurus are significant to spread new social values. They are "moral entrepreneurs" of finance.

Gurus and their advice lead individuals to believe that acting "economically" is a good action. The books and contents analyzed try to educate, and to introduce items to be mimicked. This allows for the transformation of the

23. "Mulheres em Ação" in *Bovespa*. Online.

social meanings given to people and social activities. The mechanism used by gurus transforms individuals in their collective experience and thus contributes to the (re) production of habitus (Bourdieu, 1997). The personal finance field gave legitimacy to personal activities that were not previously valued.

There is a moral influence being created that transforms attitudes and modes of action. Personal finance promoters have created a new social space, supported by performances, miraculous calculations, magic, and science, therefore, connecting happiness and satisfaction to the possession of money (Zelizer, 1994; Simmel, 1990).

> The tremendous importance of money for understanding the basic motives of life lies in the concept that money embodies and sublimates the practical relation of man to the objects of his will, his power, and his impotence; one might say, paradoxically, that man is an indirect being. I am here concerned with the relation of money to the totality of human life only in so far as it illuminates our immediate problem, which is to comprehend the nature of money trough the internal and external relationships that find their expression, their means or their effects in money (Simmel, 1990: 211).

In this sense, the segment of personal finance targeted to women highlights the setting described above. The personal finance field emphasizes that women do not enrich themselves because they focus on the needs of others, so they avoid taking the necessary "steps" to become financially independent.

"When personal finance becomes the way in which ordinary people are invited to participate in that large abstraction called the economy, a new set of signals are introduced as to how life is to be lived and what it is for" (Martin, 2002). The argument supported by Martin reinforces what happened in Brazil. The personal finance advice creates an obsession for money that dominates lifestyle, personal ambitions, and decisions. Consequently, the risk becomes part of everyday life. The moral entrepreneurs of personal finance (gurus) also use the argument that, currently, people have no more security in daily life. In a period where instability and unemployment worry the population, personal finance books show cases of business or professional success based on self-help schemes.

However, the period of crisis is an inspiring situation for personal finance gurus, because they create a new advice market about "how and where to invest in time of crisis" with a certain emotional appeal. While the rest of the world went into panic, the gurus showed how this can be the best time for financial investments. As a result, it was exactly at the period of great turbulence in financial markets that individual investors became more attracted to the stock exchange.[24]

These gurus are important to disseminate social values. They act as "moral entrepreneurs" of finance and provide advice about how to operate in times of crisis, creating new speculative manias. Their advice has increased the legitimacy of personal economic activities that were not previously valued in Brazilian society.

CONCLUSION

The literature reviewed in this chapter provides evidence that the scenario of the reconstruction of the state in Brazil made possible the legitimization of corporate governance practices; consequently, allowing the expansion of financialization in the country. Bovespa's campaign and the boom of personal finance have also shaped the Brazilian lifestyle to include increased participation in the stock market.

This context allowed the emergence of new actors—the gurus. They are moral entrepreneurs of finance, educating on ways to invest honestly to achieve economic security, if not profits, even during times of crisis. By capitalizing on instability and uncertainty, they educate how these can be the best time for the development of financial skills and economic character. Yet these institutions and agents also renew themselves and expand their market by creating speculative manias.

The expansion of this culture of investment is strongly linked to and popularized by models of self-help. This phenomenon has "magically" been consolidated into a new model of society that supports the growth of the popular investor in Brazil and legitimizes personal economic activities that were not valued in this society.

In other words, this paper calls attention to future research that may provide additional empirical evidence that self-help has been moving from a parlor game to serious initiatives that force the state to institute rules of corporate governance and thus broaden the financial market.

24. Milton Gamez, "Os investidores estão voltando." in *Revista Bovespa*, Janeiro/Março, 2006. Online.

Part IV
Shifting Global Relations

15

Brazil and the Transatlantic Community

Thomas J. Trebat

Abstract: In this study, the changing role of the Brazilian state in matters of global economic and political governance is examined in an effort to define areas of cooperation and areas of conflict between Brazil and what is referred to in the paper as the transatlantic community, i.e., basically the United States and Europe. It is appropriate to talk of cooperation and also of conflict because, on the one hand, Brazil's model of economic and political development in recent decades has drawn it ever closer to the transatlantic community in numerous ways. On the other hand, conflict and misunderstanding arise because the relative success of the Brazilian model has also fed Brazil's long-held aspirations to be an independent regional and global power-broker outside the tutelage of the wealthier countries of the North.

As the global financial crisis of 2008–2009 recedes, it seems an opportune time to reconsider relations between Brazil, an emerging market that weathered the crisis relatively well, and the broader transatlantic community, especially the United States and the European Union. Could relations between Brazil and the West improve to a point that the stability of the global economy might increase? Brazil is hardly an unfriendly nation; in fact, its close integration with the global economy suggests quite the contrary. At the same time, Brazil has changed significantly over the last two decades of economic reform and political stability. Its long-held aspirations to be an important and independent regional and global power-broker are now more in line with its resources and self-confidence. This evolution is not fully appreciated in the North though awareness is spreading.

This paper sets forth the hypothesis that a new and more productive period in Brazil's relations with the US and Europe is possible and that this improved state of relations would contribute to a more stable global economy in the future. This positive outcome derives from numerous factors, most especially Brazil's peaceful rise to a more prominent global economic role and to political changes in the United States and, prospectively, in Brazil as well which faces presidential elections in October 2010. Specifically, the arrival of the Obama administration in 2008 and its promise of a new and less muscular, less unilateral emphasis in US foreign policy has been greeted with enthusiasm in Brazil even though several irritants have cropped up in the bilateral relationships recently. Meanwhile, in Brazil itself, the 2010 presidential elections will choose a successor to President Luis Inácio (Lula) da Silva who will be provided with a natural opportunity to re-examine the state of relations between Brazil and the countries of the North that it both admires and distrusts.

Brazil's foreign policy has incorporated traditionally a strong element of nationalism, especially with respect to creating and maintaining space for an industrial sector to develop in a global economy dominated by the United States and other center economies (Lafer, 2009). This tone of foreign policy was muted during the presidential terms of Fernando Henrique Cardoso (1994–2002), but regained emphasis and vigor during the two terms of President Lula (2002–2010) (Almeida, 2009). During this Lula period, Brazil's foreign policy elite in the foreign ministry (known as Itamaraty) has experienced turmoil as diplomats considered more amenable to forging closer alliances with the West have been pushed aside in favor of those considered more attuned to the objective of creating a distinct voice for Brazil in all global matters and a leader of the global South. This more recent, more autonomous tone in Brazilian foreign policy would seem to set Brazil farther apart from the United States and Europe in matters that go beyond Western hemispheric affairs, including the standoff with Iran regarding uranium enrichment in 2010 and the ongoing peace process in the Middle East where Brazil seeks an independent role as a mediator between Israel and Palestine.

While contentious issues will arise in the relationship between Brazil and the West, three observations about Brazil suggest that a closer, more productive engagement with the West is possible given Brazil's stature in global politics and economics. First, Brazil has developed, over several decades, a role as an effective bridge to the global South and an influential voice for more inclusive global economic management. Second, the global post-2008 financial crisis and its aftermath did reveal some weaknesses in the Brazilian economy which could limit its aspirations. These include deficient levels of savings, investment, technology, and human capital. In order to address these weaknesses, which are long-standing, Brazil is keenly aware of the need for a more productive interaction with the North. Third, ambivalence permeates Brazil's approach to global reform and governance. Brazil clearly benefits from the global status quo, i.e., integration with the world market and established institutions. At the same time, Brazil is anti-status quo, seeking opportunities to distance itself from Western ideals and institutions (Schirm, 2009).

Incorporating Brazil on its terms into established institutions of global governance will be challenging, but also worth the effort. The US and the global North have recognized this already to some extent by expanding the Group of Eight (G-8) group of leading world economies to a successor Group of Twenty (G-20) that prominently includes Brazil (and several other Latin American countries).[1] For the long run, the goal for the West should be to integrate Brazil as a partner into reformed multilateral institutions (in finance, trade, and regulation) as a means of assuring stable global growth on the basis of more inclusive global management.

To understand the reasoning behind this recommendation, three issues are considered:

- the areas of common interests in foreign economic policy between Brazil and the transatlantic community;
- the roots of Brazil's traditional divergences with the North; and
- the domestic dynamics in Brazil that are leading to a change in its world view. These issues are considered in turn in this paper, followed by recommendations on how to incorporate Brazil more effectively into a transatlantic partnership.

Areas of Close Cooperation

Brazil, Europe, and the US share fundamental foreign policy goals. Dealing with the post-2008 global crisis has reinforced a need for global policy

1. The G-20 group annually gathers finance ministers and central bank presidents to consider cooperation and policy coordination in view of the state of the global economy. It has been particularly active during the global economic crisis following the collapse of Lehman Brothers in 2008. The most recent meeting was held in Busan, South Korea, in June 2010. For more on this organization, see: http://www.g20.org/.

coordination. This has been particularly clear in the area of stimulating global demand where Brazil, a large trade surplus economy prior to the onset of the global crisis, has clearly made an effort to boost consumption and investment at home, thus contributing to the global economic recovery that is underway in mid-2010 (OECD, 2009).

Brazil was able in 2009–2010 to engage in counter-cyclical fiscal and monetary policies at home that stabilized most components of domestic demand. The Central Bank of Brazil, for example, has delivered substantial monetary stimulus through an accelerated program of interest rate reductions which brought overnight rates from pre-September 2008 levels close to 12 percent down to 8.65 percent at their low point in August 2009, one of the lowest levels for interest rates in recent memory in Brazil. Meanwhile, the government announced a number of emergency fiscal measures which amounted to about 3 percent of GDP, among these significant reductions in taxes on the purchase of new vehicles, increases in the minimum wage which boosted pension payments throughout the country, an acceleration in government infrastructure spending, and a rapid expansion of credit via the lending programs of the BNDES, Brazil's national development bank (OECD, 2009).

Brazil was able to deliver this stimulus to domestic demand while still recording a primary fiscal surplus (i.e., surplus on government operations before the payment of interest on the government debt) in each month following the crisis. Thus, Brazil benefited during the crisis from a relatively strong starting position in terms of the government fiscal accounts (see Figure 15-1).

The results of the government's aggressive stimulus policies, while not without some risks of overheating the domestic economy leading to inflation, were impressive. Economic growth in Brazil was set to expand by about 7 percent in 2010 after plunging and virtually coming to a halt in late 2008 and early 2009. While Brazil experienced a great fright, this economic recovery was one of the fastest anywhere in the world in the wake of the financial crisis (see Figure 15-2 below on GDP growth). Moreover, as the financial crisis receded and GDP rebounded, the jobless rate in Brazil approached an historic low in 2010. The level of industrial production, which had plunged in the post-Lehman days of global financial turmoil, fully recovered lost ground and moved higher by mid-2010.

The most revealing indication of Brazil's contribution to global stimulus was the shift in the current account deficit of the balance of payments from

FIGURE 15-1. Government Primary Budget Surplus, 2007–2010

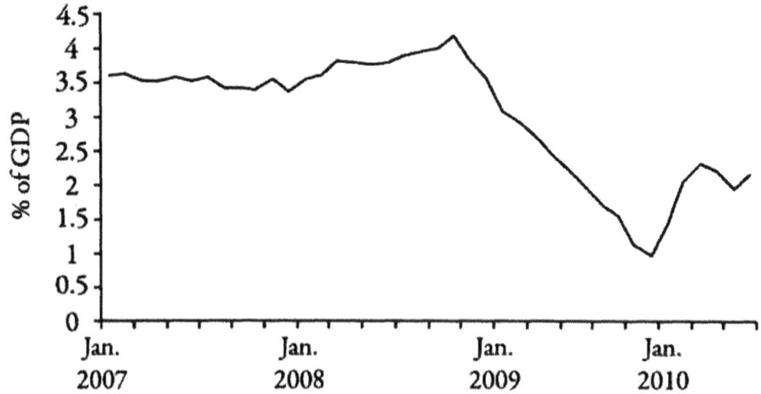

Source: Central Bank of Brazil.

a small surplus in the heady, pre-Lehman days of 2007, to a deficit estimated at about $40 billion, close to 3 percent of GDP in 2010 (see Figure 15-3). The Brazilian exchange rate which, like most non-dollar global currencies, depreciated sharply after September 2008, soon recovered to pre-crisis levels as global investors expressed confidence in the recovery prospects of the Brazilian economy (see Figure 15-4) Lula had boasted at the outset of the crisis that Brazil would be among the first economies to recover; in this respect, he appears to have been correct. In the process, Brazil not only contributed (albeit modestly because its size in the global economy is not large) to global recovery, it also strengthened its hand for future. discussions with the United States and Europe on reform of the global economy.

One of these areas for reform will be the shared governance of the main institutions of the global economy, including the International Monetary Fund (IMF). Brazil has also been an important part of global conversations to bolster the IMF as a source of emergency financial liquidity to the most vulnerable emerging economies. In 2009, Brazil agreed to subscribe to $10 billion in IMF notes in order to bolster the Fund's Special Liquidity Facility designed to help emerging economies hard hit by the global financial crisis. According to IMF Managing Director Dominique Strauss-Kahn, through this action to help other countries weather the effects of the global crisis, Brazil was not only "fulfilling the commitment of G-20 leaders," but reaffirming "its strong role as a leading emerging market economy."[2]

2. See the IMF press release: http://www.imf.org/external/np/sec/pr/2009/pr09207.htm.

FIGURE 15-2. Real GDP Growth Before and After Sept. 2008 (Quarterly Growth at Annual Rate)

Source: IBGE

While Brazil and the wealthier countries have found common ground in global finance, the level of congruence is far less in terms of global management of the world trade system. Brazil has often found itself at odds with the United States and the West, in fact, allying itself with China and India, to resist reducing tariff barriers to permit greater access to their domestic markets. At the same time, Brazil has been aggressive, within the rules of the World Trade Organization, in efforts to protect its exporters from unfair trade practices by the West. In mid-2010 Brazil and the US were locked in a dispute about subsidized US cotton production which has caused harm to Brazilian producers (the dispute was settled by the WTO in Brazil's favor in 2010 although Brazil has refrained from adopting the retaliatory measures to which it is entitled by virtue of the WTO's finding).

The recurrent conflict between Brazil and the United States on trade matters is real, but it also masks large areas of congruence in global trade. While China has moved quickly up the chart in terms of Brazil's largest export markets and may well continue to climb, trade with the developed markets of the United States and Europe is still more important for Brazil. The US and Europe as recently as 2008 still account for some 35 percent of Brazil's total trade[3] (see Table 15-1 below). Brazil obviously has an interest

3. Cooperation in trade matters should certainly not be overstated as conflicts occur frequently, often assuming a high profile in Brazil.

FIGURE 15-3. Balance of Payments Current Account 2007–2010 (Accumulated last 12 months)

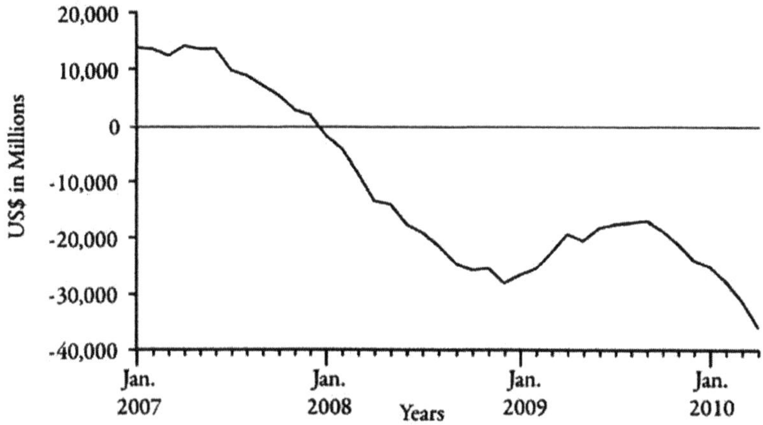

Source: Central Bank of Brazil (http://www.bcb.gov.br/?SERIEBALPAG).

in maintaining market access to these rich country markets and recognizes that the quid pro quo will be (eventually) improved access to its own market. Moreover, it is interesting that Brazil and the United States are the largest agricultural exporters in the world. While they clash on issues of industrial protection and the liberalization of trade in services, Brazil and the US have basically closed ranks in terms of the need for liberalization of global agricultural trade. It is this shared interest by US and Brazil in opening up global trade in agriculture (in particular, by breaking down protectionist barriers in Europe) that could provide the emphasis for the conclusion of the current round of global trade talks, known as the Development Round or Doha Round (these talks are basically deadlocked eight years after the launch of the Round in 2002).[4]

Foreign Investment Ties

Brazil's stable laws on foreign direct investment stand in sharp contrast to the wave of populist nationalizations of foreign and domestic companies that is occurring in Venezuela, Ecuador, Bolivia, and Argentina. Europe, the US, and Brazil are tied together as well by the accumulated stock of foreign direct investment in Brazil and the accompanying connections that this

4. In the 2008 negotiations of the Doha Round, Brazil actually broke ranks with more protectionist emerging markets, such as Argentina, China, and India, in order to support a last-minute compromise with the wealthy countries that might have given new energy to the talks.

FIGURE 15-4. Exchange Rates (Reais per Dollar), 2008-2010

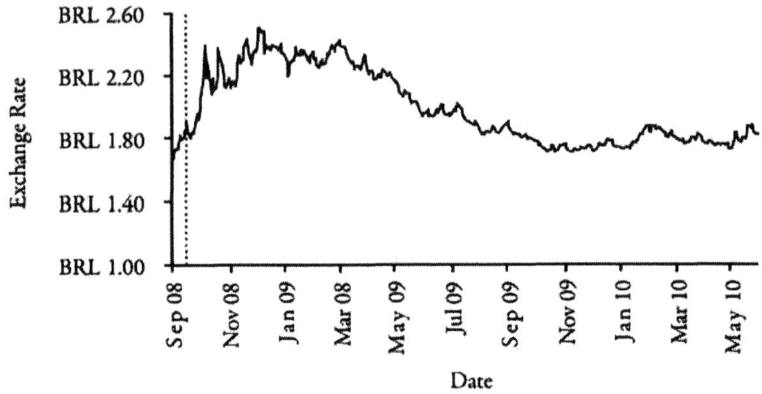

Source: Central Bank of Brazil (http://www4.bcb.gov.br/pec/taxas/port/ptaxmpesq.asp?id=txcotacao&id=txcotacao).

inflow brings in terms of access to technology, management, and global marketing networks. The overall net foreign investment in Brazil in a recent (1999-2009) period was about $265 billion; the share of the US, Europe, and Japan in the total foreign investment in Brazil is close to two-thirds, with the US accounting for the largest single-country share, followed by Spain (ECLAC, 2010: 62). Most major US and European multinationals

TABLE 15-1. Structure of Brazilian Trade in 2008

Share in world total exports (%)	1.23	Share in world total imports (%)	1.11
By main commodity group (% of total)		By main commodity group (% of total)	
Agricultural products	31.0	Agricultural products	5.6
Fuels and mining products	22.2	Fuels and mining products	23.9
Manufactures	43.7	Manufactures	70.5
By main destination (% of total)		By main origin (% of total)	
1. European Union (27)	23.5	1. European Union (27)	20.9
2. United States	14.0	2. United States	14.9
3. Argentina	8.9	3. China	11.6
4. China	8.3	4. Argentina	7.7
5. Japan	3.1	5. Japan	3.9

Source: WTO Trade Profiles 2009 (http://stat.wto.org/CountryProfile/WSDBCountryPFView.aspx?Country=BR).

have operations of some importance in Brazil; US firms have been particularly active in the expansion of Brazil's agribusiness. The huge investment push by Spanish companies in the late 1990s and early 2000s has led to the achievement by these companies of truly dominant positions in key sectors, including banking and telecommunications, led by such names as Banco Santander and Telefónica. By creating competitive pressures in areas of the Brazilian economy long dominated by US firms, the rise in the importance of Spanish firms balances the large US investment presence in Brazil and leads to new linkages for Brazil to the global economy (ECLAC, 2010).

The presence of foreign firms, mainly from the West, is expected to increase substantially in the oil sector as Brazil moves to develop its large, "pre-salt" oil reserves which are located in very deep waters off the southeastern coast. While the state-owned oil company, Petrobras, will take the lead in developing these oil reserves, Brazil will also rely substantially on foreign investment and technology in what is likely to be a gargantuan investment effort. Petrobras' own expected capital expenditure program, mostly to develop these reserves, is anticipated to be on the order of US$225 billion and that is just over the next five years. In September 2010, Petrobras raised almost US$70 billion of this amount in a single global share offering, the largest operation of its type in history. While this indicates very significant investor interest indeed in Petrobras' future, the Brazilian government will also be required to put substantial investment resources of its own into Petrobras to finance the pre-salt investment program.

Foreign oil companies will be invited to participate on a production-sharing basis in the development of these reserves, and foreign companies, mainly from the West, will be crucial to Brazil as well in the supply of drilling equipment and transportation logistics. While the emphasis in developing the pre-salt reserves will be on Petrobras and state-led investment, Brazil will be far more open to foreign participation in the pre-salt region than would be imaginable under the more restrictive foreign investment regimes in place in the oil sectors of other Latin American nations, notably Mexico and Venezuela.

While Brazil has been traditionally a recipient of foreign direct inflows, it has also emerged in the last decade as a source of direct foreign investment in other nations of growing importance. In something of a twist, Brazil has also spawned a large number of so-called "multilatinas," domestically based corporate giants such as Vale and Gerdau who have expanded aggressively into the US, Europe and elsewhere (ECLAC, 2010; Brainard et al., 2009). Petrobras is, by a wide margin, the most aggressive of the Brazilian firms in pursuing opportunities abroad, but the list of companies with important foreign operations is growing as Brazil's global connections broaden and deepen (see Table 15-2).

TABLE 15-2. Brazilian Firms with Large Foreign Operations in 2009

Firm	Sales 2009 (US$mm)	Foreign Sales (%)	Investment Abroad (%)	Workers Abroad (%)	Sector
Petrobras	101,948	29	34	10	Oil and Gas
Itaú-Unibanco	44,242	11	3	10	Banking
Vale	27,852	35	47	20	Mining
Grupo JBS	20,458	85	85	77	Agribusiness
Gerdau	15,242	53	58	46	Iron and Steel
Camargo-Correa	6,950	22	47	28	Construction
Embraer	6,812	86	45	13	Aerospace
Cia Siderurgica Nacional	6,305	23	13	6	Iron and Steel
Tam	5,780	31	5	6	Airlines
Sadia	5,577	39	40	35	Agribusiness
Marfrig	5,317	39	40	35	Agribusiness
Odebrecht	4,800	69	56	49	Construction
Andrade Gutierrez	4,500	15	10	5	Construction
Votorantim	3,110	36	48	35	Cement

Source: United Nations, ECLAC, *Foreign Direct Investment in Latin America and the Caribbean*, 2009, p. 62.

Climate Change Talks

The development of alternative energy sources and approaches to climate risk mitigation seem to be drawing Brazil closer to the transatlantic community after a long history of tense relations. Brazil is justly renowned for its pioneering research and production of biofuels; a 2007 agreement with the US pledged joint efforts to develop a global market for ethanol and other biofuels. More generally, Brazil's supply of energy has always featured a relatively high percentage of supply from renewable sources, including hydroelectricity and ethanol.

Brazil's position on climate change and deforestation has also evolved in ways that favor a global accord on the reduction of carbon emissions to move beyond the 1998 Kyoto protocol of the United Nations Framework Convention on Climate Change. Neither Brazil nor the United States ever became signatories of the Kyoto protocol, so the evolution of their respective positions in future climate talks is a matter of great international concern. At the inter-governmental climate meetings in Copenhagen in December 2009, Brazil surprised world opinion by announcing planned cuts in carbon emissions that went well beyond earlier expectations of what Brazil would be willing to offer. In announcing its intent to achieve a 35% cut in annual carbon emissions by 2020, Brazil has sought to seize the initiative by laying down a clear challenge to the rich nations (most especially, the United States) which have been reluctant to embrace such an ambitious target for emission reductions.

About one-half of Brazil's planned reduction in emissions is slated to come through a reduction in deforestation.[5] While Brazil's management of the Amazon forest is likely to remain controversial, recent advances in satellite technology to detect hot spots and improvements in land titling process in the Amazon to more clearly define ownership and discourage illegal economic activities have allowed the Brazilian government to claim a substantial reduction in rates of deforestation due to illegal logging and ranching. Brazil's evolving role toward greater cooperation with the global community in matters of climate change is more than a tactical move to deflect international criticism of its forest management policies and of its regional development policies which have featured road construction in the Amazon and dam construction which have led to flooding in vast areas. A greater ecological awareness has permeated Brazilian policy for at least the last fifteen years. As one symbol of the evolution of public opinion in Brazil on environmental matters, Lula's former minister of the environment, Marina Silva, is mounting a serious campaign for the presidency of Brazil in 2010 as a candidate of the Green Party.

DIVERGENCES WITH THE NORTH: BRAZIL'S SOUTH-SOUTH ORIENTATION

In both political and economic matters, Brazil and the global North are not always in agreement about how the world should work or be governed. Strong evidence exists, in fact, that Brazil seeks to play an important role as an independent power broker on a global scale and a bridge to the global South. In order to do so, it is not reluctant to stake out policy positions that are at odds with the United States and other global powers on important matters.

This independent role in global matters that Brazil seeks to play was clearly on view in early 2010 when Brazil, acting in close partnership with Turkey, brokered a proposed agreement on nuclear enrichment with Iran which was intended to head off tough new UN sanctions against Iran which the US had been proposing. In Brazil's view, it was acting as part of a good faith effort to promote dialogue and to avert a rush toward sanctions,

5. http://www.guardian.co.uk/environment/2009/nov/10/brazil-emissions.

increased conflict between Iran and West, and, inevitably, the possibility of another war. Obviously, its actions (along with those of its partner, Turkey) were seen as a rebuke of United States diplomacy and a criticism of faulty US intelligence which had helped pave the way to a war in Iraq which Brazil opposed. Brazil's mediation efforts in this case apparently came to naught. The US pronounced them "dangerously naïve" and the UN Security Council (with Brazil, a temporary member, opposed) promptly went ahead with broad sanctions against Iran. The upshot is that while the Brazilian-Turkish effort fell short of its goals and Brazil was exposed in its aftermath to criticism both domestic and foreign, the action did send a strong signal to the global community that Brazil's leadership ambitions are not geographically circumscribed to its own neighborhood in South America. In particular, Brazil will continue to look for ways to play a constructive role more broadly in the Middle East, including by playing a mediating role in negotiations between Israel and Palestine.

Looking more broadly at Brazilian foreign policy, areas of disagreement between the United States and Brazil in hemispheric affairs appear to abound. In the case of the Honduran political crisis of 2009, for example, Brazil refused to go along with the US decision to recognize the government elected in Honduras in November 2009 and as of mid-2010 was one of a relatively small number of Latin American nations not to have re-established relations with Honduras. Brazil's embrace of Cuba and the Castro brothers has been another bone of contention with the United States; Brazil has been a supporter of Cuba's readmission to the Organization of American States, a position clearly at odds with the long-standing policy of the United States, and maintains active trade and diplomatic relations with the island in the face of the long-standing US embargo.[6]

In other hemispheric political matters as well, Brazil does seem to be pursuing an agenda that is not consistent with US policy and which is designed to maintain a certain distance between the two countries. For example, Brazil is the chief architect between a new regional organization created in 2008 and known as the South American Union of Nations (or UNASUR using the Spanish acronym) which specifically excludes the United States (and Mexico, too, a potential rival for regional leadership which Brazil perceives as too close to the United States).[7] UNASUR could be seen as a regional structure to mediate conflicts in South America and, as such, an

6. In 2009, Brazil was a strong supporter of an OAS decision to lift Cuba's suspension from the OAS, though this did not automatically open the door to renewed membership (see: http://www.cnn.com/2009/WORLD/americas/06/04/cuba.oas/index.html).

alternative to the Organization of American States, long dominated by the United States and US foreign policy concerns.

Still other examples of Brazil's regional assertion of leadership would be its decision, backed by Argentina, to invite Venezuela to join Mercosul, the customs union arrangement comprised heretofore of Argentina, Brazil, Paraguay, and Uruguay. The action was probably intended as a counterpoint to US policies to isolate and ignore President Hugo Chavez of Venezuela. Along similar lines, Brazil has expressed its concern to the United States regarding the proposed creation of US military bases in Colombia. In all these matters of political governance in the hemisphere, Brazil seems to be signaling that while it values good relations with the United States, it also feels free to challenge the US position as it sees fit.

Similarly in many issues of global economic diplomacy, Brazil can often seen to be at odds with the United States, and the West more generally, even while valuing the benefits of closer integration with the global economy.

The predominant economic ideology underlying Brazil's approach in economic matters could be referred to as a national development mindset, rooted in a world view that global economic relations reinforced an unequal power distribution between the developed and richer countries of the center North and the capital-dependent and technology-challenged countries of the periphery South. The traditional foreign policy framework of a large divide between the North and South (also characterized as a division between industrial powers and commodity producers such as Brazil and most of the other economies of Latin America) has led Brazil practically since the 1930s to be very protectionist in terms of trade policies to promote development of its industrial sector, in particular, by shielding industry in São Paulo (and elsewhere in Brazil, of course) from competition deemed to be unfair coming from companies based in the North (Baer, 2008).

Buffered from foreign competition by a complex set of tariffs, non-tariff barriers, and export promotion schemes, the favored sectors in Brazilian industry have always included automobiles, electric and electronic devices, textiles, clothing, and footwear (Motta Veiga, 2009). While tariffs were reduced unilaterally through a broad program of trade liberalization introduced by the Collor administration in the early 1990s, protection from international trade competition remains relatively high in Brazil.

7. For more on UNASUR, see: http://www.upi.com/Top_News/Special/2010/06/16/Ambitious-UNASUR-seeks-to-make-impact-without-conflict/UPI-62331276717712/.

To be fair, the value-added weighted-average tariff in Brazil has been reduced substantially since the late 1980s, from 57% to about 13% in the early 2000s (Moreira, 2009: 139). While the subsequent years under Lula saw some reversal in trade policy liberalization, including an increase in tariffs to 35% for some apparel and footwear, the Lula administration has not significantly increased protection. However, it should be emphasized that protection remains relatively high in international comparative perspective and that Brazil has ruled out any further reduction or rationalization of its tariff structure unless and until a broad multilateral agreement is reached in the context of the Doha Round. Moreover, the stated level of average protection does understate, in some cases significantly understate, the actual protection provided to Brazilian industry. If the concept of effective protection is used, which takes into account not only tariffs on final products, but tariffs as well on the inputs used to produce these products, protection for certain important branches of Brazilian industry is extraordinarily high, e.g., almost 140% in the case of passenger cars and light trucks (Moreira, 2009: 142-43). While economists would argue that tariffs of these levels is damaging to economic growth, the need to maintain protection is close to an article of faith among both São Paulo elites and general public opinion in Brazil.

The deeply ingrained belief in Brazil that increased global engagement with the North will inevitably (and unfairly) reduce the "space" for autonomous industrial development has been reinforced by a general onset of "reform fatigue" that followed the Cardoso era in which an aggressive pace of economic reform failed to raise the level of Brazilian economic growth. This belief has stiffened Brazil's inherent tendency to be dubious about the benefits of bilateral or regional free trade agreements with the North. In the post-2002 period of the Lula administration, this traditional tendency is most in evidence in the downgrading of bilateral US-Brazil trade talks and discussions between Mercosul and the European Union on a free trade agreement. Of course, and in addition, Brazil's opposition to the mid-1990s US initiative to negotiate a Free Trade Area of the Americas (or FTAA) eventually and inevitably led to a sidelining of the initiative and its eventual abandonment.

Tensions on trade issues are also evident at the multilateral or global level. Brazil has resisted efforts to negotiate new disciplines in the World Trade Organization in such sensitive areas as investment, trade in services, and government procurement, all of which are intended to remove non-tariff barriers to global trade in goods and services. As Schirm reminds us, Brazil has been instrumental in successfully organizing a larger group of emerging market economies (including India and China) in the context of the Doha Round talks to oppose particular European Union and United States initiatives seen as tilting the deck in favor of developed country interests at the expense of the South (Schirm, 2009).

Brazil has complemented what might be perceived as something less than wholehearted engagement in global trade talks by pursuing other, more limited and region-specific accords that further its goal of being seen as a leader of the global South interested above all in South-South economic cooperation. Brazil has embraced its association with the so-called BRIC group of nations (including Russia, India, and China) and promoted greater collaboration in trade and economic matters among this potentially powerful set of economies in a series of trade initiative international summits which have taken place since 2008. Brazil's India-Brazil-South Africa Initiative is an innovative structure launched in 2006 which seeks to knit together south economies which traditionally have had very limited trade and commercial interaction.[8] Brazil has reached out to sign agreements with minor countries as well, including Cuba and Morocco, with which even the potential for trade is limited. More broadly, Brazil has engaged in an ambitious program to build its diplomatic presence through Africa as a means to improve trade relations and to seek the support of these nations for Brazilian initiatives in international forums, such as the United Nations.

To round out the picture, various Brazilian initiatives in South America also embody the South-South thrust in foreign policy. Obviously, Brazil has worked hard to keep the Mercosul arrangement together despite a slow pace of growth in trade between Brazil and Argentina over the last decade and despite the unhappiness with the regional tariff structure expressed by the more junior partners, especially Uruguay, but also Paraguay. As mentioned, the initiative to invite Venezuela to participate reflects Brazil's long-term foreign policy goals although the economic rationale to include Venezuela in the arrangement is not crystal clear as trade ties are quite limited. The UNASUR arrangement, mentioned above, also has an economic component in that it is designed to help promote infrastructure projects, in energy and transportation especially, that would lead to a greater integration of the South American economies traditionally separated by vast physical distances.

To conclude this section on Brazil's South-South orientation and how this sets the country apart from the agenda of the richer nations, one might

8. For more on IBSA, see http://www.ibsa-trilateral.org/.

consider Brazil's evolving role in the G-20 group of powerful economies, the successor to the G-7, an informal club of the largest economies in the world. Along with China, Brazil seems destined to be the influential voice on behalf of the global issues of greatest concern to the emerging nations. These issues would include liberalization in agricultural trade, which would benefit most of the poorer nations of the world, while including also Brazil. The issues would include reform of the leading institutions of international economic governance, especially the International Monetary Fund and the World Bank, in which the voting power has always tilted heavily toward the US, Europe, and Japan. Brazil has long called for a larger voting share in both the Fund and the Bank with the stated intent of altering the mission of these institutions toward development and economic assistance issues which are of primary concern to the developing countries.

BRAZIL'S CHANGING WORLD VIEW

In the first two sections, two somewhat opposing forces shaping Brazil's role in global economy and politics have been examined. In Part I, the numerous and powerful forces leading to a greater integration of Brazil within the global community seem to indicate clearly that the country has much to gain indeed from greater globalization. In Part II, the strong pull of Brazil's history, including decades-long traditions of foreign policy, seems to set up countervailing pressures upon Brazil to set itself apart from the North and to assert its leadership of the global South. The interplay of these two factors could, at first glance, create a somewhat muddled image for Brazil in global affairs. In particular, is this new Brazil a reliable partner for the United States and the transatlantic community? Or is it an emerging new power with its own distinct policy goals and also with the resources and confidence to pursue an agenda that might conflict with the West in important areas?

The answer to this apparent puzzle is likely to be found in dynamics within Brazil itself, in particular, in profound alterations in Brazil's view of the world and its role within it. On balance, understanding this changing perception requires a closer look at what is happening within Brazil itself. The argument will be made that these changes, which are unfolding in Brazil and shaping both elite and popular opinion, are likely to move Brazil more firmly into the transatlantic community with benefits for both.

The changing nature of the Brazilian economy itself is one factor favoring greater, rather than lesser, integration with the West. One of these factors has already been alluded to—Brazil recognized the need for shared management of global risks in the post-2008 financial crisis and has been able to make positive contributions to domestic and international stability despite the serious nature of the shock Brazil endured. One of the reasons for Brazil's relatively safe passage through the global crisis is the economic stability produced over at least the two decades (or, roughly, since the Collor administration in the early 1990s) by the application of a rules-based approach to economic management. These rules, or economic practices, have consolidated in Brazil a model of economic management that approximates the Western ideal of a market-oriented economy with an important role for government as a regulator of economic activity and provider of social services.

Some of the hallmarks of Brazilian economic management have included a concern for macroeconomic stability as one of the foundations of sustained economic growth. This stability had eluded Brazil in the decades that followed the decline of the import-substitution model of economic growth after the 1970s. The essential policy components have included fiscal, monetary, and exchange rate policies that have produced in Brazil relatively low government budget deficits, a reduced risk of sovereign debt problems, low and stable rates of inflation, and a large supply of foreign exchange reserves. The overall impact of these policies was to permit a period of strong economic growth in Brazil in the period from 2003–2008. While growth plunged in 2009 in line with the downturn in the global economy, Brazil's resilience because of its improved economic policies and the large accumulated stock of international reserves effectively buffered Brazil during the global turmoil of 2008–2009. In 2008, one of the major rating agencies recognized the policy improvements in the Brazilian economy by assigning an investment-grade rating for Brazil's sovereign debt which has meant that Brazil can now access international capital markets (on which it is dependent for development finance) on more favorable terms.

Important changes are occurring in the external structure of the Brazilian economy that are leading to a fuller engagement with the world economy. Following the strong surge in exports in 2003-08, much of it the result of Chinese demand for the commodity exports in which Brazil specializes, the importance of the external sector to Brazil's growth and stability is now more evident. Combined with a very vigorous growth in imports during the same period of the early 2000s, the surge in exports has contributed to boosting the openness of the Brazilian economy; the ratio of external trade to GDP, the main measure of how open an economy is, has increased to 25 percent of GDP in the late 2000s, close to the level of other large economies, and almost twice the level of a decade ago in Brazil when Brazil was far more closed to the outside world in economic terms.[9]

Much of Brazil's export growth is commodity-based, including both industrial raw materials, such as iron ore and agricultural products, including soybeans and meat products. Motta Veiga reports that agribusiness exports grew at annual rates in excess of 16 percent in the mid-2000s, with significant diversification occurring in terms of markets reached and products exported (2009: 125-26).[10] The author further observes that Brazil is the world leader in such exports as sugar, ethanol, beef, and chicken and among the top exporters of soybeans and orange juice.

In the past, Brazil may have been reluctant to embrace this role of a food and raw material exporter to the rest of the world as it seemed that the economy would be limited by a specialization in sectors involving low levels of technology and innovation and, consequently, generating few spillover benefits to the rest of the economy. This attitude seems to be fading as export growth, based on both agribusiness and industrial exports, is seen not only as a means of relieving Brazil's chronic foreign exchange problems, effectively insulating the economy from the periodic external shocks which in the past, such as in the 1980s and again in the late 1990s, have cut off capital inflows to Brazil and interrupted economic growth. In other words, Brazil's growing success as an exporter has allowed the country to diminish one of the principal obstacles to sustained growth which in the past has been the perception by international investors that the country was permanently on the cusp of sovereign debt problems. It has probably also helped that the agribusiness boom has acted to spread prosperity regionally across many areas of the interior of Brazil and that much of the boom has been based on the successful application of technology to permit the cultivation of semi-arid land. Much of the research on which this technology has been based is authentically Brazilian having been produced in the laboratories of EMBRAPA, a state-supported research entity dedicated to agriculture (Mueller, 2009).

9. Ipeadata. The overall level of openness of the Brazilian economy is still relatively low compared to other fast growing emerging economies, however.

10. In the period from 2001-2005, for example, growth to developing markets (including, importantly, China) grew at even higher rates of 26 percent annually.

With the success of Brazil's trade policies and the growth and global integration of the economy, new forces may be emerging within the Brazilian business community which could be in favor of freer trade, possibly countering to some extent the still strong influence of the São Paulo elites and the foreign policy establishment. Motta Veiga cites the example of the Confederação Nacional de Indústria (CNI, or National Confederation of Industry) which in 2006 produced an important document arguing for a new strategy of trade negotiations with countries such as Mexico which would be based solely on the economic benefits accruing to Brazil, including greater access to larger markets for its exports. He adds: "It is the first time that the Brazilian manufacturing sector has formally adopted an offensive stance in trade negotiations and pushed for a comprehensive and ambitious agreement" (Motta Veiga, 2009: 127).

Moreover, the emergence of a global agribusiness based in Brazil has raised the profile of sectors which would benefit very importantly from greater liberalization of global trade, thus infusing what is called an offensive or market-opening element in Brazil's global trade posture as opposed to the more traditional, defensive agenda focused on protecting Brazilian industry from external competition.

Along the same lines, the important growth of the large Brazilian companies with a global reach, companies such as Gerdau, Odebrecht, and Vale, is also challenging the way in which Brazilians think about the role of multinational enterprise and the ease with which it should be allowed to cross and operate beyond borders. While Brazil does not have an official policy to support the expansion of private-sector firms abroad, the growing success of these firms and their increasing presence abroad is a matter of national pride. As a matter of conjecture, the growth of these "national champions" in international markets is likely to make Brazil more, rather than less, likely to back global efforts to facilitate international investment flows.

The case of the state-owned oil company, Petrobras, is a special case of a multinational which shows the extent to which Brazil's role in international investment flows is changing from passive recipient to active participant exposed to the risks and rewards of such activity. Petrobras was, by a large margin, the most important investor in oil and gas properties in neighboring Bolivia when the newly elected government of President Evo Morales in May 2006 nationalized all fields and ordered the army to occupy all foreign-owned facilities. At the time, Petrobras' investment in gas properties in Bolivia was valued at about $1.5 billion. Resisting calls to take harsh measures against Bolivia to retaliate for the nationalization, Brazil eventually negotiated an agreement later in 2006 that essentially acquiesced in Bolivia's sovereign actions in exchange for a share of profits and a continued management role in the subsidiary. The company continues to operate in Bolivia and remains responsible for the flow of most gas exports to Brazil.

An Agenda for Cooperation

In sum, the argument is that while Brazil will continue to seek a "world without the West" and to strengthen its South-South ties, the factors promoting Brazil's greater global integration are very powerful. The predominant tendency for Brazil in the future is in this light likely to be one of increasing cooperation, rather than confrontation with the United States and the richer countries of the West. Because Brazil's long-term strategic interests overlap to an important degree with those of the North, it makes sense for the transatlantic community to incorporate and accommodate Brazil within the institutions that govern the global economy rather than exclude or isolate Brazil. A number of policy areas come to mind where greater inclusion of Brazil would be helpful. Some of these are reviewed below by way of conclusion.

Reform of global governance

Brazil has been a leading voice for increased representation of the developing countries in global economic decision-making and norm-setting. Reform of the IMF is the starting point. The reform agenda includes increasing the resources of the Fund, revising conditionality requirements, and improving its governance to increase the voting shares of countries other than the United States, Europe, and Japan. The idea that the IMF should be governed more democratically so that its actions more appropriately reflect the interests of the global economic community, not just the wealthier countries, gained new urgency in the context of the post-2008 global financial crisis. Provided that its own voting share increased in the Fund were to increase, Brazil would be very supportive of reforms to place the IMF at the center of global policy coordination with an enhanced ability to lend more freely to poorer economies grappling with sharp declines in government revenues and export earnings following future global financial crises.

Reform of global financial regulation

Global financial sector reform is needed to create a well functioning network of national and regional authorities to prevent a reoccurrence of the 2008 financial crisis attributed to poor financial regulation and excessive risk-taking by international banks. In this area of international financial flows in which North-South cooperation is essential, Brazil has been in the forefront of this debate to provide truly international supervision of financial institutions with a global reach as these institutions have proven to be channels by which financial shocks originating in the North are transmitted quickly to the South. Brazil's credibility in this area was enhanced by the relatively smooth passage of its own financial sector through the post-2008 financial crisis which was attributable to the broad ranging nature of financial regulation in Brazil. Some of the elements of the Brazilian regulatory framework, such as the comprehensive oversight of all financial institutions by a single regulator (the Central Bank) are aspects of financial reform that were absent in the regulatory systems of the United States and other richer nations prior to the financial crisis (Meirelles, 2010).

A new consensus on global trade liberalization

An obvious area for cooperation would be for the transatlantic community to enlist Brazil's support in stemming the tide toward increased protectionism that has been spawned by the decline of global trade in 2009. Brazil is well placed in global trade talks to bridge longstanding differences between North and South particularly in the areas of market access and agricultural trade. Elements of a global grand bargain are liberalized trade in agricultural products, including ethanol, in exchange for significant movement by emerging economies on industrial sector liberalization and trade-related disciplines, such as government procurement. The evolution of trade strategy in Brazil itself points in this direction (Motta Veiga, 2009: 128-36) If so, and if Brazil signals a clearer intent to make concessions in exchange for benefits, it could have a powerful impact on the G-20 grouping of nations within the broader WTO talks.

A global framework on energy and climate change

Brazil plays an important role in global energy and climate change discussions, policy areas where more North-South collaboration is needed. Brazil is a leader in the use and production of biofuels, including ethanol, and is committed to further research and to the development of global markets for trade in greener forms of energy. In March 2007, the US and Brazil reached a landmark agreement for shared research and technology in the production and international trade of biofuels.[11] These types of agreements between the world's leading producers of ethanol could well be revisited and to expanded to include other countries. On climate change, Brazil plays a role as steward of the resources of the Amazon region. Perhaps because of this global responsibility and the perception that this responsibility places limits on its own domestic development objectives, Brazil has not been an enthusiastic participant in climate change discussions. As discussed earlier, however, Brazilian public opinion and public policies appear to be changing. Brazil made a bold policy proposal at the 2009 Copenhagen meetings to success a successor global agreement to the Kyoto Protocol. This change in Brazilian policies has coincided with the advent of the Obama administration in the United States and its greater amenability to accepting limits on emissions as part of a global compact.

Development beyond trade: new sources of financing for emerging economies

The post-2008 global crisis has pointed to the need for more secure sources of long-term financing for low-income emerging economies, especially in periods during which private financing via bank lending or bond markets dries up. Brazil itself in 2008 benefited during the crisis from availability of dollar financing in a currency swap arrangement with the Federal Reserve Bank of the United States. In part, the global task involves creating a more important and permanent role for multilateral and regional development banks, a position that Brazil has favored through increasing the capital of these global institutions. Obviously, strengthened capital for the World Bank and the Inter-American Development Bank, among other institutions, would improve their ability to extend loans for development purposes. These entities could also prove useful, as they have in the case of Brazil, in helping Latin American economies to strengthen their financial markets and develop their own bond markets.

The point is that a more balanced flow of investment financing, one which assures a more reliable source of credit to the emerging economies

11. For background, see http://www.nytimes.com/2007/03/03/business/worldbusiness/03ethanol.html.

than private markets are capable of providing, could produce a more stable world economy by directing more surplus savings to economies (such as Brazil's) where the rates or return on investment are the highest. Besides being an advocate for less developed emerging economies, Brazil itself could obviously benefit from a more powerful and better capitalized network of multilateral and regional official lenders as it seeks to overcome chronically low levels of public investment, including poor economic and social infrastructure.

While for Brazil and for many developing countries, the issue of greater reliance for development finance on official lenders raises longstanding issues of conditionality, i.e., that increased lending will come with demands for changed public policies that developing countries will view as impinging on their sovereignty. In part, these concerns could be addressed by increasing the voting rights of the developing countries. In part, as well, conditionality may be for developing countries the lesser of two evils for developing economies, especially when private sector financing is suddenly not available due to a global financial crisis and the poorer economies have limited resources of their own to fall back upon.

CONCLUSIONS

Brazil's peaceful rise in global affairs makes it an attractive partner in global initiatives for the US and the EU. While often wishing to project an image of anti–status quo, the argument here is that Brazil actually would welcome a more meaningful role in managing and reforming the institutions and practices of global governance. Indeed, the main objective of its foreign policy has long been to obtain a permanent seat on the Security Council of the United Nations. While this may or may not be a realistic goal in the foreseeable future, it does demonstrate Brazil's commitment to multilateralism and the objective should not be seen as an impediment to improved cooperation between Brazil and the United States. The shock of the global crisis underlines needed reforms in global governance and the positive role that Brazil can play as a nation closely tied to the West and yet able and willing to act as a bridge to the global South.

16

Regional Integration: Political Uses of Energy Policy

Christine A. Gustafson and Leslie Elliott Armijo

Abstract: This chapter analyzes the role of the Brazilian state in regional energy policy from 1990 to 2009. It compares Brazil's vision of energy cooperation in the Americas with those of two other important states, the United States and Venezuela. It finds that in each case, energy policy forms an integral piece of the countries' larger plans for organizing the region. It argues further that the Brazilian government's vision of "South American" energy integration may be more likely to be realized than either the "hemispheric" integration plans of the United States or the "Latin/Caribbean" energy framework of Venezuela.

State goals for the energy sector are important to any consideration of the contemporary economic role of the Brazilian state. This chapter examines one often-overlooked aspect of national energy planning. We ask how the ongoing competition among Western Hemisphere governments over the contours of 21st century international cooperation has influenced energy sector development. That is, we analyze energy policy from the perspective of foreign policy. We find, first, that contemporary "national" energy strategies form integral pieces of states' larger plans for organizing the region. Thus the United States, Venezuela, and Brazil each promote distinct regional cooperation projects that imply non-trivial differences in hemispheric energy integration. Our second, and subsidiary, thesis is necessarily speculative, foreshadowing rather than reporting on actual events. Our reading of evidence suggests that key aspects of the Brazilian government's vision of "South American" energy integration may be more likely to be realized than either the "hemispheric" integration plans of the US or the "Latin/Caribbean" energy framework envisioned by Venezuela.

The chapter has six parts. Following section one's brief review of the history of regionalism in the Americas, section two provides essential empirical information about energy production, consumption, investment, and trading patterns in the Western Hemisphere. The third through fifth sections analyze three competing visions of regional energy integration. We end with tentative conclusions about a still unfolding process.[1]

REGIONALISM IN THE AMERICAS

Efforts at regional cooperation and economic integration have a long history in the Americas. Mace and Thérien (2007) identify three periods of hemispheric cooperation, the first beginning with the first Pan-American conference in 1889-90, the second with the formation of the Organization of American States (OAS) in 1948, and the most recent era commencing in 1994 with the first Summit of the Americas meeting. Mace and Thérien note a cyclical pattern in which each period began strongly, with enthusiasm and real cooperative gains, and then lost steam as balance of power disparities and true differences in national interests came ineluctably to the fore.

Regarding the more specific issue of regional *economic* integration,[2] scholars identify two periods (Devlin and Estevadeordal, 2001; Gómez-Mera, 2008; Grugel, 2006). The first, today called the "old regionalism," began just after the Second World War and lasted until the 1980s. The old regionalism was greatly influenced by the developmentalist ideology of the United Nations Economic Commission for Latin America (ECLA—now the Economic Commission for Latin America and the Caribbean or ECLAC),

1. The authors thank Sean Burges, Maxwell Cameron, Laura Gómez-Mera, Eric Hershberg, Anil Hira, Andrew Hurrell, Alberto Pfeifer, Shawn Smallman, Maria Regina Soares de Lima, Laura Randall, and William Smith for their comments on previous versions of this work.

2. Regional economic integration is the process by which two or more countries become increasingly interlinked via trade, production, or finance. Formal integration arrangements range from "free trade areas" to "common markets." A "free trade area" consists of a group of countries that have free trade with one another but maintain separate trade policies with outside countries. A "customs union" unites countries that have free trade with one another and a common external tariff for trade outside the group. A "common market" exists when a group of countries forms a customs union, and in addition allows free movement of labor and capital among group members (Black, Hashimzade and Myles, 2009).

founded in 1948.[3] ECLA economists saw regional integration as a strategy for promoting import substitution industrialization (ISI). They believed that eliminating tariff barriers among the member nations of the regionally integrated area, while maintaining them against other nations, would increase the size of markets and thus allow industries to take advantage of economies of scale, lower "unit costs," and enjoy "protection against imports from third countries" (Bulmer-Thomas, 1994: 299). Although three regional trade organizations (RTOs) formed in the 1960s under this rationale—the Latin American Free Trade Association (LAFTA), the Andean Pact (AP), and the Central American Common Market (CACM)—none were very successful. Although the CACM increased industrialization, its members were the least developed in the region, and therefore even modest gains seemed huge. All of the RTOs also struggled with distributing benefits equitably, with finding reliable mechanisms for compensating their poorest members, and with agreeing on tariff reductions for key products (Felix, 1969). By 1975, intraregional trade's share in total exports was only about 18 percent (Bulmer-Thomas, 1994: 305). By the early 1980s, the old regionalism was moribund. The RTOs continued to exist, some with new names (LAFTA became the Latin American Integration Association or ALADI in 1980), but integration as a development strategy seemed to get scrapped along with ISI when the pro-market or "neoliberal" economic ideology took hold in Latin America following the 1980s debt crisis (Kearney, 2001).

The second period, called the "new regionalism," began in the late 1980s and continues to the present. It emerged as part of neoliberalism's emphasis on macroeconomic stabilization and structural reform of the national economic regulatory framework. The International Monetary Fund (IMF) and World Bank promoted regional integration, not as a means of stimulating industrialization, but rather with the goals of advancing free trade and locking in other liberalization efforts. What became known as "open regionalism," both in Latin America and East Asia, was an ideology that championed the private sector and favored the withdrawal of the state from economic activity. The new regionalism coincided with the conclusion of the Uruguay Round in 1994 and the acceleration of market liberalization and integration worldwide after the end of the Cold War. In this new ideological and global economic climate, some of the old RTOs reinvented

3. Developmentalism in the Latin American context is an ideology asserting that the shortest path to economic growth and prosperity for poor countries is through industrialization, usually led by the state and with the protection of high tariffs (Bulmer-Thomas, 1994: 278-279).

themselves as free trade associations, while others disbanded and formed new groupings. The Central American Common Market endured, but with new goals; the countries of the Southern Cone formed the Common Market of the South (MERCOSUR) in 1991; the Andean countries created the Andean Community (CAN) in 1993; and the United States, Canada, and Mexico inaugurated the North American Free Trade Agreement (NAFTA) in 1994. Devlin and Estevadeordal (2001: 25-35) argue that these newer RTOs contrast markedly with those of the old regionalism: they are market driven rather than state driven; they aim to attract foreign investment rather than restrict it; they are outward-looking, creating demand for greater rather than less participation in extra-regional trade forums; they are very little concerned with special and differential treatment of members; and their institutional architecture is much scaled down in comparison to the RTOs of the 1960s and 1970s (see also de la Reza, 2006).

The cross-regional comparative literature, much of which has focused on Western European integration, also stresses the more pro-market, globally-integrated forms of economic regulation today as compared to integration efforts of the 1950s and 1960s. It suggests that the *politics* of the integration process are notably less state-centric and more reliant on leadership from private business and transnational groups, as well as more influenced by existing international institutions, than in the past (Katzenstein, 2005; Buzan and Waever, 2003; Acharya, 2007). Observers of Latin America, in contrast, highlight the continuing dominance of the state in integration decisions (Gómez-Mera, 2008; Hurrell, 2005).[4] Moreover, the straightforward division of "old regionalism" as representing the structuralist vision of ECLA, and "new regionalism" as embodying neoliberalism and the embrace of globalization, describes NAFTA better than the universe of contemporary integration options in South America.

At present, there are multiple formal institutions in the Americas that embody aspects of political cooperation and economic integration. Nonetheless, they may be summarized into three distinct regional integration projects or visions for the hemisphere (cf. Burges, 2007).[5] Each has both political and economic dimensions, and each is championed by one of the hemisphere's important states. The United States prefers a vision of regional

---

4. Structuralism is related to developmentalism. It has several meanings, but we refer here to the idea that the world economy is structurally biased against poor countries. Specifically, the terms of trade between primary product exporters (normally poor countries) and exporters of manufactures (normally rich countries) tend to decline over time—the Singer-Prebisch thesis. Thus, in order to grow and prosper, primary product exporters must industrialize, usually via state-sponsored import-substituting policies (Prebisch, 1949; Furtado, 1959).

integration, embodied in NAFTA, that incorporates all countries in the Western Hemisphere, excepting Cuba, and in which the US is the dominant player. Venezuela promotes a Latin American vision that explicitly excludes the US and Canada, but includes Cuba and other Caribbean nations whose friendship can help Venezuela in its aspirations for regional leadership. Its institutional manifestation is the Bolivarian Alliance for the Americas (ALBA). Brazil's preferred regional design is manifest in the Union of South American Nations (UNASUR). It includes all of South America, but locates both North and Central America, including the island states of the Caribbean, outside.

What is interesting for a volume on the future role of the Brazilian state is that the three integration alternatives currently in play in the Americas offer three distinct visions of the state's appropriate economic role. Together they evoke a rough right-to-left political continuum, running from NAFTA through UNASUR to ALBA, though there is also considerable overlap among them (Burges, 2007; Kellogg, 2007). Each of these integration alternatives began as a vision of *trade integration*, involving mechanisms to promote the exchange of goods and services among members, and of the group with the outside world. But each of these contemporary regional integration initiatives also involves a number of other dimensions, including explicit and implicit promotion of foreign direct investment (FDI), collaborative infrastructure, harmonization of domestic regulatory frameworks, joint political positions in international affairs, and transnational citizen links. Rather than examining tariff arrangements or trade-related negotiations per se, we prefer to explore an issue arena that clearly possesses profound regional and international dimensions, but that is less often addressed by the regional integration literature. This chapter's task, then, is to treat energy integration (a work in progress, by definition) as a critical case study for understanding the region's broader integration dynamics.

5. Laura Randall, in an e-mail communication in late 2009, noted the striking similarities between the three contemporary regional integration visions profiled here and the colonial governance structure, centered in present-day Mexico but including much of what is now US territory (Viceroyalty of New Spain, established 1535), the Andes (the Viceroyalty of Peru, established in 1544, from which the Viceroyalty of New Granada, headquartered in Caracas, separated off in 1717), and Brazil (the Viceroyalty of Brazil, governed from Portugal after 1640).

ENERGY IN THE WESTERN HEMISPHERE

This section provides a brief factual overview of Latin America's contemporary energy profile in terms of production, consumption, and resource endowments. It compares the region's situation in the early 1990s with data from the latest available sources. In accordance with statistical norms, we consider "Latin America," and sometimes "Latin America and the Caribbean," as the relevant region.

In 1991, Latin America's total energy production was 13.9 million boe/d (barrels of oil equivalent per day), distributed among the major countries as shown in Table 16-1. Total production was 59% petroleum, 16% natural gas, 6% hydroelectric, 4% coal, and half a percent nuclear, with the remaining 14% dispersed among firewood, sugarcane products, geothermal, and a host of other nontraditional sources. Energy resources were unequally distributed: Venezuela and Mexico together accounted for 92% of Latin America's proven oil reserves[6] and 70% of oil production, while countries like Paraguay and Uruguay had no oil at all. In terms of total energy consumption, in the early 1990s fossil fuels dominated, as shown in Table 16-1.

TABLE 16-1. Energy Production and Use in Latin America, 1992 and 2006

	Energy imports, net (% of energy use)		Energy Production (kilotons of oil equivalent)		Energy use (kg of oil equivalent per capita)		Fossil fuel energy consumption (% of total)	
	1992	2006	1992	2006	1992	2006	1992	2006
Argentina	-8.7	-21.4	54,322	83,865	1,491.5	1,765.7	88.8	88.4
Bolivia	-68.5	-144.3	5,058	14,290	429.8	625.3	70.8	83.1
Brazil	27.6	7.8	104,280	206,717	933.0	1,183.8	52.7	53.7
Chile	47.2	66.5	8,412	9,970	1,166.4	1,811.9	69.3	73.5
Colombia	-84.9	-180.0	48,443	84,588	759.3	695.5	69.9	73.4
Ecuador	-186.9	-165.3	18,355	29,819	595.8	851.4	80.4	88.2
Mexico	-53.1	-44.3	200,321	255,967	1,514.7	1,702.4	88.0	89.1
Paraguay	-42.7	-68.9	4,520	6,708	709.9	660.1	24.0	30.5
Peru	-0.9	15.4	9,597	11,470	420.4	491.3	65.1	68.5
Uruguay	53.3	75.4	1,261	784	856.9	962.4	64.0	67.8
Venezuela	-226.4	-214.3	165,780	195,547	2,458.5	2,301.9	90.9	88.2

Source: World Bank, 2009.

Nonetheless, almost 72% of Latin America's electricity came from hydropower plants. Table 16-2 shows that every South American country used

6. Proven oil reserves are "those quantities of petroleum which, by analysis of geological and engineering data, can be estimated with a high degree of confidence to be commercially recoverable from a given date forward, from known reservoirs and under current economic conditions" (CIA World Factbook 2009, https://www.cia.gov/library/publications/the-world-factbook).

hydropower as a principal source for electricity, a fact that has created supply problems in times of drought (Wu, 1995: 1-5).

Latin America in the early 1990s had a net energy surplus with the rest of the world. In 1991, the region's net energy exports were about 4 million boe/d, representing 26% of all energy produced in the region. With about 12% of the world's proven oil reserves (124 billion barrels in 1992), and 12% of world crude oil production, Latin America was a net exporter of oil, refined petroleum products, and coal. 73% of Latin American oil exports went to the United States, with Western Europe taking 19%, and the Asia-Pacific region another 5%. Venezuela, Mexico, Colombia, and Ecuador

TABLE 16-2. Energy Production by Source in Latin America, 1992 and 2006

	Hydroelectric (% of total)		Oil (% of total)		Natural Gas (% of total)		Coal (% of total)		Nuclear (% of total)	
	1992	2006	1992	2006	1992	2006	1992	2006	1992	2006
Argentina	34.7	33.0	13.7	7.0	37.3	50.2	1.5	1.8	12.7	6.7
Bolivia	52.4	40.8	6.3	16.7	38.1	39.3	0.0	0.0	0.0	0.0
Brazil	92.4	83.2	2.6	3.0	0.0	4.4	2.1	2.4	0.7	3.3
Chile	82.2	59.5	3.8	1.6	1.2	19.9	10.6	17.1	0.0	0.0
Colombia	67.6	78.7	2.2	0.2	15.0	12.4	14.0	7.5	0.0	0.0
Ecuador	69.1	46.3	30.9	44.1	0.0	9.6	0.0	0.0	0.0	0.0
Mexico	19.8	12.2	54.0	21.6	12.5	45.5	6.3	12.7	3.0	4.4
Paraguay	99.9	100.0	0.0	0.0	0.0	0.0	0.0	0.0	0.0	0.0
Peru	73.8	78.5	23.8	8.4	1.4	9.5	0.0	3.0	0.0	0.0
Uruguay	89.0	64.0	10.3	35.1	0.0	0.1	0.0	0.0	0.0	0.0
Venezuela	70.1	72.0	6.8	14.6	23.1	13.4	0.0	0.0	0.0	0.0

Source: World Bank, 2009.

were the main oil exporters, and Chile and Brazil the main importers. All of the natural gas produced in the region was consumed in the region, with Bolivia being the only net exporter, and Argentina the only net importer. Coal represented only 2% of total net energy exports (Wu, 1995: 1-5).

The energy scenario at the end of the first decade of the 21st century reveals subtle but important differences from the early 1990s. Given economic growth, both production and consumption have increased. Total Latin American consumption reached 3.6 million kbep (thousands of barrels of oil equivalent) in 2006 (World Energy Council, 2008; OLADE, 2007), with Mexico accounting for about 21% of Latin American consumption and Brazil 36% (OLADE, 2007). Fossil fuels still dominate both total regional energy production and total consumption, with oil products now accounting for about 50% of energy consumption on average in all countries. Firewood is still a major factor in Paraguay (40% of the energy mix). Venezuela uses virtually no natural gas, while in Argentina it is 50 percent of energy use. Coal is not significant in the region. In contrast, biofuels have become much more important, especially in Brazil over recent decades. Brazil produced 46% of world ethanol in 2006, and flex fuel cars in the same year accounted for 65% of Brazilian car manufactures (World Energy Council, 2008: 10-11). As before, hydroelectric dams generate the majority of electricity in Latin America, especially throughout South America.

TABLE 16-3. Estimated Oil and Gas Reserves in Latin American, Jan. 2010

	Oil		Gas	
	Volume (billion barrels)	% Total	Volume (trillion cubit feet)	% Total
Argentina	2.5	1.9	14.1	2.4
Bolivia	0.5	0.3	26.5	4.5
Brazil	12.8	9.5	12.9	2.2
Chile	0.2	0.1	3.5	0.6
Colombia	1.4	1.0	4.0	0.7
Ecuador	6.5	4.8	0.3	0.0
Mexico	10.4	7.7	12.7	2.2
Peru	0.4	0.3	11.8	2.0
Suriname	0.1	0.1		
Trinidad and Tobago	0.7	0.5	15.4	2.6
Venezuela	99.4	73.7	176.0	30.0
Total	134.8		586.1	

Source: Radler, 2009.

Some individual countries within the region have become more energy-independent, but others less so. Venezuela still has the largest proven oil reserves by far and is the region's largest producer of oil and oil products. Until recently, Mexico came second in terms of proven reserves, but recent discoveries off the Brazilian coast already have pushed Brazil to second place, as shown in Table 16-3. Venezuela and Mexico remain the region's top producers and net exporters of oil and oil products. In 2008, they ranked tenth and seventh in the world respectively for oil production, and eighth and thirteenth in the world respectively for net oil exports (US Energy Information Administration, 2010). Argentina and Bolivia are the region's top natural gas exporters (Sullivan, Rush, and Seelke, 2008). Looking at relative changes, Table 16-1 shows that net imports as a share of domestic energy consumption are up since 1992 in Chile, Peru, and Uruguay, while Mexico, Ecuador, and even Venezuela are exporting somewhat smaller shares of their production. In contrast, Argentina, Bolivia, Brazil, Colombia, and Uruguay all have bettered their national net energy positions since 1992. In absolute terms, Venezuela, Ecuador, Bolivia, and perhaps Colombia can fairly be described as natural resource economies, with

93, 59, 49, and 38%, respectively, of their merchandise exports in 2006 consisting of fuel exports (World Bank, 2009). Mexico, Argentina, and surprisingly also Paraguay (due to its share in the hydropower from the Itaipú Dam) are all comfortable net energy exporters, although energy provides less than 20% of their merchandise exports. Brazil too is rapidly approaching energy balance, and may soon become a net energy exporter. Net energy importers currently include Brazil, Peru, Chile, and especially Uruguay (World Bank, 2009).

In 2009, Latin America as a whole still had a net energy surplus and was a net exporter of energy to the rest of the world. Latin American proven oil reserves were down slightly from the early 1990s as a percentage of the world's total, constituting approximately 11% in 2009 (US Energy Information Administration, 2009a). The United States remained the region's most important customer. Some 60% of Venezuela's oil exports, for example, went to the United States in 2006 (Sullivan, Rush, and Seelke, 2008; Caspary, 2007). But China is rapidly becoming an important consumer of Latin American energy. For example, in May 2009 the China Development Bank and Sinopec, a Chinese oil company, lent Petrobras, Brazil's state oil company, US$10 billion. In exchange, China will receive up to 200,000 barrels per day of crude oil for ten years from Brazil's new deep-sea oil fields. China and Venezuela have also set up a joint investment fund. Formed in 2007, the fund was increased to US$12 billion in February 2009, with the China Development Bank lending two thirds of the total. The goal is for Chinese companies to use this fund to invest in the Venezuelan energy sector and, ultimately, to increase Venezuelan oil exports to China ("The Dragon in the Backyard," 2009: 19-21).

Industry observers have characterized Latin America as having vast untapped energy potential, but as suffering from a lack of investment. *The Banker* estimated in 2008 that from now until 2030, the region will be the site of about 7% of global project investments in energy, and that, of these investments, Brazil will probably garner about one third (Rumsey, 2008). The President of the Inter-American Development Bank (IDB) has said that in order to meet demand, investment in Latin America's energy sector will need to be $1,380 billion by 2030 (Moreno, 2008), while the International Energy Agency has cited a figure of US$1,337 billion for the same period (IEA, 2003). Over the past two decades, however, energy projects have made up only about 20% of foreign direct investments. For this reason, supply, distribution and service have been unreliable. Some blame this situation on the regulatory systems of South American governments, which arguably tilted more toward resource nationalism in the first decade of the 21st century (Rumsey, 2008).

Some analysts also view investment in the renewable energy sector as insufficient, but note that many efforts are currently being made to stimulate it.[7] 21 countries signed the Brasilia Platform on Renewable Energies in 2003.[8] They agreed that 10% of energy should be derived from renewable energy sources. The wording of the agreement, however, is loose, saying that the countries should try to meet the target "on the basis of voluntary efforts and taking into account the diversity of national situations" (Rumsey, 2008). Local private investment in the sector faces obstacles, such as failure of governments to provide subsidies and lack of access to loans. Problems of scale and newness of technology are also important. Multilateral institutions and state development banks, however, are filling the gap. The IDB, for example, wants to spend $300 million on renewable energy in Latin America over the next five years. It is actively promoting programs on sustainable biofuels, energy efficiency, solar and wind power, small-scale hydropower, and energy from waste. In Brazil, the National Development Bank (BNDES) is taking a leading role, especially in cases where local currency is needed and commercial banks have trouble hedging their foreign exchange risk on long-term contracts (Rumsey, 2008).[9]

In this discussion of investment, however, we do not wish to imply that foreign investment is essential in order to meet the region's future energy needs and goals. First, if investment is to be subsidized by local or multilateral development banks, it is not clear why foreign direct investors, rather than local ones, should be the main private sector partners, or why other sectors of the economy should not take precedence over the energy sector. Second, such investment might not be needed if domestic tax systems and the pricing of energy products could be designed and managed better by Latin American governments.[10]

---

7. Renewable energy is any energy source that is "naturally regenerated" and "virtually inexhaustible," but whose flow may be limited. Sources include "biomass, hydro, geothermal, solar, wind, ocean thermal, wave action, and tidal energy" (US Energy Information Administration, 2010, http://www.eia.doe.gov).

8. For more information on the Brasília Platform, see ECLAC's web page on the agreement: http://www.eclac.cl/cgi-bin/getProd.asp?xml=/dmaah/noticias/discursos/5/13555/P13555.xml&xsl=/dmaah/tpl-i/p4f.xsl&base=/tpl/top-bottom.xslt.

9. Energy investments, especially in developing countries tend to be risky. They involve large amounts of capital, take a long time to yield a profit, often involve many investors, and are subject to changes in host-country government policies and economic climate (such as exchange rates). For more information, see Razavi (1996).

10. The authors thank Laura Randall for these insights.

Energy integration—the process of interlinking states' energy infrastructure, institutions, and investments—has been on the agenda in Latin America for decades now. Several regional organizations have been created. In the 1960s and 1970s, the Regional Association of Oil and Natural Gas Companies in Latin America and the Caribbean (ARPEL), the Regional Electrical Integration Commission (CIER), and the Latin American Energy Organization (OLADE) formed. All have regional integration as priorities in their mission statements (Caro, 2008). Energy integration has also been a priority of multilateral lending institutions, such as the IDB and the World Bank. More recently, initiatives emerged from the Summits of the Americas process, the most important being the "Hemispheric Energy Initiative" now overseen by the OAS. Finally, the first South American Presidential Energy Summit took place in April 2007. Its purpose was to begin developing a joint energy strategy for the region and to institute regular meetings (Caro, 2008). The following sections review how the United States, Venezuela, and Brazil view these efforts.

THE UNITED STATES' VISION: NAFTA-PLUS

We use the term "NAFTA-plus" to describe the United States' approach to hemispheric policy, as the US's goal has been to embrace the entire hemisphere within trade and investment rules that closely parallel those embodied in the North American Free Trade Agreement among the US, Canada, and Mexico. The NAFTA-plus vision's principal incarnation has been the Free Trade Area of the Americas (FTAA), an initiative first launched by US President George H. W. Bush at the 1992 Summit of the Americas in Miami.[11] Since the stalling of the FTAA in November 2005, the United States instead has pursued bilateral trade and investment agreements.[12] While some hoped the 2008 election of Barack Obama would jumpstart the Summit process, as of late 2009 they had been disappointed (LeVine, 2009).

11. There have been five Summits to date: Miami (1994); Santiago, Chile (1998); Quebec City, Canada (2001); Mar del Plata, Argentina (2005); and Port-of-Spain, Trinidad and Tobego (2009). The sixth is scheduled for 2013 in Colombia.

12. The main reason for the halt has been disagreements between the United States and Brazil, but Venezuelan inflexibility and rhetorical attacks on other member states have also been factors. Brazil and the United States are the co-chairs of the FTAA. At a trade meeting in Miami in 2003, they changed the basis of the FTAA from a "comprehensive, single undertaking principle" to "a two-tier framework comprising a set of 'common rights and obligations' for all countries, combined with voluntary plurilateral arrangements with country benefits related to commitments" (Hornbeck, 2005: 1).

The US approach to regional integration is broad and deep. US negotiators seek market access through both bilateral and multilateral free trade agreements covering all aspects of trade, and extending the major provisions of the North American Free Trade Area to the Caribbean, Central America, and South America. NAFTA-plus is notably friendly to transnational business interests, often requiring that trade agreements include the obligation to submit any disputes with transnational investors to international arbitration, rather than trying them in home-country courts. At the same time, the proposed FTAA places special emphasis on "harmonizing" foreign direct investment, intellectual property, and government procurement rules. The US strategy is sometimes termed "competitive liberalization," as its focus is less on traditional merchandise trade and more on encouraging countries to compete with one another to liberalize their domestic regulatory regimes sufficiently to attract the most foreign investment. More recently, additional issues have been added to this deep trade and market access agenda. The US Congress has been debating the labor and environmental standards that future free trade agreements must protect. It has agreed basically that US trade partners must comply with International Labor Organization (ILO) rules, as well as with any multilateral environmental agreements to which the US is a signatory (ECLAC, 2008: 125-127).

The United States' approach to energy policy in particular is much influenced by its status as the world's largest consumer of oil. As of 2006, the United States consumed about 21 million barrels of oil per day (mbd). Net oil imports were about 12 mbd or 60% of this total. Latin America supplied about 32% of total US crude oil imports in 2007, with Venezuela alone accounting for 12% and Mexico 14%. South America provided about 17% (Sullivan, Rush, and Seelke, 2008). The energy needs of the United States are enormous, and its dependence on foreign oil is a crucial component of its foreign policy. South America is an important part of the mix.

Not surprisingly, energy security is a crucial element of President Barack Obama's foreign policy. Reducing dependence on foreign oil, especially from the Middle East, is critical. There is disagreement among the US elite as to how this goal should be accomplished, but most proposals include cultivating sources closer to home, which includes Latin America, as well as developing renewables. The US prefers energy initiatives that are hemisphere-wide, market based, and led by the private sector. The Obama administration also has added a greater concern with climate change. When Senator Hillary Clinton was being vetted for the post of Secretary of State, she echoed all of these positions. She assured the Senate Foreign Relations Committee that she would work to reduce US dependence on foreign oil and to form partnerships with other countries to overcome threats to the environment. Clinton said that in this regard Obama wants an energy partnership with Latin America, "looking to find ways through technology and other activities [that] we can work together to become more energy independent in this hemisphere" (Snow, 2009: 28). She added that this partnership would require overcoming resource nationalism disputes with key oil and natural gas exporting states like Venezuela and Bolivia, as well as helping other countries to meet their energy supply needs. The Secretary of State also voiced an interest in working through the International Energy Agency (IEA), noting that demand for energy is shifting from the developed to the developing world, and arguing that it will be important to have developing countries, particularly China and India, involved in "agreeing on energy standards and principles such as transparent energy markets, to ensure the coordinated release of strategic petroleum reserves during a major market disruption, and to maintain IEA's position as the voice of the world's major energy consuming nations" (Snow, 2009: 28).

Clinton also echoed the usual US concern for promoting the private sector, and called attention to problems with resource nationalism in Latin America and other developing countries. She said, "Most of the required investment [for energy] . . . must come from the private sector. In order to mobilize that investment, major policy and regulatory reforms are needed in many countries. Neither public nor private utilities and their investors can generate the capital required to expand access to clean, sustainable energy supplies, for example, when regulatory regimes prevent them from recovering their direct and indirect operating costs" (Snow, 2009: 28). She offered two kinds of assistance to developing countries willing to reform their energy sectors: technical assistance to "establish the overall regulatory and policy environment to stimulate new public and private investments," and "project-based financial guarantees [that] can help to reduce the perceived risks and costs of mobilizing the much larger flows of private sector financing [which will be] required" (Snow, 2009: 28).

However, resource nationalism in Venezuela, Bolivia, and Ecuador has dogged US attempts to see its energy vision realized in the hemisphere. Although the United States had great hopes for the Summits of the Americas process in general, and specifically for its "Hemispheric Energy Initiative," the Summits forum has stagnated in recent years. Venezuela's

President Hugo Chávez has been perceived in the US as a particular cause for concern. Since taking office in 1999, he has increased state control of Petróleos de Venezuela (PDVSA). He has directed its earnings and projects toward social purposes and asserted control over foreign investment. By early 2006, President Chávez had forced the conversion of operating agreements with foreign oil companies into joint ventures in which the Venezuelan state retained the upper hand. The new joint ventures also carry an income tax increase from 34 to 50%. Some companies voluntarily turned operating agreements over to PDVSA, but Chávez confiscated two operations when companies rejected his terms, and in 2007 also altered associations with foreign companies in the Orinoco River Basin. Three of the six companies involved were based in the United States (ExxonMobil, ConocoPhillips, and Chevron). ExxonMobil entered into a long dispute over its compensation, filing a request for arbitration with the International Center for Settlement of Investment Disputes in 2007. Other Andean governments also recently have challenged the property rights of multinational energy firms. Bolivia's President Evo Morales nationalized his country's gas sector, which is substantial and had strong involvement from US companies. Ecuador increased its share of windfall profits from foreign oil companies and also terminated the contract of Occidental Petroleum after a lengthy disagreement over the sale of drilling rights (Sullivan, Rush, and Seelke, 2008: 7-8).

As a result, US companies are looking for investments in other parts of the region and the world. Moreover, the US government and think tanks have expressed concern about what Chávez and his followers mean for energy security in the region. Senator Richard Lugar (R-Ind), the ranking member of the Senate Foreign Relations Committee, has sponsored two bills. The Energy Diplomacy and Security Act of 2007 contained a proposal for establishing a "Western Hemisphere Energy crisis mechanism" and a ministerial forum called the "Hemisphere Energy Cooperation Forum" (Sullivan, Rush, and Seelke, 2008: 19). Lugar also sponsored the United States-Brazil Energy Cooperation Pact of 2007. This bill calls on the Secretary of State to "accelerate the development of biofuels production, research, and infrastructure" (Sullivan, Rush, and Seelke, 2008: 19). A US business association, the Council of the Americas, has issued a report specifically recommending hemispheric energy cooperation as an engine for regional development and growth. The group favors expanding on the

NAFTA framework. Finally, the US Southern Command has taken up energy security as a key concern (Sullivan, Rush, and Seelke, 2008: 17).

In sum, the United States' NAFTA-plus vision of energy integration would (ideally) use the proposed FTAA or similar bilateral agreements to tie Latin American energy producers to the US market by a combination of long-term contracts and foreign direct investment. It envisions a minimal role for the state in managing the energy sector. The state would regulate, but only with the goals of protecting property rights, enforcing contracts, and, perhaps, ensuring basic labor and environmental standards. The bulk of the investment, exploration, extraction, and distribution of energy would be left to private actors.

THE VENEZUELAN VISION: THE BOLIVARIAN ALLIANCE (ALBA)

The second integration option prominent today is the Bolivarian Alliance for the Americas (ALBA), the brainchild of Venezuelan President Hugo Chávez Frías (Burges, 2007; Kellogg, 2007). Chávez first mooted ALBA in December 2001 at a Summit of the Association of Caribbean States, and formally launched it in December 2004 in a joint declaration with Cuba's Fidel Castro. Bolivia's New Left President Evo Morales formalized Bolivia's entrance into ALBA in April 2006. Nicaragua joined the group in January 2007, just as ALBA was holding its fourth leaders' summit. A fifth summit took place in April 2007, and the governments of Haiti, Ecuador, Uruguay, Dominica, Saint Kitts and Nevis, and Saint Vincent and the Grenadines sent representatives, after which Dominica became a full member. Ecuador and St. Vincent and the Grenadines joined in 2009.

ALBA is Chávez's alternative to the United States' plan for a Free Trade Area of the Americas. David Harris and Diego Azzi note enthusiastically, "[ALBA] includes the promotion of trade relations between countries, and even the elimination of tariff barriers on certain products, but its core purpose goes far beyond this. The explicit aim of ALBA is to promote the 'social' side of development, eliminating poverty and combating social exclusion in a cooperative effort by Latin American states" (Harris and Azzi, 2006: 6). More skeptically, Sean W. Burges characterizes ALBA as a realist strategy designed to protect Chávez from internal and external enemies. By sharing Venezuelan petro-profits with neighbors, forging alliances with like-minded regional allies, and employing the rhetoric of the historic liberator Simón de Bolívar,

Chávez hopes to secure his domestic rule and counteract US hegemony (Burges, 2007). Indeed, the ideological symbolism of ALBA is strong, and reactions to it tend to fall clearly along ideological lines.

Of the three visions for regional energy policy, Venezuela's is the most explicitly political and social. Energy policy is a tool for development, but more importantly it is a weapon for fighting imperialism and inequality. President Hugo Chávez's proposals for energy integration thus follow closely the lines set out in his Bolivarian vision (ALBA). ALBA's stated goals are wide ranging. They include: fostering trade and investment "based on cooperation, and with the aim of improving people's lives, not making profits;" providing universal free healthcare and education; integrating members' energy sectors "to meet people's needs;" creating alternative media outlets "to counterbalance the US and regional neo-liberal media and promote an indigenous Latin American identity;" promoting land redistribution and food security; founding state-owned enterprises; developing basic industries "so that ALBA member states can become economically independent;" supporting "workers' movements, student movements, and social movements;" and ensuring that ALBA projects are environmentally sustainable (Hattingh, 2008).

Venezuela has the largest proven oil reserves and oil exports in Latin America (see Tables 16-1 and 16-3), and President Chávez has endeavored to use this wealth to build an anti-imperialist coalition in the region. There are several examples of this policy. First, as already mentioned, Chávez thoroughly restructured PDVSA, nationalizing it and reorienting its mission toward achieving social development goals. At the same time, Chávez fired the majority of PDVSA senior executives and many workers, horrifying many Venezuelan and foreign elites, (Dittrick, 2009). Second, there is PetroCaribe, an initiative launched in 2005. Through it, Venezuela supplies poor countries in the region with oil on preferential terms.[13] PetroCaribe aims to establish "a regional supply, refining, and transportation and storage network," and it includes a development fund for participating countries (Sullivan, Rush, and Seelke, 2008: 14). As of late 2009, PetroCaribe included most Caribbean countries plus Nicaragua and Honduras. Third, Venezuela has formed an accord with Bolivia, called PetroAndina, which will supply about 8,300 bpd to Bolivia via a joint venture. Fourth, PDVSA

13. PetroCaribe is just the latest in a long line of such programs, however, and some of them predate Chávez. Also, Chávez, through PDVSA's US-based refining subsidiary, Citgo, Venezuela even has provided low-cost heating oil to needy families in the US (Sullivan, Rush, and Seelke, 2008; James, 2006).

has spearheaded the Petroamerica initiative, the aim of which is to use the region's vast energy reserves in hydroelectric power and fossil fuels as the "backbone" for a modern regional economy and continental integration (Wertheim, 2004). Finally, Venezuela has invested in the energy sectors of several of its Latin American neighbors. It has plans to invest $1.5 billion in the Bolivian gas industry, has an agreement with Ecuador for joint ventures in oil, gas and refining, and has a refinery project in Northeastern Brazil that began construction in 2007. In 2006, Venezuela and Colombia agreed to construct a gas pipeline project. There is a joint hydrocarbon exploration and development project with Argentina (signed in 2006), and numerous cooperative projects in Cuba (Sullivan, Rush, and Seelke, 2008).

Another of President Chávez's strategies for securing regional leadership has been to cultivate outside allegiances, particularly with US rivals. Venezuela was a founding member of the Organization of Petroleum Exporting Countries (OPEC) in 1960, well before Chávez's time, but since taking office he has tried to use the organization to promote his socialist goals and to criticize the United States (Williams and Chmaytelli, 2007). He has also sought closer ties with Russia, based on the commonality of being major energy producing states. He has said he would offer Russia a military base in Venezuela if President Medvedev wants one. The two countries have formed a "strategic partnership," which seems mainly to consist of Russia selling arms to Venezuela. Chávez has also tried to cultivate Iran. All three countries dislike the United States and all three have an interest in trying to keep energy prices from falling too much. The point, however, is the strong symbolism and the recurring anti-American theme in Venezuela's regional vision (Watkins, 2008).

Despite ALBA's rhetorical commitment to building "21st Century Socialism," Venezuela's petroleum wealth clearly provides much of the organization's glue, a fact that makes Chávez's regional plans dependent on the world oil market. Oil is 90% of Venezuelan exports and provides over half of government income. "For each $10 drop in the oil price, the government gets $5 billion (1.4% of GDP) less in revenue" ("An Axis in Need of Oiling," 2008: 71-72). World petroleum prices have been highly volatile in the past decade, rising from about US$17 dollars per barrel in 1998 to over $95 dollars per barrel in 2007, then plummeting by mid 2009 to below US$50 dollars per barrel.[14] During the crash that began in early 2008, many proj-

14. All figures are in constant 2008 dollars. See "Oil price history and analysis" and the table "Crude Oil Prices, 1947-August 2009" at www.wtrg.com, accessed 26 February 2010.

ects advocated by President Chávez stalled, including a continental gas pipeline from Venezuela to Argentina, and as many as eight refineries throughout the region. Venezuelan aid to its neighbors also became more difficult. In May 2009, *The New York Times* reported that Venezuela was expected to spend only US$6 billion overseas in 2009, compared with US$79 billion in 2008, and noting further that Venezuelan allies like Argentina and Ecuador were looking elsewhere for support ("Venezuela's Hope," 2009: A8). In 2009 Argentina closed a trade deal with China, Ecuador renewed relations with the IMF and the United States, and even Cuba began exploring improved ties with Washington and the new Obama administration. The larger countries in Latin America have also seemed to be cultivating energy relationships away from Venezuela, turning to Russia, Trinidad and Tobago, and even Brazil, with its new deep sea oil and natural gas discoveries ("Venezuela's Hope," 2009: A8). Whether these efforts were politically motivated or the result of economic prudence (or both), however, is not clear.

The 2008-2009 drop in world oil prices, combined with President Chávez's management of his domestic oil sector, has also created problems for him at home. In 2010, Venezuela suffered from high inflation, labor union tension, and slowing economic growth. The oil industry is still reeling from Chávez's nationalizations of PDVSA and foreign oil contracts, and there is insufficient technology and expertise to develop the Orinoco fields or to embark on further off shore exploration. There is also illegal smuggling of fuel to Colombia, export delays, and increasing debts. In early 2008, Chávez seized the assets of several domestic and foreign oil contractors rather than pay more than $10 billion in debts owed to them ("Venezuela's Hope," 2009: A8). All of these factors reflect the vulnerability of Venezuela's regional vision to the vagaries of the world oil market.

Nevertheless, Venezuela still has a great deal of influence, and a strengthening of world oil prices, as now seems to be occurring, can significantly improve both Venezuela's domestic economic prospects and its ability to fund ALBA's energy vision. As of early 2010, energy prices seem to be rising again, with oil futures on the New York Mercantile Exchange (NYMEX) increasing steadily from $34 dollars per barrel in March 2009 to $78 dollars per barrel in February 2010.[15] Venezuela has closed deals with both Russia and China to exploit the Orinoco fields (Tockman, 2009), and in February 2010 once again awarded contracts to western foreign oil companies,

15. From graph of "NYMEX Crude Oil Futures" at www.wtrg.com, accessed 26 February 2010.

including Chevron (Romero, 2010). Many Central American and Caribbean countries are dependent on Venezuelan oil subsidies and special payment arrangements. In 2008, they had debts to Venezuela of $5.5 billion. Venezuela's idea for a Bank of the South also seems to be making progress, though there is no set starting date for operations. And ALBA still has wide ideological appeal, especially to the region's poorest countries ("Venezuela's Hope," 2009: A8). Finally, the smaller and poorer countries of the hemisphere question the ability of Obama to offer an alternative attractive to them (Weisbrot, 2009).

With regard to the role of the state in the energy sector, the ALBA vision is the most state-directed of the three visions we discuss. ALBA explicitly calls for the state to use energy wealth to improve social welfare and reduce inequality. Market considerations, and the interests of private actors are clearly subordinate to the "social good." If Chávez's domestic energy policies are indicative of his broader regional vision, then the role for private capital in regional energy extraction and distribution would be tightly circumscribed by states. The energy assets themselves also would not be left in the hands of private companies, but rather, administered by states in the name of their people.

THE BRAZILIAN VISION: FROM MERCOSUR TO UNASUR

We use "UNASUR approach" to describe the efforts at regional cooperation pursued by the countries of MERCOSUR and the Andean Community. These efforts culminated in the creation of UNASUR in 2008, although the idea for such a union existed as early as 2004. UNASUR was formalized in the Constitutive Treaty of the South American Union of Nations, signed by the MERCOSUR and Andean countries, as well as Chile, Guyana, and Suriname. Its goals are very ambitious, moving well beyond economic cooperation and integration. Its preamble states that UNASUR will work "to eliminate socio-economic inequality, achieve social inclusion and civil-society participation, strengthen democracy, and reduce asymmetries" (ECLAC, 2008: 103). It also has a range of more specific goals, including energy integration. UNASUR's institutions include four bodies: the Council of Heads of State and Government, the Council of Ministers of Foreign Affairs, the Council of Delegates, and the General Secretariat. The General Secretariat is to be headquartered in Quito. However, as of early 2010, UNASUR's constitutive treaty had yet to be signed and ratified by member countries.[16]

Brazil has been a prime mover in the formation of UNASUR, just as it was in the formation of MERCOSUR in 1991 (Armijo and Kearney, 2008). At the same time, UNASUR's proposed institutions and even its name reflect accommodations with the sensitivities of other states, particularly Venezuela. Even so, UNASUR's incipient approach to regionalism reflects to a large extent Brazil's approach to regional and economic development, which puts the state, as well as political interests, front and center. Scholars have noted MERCOSUR's deviation from the "new regionalism" model of bottom-up, market, and civil-society generated integration (Gómez-Mera, 2008). MERCOSUR began and has continued to be as much about political alliances and state building as it has been about freer trade per se. With its weak institutionalization, low participation of economic interest groups, and reliance on government leaders to keep it alive, MERCOSUR retains elements of the "old regionalism" (Grugel, 2006; Gómez-Mera, 2008). In a similar vein, Brazil's vision of regionalism, as manifest in the UNASUR initiative, retains a strong role for state leadership in economic development (Burges, 2006). Where the NAFTA-plus vision focuses on regulatory integration of all of the hemisphere's economies by rewriting domestic economic legislation to give transnational businesses a stable environment for investment, Brazil's UNASUR vision represents a contemporary, more pro-market incarnation of South America's tradition of structuralism, which recognizes that the state has an ongoing and crucial role to play in guiding and promoting economic development (Prebisch, 1949; Furtado, 1959).

Brazil's preferences for the energy sector lie between those of the United States and Venezuela. Brazil has regional and global leadership aspirations, but it takes a pragmatic approach. Its attitude toward the United States is conciliatory but firm, as reflected in a recent statement by foreign minister Celso Amorim: "We want to have a good relationship with the United States. But we don't depend on external tutelage" ("The Samba Beat," 2008: 57). Brazil takes a middle position in the debate over whether the state or the private sector should take the lead in the energy sector, emphasizing

16. In using UNASUR as a short hand for Brazil's vision of regionalism, we do not wish to suggest that all of the countries that signed the treaty agree with Brazil's vision of economic and energy integration. Both CAN and MERCOSUR have been plagued by internal divisions, Chile has initiated and terminated associations with both groups, and UNASUR itself is already experiencing disagreements. For more extensive treatment of these dynamics see Gómez-Mera (2008), Malamud (2005), and ECLAC (2008).

that there is a role for both. Petrobras, Brazil's leading oil company, is evidence of this stance, being mostly state-owned but having a substantial number of private shareholders too.[17] In terms of scope, Brazil privileges South American initiatives over hemispheric ones, and on the social welfare aspects of energy policy, it shows more explicit concern than does the United States, but is far less militant and populist than Venezuela. In an interview with Newsweek, for example, President Lula mildly noted that recent Brazilian oil discoveries are important because they can be used to help overcome social problems like poverty and lack of education ("Lula Wants to Fight," 2009: 43).[18]

Like Venezuela, Brazil has significant energy wealth. As of January 1, 2010, its estimated proven oil reserves were 12.8 billion barrels and its natural gas reserves were 12.8 trillion cubic feet, ranking fourth and seventh largest respectively in the western hemisphere (Radler, 2009). Brazilian oil reserves were only about 1% of the world's estimated total in 2007, but recent discoveries in pre-salt fields[19] off the southern coast may amount to as much as 40 billion barrels, which would place Brazil eighth in the world ("More Bounty," 2008: 82; IEA, 2009). Brazil is also significant in terms of production and consumption. In 2006, Brazil was the third largest producer of oil after Venezuela and Mexico, and the fifth largest producer of natural gas after Mexico, Argentina, Venezuela, and Trinidad and Tobago. It had the largest installed capacity for the generation of electricity (about 36 % of the regional total), and it accounted for well over a third of Latin America's total final energy consumption (OLADE, 2007). Currently, Brazil is one of the top ten oil consumers in the world (IEA, 2009).

Brazil is also an important energy actor because of its industry leadership. Petrobras, the state oil company, is Brazil's largest company. Founded in 1953, it was instrumental in the development of Brazil's capital goods industry, and it currently has projects and investments in more than 25 countries, including almost all of the countries in South America. Projects involve exploration and production, refining, marketing and transportation, petrochemicals, distribution, biofuels, and natural gas. Its proven reserves in 2007 were the equivalent of 15 billion barrels of oil (boe). It also

17. The structure of Petrobras is complex, and includes multiple subsidiaries. See the Petrobras website: http://www2.petrobras.com.br/ingles/index.asp.

18. Some in the Brazilian Congress, however, think that President Lula's plan for tying Brazil's health and education funding to Petrobras' revenues will place these programs' future funding at risk ("Brazil's Lula meets foes," 2009).

19. The fields are called "pre-salt" because the oil is located deep beneath the ocean floor under a thick layer of salt, which makes extracting it difficult.

had 15 refineries, thousands of kilometers of ducts and close to 6000 service stations. Petrobras' net income in 2007 was $13 billion, which enabled it to fund investments of $21 billion. It plans to invest $174.4 billion between 2009 and 2013, with an annual average of $34.9 billion in Brazil and $3.2 billion abroad. The company actively seeks partnerships with companies in other countries ("New Horizons," 2009) Petrobras' investments abroad may be one of the reasons that for the first time, in January 2008, Brazil became a net foreign exchange creditor (Parra-Bernal and Pimentel, 2008). The Brazilian National Development Bank (BNDES) also provides a significant amount of financing for energy projects in the region, lending not only to Brazilian entities, but also to foreign governments, as in a recent controversial case with the government of Ecuador involving a hydropower project (discussed further below). The BNDES also partners with multilateral lending agencies, such as the Inter-American Development Bank, which is a major sponsor of the IIRSA initiative (also discussed below).

Brazilian companies are also large players in energy construction. At the South American Presidential Summit in August of 2000, the Brazilian government began to promote a plan called Integração da Infraestrutura Regional na América do Sul (IIRSA, South American Regional Infrastructure Integration), whose purpose is to create "axes of development" that will connect different regions of South America via "corridors" of energy, transportation, and communications infrastructure. The idea is to foster "regional production chains" that will help South America exploit its global competitive advantages (Burges, 2006). Energy is a big part of IIRSA, and companies like Odebrecht are involved in building power plants and dams throughout the region. Odebrecht is the largest construction company in Latin America and the third largest company in Brazil. It was founded in 1944, operates in 20 countries—including all of the South American countries—and had recorded earnings in 2007 of $17 billion (Zibechi, 2009: 3). As Raúl Zibechi (2009) notes, this figure is more than the GDPs of Bolivia and Paraguay combined. Overall, Brazilian foreign direct investment (FDI) was $71 billion by 2005, much of it in Latin America. By comparison, Mexico was a distant second with FDI of only $28 billion (Zibechi, 2009: 1).

The regional energy projects and partnerships that involve Brazil are far too numerous to list here. But several have been in the news recently due to disputes with other countries. As the Brazilian economy continues to grow and strengthen, and Brazilian companies engage in foreign investment, other Latin American countries are making accusations of imperialism, which Brazil's neighbors periodically have leveled against it since the nineteenth century. The Andean countries have been the most vocal, perhaps inspired by Hugo Chávez and his Bolivarian socialist ideology. In 2006, Bolivia nationalized two Brazilian oil refineries built by Petrobras, as part of a more general effort on the part of President Morales to gain national control over energy production ("The Samba Beat," 2008: 57). In September 2008, Ecuador had a significant dispute with Odebrecht regarding a hydroelectric plant it failed to build to specification, which resulted in power losses due to dam shutdowns, as well as damage to aquifers and springs. President Rafael Correa had the Army surround four Odebrecht projects, froze the company's assets, and threatened to stop payment on a $243 million loan from the Brazilian national development bank. Correa then kicked Odebrecht out of the country and said he would oust other Brazilian companies too, including Petrobras. He accused the Brazilians of "disrespecting national sovereignty" (Margolis, 2008: 52-53). Shortly thereafter, in November 2008, Venezuela's President Chávez charged Odebrecht with $282 million in "extra" taxes, leading to a serious dispute with the Brazilian government. The company claimed it had already paid its full tax bill, and there was speculation that the additional taxes were levied as punishment for the company's behavior in Ecuador ("Update 2," 2008). Regarding Venezuelan accession to MERCOSUR, Chávez also called the Brazilian Congress "Washington's parrot" (Margolis, 2008: 52-53).

Brazil has also had conflicts with Paraguay. Paraguay's president, Fernando Lugo, ran on an "energy independence" platform, and upon election embarked on negotiations with Brazil over the Itaipú dam, which the two countries share. Paraguay has long held that Brazil does not pay enough for power imports from the plant. When construction began on the dam in 1973, the two countries signed a treaty specifying that each country had a right to 50% of the energy generated by the dam's power plant, but that they had to sell any unused energy to one another. The power plant began generating electricity in 1984, and for its entire history, Paraguay has used far less of its electricity than has Brazil. It is estimated that 90% of the plant's electricity goes to Brazilian industry. In 1985, Paraguay agreed to sell its unused electricity to Brazil at below-market prices in order to help Brazil with its balance of payments problems. This situation continued, however, until very recently, and was the focus of President Lugo's complaints to Brazil. He wanted Brazil to pay Paraguay more for Itaipú electricity, and he wanted the right to sell electricity to third parties (Barrionuevo, 2009; Margolis, 2008).

On the surface, Brazil seems not to do much about actions from neighboring countries that seemingly threaten its interests. Unlike its reactions to industrialized countries, where it has not hesitated to bring World Trade Organization (WTO) cases, with Latin American countries Brazil appears tolerant. In the Paraguayan case just discussed, although Brazil at first refused to renegotiate the Itaipú agreement, it ultimately relented in July 2009. The two countries signed a new deal, which will triple what Brazil pays yearly for Paraguay's unused electricity (from $124 million to $360 million) and allow Paraguay to sell electricity directly to the Brazilian market, bypassing Brazilian state electricity companies. Referring to the deal, Lula said in a speech in Asunción, "Brazil is not interested in growing and developing if its partners don't grow and don't develop" (Barrionuevo, 2009: A10). When Bolivia nationalized Petrobras' refineries, Brazilian officials said that Morales was "exercising his country's sovereign rights" (Margolis, 2008: 52-53). Lula asked rhetorically, "What do you want us to do, invade Bolivia?" (Margolis, 2008: 52-53). He said further that powerful countries like Brazil "must show solidarity with the poorer countries" (Margolis, 2008: 52-53).

On the one hand, Brazil seems to understand that these outbursts are the price of success. Brazil's diplomats note that their country's rising economic power means that at every meeting on trade, they are confronted with a demand to do more for their neighbors ("The Samba Beat," 2008: 57). At the same time, these neighbors are supplying Brazil with essential resources, and Brazil cannot afford to alienate them. Perhaps for this reason Brazil refrains from open criticism. Lula refuses to be bated into criticizing Venezuelan democracy, for example. There are Brazilians that want their country to do more in the face of these actions by neighbors. Brazilian political analyst Amaury de Souza has said, "We're getting our butts kicked by mice" ("The Samba Beat," 2008: 57). Also, in October 2008, the Brazilian Defense Ministry formulated a new National Mobilization Strategy, which Lula has signed. It has stronger rules for responding to "rogue nations" and "actions that damage national sovereignty" (Margolis, 2008: 52-53). For the most part, however, Brazil is subtle. "Brazil never criticises Mr. Chávez in public but it increasingly seeks to outflank him" ("The Samba Beat," 2008: 57).

Two final energy issues concerning Brazil's role in the region are worth mentioning. First, as discussed above, Brazil has taken the lead on efforts to promote biofuels and renewable energy. Given the currently large and growing demand internationally in this sector, the Brazilian government views expansion as both imperative and highly lucrative. Brazil has actively pursued greater market access for its sugar and ethanol exports in international trade fora, winning a 2004 case in the WTO against European Union (EU) sugar subsidies. It has also made sugar and ethanol part of a broader agricultural export drive, one that has been highly successful. Finally, at home and abroad Brazilian policy makers have been pushing ethanol as a substitute for gasoline, on both economic and environmental grounds. Brazil has even agreed to help other poor countries, such as Jamaica and India, develop their own self-sustaining ethanol industries (Beattie, 2006). Brazil sponsored the Brasília Platform on Renewable Energies in 2003, and in 2007 partnered with the United States to promote biofuels in the western hemisphere.

Second, Brazil is thinking of joining OPEC. Lula has recently said that Brazil will participate very soon. The initial invitation from Saudi Arabia came in September of 2008. The renewed invitation came in March 2009. Brazil initially declined, saying that it planned to export refined petroleum products like gasoline and not crude oil. Lula reiterated this intention earlier this year. If Brazil joins OPEC, it could mark a major shift in policy. At any rate, Brazil cannot join immediately because it would not be able to implement OPEC production cuts. Brazil uses all the oil it produces and still imports oil (Watkins, 2009).

CONCLUSIONS

As we noted in this chapter's beginning, energy integration in the Americas is incipient but likely to be on going and ultimately profound. We have described three visions for regional integration, each promoted by an important state, and each with a distinct vision of energy policy. The United States' NAFTA-plus approach is in general pro-private enterprise and pro-market. For energy integration, it would use multilateral and bilateral free trade agreements to tie Latin American energy producers to the US market by a combination of long-term contracts and foreign direct investment. It sees the proper role for the state in the economy as a minimal, regulatory one. Venezuela's ALBA vision takes much the opposite view. The role for the state is extensive, both in its general integration vision and its energy policy initiatives. It would use Chávez-brokered deals to exchange subsidized energy or finance for other goods and services, such as Cuban medical personnel, and political support for Venezuela-centric energy infrastructure. The stated goal in all cases would be to improve social welfare. Finally,

Brazil's UNASUR vision lies between the two extremes. Regional integration would have roles for both states and private actors. For energy policy specifically, it would involve a perhaps uneasy coexistence of "green energy" promotion and a push for continental energy infrastructure, such as binational or multinational hydroelectric projects built via the IDB-funded IIRSA initiative.

For several reasons, we find that Brazil's vision of energy integration is the most likely to endure in South America. First, there is the seriousness of Brazil's commitment to South America. One sign of this is Brazil's allocation of diplomatic resources over the past seven years. Since 2002, the number of diplomats from Itamaraty (Brazil's foreign ministry) posted in South America has nearly doubled, while the number in Europe has declined substantially. Brazil hopes regional involvement will promote better relations with Argentina, strengthen democracy and political stability in the region, and "consolidate regional support for the expansion of [Brazil's] presence in world affairs" (Soares de Lima and Hirst, 2006: 31). In achieving all of these goals, Brazilian participation and financing of infrastructure and energy projects are important bargaining tools. Not only do improvements in these areas help insure Brazil's continued economic health and expansion, but they also offer opportunities to Brazil's poorer neighbors, and they potentially foster good will in regional inter-governmental relations (Burges, 2006). Countries in the region have had specific disputes with Brazilian corporations and with the Brazilian government, but these do not seem to have detracted from the broader appeal of Brazil's vision and leadership. Brazil's low-key management of its power has helped it to weather disputes and maintain good relations with neighbors, while Lula in particular has been a popular and revered role model (Margolis, 2008).

Second, contemporary economic debates may favor Brazil's model, especially as the larger emerging markets seek to deepen their investments in infrastructure and energy. Commitment from multilateral institutions like the IDB to the energy and infrastructure projects of the IIRSA is already strong. With world class institutions like Petrobras and the BNDES offering partnerships or deals to private firms, foreign governments, and international governmental institutions alike, Brazil's integration plans may well have the best chance of surviving tough economic times—especially given new discoveries and growing demand in the region.

Third, but perhaps least recognized in the often highly-technical debates over economic integration, is the fact that the UNASUR vision, and Brazil's prominent but not overwhelming role within the UNASUR institutional framework, receives enormous political benefits in the other capitals of South America by the existence of realistic, but potentially more threatening, integration alternatives both to the right and to the left. The UNASUR approach to energy integration is notable for the moderate stance it strikes between the perhaps overly private-enterprise-friendly positions of the United States on the one hand, and the anti-market hostility of Venezuela on the other. Brazil has a long history of state economic management, production, investment, and regulation, and pragmatism is widely agreed to characterize Brazil's overall foreign policy stance. Evidence from the energy sector suggests that South America is rather likely to integrate with a continental, rather than a Latin/Caribbean or a hemispheric scope.

APPENDIX ECONOMIC AND SOCIAL INDICATORS

Laura Randall

Table A-1: Brazil Economic Indicators, 1980–2009

	Brazil GDP per capita, PPP[a]	World GDP per capita, PPP[a]	GDP growth (annual%) PPP[a]	Gross capital formation (% GDP)	Gross fixed capital formation (% GDP)	Gross savings (% GDP)	FDI[b], Net inflow (% GDP)	FDI[b], Net outflow (% GDP)
1980	7,572	5,949	9.11	23.35	22.90	17.87	0.81	0.16
1981	7,072	5,961	-4.39	23.08	22.94	18.64	0.96	0.08
1982	6,950	5,890	0.58	21.09	21.44	15.29	1.03	0.13
1983	6,562	5,939	-3.41	16.68	18.13	13.32	0.79	0.09
1984	6,756	6,107	5.27	15.74	16.89	15.76	0.76	0.02
1985	7,139	6,224	7.95	19.20	16.95	19.09	0.65	0.04
1986	7,554	6,327	7.99	19.09	19.09	17.12	0.13	0.05
1987	7,674	6,448	3.60	22.30	22.30	21.81	0.40	0.05
1988	7,524	6,627	-0.10	22.72	22.72	23.94	0.85	0.05
1989	7,632	6,755	3.28	26.90	26.90	35.81	0.27	0.12
1990	7,179	6,813	-4.30	20.17	20.66	18.92	0.21	0.14
1991	7,168	6,796	1.51	19.77	18.11	18.66	0.27	0.25
1992	7,022	6,807	-0.47	18.93	18.42	20.09	0.53	0.04
1993	7,238	6,822	4.66	20.85	19.28	20.18	0.29	0.11
1994	7,510	6,934	5.33	22.15	20.75	21.27	0.56	0.19
1995	7,724	7,054	4.42	18.03	18.32	15.54	0.63	0.18
1996	7,771	7,213	2.15	17.04	16.87	14.08	1.33	-0.06
1997	7,913	7,397	3.37	17.43	17.37	13.58	2.26	0.12
1998	7,799	7,475	0.04	17.03	16.97	13.03	3.78	0.32
1999	7,704	7,637	0.25	16.38	15.66	12.06	4.87	0.29
2000	7,921	7,883	4.31	18.25	16.80	13.94	5.08	0.35
2001	7,911	7,951	1.31	18.03	17.03	13.81	4.06	-0.41
2002	8,010	8,058	2.66	16.20	16.39	15.16	3.29	0.49
2003	7,994	8,239	1.15	15.77	15.28	17.99	1.84	0.05
2004	8,344	8,547	5.71	17.12	16.10	20.36	2.74	1.43
2005	8,505	8,825	3.16	16.21	15.94	18.79	1.71	0.29
2006	8,744	9,166	3.96	16.77	16.43	18.68	1.72	2.59
2007	9,181	9,530	6.09	17.31	17.10	17.66	2.53	0.52
2008	9,559	9,688	5.14	18.21	18.26	16.86	2.75	1.25
2009	9,455	9,514	-0.18	16.60	16.22	14.78	1.65	-0.64

Notes: [a] Purchasing Power Parity in constant 2005 international dollars. [b] Foreign Direct Investment
Source: http://data.worldbank.org/country/brazil.

Table A-1: Brazil Economic Indicators, 1980–2009

	Exports (% of GDP)	Imports (% of GDP)	Current account balance (% of GDP)	Money and quasi money (% of GDP)	Total debt services (% of exports)[a]	Interest payments on external debt (% of exports)[a]	Total reserves (% total external debt)	Tariff rate (%)[b]	Official exchange rate[c]	Inflation, GDP deflator (annual%)
1980	9.05	11.31	-5.46	18.49	63.25	33.90	9.61	–	0.05	87.31
1981	9.42	9.80	-4.46	18.53	66.22	38.71	9.18	–	0.09	107.21
1982	7.61	8.27	-5.79	18.97	81.76	49.50	4.26	–	0.18	104.83
1983	11.42	9.01	-3.36	20.75	54.62	39.54	4.63	–	0.58	140.20
1984	13.55	7.92	0.02	20.89	45.34	30.94	11.52	–	1.85	212.79
1985	12.25	7.10	-0.13	21.26	39.10	31.06	11.21	–	6.20	231.72
1986	8.82	6.35	-1.98	16.03	46.19	30.96	6.19	–	13.66	145.27
1987	9.46	6.19	-0.49	11.87	41.59	25.52	6.24	–	39.23	204.10
1988	10.89	5.69	1.26	38.71	45.72	34.29	6.89	–	262.38	651.11
1989	8.93	5.46	0.24	58.44	36.29	13.42	7.63	42.92	0.00	1,209.12
1990	8.20	6.96	-0.83	17.25	22.13	6.13	7.68	33.50	0.00	2,735.49
1991	8.68	7.91	-0.36	20.43	22.55	9.57	7.24	27.53	0.00	414.24
1992	10.87	8.39	1.56	32.11	20.23	8.91	18.03	23.45	0.00	968.18
1993	10.50	9.10	0.00	48.21	23.64	8.80	22.04	15.73	0.03	2,001.35
1994	9.51	9.16	-0.21	24.62	30.04	11.68	25.26	14.46	0.64	2,251.70
1995	7.26	8.78	-2.36	27.48	36.57	17.84	32.08	13.23	0.92	93.52
1996	6.57	8.37	-2.77	31.36	42.22	17.50	32.92	15.05	1.01	17.09
1997	6.82	9.02	-3.50	34.72	62.64	18.46	26.05	14.42	1.08	7.64
1998	6.93	8.93	-4.01	38.10	79.45	23.90	18.18	17.15	1.16	4.23
1999	9.41	10.82	-4.33	40.37	117.81	29.40	14.89	15.89	1.81	8.48
2000	9.98	11.74	-3.76	43.37	93.55	24.68	13.67	16.55	1.83	6.18
2001	12.18	13.50	-4.19	45.27	75.72	23.86	15.66	14.80	2.35	8.97
2002	14.10	12.58	-1.51	44.02	69.40	19.94	16.38	14.56	2.92	10.55
2003	14.99	12.08	0.76	44.40	65.56	18.37	20.99	14.37	3.08	13.72
2004	16.43	12.55	1.77	46.38	46.63	12.82	24.12	13.28	2.93	8.04
2005	15.13	11.52	1.59	49.62	44.73	9.48	28.70	12.39	2.43	7.21
2006	14.37	11.47	1.25	53.58	37.30	8.87	44.36	12.20	2.18	6.15
2007	13.35	11.85	0.11	56.63	27.81	7.53	75.94	12.22	1.95	5.87
2008	13.79	13.63	-1.72	59.12	22.73	6.49	75.81	13.08	1.83	7.39
2009	12.83	13.29	-1.55	–	–	–	–	–	2.00	4.79

Notes: [a] Percent of exports of goods, services and income. [b] Applied, simple mean, all products, [c] LCU per US$, period average.
Source: http://data.worldbank.org/country/brazil.

I

Table A-1: Brazil Economic Indicators, 1980–2009

	Alternative and nuclear energy (% of total energy use)	GDP per unit of energy use (constant 2005 PPP $per kg of oil equivalent)	Agricultural land (% of land area)	Fuel Imports (% merchandise imports)	Fuel Exports (% merchandise exports	Labor participation rate, female (% of female pop. ages 15+)	Labor participation rate, total (% of total pop. ages 15+)
1980	9.74	8.09	26.51	23.35	9.11	38.20	61.50
1981	10.32	8.08	26.69	23.08	-4.39	39.40	62.10
1982	10.98	8.01	26.97	21.09	0.58	40.00	62.40
1983	11.45	7.52	27.05	16.68	-3.41	41.00	63.00
1984	12.20	7.45	27.18	15.74	5.27	41.30	63.10
1985	12.56	7.53	27.31	19.20	7.95	41.30	63.10
1986	11.64	7.77	27.67	19.09	7.99	41.60	63.30
1987	11.56	7.75	27.87	22.30	3.60	43.50	64.50
1988	12.15	7.64	28.10	22.72	-0.10	43.80	64.50
1989	12.49	7.75	28.30	26.90	3.28	43.90	64.50
1990	13.16	7.70	28.56	20.17	-4.3	44.70	64.70
1991	13.44	7.67	28.95	19.77	1.51	48.50	66.50
1992	13.69	7.55	29.16	18.93	-0.47	52.20	68.40
1993	13.81	7.71	29.49	20.85	4.66	52.30	68.30
1994	13.48	7.72	29.72	22.15	5.33	52.90	68.50
1995	14.04	7.80	30.55	18.03	4.42	53.60	68.60
1996	13.92	7.56	30.62	17.04	2.15	51.80	66.90
1997	13.95	7.41	30.68	17.43	3.37	52.80	67.60
1998	14.22	7.24	30.75	17.03	0.04	53.20	67.60
1999	14.04	7.07	30.82	16.38	0.25	54.80	68.30
2000	14.70	7.29	30.90	18.25	4.31	54.70	68.00
2001	14.09	7.34	31.14	18.03	1.31	54.70	67.80
2002	14.44	7.33	31.16	16.20	2.66	56.20	68.60
2003	15.02	7.30	31.16	15.77	1.15	56.60	68.70
2004	14.62	7.31	31.18	17.12	5.71	57.60	69.40
2005	14.70	7.34	31.21	16.21	3.16	58.50	70.10
2006	15.12	7.38	31.21	16.77	3.96	59.50	70.80
2007	15.10	7.41	31.15	17.31	6.09	59.10	70.30
2008	–	–	–	18.21	5.14	59.90	70.70
2009	–	–	–	16.60	-0.18	–	–

Source: http://data.worldbank.org/country/brazil

Table A-2: Brazil Population and Social Indicators, 1980–2009

	Population growth rate	Rural Population (% of total population)	Telephone lines (per 100 people)	Fertility rate (births per woman)	Birth rate, crude (per 1,000 people)	Death rate, crude (per 1,000 people)	Life expectancy at birth (years)	Life expectancy at birth, female (years)	Population ages 0-14 (% of total)	Population ages 65 and above
1980	2.34	32.60	4.07	4.07	31.95	8.67	62.49	65.30	38.08	4.11
1981	2.34	31.82	4.28	3.97	31.53	8.50	62.89	65.87	37.81	4.12
1982	2.32	31.04	4.57	3.85	30.99	8.33	63.28	66.43	37.59	4.12
1983	2.28	30.26	4.83	3.72	30.34	8.15	63.66	66.96	37.40	4.12
1984	2.22	29.48	5.03	3.59	29.57	7.98	64.04	67.47	37.20	4.13
1985	2.13	28.70	5.29	3.45	28.71	7.80	64.42	67.95	36.98	4.15
1986	2.04	28.00	5.36	3.31	27.78	7.63	64.80	68.40	36.72	4.18
1987	1.96	27.30	5.51	3.17	26.82	7.47	65.17	68.84	36.43	4.22
1988	1.88	26.60	5.73	3.04	25.88	7.31	65.54	69.27	36.10	4.28
1989	1.80	25.90	5.98	2.92	25.00	7.17	65.92	69.70	35.72	4.35
1990	1.73	25.20	6.29	2.81	24.20	7.05	66.30	70.13	35.29	4.43
1991	1.65	24.60	6.63	2.72	23.52	6.94	66.69	70.57	34.80	4.53
1992	1.58	24.00	7.02	2.64	22.97	6.83	67.09	71.01	34.26	4.64
1993	1.53	23.40	7.21	2.58	22.53	6.74	67.49	71.44	33.69	4.75
1994	1.51	22.80	7.70	2.54	22.20	6.66	67.91	71.88	33.10	4.87
1995	1.51	22.20	8.20	2.50	21.95	6.59	68.32	72.30	32.49	4.97
1996	1.51	21.52	9.20	2.47	21.76	6.53	68.72	72.71	31.89	5.08
1997	1.51	20.84	10.22	2.45	21.59	6.48	69.11	73.10	31.28	5.17
1998	1.50	20.16	11.82	2.43	21.41	6.44	69.49	73.47	30.68	5.27
1999	1.47	19.48	14.55	2.40	21.18	6.41	69.85	73.82	30.12	5.37
2000	1.44	18.80	17.76	2.36	20.88	6.39	70.19	74.15	29.60	5.49
2001	1.42	18.20	21.19	2.32	20.48	6.37	70.50	74.45	29.13	5.61
2002	1.38	17.60	21.67	2.27	20.00	6.36	70.81	74.72	28.71	5.75
2003	1.34	17.00	21.60	2.21	19.44	6.35	71.10	74.99	28.31	5.89
2004	1.27	16.40	21.53	2.14	18.82	6.34	71.38	75.23	27.93	6.03
2005	1.19	15.80	21.42	2.08	18.15	6.34	71.65	75.47	27.55	6.17
2006	1.11	15.34	20.62	2.01	17.48	6.35	71.91	75.70	27.16	6.30
2007	1.04	14.88	20.72	1.94	16.81	6.36	72.16	75.93	26.77	6.44
2008	0.97	14.42	21.43	1.88	16.19	6.38	72.40	76.16	26.36	6.58
2009	0.91	13.96	–	–	–		–	–	25.93	6.73

Source:http://data.worldbank.org/country/brazil.

Table A-2: Brazil Population and Social Indicators, 1980–2009

	Unemployment, total (% of total labor force)	Unemployment, male (% of male labor force)	Unemployment, female (% of female labor force)	Female labor force (% of total labor)	Poverty gap at $1.25 a day (PPP) (%)	Poverty gap at $2 a day (PPP) (%)	Poverty headcount ratio at $1.25 a day, PPP (% of population)	Poverty headcount ratio at $2 a day, PPP (% of population)
1980	–	–	–	31.27	–	–	–	–
1981	4.30	4.20	4.40	31.96	5.18	12.38	17.10	31.12
1982	–	–	–	32.32	5.46	12.68	17.52	31.32
1983	4.90	4.90	4.80	32.85	6.64	14.96	20.86	36.01
1984	4.30	4.10	4.60	33.08	6.36	14.74	20.56	36.08
1985	3.40	3.20	3.90	33.12	5.33	12.63	17.51	31.48
1986	2.40	2.20	2.70	33.29	3.13	8.99	12.29	24.80
1987	3.60	3.30	4.00	34.20	5.47	12.15	16.68	29.42
1988	3.80	3.50	4.30	34.47	5.93	12.83	17.66	30.48
1989	3.00	3.00	3.00	34.58	4.29	10.53	14.59	26.75
1990	3.70	3.80	3.50	35.14	4.81	11.22	15.49	27.83
1991	–	–	–	37.13	–	–	–	–
1992	6.40	5.40	7.90	38.89	4.30	9.81	13.29	24.42
1993	6.00	5.20	7.30	39.05	3.78	9.49	12.97	24.69
1994	–	–	–	39.41	–	–	–	–
1995	6.00	5.10	7.20	39.90	2.56	7.74	10.51	21.92
1996	6.80	5.50	8.60	39.56	3.05	8.36	11.43	22.64
1997	7.70	6.20	9.80	39.93	3.31	8.75	11.98	23.32
1998	8.90	7.10	11.50	40.24	2.78	8.10	11.03	22.55
1999	9.60	7.80	12.10	41.04	2.76	8.20	11.15	23.00
2000	–	–	–	41.17	–	–	–	–
2001	9.30	7.50	11.90	41.30	2.83	8.06	10.96	22.28
2002	9.10	7.30	11.50	41.96	2.24	7.30	9.81	21.32
2003	9.70	7.80	12.30	42.22	2.60	7.71	10.43	21.74
2004	8.90	6.80	11.70	42.55	3.84	7.58	11.68	20.93
2005	9.30	7.10	12.20	42.80	1.59	5.93	7.76	18.34
2006	8.40	6.40	11.00	43.11	1.84	5.62	7.36	16.38
2007	9.30	7.40	11.60	43.14	1.26	4.15	5.21	12.69
2008	7.90	6.10	10.00	43.50		–	–	–
2009	–	–	–	–		–	–	–

Source:http://data.worldbank.org/country/brazil.

Abbreviations and Acronyms

ABDI	Agência Brasileira de Desenvolvimento Industrial (Brazilian Agency of Industrial Development)
ABI	Associação Brasileira de Imprensa (Brazilian Press Association)
ABONG	Associação Brasileira de Organizações Não Governamentais (Brazilian Association of Non-Govermental Organizations)
AIG	American International Group
ALADI	Associação Latino-Americana de Integração (Latin American Integration Association)
ALBA	Alianza Bolivariana para los Pueblos de Nuestra América (Bolivarian Alliance for the Americas)
ANP	Agência Nacional do Petróleo (National Petroleum Agency)
ARPEL	Asociación Regional de Empresas de Petróleo y Gas Natural en Latinoamérica y el Caribe (Regional Association of Latin American and Caribbean Oil and Natural Gas Companies)
BIB	Banco de Investimentos do Brasil (Investment Bank of Brazil)
BNDE	Banco Nacional de Desenvolvimento Econômico (National Bank of Economic Development)
BNH	Banco Nacional da Habitação (National Bank of Housing)
Bovespa	São Paulo Stock Exchange

CACM	Central American Common Market
CAR	Centros Administrativos Regionais (Regional Administrative Centers)
CDES	Conselho de Desenvolvimento Econômico e Social (Council of Economic and Social Development)
CEF	Caixa Econômica Federal (Federal Savings and Loans Bank)
CETIP	S.A. Balcão Organizado de Ativos e Derivativos (Over-the-Counter Fixed Income and Derivatives Trading and Custody Organization)
CFEMEA	Centro Feminista de Estudos e Assessoria (Feminist Center for Studies and Consulting)
CGL	Comitê Gestor Local (Local Managing Committee)
CIER	Comisión de Integración Energética Regional (Regional Electrical Integration Commission)
CLT	Consolidação das Leis do Trabalho (Labor Code)
CNDI	Conselho Naciuonal de Desenvolvimento Industrial (National Council of Industrial Development)
CNDM	Conselho Nacional dos Direitos das Mulheres (National Council of Women's Rights)
CNI	Confederação Nacional da Indústria (National Confederation of Industry)
COAF	Conselho de Controle de Atividades Financeiras (Council for Control of Financial Activities)
COAL	Coordenadoria de Assuntos Legislativo (Coordination Office for legislative Affairs)
COP	Comitê do Orçamento Participativo (The Participatory Budgeting Committee)
CPAIMC	Centro de Pesquisa de Assistência Integrada à Mulher e à Criança (Center for Research and Integral Assistance to Women and Children)
CSN	Companhia Siderúrgica Nacional (National Steel Company)
CSSF	Comissão de Seguridade Social e Familia (Health, Security and Family Committee)
CUT	Central Única dos Trabalhadores (Unified Worker's Central)
DASP	Departamento Administrativo do Serviço Público (The Public Service Management Department)
DPHAN	Department of Historical and Artistic Patrimony
ECLAC	United Nations Economic Commission for Latin America and the Caribbean
EMBRAPA	Empresa Brasileira de Pesquisa Agropecuária (Brazilian State Company for Research in Agriculture)
EMBRATEL	Empresa Brasileira de Telecomunicações (Brazilian Telecom Company)

ERP	European Recovery Program (Marshall Plan)
FAT	Fundo de Amparo ao Trabalhador (Workers Assistance Fund)
FEBRABAN	Federação Brasileira de Bancos (Brazilian Federation of Banks)
FGC	Fundo Garantidor de Crédito (Federal Deposit Insurance Fund)
FGTS	Fundo de Garantia de Tempo de Serviço (Social Security Fund)
FIESP	Federação das Indústrias do Estado de São Paulo (Federation of Industries of the State of Sao Paulo)
FINATEC	Fundação de Empreendimentos Científicos e Tecnológicos (Foundation for Scientific and Technological Projects)
FIU	Financial Intelligence Unit
FTAA	Free Trade Area of the Americas
GATT	General Agreement on Tariffs and Trade
GDP	Gross Domestic Product
GNP	Gross National Product
IBGE	Instituto Brasileiro de Geografia e Estatística (Brazilian Institute of Geography and Statistics)
IDB	Inter-American Development Bank
IEA	International Energy Agency
IEDI	Instituto de Estudos para o Desenvolvimento Industrial (Institute for the Study of Industrial Development)
ILO	International Labor Organization
IMF	International Monetary Fund
INTAL	Institute for the Integration of Latin America and the Caribbean
IPEA	Instituto de Pesquisas Econômicas Aplicadas (Applied Economic Research Institute
IPAC	Institute of Cultural and Artistic Patrimony
IPHAN	Institute of National Artistic and Historical Patrimony
IPI	Imposto sobre Produtos Industrializado (Tax on Industrialized Products)
ISI	Import-Substituting Industrialization
ITO	International Trade Organization
LAFTA	Latin American Free Trade Association
LIBOR	London Interbank Offering Rate
MARE	Ministério da Administração Federal e Reforma do Estado (Ministry of Federal Administration and State Reform)
MERCOSUR	Mercado Común del Sur (Common Market of the South)
NAFTA	North American Free Trade Agreement
NATO	North Atlantic Treaty Organization
NPM	New Public Management

NYMEX	New York Mercantile Exchange
OAB	Ordem dos Advogados do Brasil (Brazilian Bar Association)
OAS	Organization of the American States
OECD	Organization for Economic Co-operation and Development
OLADE	Organización Latinoamericana de Energía (Latin American Energy Organization)
ONIP	Organização Nacional da Indústria do Petróleo (National Organization of Industry and Petroleum)
OP	Orçamento Participativo (Participatory Budgeting)
OPEC	Organization of the Petroleum Exporting Countries
ORTN	Obrigação Reajustável do Tesouro Nacional - Inflation Adjusted Treasury Note
OSCIP	Organizações da Sociedade Civil de Interesse Público (Civil Society Organization of Public Interest)
PAC	Programa de Acelaração do Desenvolvimento (Accelerated Growth Program)
PAEG	Plano de Ação Econômica do Governo (Plan for Government Economic Action)
PAISM	Programa de Assistência Integral à Saúde da Mulher (Complete Assistance Health Program for Women)
PDVSA	Petróleos de Venezuela (Venezuelan Petroleum Company)
Petrobras	Petróleo Brasileiro S/A (State Oil Company)
PIS	Plano de Integração Social (Plan for Social Integration)
PITCE	Programa de Inovação Tecnológica e Comércio Exterior (Industrial, Technological, and Trade Policy)
PMDB	Partido do Movimento Democrático Brasileiro (Party of the Brazilian Democratic Movement)
PMN	Partido da Mobilização Nacional (National Mobilization Party)
PNAD	Pesquisa Nacional por Amostra de Domicílio (Household National Sample Survey)
PND II	Plano Nacional do Desenvolvimento II (National Plan for Development II)
PRONA	Partido da Reedificação da Ordem Nacional (Party of the Reedification of National Order)
PR	Partido da República (Party of the Republic)
PROEF	Programa de Fortalecimento dos Bancos Federais (Program for the Strengthening of Federal Banks)
PROER	Programa de Estímulo à Reestruturação e ao Fortalecimento do Sistema Financeiro Nacional (Stimulus Program for the Restructuring and Strengthening of the Brazilian Financial System)

PROES	Programa de Incentivo à Redução do Estado na Atividade Bancária (Stimulus Program for the Reduction of State Involvement in Banking Activities)
PSB	Partido Socialista Brasileiro (Brazilian Socialist Party)
PSDB	Partido da Social Democracia Brasileira (Brazilian Social Democratic Party)
PSoL	Partido de Socialism e Liberdade (Party of Socialism and Liberty)
PSTU	Partido Socialista dos Trabalhadores Unificado (Unified Socialist Labor Party)
PT	Partido dos Trabalhadores (Workers' Party)
PTB	Partido Trabalhista Brasileiro Brazilian Labor Party
SAL/MJ	Secretaria de Assuntos Legislativos/Ministerio de Justiça (Legislative Affairs section at the Justice Ministry)
SELIC	Sistema Especial de Liquidação e Custódia (Special System for Trading and Custody)
SENASP	Secretaria Nacional de Segurança Pública (National Secretariat for Public Safety)
SMCPGL	Secretaria Municipal de Coordenação Política e Governança Local (Secretariat for Political Coordination and Local Solidarity Governance)
SPHAN	National Artistic and Historical Patrimony Service
SPM	Secretaria Especial para Políticas para Mulheres (Special Secretariat for Women's Policies)
STF	Supremo Tribunal Federal (The national level Supreme Court)
STJ	Superior Tribunal de Justiça (Highest level federal appeals court)
TSE	Tribunal Superior Eleitoral (Brazil's national level election)
SUMOC	Superintendência da Moeda e do Crédito (Superintendency for Money and Credit)
SUS	Sistema Unico de Saude (Unified Health System)
SVS	Secretaria de Vigilância em Saúde (Secretariat for Health Surveillance)
TELEBRAS	Telecomunicações Brasileiras (State Telephone Company)
UAMPA	União das Associações de Moradores de Porto Alegre (Union of Neighborhood Associations of Porto Alegre)
UNASUR	Unión de Naciones Suramericanas (Union of South American Nations)
UNCTAD	United Nations Conference on Trade and Development
UNESCO	United Nations Educational, Scientific and Cultural Organization
URV	Unidade Real de Valor (Unit of Real Value)

BIBLIOGRAPHY

Abers, Rebecca Neaera. 2000. *Inventing Local Democracy: Grassroots Politics in Brazil.* Boulder, Colo.: Lynne Rienner Publishers.

Aberbach, Joel, R. Putnam, and B. Rockman. 1981. *Bureaucrats and Politicians in Western Democracy.* Cambridge, Massachussets: Harvard University Press.

Abranches, Sérgio. 1988. "O presidencialismo de coalizão: o dilema institucional brasileiro," *Dados*, 31(1): 5-33.

——. 1996. "Governabilidade e reformas: dilemas de transição." In J.P. Reis Velloso, ed., *O Real, O Crescimento e as Reformas.* Rio de Janeiro, Brazil: José Olympio.

Acharya, Amitav. 2007. "The Emerging Regional Architecture of World Politics." *World Politics* 59 (4): 629-52.

Aggarwal, Reena 2003. "Capital Market Development and Nurturing," In Litan, Pomerleano and Sundararajan, eds., *The Future of Domestic Capital Markets in Developing Countries.* Washington, D.C.: Brookings Institution Press.

Akitoby, Bernardin and Thomas Stratmann. 2008. "Fiscal Policy and Financial Markets." *Economic Journal* 118: 1971-85.

Aldcroft, Derek H. 1977. *From Versailles to Wall Street. 1919-1929.* London, U.K.: Allen Lane Penguin Books.

Almeida, Paulo Roberto de. 2009. "Lula's Foreign Policy: Regional and Global Strategies." In Joseph L. Love and Werner Baer, eds., *Brazil Under Lula: Economy, Politics, and Society under the Worker-President.* New York, N.Y.:

Palgrave-MacMillan, 167-186.

Almeida, Rodrigo. Forthcoming. "Entrando no clube: o BNDES e a inserção Brasileira no capitalismo internacional." In Renato Boschi ed., *Variedades de capitalismo: política e desenvolvimento na América Latina.* Belo Horizonte, Brazil: Ed.UFMG/IUPERJ.

Alvarez, Sonia E. 1990. *Engendering Democracy in Brazil: Women's Movements in Transition Politics.* Princeton, N.J.: Princeton University Press.

——. 1998. "Latin American Feminisms 'Go Global': Trends of the 1990s and Challenges for the New Millennium." In Sonia E. Alvarez, Evelina Dagnino, and Arturo Escobar, eds., *Cultures of Politics/Politics of Cultures: Re-visioning Latin American Social Movements.* Boulder, Colo.: Westview Press.

Alves, Branca Moreira, Leila Linhares Barsted, Sandra Azeredo Boschi, Jacqueline Pitanguy, and Mariska Ribeiro. 1981. *Espelho de Vênus: identidade social e sexual da mulher.* São Paulo, Brazil: Grupo Ceres, Editora Brasiliense.

Amable, Bruno. 2003. *The Diversity of Modern Capitalism.* Oxford, London: Oxford University Press.

Amsberg, Joachim von, Peter Lanjouw, Kimberly Nead. 2000. "A focalização do gasto social sobre a pobreza no Brasil." In R. Henriques, ed. *Desigualdade e pobreza no Brasil.* Rio de Janeiro, Brazil: IPEA, pp. 685-718.

"An Axis in Need of Oiling: the Anti-West." 2008. *The Economist*, 25 October: 71-72.

ANAPP. 2008. *Estatísticas de Mercado.* December. www.anapp.org.br.

Anastasia, Fátima, Carlos Ranulfo Melo, and Fabiano Santos. 2004. *Governabilidade e representação política na América do Sul.* São Paulo, Brazil: Editora da UNESP/Fundação Konrad Adenauer.

Anastassakis, Zoy. 2008. "Um projeto de design nacional: Aloisio Magalhães e o Centro Nacional de Referencia Cultural." Anais do 8o Congresso Brasileiro de Pesquisa e Desenvolvimento em Design. São Paulo, Brazil: AEND.

Andrade, Mário de. 1968. "O movimento modernista" In Gilberto Freyre, ed., *Temas Brasileiros.* Rio de Janeiro, Brazil: Casa do Estudante do Brasil.

——. 1993. "Anteprojeto do patrimônio." In Lauro Cavalcanti, ed., *Modernistas na repartição.* Rio de Janeiro, Brazil: Editora UFRJ, 39-56.

Assef, Andrea and Mara Luquet. 2006. *Meninas normais vão ao shopping—meninas iradas vão à bolsa.* São Paulo, Brazil: Editora Saraiva.

Andrews, Edmund and Larry Rohter. 2007. "U.S. and Brazil Seek to Promote Ethanol in West." *The New York Times*, 3 March.

Apolinário, Alessandro A., Alessandro Rocha da Silva, Carlos Eduardo Marinho Diniz, Erica Pelicano Ribeiro, and Emerson de Oliveira Capistrano. 2002. "O impacto do FGTS na alavancagem do mercado de capitais brasileiro." Paper presente at the "XXII Encontro Nacional de Engenharia de Produção," Curitiba, Brazil, October 23-25.

Apostolik, Richard, Christopher Donohue, and Peter Went. 2009. *Foundations of Banking Risk.* Hoboken, N.J.: Wiley, John & Sons, Inc., 68-70.

Araújo, Clara. 2001. "As cotas por sexo para a competição legislativa: o caso brasileiro e comparação com experiências internacionais." *Dados*, 44 (1): 155-94.

Arbix, Glauco. 2000. "Beyond Market Fundamentalism and the Developmental State." Paper presented at the conference, "Regional Powers, New Developmental States, and Global Governance: BRICS in the New World

Order," Watston Institute for International Studies, Brown University, March 13-14.

Arbix, Glauco and Zil Miranda. 2009. "Tecnologia e internacionalizacão." *Folha de São Paulo*, 19 October.

Arbix, Glauco and João A. Negri. 2006. "Uma nova competitividade da indústria e o novo empresariado: uma hipótese de trabalho." *São Paulo em Perspectiva* 19 (2).

Armijo, Leslie Elliott and Christine A. Kearney. 2008. "Does Democratization Alter the Policy Process? Trade Policymaking in Brazil." *Democratization* 15 (5): 991-1017.

Arretche, Marta. 2004. "Toward a Unified and More Equitable System: Health Reform in Brazil." In Robert R. Kaufman and Joan Nelson, eds., *Crucial Needs, Weak Incentives: Social Sector Reform, Democratication, and Globalization in Latin America*. Baltimore, Md. and London, U.K.: Johns Hopkins University Press, 155-88.

Asad, Talal. 2002. "Ethnographic Representation, Statistics, and Modern Power." In Brian Axel, ed., *From the Margins: Historical Anthropology and its Futures*. Durham, N.C.: Duke University Press, 66-94.

Avelar, Lúcia, and Antônio Cintra, ed. 2007. *Sistema político Brasileiro: uma introdução*. 2nd Ed. São Paulo, Brazil: UNESP/Konrad Adenauer Stiftung.

Avritzer, Leonardo. 2009. *Participatory Institutions in Democratic Brazil*. Baltimore, MD: The Johns Hopkins University Press.

Avritzer, Leonardo, and Fátima Anastásia, ed. 2006. *Reforma política no Brasil*. Belo Horizonte, Brazil: Editora da UFMG.

Baaklini, Abdo and Antonio Carlos Pojo do Rego. 1988. "The Congress and the National Policy on Computer Science." *Revista de Administração Pública* 22 (2).

Babington, Deepa and Jane Barrett. 2007. "Santander sells Antonveneta to M. Paschi." Reuters, 8 November.

Baccaro, Lucio. 2002. "Negotiating the Italian Pension Reform with the Unions: Lessons for Corporatist Theory." *Industrial and Labor Relations Review* 55 (3): 413-431.

Baer, Werner. 1995. *The Brazilian Economy: Growth and Development.*. 4th Ed. Westport, Conn.: Praeger Publishers.

——. 2008. *The Brazilian Economy: Growth and Development*. 6th Ed. Boulder, Colo.: Lynne Rienner Publishers.

Baer, Werner and Nader Nazmi. 2000. "Privatization and Restructuring of Banks in Brazil." *The Quarterly Review of Economics and Finance* 40 (1).

Baier, Scott L., Jeffrey H. Bergstrand, and Erika Vidal. 2007. "Free Trade Agreement in the Americas: Are the Trade Effects Larger than Anticipated?" *World Economy* 30 (9): 1347-77.

Baiocchi, Gianpaolo. 2005. *Militants and Citizens: The Politics of Participatory Democracy in Porto Alegre*. Stanford, Calif.: Stanford University Press.

Banco Central do Brasil. 2008. *Financial Stability Report 7.1*. Brasília, Brazil: BCB.

——. *Informações Contábeis, 50 Maiores Bancos*. www.bcb.gov.br.

——. *Operações de crédito do sistema financeiro, saldos com recursos livres e direcionados*. www.bcb.gov.br.

——. *Series temporais*. http://www.bcb.gov.br/?SERIETEMP.

——. *Sistema financeiro nacional. relatório de ativos*. www.bcb.gov.br.

Banco do Brasil S.A. 2009. "Conclusion of Banco Votorantim Strategic Partnership." Press Release, 28 September.

BIS. 2004. *International Convergence of Capital Measurements and Standards: A Revised Framework*. Basel, Switzerland: Bank of International Settlements.

BID. 2009. *INTAL - Carta Mensal no. 152*, March.

Banco Santander, 2009. "Material Fact, Complementary Information on IPO of Banco Santander (Brasil) S.A," 10 November. www.santander.com.

Bandeira, Lourdes. 1998. "O que faz da vítima, vítima?" In Ricardo Limam, Djaci Oliveira, and Elen Geraldes, eds., *A Primavera já Partiu*. Petrópolis, Brazil: Ed. Vozes e M.N.D.H.

——. 2005. *Brasil: fortalecimento da Secretaria Especial de Políticas para as Mulheres avançar na transversalidade da perspectiva de Gênero nas Políticas*. Brasília, Brazil: CEPAL and SPM.

Baratta, Alessandro. 1999. *Criminologia crítica e crítica do Direito Penal*. Rio de Janeiro, Brazil: Instituto Carioca de Criminologia.

Barbosa, Fernando. 2008. "Jogo de Ponzi, PROER e FCVS," *Revista de Economia Política* 28 (1).

Barreto, Leonardo, and David Fleischer. 2008. "Reformas políticas y democracia en Brasil." In Daniel G. Zovatto, and José Henríquez, eds., *Reforma política y electoral en América Latina*. México: UNAM and IDEA, 315-52.

Barrionuevo, Alexei. 2009. "Energy Deal with Brazil Gives Boost to Paraguay." *New York Times*, 27 July: A10.

Barros, Ricardo and Miguel Foguel. 2000. "Focalização dos gastos públicos sociais e erradicação da pobreza no Brasil." In *Desigualdade e pobreza do Brasil*. Rio de Janeiro, Brazil: IPEA.

Barsted, Leila Linhares. 2007. "O movimento de mulheres e o debate sobre o aborto." Presented at the "Seminário Estudos sobre a Questão do Aborto." Campinas, Brazil: Unicamp.

Beattie, Alan. 2006. "Ethanol Puts Power in Brazil's Tank." *The Financial Times* (London), 16 May.

Becker, Howard S. 1997. *Uma teoria da ação coletiva*. Rio de Janeiro, Brazil: Zahar.

Becker, Uwe. 2007. "Open Systemness and Contested Reference Frames and Change: A Reformulation of the Varieties of Capitalism Theory." *Socio-Economic Review* 5.

Beltrão, Hélio. 1984. *Descentralização e liberdade*. Rio de Janeiro, Brazil: Record.

Benevides, Maria Victória. 1976. *Governo Kubitschek: desenvolvimento econômico e estabilidade política*. São Paulo, Brazil: Brasiliense.

Benevides, Maria Victória, Paulo Vannuchi, and Fábio Kerche, eds. 2003. *Reforma política e cidadania*. São Paulo, Brazil: Fundação Perseu Abramo.

Beras, Cesar. 2008. "Orçamento participativo de Porto Alegre e a democratização do Estado: a configuração especifica do caso de Porto Alegre: 1989-2004." Ph.D. Diss. Universidade Federal do Rio Grande do Sul.

Besley, Timothy and Burgess, Robin. 2003. "Halving Global Poverty." *Journal of Economic Perspectives* 17 (3): 3-22.

Besse, Susan. 1996. *Restructuring Patriarchy: The Modernization of Gender Inequality in Brazil, 1914-1940*. Chapel Hill, N.C.: University of North Carolina Press.

Black, John, Nigar Hashimzade, and Gareth Myles. 2009. *A Dictionary of Economics*. Oxford, London: Oxford University Press.

Bomeny, Helena Bousquet. 1995. "O patrimônio de Mário de Andrade." In Márcia Chuva et al., eds. *A invenção do patrimônio: continuidade e ruptura na constituição de uma política oficial de preservação no Brasil.* Rio de Janeiro, Brazil: Minc/IPHAN.

Boschi, Renato. 2004. "Instituciones políticas, reformas estructurales y ciudadanía: dilemas de la democracia en Brasil." *Política* 42.

——. 2006. "Setor privado, reestruturação econômica e democratização na América Latina." In José M. Domingues and María Maneiro eds., *América Latina hoje.* Rio de Janeiro, Brazil: Civilização Brasileira.

——. 2008. "Capacidades estatales y políticas de desarrollo en Brasil: Tendencias Recientes." In Manuel Alcántara Sáez and Carlos Ranulfo Melo eds., *La democracia Brasileña, balance y perspectivas para el siglo XXI.* Salamanca, Spain: Ediciones Univesidad de Salamanca.

——. 2009. "Elites parlamentares e a agenda pós-neoliberal: Brasil e Chile." In Fátima Anastasia et al. eds., *Elites parlamentares na América Latina.* Belo Horizonte, Brazil: Ed. Argvmentvm.

Boschi, Renato and Flávio Gaitan. 2008a. "Intervencionismo estatal e políticas de desenvolvimento na América Latina." *Caderno CRH* 21 (53): 301-17.

——. 2008b. "Gobiernos progresistas, agendas neodesarrollistas y capacidades estatales: la experiencia reciente en Argentina, Brasil y Chile." In Maria Regina S. de Lima, ed., *Desempenho de governos progressistas no Cone Sul.* Rio de Janeiro, Brazil: Edições IUPERJ.

——. 2009. "Outra volta no parafuso desenvolvimentista: um manifesto." *INSIGHT Inteligencia* 45: 131-45.

Boschi, Renato and Maria Regina S. de Lima. 2002. "O Executivo e a construção do Estado no Brasil: Do Desmonte da Era Vargas ao Novo Intervencionismo Regulatório." In Luiz Werneck Vianna ed., *A democracia e os três poderes no Brasil.* Belo Horizonte, Brazil: Ed. UFMG/IUPERJ.

Bourdieu, Pierre. 1997. "Le Champs Économique." *Actes de la Recherché en Sciences Sociales* 119: 15-57.

Bouzan, Ary. 1975. *Os bancos comerciais do Brasil (1964-1972).* São Paulo, Brazil: FEBRABAN.

Boyer, Robert. 2005. "How and Why Capitalisms Differ." *Economy and Society* 34 (4): 509-57.

Braga, Isabel. 2003. "Bancada evangélica pressiona o governo contra a reforma política." *O Globo*, 13 July: 4.

Bragon, Ranier, and Maria Clara Cabral. 2009. "Troca-troca engorda PSC e PR; oposição encolhe 17%." *Folha de São Paulo*, 3 October.

Brainard, Lael and Leonardo Martinez-Diaz, eds. 2009. *Brazil as an Economic Superpower? Understanding Brazil's Changing Role in the Global Economy.* Washington, D.C.: Brookings Institution Press.

Brasil Jr., Olavo. 1998. "As reformas administrativas no Brasil: modelos, sucessos e fracassos." 49 (2).

"Brazil's Lula meets foes to new oil plan." 2009. *Reuters*, 31 August. www.reuters.com.

Bresser-Pereira, Luiz Carlos. 1972. *Tecnoburocracia e contestação.* Petrópolis, Brazil: Editora Vozes.

——. 1977. *Estado e desenvolvimento industrializado.* São Paulo, Brazil: Brasiliense.

——. 2000a. *The New Left and the Moving Center.* Brasília, Brazil: Instituto Teotônio Vilela.

——. 2000b. "State Reform in the 1990s: Logic and Control Mechanisms." In Leonardo Burlamaqui, Ana Célia Castro, Ha-Joon Chang, eds., *Institutions and the Role of the State.* Cheltenham, U.K.: Edward Elgar, 175-219.

——. 2004. "O novo desenvolvimentismo." *Folha de S. Paulo*, 19 September.

——. 2005. "Proposta de desenvolvimento para o Brasil." In João Sicsú, Luís Fernando de Paula and R. Michel, eds., *Novo-desenvolvimentismo: um projeto nacional de crescimento com eqüidade.* São Paulo, Brazil: Editora Manole.

——. 2006. "O novo desenvolvimentismo e a ortodoxia convencional." *São Paulo em Perspectiva* 20(1).

——. 2009. *Mondialisation et Competition: Pourquoi Certains Pays Émergents Réussissent et d'Autres Non.* Paris, France: Editions la Découverte.

Bresser-Pereira, Luiz Carlos, and Nuria C. Grau. 1999. "Entre o Estado e o mercado: o público não estatal." In L.C. Bresser-Pereira and Nuria C. Grau, eds., O *público não-estatal na reforma do Estado.* Rio de Janeiro, Brazil: Editora FGV, 15-48.

Brooks, Sarah M. 2009. *Social Protection and the Market in Latin America: the Transformation of Social Security Institutions.* New York, N.Y.: Cambridge University Press.

Bulmer-Thomas, Victor. 1994. *The Economic History of Latin America Since Independence.* Cambridge, Mass.: Cambridge University Press.

Burges, Sean. 2006. "Without Sticks or Carrots: Brazilian Leadership in South America During the Cardoso Era, 1992-2003." *Bulletin of Latin American Research* 25 (1): 23-42.

——. 2007. "Building a Global Southern Coalition: the Competing Approaches of Brazil's Lula and Venezuela's Chavez." *Third World Quarterly* 28 (7): 1343-58.

Burgos, Raúl. 2002. "The Gramscian Intervention in the Theoretical and Political Production of the Latin American Left." *Latin American Perspectives* 29 (1): 9-37.

——. 2007. "Da democratização política à radicalização da democracia: novasdimensões estratégicas dos movimentos sociais." In Evelina Dagnino and Luciana Tatagiba, eds., *Democracia, sociedade civil e participação.* Chapecó, Brazil: Argos, 125-66.

Busatto, Cézar. 1991. "Notas sobre desenvolvimento, Estado, planejamento e orçamento." In Cézar Busatto, ed., *Democracia, prosperidade e responsabilidade social.* Porto Alegre, Brazil: Editora Sulina, 38-57.

——. 1998. *Anjos anônimos: exemplo de luta e solidariedade humana.* Porto Alegre, Brazil: L&PM Editores.

——. 1999a. "O significado histórico do Governo Britto." *Democracia: Cadernos de Reflexão Política* 3: 94-106.

——. 1999b. "Política e desenvolvimento paraviver melhor." In Cézar Busatto, ed., *Democracia, prosperidade e responsabilidade social.* Porto Alegre, Brazil: Editora Sulina. 15-36.

——. 1999c. *Democracia, prosperidade e responsabilidade social.* Porto Alegre, Brazil: Editora Sulina.

——. 2001. *Responsabilidade social: revolução do nosso tempo.* Porto Alegre, Brazil:

CORAG.

——. 2008. Personal Interview. August 31.

Busatto, Cézar, and Jandira Feijó. 2006. *A era dos vagalumes: o florescer de uma nova cultura política*. Porto Alegre, Brazil: Universidade Luterana do Brasil.

Busatto, Cézar, and Plíno Zalewski. 2004. *Governça Solidária Local: fundamentos políticos da mundança em Porto Alegre*. Porto Alegre, Brazil: Prefeitura Municipas de Porto Alegre.

Buzan, Barry and Ole Waever. 2003. *Regions and Powers: The Structure of International Security*. Cambridge, Mass.: Cambridge University Press.

"Caderno Economia."*O Globo*, 2006. 3 August.

Caiado, Ronaldo. 2007. "Com o atual sistema, não há salvação." *Plenarium* [Câmara dos Deputados] 4 (2): 4-29.

Caldeira, Jorge. 1995. *Mauá empresário do Império*. São Paulo, Brazil: Editora Schwartz.

Calógeras, João P. 1939. *A History of Brazil*. Chapel Hill, N.C.: University of North Carolina Press.

Câmara dos Deputados. 2007. "Reforma política." *Plenarium* 4.

Campbell, John L. and Ove Pedersen. 2007. "The Varieties of Capitalism and Hybrid Success: Denmark in the Global Economy." *Comparative Political Studies* 40 (3): 307-32.

Campello de Souza, Maria do Carmo. 1976. *Estado e partidos políticos no Brazil*. São Paulo, Brazil: Editora Alfa-Omega.

Campos, Carmen. 2001. "Violência doméstica no espaço da Lei." In Cristina Bruschini, and Céli Pinto, eds., *Tempos e Lugares de Gênero*. São Paulo, Brazil: Fundação Carlos Chagas and Editora 34.

Cardoso, Fernando Henrique. 1975. *Autoritarismo e democratização*. Rio de Janeiro, Brazil: Paz e Terra.

——. 2001. *Charting a New Course: The Politics of Globalization and Social Transformation*. Maurício Font, ed., New York, N.Y.: Rowman and Littlefield.

Cardoso, Ruth. 1992. "Popular Movements in the Context of Democracy in Brazil." In Escobar and S. Alvarez, eds., *The Making of Social Movements in Latin America: Identity, Strategy and Democracy*. Boulder, Colo.: Westview Press.

Caro, Ariela Ruiz. 2008. "Energy Integration and Security in Latin America and the Caribbean." Americas Policy Program 27 March. www.americas.irc-online.org.

Carrara, Sérgio, Adriana Vianna, and Ana Lúcia Enne. 2000. "Crimes de Bagatela: a violência contra a mulher na justiça do Rio de Janeiro." In Mariza Corrêa, ed., *Gênero e cidadania*. São Paulo, Brazil: Unicamp.

Carvalho, Antonio G. 2002. "Governança corporativa no Brasil em perspectiva." *Revista de Administração de Empresas* 37: 19-32.

Carvalho, José Murilo. 1997. "Mandonismo, coronelismo, clientelismo: uma discussão conceitual." *Revista Dados* 40(2), Rio de Janeiro, Brazil.

Caspary, Georg. 2007. "The Energy Sector in Latin America: Key Prospects, Risks and Opportunities." Latin America Current Issues, Deutsche Bank Research, 7 September.

Castañeda, Jorge. 2006. "Latin America's Left Turn." *Foreign Affairs*, May-June.

Castro, Mônica. 2006. "Cláusula de barreira." In Leonardo Avritzer, and Fátima

Anastásia, eds., *Reforma política no Brasil.* Belo Horizonte: Editora da UFMG, 188-91.

Cavalcanti, Amaro. 1983. *Meio circulante nacional (1808-1835).* Brasília, Brazil: Editora Universidade de Brasília.

Cavalcanti, Lauro. 1999. "Modernistas, arquitetura e patrimônio." In Dulce Pandolfi, ed., *Repensando o Estado Novo.* Rio de Janeiro, Brazil: Editora FGV, 178-196.

Cavalcanti, Maria Laura and Maria Luiza Heilborn. 1985. "SOS—Mulher do Rio de Janeiro: uma entrevista." In Bruna Franchetto, Maria Laura Cavalcanti e Maria Luiza Heilborn, eds., *Perspectivas antropológicas da mulher: sobre mulher e violência.* Rio de Janeiro, Brazil: Zahar Editores.

Cechin, J. 2002. "A previdência social reavaliada-II." *Conjuntura Social* 13 (1): 7-54.

"Central Planning: Rediscovering the Charms of BNDES." 2009. *The Economist*, 16 April.

Cerbasi, Gustavo. 2004. *Casais Inteligentes Enriquecem Juntos.* São Paulo, Brazil: Editora Gente.

Cesar, Benedito Tadeu. 2002. "O projeto político-societário petista." In *PT: a contemporaneidade possível. base social e projeto político (1980-1991).* Porto Alegre: Editora Universidade Federal do Rio Grande do Sul.

CFEMEA. 1994. *Jornal Fêmea.* nº11, January.

Chacon, Vamireh. 2001. *A construção da brasilidade: Gilberto Freyre e sua geração.* São Paulo, Brazil: Marco Zero.

Chang, Ha-Joon. 2002. *Kicking Away the Ladder: Development Strategy in Historical Perspective.* London, U.K.: Anthem Press.

——. 2003. *Globalization, Economic Development and the Role of the State.* London, U.K.: Zed Books.

——. 2007. *Bad Samaritans: Rich Nations, Poor Policies, and the Threat to the Developing World.* London, U.K.: Random House.

Chaui, Marilena. 2000. *Brasil: mito fundador e sociedade autoritaria.* São Paulo, Brazil: Fundação Perseu Abramo.

CIA World Factbook. 2009. Washington, D.C.: Central Intelligence Agency.

CIDADE. 2007. "Renovação de lideranças e democracia: uma reflexão necessária." *Boletim Cidade* VI (39).

——. 2008. "Um fantasma assombra o governo municipal." *Boletim Cidade* VII (43).

Cintra, Antônio. 2008. "Majoritário ou proporcional? Em busca do equilíbrio na construção de um sistema eleitoral." In João Paulo Viana, and Gilmar Nascimento, eds., *O sistema político brasileiro: continuidade ou reforma.* Porto Velho, Brazil: Edufro, 17-46.

CNDM. 1986. Carta das Mulheres. Brasília, Brazil.

Coates, David. 2005. *Varieties of Capitalism, Varieties of Approaches.* New York, N.Y.: Palgrave McMillan.

Código Penal Atualizado. 1940. Decreto-Lei no 2.848, de 7 de Dezembro.

Cohen, Jean L. and Andrew Arato. 1992. *Civil Society and Political Theory.* Cambridge, Mass.: MIT Press.

Cohn, Gabriel. 1968. *Petróleo e nacionalismo.* São Paulo, Brazil: DIFEL.

——. 1984. "A concepção oficial da política cultural nos anos 70." In Sérgio Miceli, ed., *Estado e cultura no Brasil.* São Paulo, Brazil: Difel, 85-96.

Collins, John. 2008a. "'But What if I Should Need to Defecate in Your Neighborhood, Madame?' Empire, Redemption and the 'Tradition of the Oppressed' in a Brazilian Historical Center." *Cultural Anthropology* 23: 279-328.

——. 2008b. "Patrimony, Public Health, and National Culture: The Commodification and Redemption of Origins in Neoliberal Brazil." *Critique of Anthropology* 28: 237-55.

——. Forthcoming. *The Revolt of the Saints: Memory and Redemption in the Twilight of Brazil's 'Racial Democracy.'* Durham, N.C.: Duke University Press.

Comaroff, Jean and John Comaroff. 2009. *Ethnicity, Inc.* Chicago, Ill.: University of Chicago Press.

Constanzi, Rogério N. 2009. "Crise global e impactos no Brasil: o problema da estabilidade da instabilidade financeira," *Informações FIPE*, August.

Correio Braziliense. 2000. 28 August: 6.

Costa, Ana Maria. 1996. "Planejamentofamiliar no Brasil." *Revista Bio* 2 (4).

Costa, Vanda Maria Ribeiro. 2006. "Os conselhos do CDES: experimento sem conclusão." *Insight Inteligência* 32: 146-61.

Crotty, James R. 2003. "The Neoliberal Paradox: the Impact of Destructive Product Market Competition and Impatient Finance on Nonfinancial Corporations in the Neoliberal Era." PERI *Research Brief.* Amherst, Mass.: University of Massachusetts Press.

Crouch, Colin. 2005. *Capitalist Diversity and Change: Recombinant Governance and Institutional Entrepreneurs.* Oxford, London: Oxford University Press.

Crouch, Colin and Henry Farrell. 2004. "Breaking the Path of Institutional Development? Alternative to the New Determinism." *Rationality and Society* 16 (5): 5-43.

Cruvinel, Tereza. 2003. "Regras próprias." *O Globo*, 15 July: 2.

"Cuba rejects OAS membership, official says." 2009. *CNN*, 4 June. http://www.cnn.com/2009/WORLD/americas/06/04/cuba.oas/index.html.

Cunha, Anna Lucia. 2007. "Pessoa e direito, corpo e ciência: negociando preceitos cosmológicos em torno da legalizaçao do aborto." M.A. Diss. Universidade de Brasília.

Cunha, Eleonora Schettini Martins. 2007. "O potencial de conselhos de políticas e orçamentos participativos para o aprofundamento democrático." In Evelina Dagnino and Luciana Tatagiba, eds., *Democracia, sociedade civil e participação.* Chapecó, Brazil: Argos, 25-44.

Cunha, Olívia Maria Gomes da. 2000. "Sua alma em sua palma: identificando a 'raça' e inventando a nação." In Dulce Pandolfi, ed., *Repensando o Estado Novo.* Rio de Janeiro, Brazil: Editora FGV.

D'Araujo, Maria Celina. 1982. *O segundo governo Vargas (1951-54).* Rio de Janeiro, Brazil: Zahar Editores.

——. 2007. "Governo Lula: contornos sociais e políticos da elite do poder." *CPDOC/FGV.*

Dacanal, José Hildebrando. 1999. *A nova classe no poder.* Porto Alegre, Brazil: Editora Novo Século.

Dagnino, Evelina. 2004. "Sociedade civil, participação e cidadania: de que estamos falando?" In Daniel Mato, ed., *Políticas de ciudadanía y sociedad civil en tiempos de globalización*. Caracas, Venezuela: FACES, Universidad Central de Venezuela, 95-110.

——. 2007. "Citizenship: A Perverse Confluence." *Development in Practice* 17 (4 and 5): 549-56.

Dagnino, Evelina, Alberto J. Olvera, and Aldo Panfichi. 2006. "Para uma outra leitura da disputa pela construção democrática na América Latina." In Evelina Dagnino, Alberto J. Olvera and Aldo Panfichi, eds., *A disputa pela construção democrática na América Latina*. São Paulo, Brazil: Editora Paz e Terra, 13-91.

Dalland, Robert. 1968. *Brazilian Planing*. Chapel Hill: University of North Carolina Press.

DATASUS. Ministério de Saúde. http://www2.datasus.gov.br/DATASUS/index.php.

Dávila, Jerry. 2003. *Diploma of Whiteness: Race and Social Policy in Brazil, 1917-1945*. Durham, N.C.: Duke University Press.

Davis, Steven. 2000. *Bank Mergers: Lessons for the Future*. London, U.K.: MacMillan Press.

De la Reza, Germán A. 2006. *Integración económica en América Latina: hacia una nueva comunidad regional en el siglo XXI*. Mexico City, Mexico: Universidad Autónoma Metropolitana Azcapotzalco; Plaza y Valdés.

De Vries, Margaret G. 1972. *The International Monetary Fund. 1945-1970*. Washington, D.C.: International Monetary Fund.

Deeg, Richard. 2005. "Path Dependency, Institutional Complementarity, and Change in National Business Systems." In Glenn Morgan, Richard Whitley and Eli Moen, eds., *Changing Capitalisms? Internationalization, Institutional Change, and Systems of Economic Organization*. Oxford, London: Oxford University Press.

Deeg, Richard and Gregory Jackson. 2007. "The State of the Art: Towards a More Dynamic Theory of Capitalist Variety." *Socio Economic Review* 5:149-79.

Devlin, Robert and Antoni Estevadeordal. 2001. "What's New in the New Regionalism in the Americas?" In Victor Bulmer-Thomas, ed., *Regional Integration in Latin America and the Caribbean: the Political Economy of Open Regionalism*. London, U.K.: Institute of Latin American Studies, 17-44.

Dezalay, Yves and Bryant G. Garth. 2002. *The Internationalization of Palace Wars: Lawyers, Economists, and the Contest to Transform Latin American States*. Chicago, IL: University of Chicago Press.

Diebold, William Jr. 1952. "The End of ITO." *Princeton Essays in International Finance* 16.

Diniz, Eli. 1997. *Crise, reforma do Estado e governabilidade*. Rio de Janeiro, Brazil: Fundação Getulio Vargas

——. 2000. Globalizacão, reformas econômicas e es empresariais. Rio de Janeiro, Brazil: FGV Editora.

Diniz, Eli and Renato Boschi. 2003. "Empresariado e estratégia de desenvolvimento." *Revista Brasileira de Ciências Sociais* 18 (52).

——. 2004. *Empresários, interesses e mercado: dilemas do desenvolvimento no Brasil*. Belo Horizonte, Brazil: Ed. UFMG.

——. 2007. *A difícil rota do desenvolvimento: empresários e a agenda pós-neoliberal*. Belo Horizonte, Brazil: Ed. UFMG.

Dion, Michelle and Andrew Roberts. 2008. "Sources of Support for Pension Reform: A Cross-National Perspective." Center for Retirement Research at Boston College Working Paper Series 23.

Dittrick, Paula. 2009. "Latin American oil, gas policies remain in flux." *Oil and Gas Journal*, 13 April: 20.

Domingues, José Maurício. 2008. *Latin America and Contemporary Modernity: A Sociological Interpretation*. New York, N.Y./London, U.K.: Routledge.

Doner, Richard F. and Ben Schneider. 2000. "Business Associations and Economic Development: Why Some Associations Contribute More Than Others." *Business and Politics* 2 (3).

"The Dragon in the Backyard." 2009. *The Economist*, 15 August: 19-21.

Draibe, Sônia M. 1985. *Rumos e metamorfoses: um estudo sobre a constituição do Estado e as alternativas industriais no Brasil (1930-1960)*. Rio de Janeiro, Brazil: Paz e Terra.

——. 2004. "Federal Leverage in a Decentralized System: Education Reform in Brazil." In Robert R. Kaufman and Joan M. Nelson, eds., *Crucial Needs, Weak Incentives: Social Sector Reform, Democratization, and Globalization in Latin America*. Baltimore, M.D.: Johns Hopkins University Press.

Drucker, Peter F. 1986. *The Frontiers of Management. Where Tomorrow's Decisions are Being Shaped Today*. New York, N.Y.: Penguin Putnam Inc.

Easton, David. 1965. *A System Analysis of Political Life*. New York, N.Y.: Wiley.

ECLAC. 2008. *Latin America and the Caribbean in the World Economy 2007, 2008 Trends*. Santiago, Chile: United Nations.

——. 2010. *Foreign Direct Investment in Latin America and the Caribbean, 2009*. New York, N.Y.: United Nations.

Erickson, Kenneth. 1977. *The Brazilian Corporative State and Working-Class Politics*. Berkeley, Calif.: University of California Press.

Erturk, Ismail, Julie Froud, Sukhdev Johal, Adam Leaver, and Karel Williams. 2007. "The Democratisation of Finance? Promises, Outcomes, Conditions." *Review of International Political Economy* 14 (4): 553-75.

——. 2008. *Financialization at Work: Key Texts and Analysis*. New York, N.Y.: Routledge.

Esping-Andersen, Gosta. 1985. *Politics Against Markets: The Social Democratic Road to Power*. Princeton, N.J.: Princeton University Press.

Estatuto do Desarmamento Comentado. Lei n° 10.826, de 22 de Dezembro de 2003. http://www.deolhonoestatuto.org.br/downloads/biblioteca/002.pdf

Evans, Peter. 1992. "The State as Problem and Solution: Predation, Embedded Autonomy, and Structural Change." In Haggard and Kaufman, eds., *The Politics of Economic Adjustment: International Constraints, Distributive Conflicts and the State*. Princeton, N.J.: Princeton University Press, 139-81.

——. 1995. *Embedded Autonomy, States & Industrial Transformation*. Princeton, N.J.: Princeton University Press.

——. 1997. "The Eclipse of the State? Reflections on Stateness in an Era of Globalization." *World Politics* 50 (1) :62-87.

——. 2005a. "Harnessing the State: Rebalancing Strategies for Monitoring and Motivation." In Matthew Lange and Dietrich Rueschemeyer eds., *States and Development: Historical Antecedents of Stagnation and Advance*. New York, N.Y.: Palgrave MacMillan.

——. 2005b. "Neoliberalism as a Political Opportunity: Constrain and

Innovation in Contemporary Development Strategy." In K. Gallagher ed., *Putting Development First: The Importance of Policy Space in the WTO and International Financial Institutions*. London, U.K.: Zed, 195-215.

——. 2008. "Constructing the 21st century Developmental State: Potentialities and Pitfalls." Presentation delivered at the DBSA/HSRC conference on "The Potentials for and Challenges of Constructing a Democratic Developmental State in South Africa," Magaliesburg, South Africa, 4 June.

Faletto, Enzo. 1996. "La CEPAL y la sociologia del desarrollo." *Revista de La CEPAL* 58.

Fausto, Boris. 2001. *História concisa do Brasil*. São Paulo, Brazil: Edusp e Impresa Oficial.

Fedozzi, Luciano. 1999. *Orçamento Participativo: reflexões sobre a experiência de Porto Alegre*. 2nd ed. Porto Alegre, Brazil: Tomo Editorial.

Feijó, Jandira. 2008. "My View Is Perplexed." In Jandira Feijó and Augusto de Franco, eds., *Views on the Local Solidary Governance in Porto Alegre. Porto Alegre, Brazil*. Porto Alegre, Brazil: EDIPUCRS.

Feinberg, Richard E. with Paul Haslam. 2007. "Problem of Coordination: the OAS and the IADB." In G. Mace, J.P. Thérien, and P. Haslam, eds., *Governing the Americas: Assessing Multilateral Institutions*. Boulder, Colo.: Lynne Rienner, 68-94.

Felix, David. 1969. "The Political Economy of Integration in Latin America." *Studies in Comparative International Development* 5 (5): 87-102.

Ferraz Junior, Vitor Emanuel. 2008. "Poder judiciário e competição política no Brasil: uma análise das decisões do TSE e do STF sobre as regras eleitorais." Ph.D. Diss. PUC, São Paulo. www.sapientia.pucsp.br//tde_busca/arquivo.php?codArquivo=7260.

Ferreira, Carlos Roberto. 2003. "Participação das aposentadorias e pensões na desigualdade da distribuição de renda no período de 1981 a 2001." Ph.D. Diss. Escola Superior de Agricultura Luís de Queirós da Universidade de São Paulo.

Figueiredo, Argelina, and Fernando Limongi. 1999. *Executivo e legislativo na nova ordem constitucional*. Rio de Janeiro/São Paulo: Editora FGV/FAPESP.

Filgueira, Carlos H. and Fernando Filgueira. 2002. "Models of Welfare and Models of Capitalism: The Limits of Transferability." In Evelyne Huber, ed., *Models of Capitalism: Lessons for Latin America*. University Park, Pa.: Penn State University Press, 127-158.

Filho, Adauto, Maria de Fátima Souza, and Cynthia Gazal-Carvalho. 2007. "Análise da mortalidade por homicídios no Brasil." *Epidemiol. Serv. Saúde* 16 (1): 7-18.

Filho, Nelson S. and Carla S. Silva. 2001. "As grandes empresas nos anos 90: respostas estratégicas a um cenário de mudanças." Banco Nacional de Desenvolvimento Econômico, Working Paper: 375-410. http://www.bndes.gov.br/SiteBNDES/export/sites/default/bndes_pt/Galerias/Arquivos/conhecimento/livro/eco90_11.pdf.

Fine, Ben. 1999. "The Developmental State is Dead—Long Live Social Capital?" *Development and Change* 30: 1-19.

Fleischer, David. 1998. "Reelección a Brasileña: las elecciones generales de 1998." *Contribuciones* 15 (4): 175-95.

——. 2002. "As eleições municipais no Brasil: uma análise comparativa (1982-

2000)." *Opinião Pública* 8 (1): 80-105.

——. 2004a. "Political Reforms: Cardoso's 'Missing Link.'" In Mauricio Font, and Anthony Spanakos, eds., *Reforming Brazil.* Lanham, Md.: Rowman & Littlefield, 112-39.

——. 2004b. "O impacto da reforma política sobre a Câmara dos Deputados." Plenarium [Brasília] 1: 123-41.

——. 2004c. "Reforma política en Brasil: una historia sin Fin." *América Latina Hoy* 37: 81-99.

——. 2006. "A política de coligações no Brasil—antes e depois da verticalização: impactos sobre os partidos." Paper presented at the "VII Congress of the Brazilian Studies Association," Nashville, Tennessee, 13-16 October.

——. 2007a. "Os partidos políticos." In Lúcia Avelar, and Antônio Cintra, ed., *Sistema político Brasileiro: uma introdução.* 2nd Ed. São Paulo: UNESP/Konrad Adenauer Stiftung, 303-48.

——. 2007b. "Reforma política no Brasil: os partidos políticos em questão." In Lúcio Rennó, ed., *Reforma política em questão.* Brasília: Editora da UnB, 163-90.

Fligstein, Neil. 2001. *The Architecture of Markets: an Economic Sociology of Twenty-First Century Capitalist Societies.* Princeton, N.J.: Princeton University Press.

Fonseca, Marcia Cecilia Londres. 1997. *O patrimônio em processo: trajetória da política federal de preservação no Brasil.* Rio de Janeiro, Brazil: UFRJ/Minc.

Font, Mauricio A. 2002. *Transforming Brazil: A Reform Era in Perspective.* Boulder and New York: Rowman & Littlefield.

Font, Mauricio A. and Anthony Spanakos, eds. 2004. *Reforming Brazil.* Boulder and New York: Lexington Books.

Fourcade-Gourinchas, Marion and Sarah L. Babb. 2002. "The Rebirth of the Liberal Creed: Neoliberal Transitions in England, France, Mexico and Chile." *American Journal of Sociology* 108 (3): 533-79.

Franco, Augusto de. 2008. "My View on Local Solidary Governance." In Jandira Feijó and Augusto de Franco, eds., *Views on the Local Solidary Governance in Porto Alegre.* Porto Alegre, Brazil: EDIPUCRS, 91-114.

Frankenberg, Louis. 2001. *Seu futuro financeiro.* Rio de Janeiro, Brazil: Campus Elsevier.

Fraser, Nancy. 1993. "Rethinking the Public Sphere: A Contribution to the Critique of Actually Existing Democracy." In B. Robbins, ed., *The Phantom Public Sphere.* Minneapolis: University of Minnesota Press.

French, John. 1992. *The Brazilian Workers' ABC: Class Conflict and Alliances in Modern São Paulo.* Chapel Hill, N.C.: University of North Carolina Press.

Freyre, Gilberto. 1996. *Manifesto regionalista.* Recife, Brazil: Fundação Joaquim Nabuco.

Frischtak, Claudio R. 1986. "Brazil." In Francis W. Rushing and Carole B. Brown, eds., *National Policies for Developing High Technology Industries: International Comparisons.* Boulder, Colo.: Westview Press, 31-70.

Furtado, Celso. 1959. *Formação econômica do Brasil.* São Paulo, Brazil: Companhia Editora Nacional.

——. 1976. *Economic Development of Latin America-Historical Background and contemporary problems.* 2nd Ed. Cambridge, Mass.: Cambridge University Press.

Gallagher, Kevin, ed. 2005. *Putting Development First: The Importance of Policy Space in the WTO and International Financial Institutions*. London, U.K.: Zed.

Galle, Juliano Morais and Sandro Bertolli. 2004. "As finanças públicas brasileiras do início da década de 1980 até a implantação do Plano Real," *Intertemas* 8 (8).

Garcia, Marco Aurélio. 1996. "Esquerdas: rupturas e continuidades." In Evelina Dagnino, ed., *Os anos 90: política e sociedade no Brasil.* São Paulo, Brazil: Editora Brasiliense, 119-36.

Gardner, Richard N. 1956. *Sterling-Dollar Diplomacy*. Oxford, London: Clarendon Press.

Geddes, Barbara. 1990. "Building State Autonomy in Brazil, 1930-1964," *Comparative Politics* 22(2): 217-235.

——. 1996. *Politician's Dilemma: Building State Capacity in Latin America*. Berkeley, Calif.: University of California Press.

Gerschenkron, Alexander. 1962. *Economic Backwardness in Historical Perspective.* Cambridge, Mass.: Belknap Press.

Giambiagi, Fabio, Ana Claudia Além. 1999. *Finanças públicas teoría e práctica no Brasil.* Rio de Janeiro, Brazil: Campus.

Giambiagi, Fábio and Paulo Tefner. 2010. *Demografia a ameaça invisível.* São Paulo, Brazil: Campus Elsevier.

Giambiagi, Fábio and Lavínia Barros de Castro. 2003. "Previdência social: diagnósticos e propostas." *Revista do BNDES* 10 (19): 265-292.

Giambiagi, Fabio, Hélio Zylbersztajn, Luís Eduardo Afonso, André Portela Souza, and Eduardo Zylbersztajn. 2007. "Impacto de reformas paramétricas na previdência social brasileira: simulações alternativas." *Pesquisa e Planejamento Econômico* 37 (2).

Glatzer, Miguel and Dietrich Rueschemeyer, eds. 2005. *Globalization and the Future of the Welfare State.* Pittsburgh, PA: University of Pittsburgh Press.

Global Property Guide. 2010. 7 February. www.globalpropertyguide.com/Chile.

Goertzel, Ted G. 2002. *Fernando Henrique Cardoso e a reconstrução da democracia no Brasil.* São Paulo, Brazil: Saraiva.

Goldberg, Anette. 1987. "Feminismo e autoritarismo: a metamorfose de uma utopía de liberação em ideología liberalizante." M.A. Diss. Universidade Federal do Rio de Janeiro.

——. 1991. "Le Dire et Le Faire Feministes: une approche socioculturelle du Brésil Contemporain." Ph.D. Diss.Université de Paris VII.

Goldfajn, Ilan. 2003. "The Brazilian Crisis, the Role of the IMF and Democratic Governability." Pontifícia Universidade Católica do Rio de Janeiro, 19 October. www.econ.puc-rio.br

Goldsmith, Raymond W. 1986. *Desenvolvimento financeiro sob um século de inflação: Brasil 1850-1984*. São Paulo, Brazil: Bamerindus.

Gómez-Mera, Laura. 2008. "How 'new' is the 'New Regionalism' in the Americas? The Case of Mercosur." *Journal of International Relations and Development* 11 (3): 279-308.

Gonçalves, José Reginaldo Santos. 1996. *A retórica da perda: os discursos do patrimonio cultural no Brasil.* Rio de Janeiro, Brazil: Editora UFRJ/Ministério da Cultura-IPHAN.

Gourevitch, Peter Alexis. 1986. *Politics in Hard Times.* Ithaca, N.Y.: Cornell University Press.

Gourevitch, Peter Alexis and James Shinn. 2005. *Political Power and Corporate Control: The New Global Politics of Corporate Governance.* Princeton, N.J.: Princeton University Press.

Gouveia, Gilda. 1994. *Burocracia e elites burocráticas no Brasil.* São Paulo, Brazil: Editora Sumaré.

Gregori, María F. 1993. *Cenas e queixas: um estudo sobre mulheres, relações violentas e a prática feminista.* São Paulo, Brazil: Paz e Terra.

Gret, Marion, and Yves Sintomer. 2005. *The Porto Alegre Experiment: Learning Lessons for Better Democracy.* London, U.K.: Zed Books.

Grugel, Jean. 2006. "Regional Governance and Transnational Collective Action in Latin America." *Economy and Society* 35 (2): 209-31.

Grün, Roberto. 2003. "Atores e ações na construção da governança corporativa Brasileira." *Revista Brasileira de Ciências Sociais* 18: 139-61.

——. 2004. "A evolução recente do espaço financeiro no Brasil e alguns reflexos na cena política." *Revista Brasileira de Ciências Sociais.* 47: 5-47.

——. 2007. "Decifra-me ou te devoro! As finanças e a sociedade Brasileira." *MANA* 13: 381-410.

——. 2009. "A crise, a guerra cultural e as surpreendentes transformações do espaço econômico brasileiro em 2009." Paper presented at the "Colóquio Internacional—A internacionalização das ciências sociais francesas e a cooperação científica com o Brasil." http://www.fe.unicamp.br/focus/textos/GRUN-Coloquio2009.pdf

Guerreiro, Gabriela. 2009. "Ministros entregam ao Congresso proposta de reforma política sem brecha para 3° mandato." *Folha de São Paulo,* 10 February.

Guzzo Decca, Maria Auxiliadora. 1987. *A vida fora das fabricas: cotidiano operario em São Paulo, 1920-1934.* São Paulo, Brazil: Paz e Terra.

Haggard, Stephan and Robert R. Kaufman, eds. 1992. *The Politics of Economic Adjustment.* Princeton, N.J.: Princeton University Press.

Haggard, Stephan and Robert R. Kaufman. 2008. *Development, Democracy, and Welfare States: Latin America, East Asia, and Eastern Europe.* Princeton, N.J.: Princeton University Press.

Hagopian, Francis and Scott Mainwaring, eds. 2005. *The Third Wave of Democratization in Latin America: Advances and Setbacks.* New York, N.Y.: Cambridge University Press.

Hall, Peter. 2007. "The Evolution of Varieties of Capitalism in Europe." In Bob Hancké, Martin Rhodes and Mark Thatcher eds., *Beyond Varieties of Capitalism: Conflict, Contradictions, and Complementarities in the European Economy.* Oxford, London: Oxford University Press.

Hall, Peter, and David Soskice, eds. 2001. *Varieties of Capitalism: The Institutional Foundations of Comparative Advantage.* Oxford, London and New York, N.Y.: Oxford University Press.

Harrington, Brooke. 2008. *Pop Finance: Investment Clubs and the New Investor Populism.* Princeton, N. J.: Princeton University Press.

Harris, David, and Deigo Azzi. 2006. "ALBA: Venezuela's Answer to 'Free Trade': The Bolivarian Alternative for the Americas." Focus on the Global South, Occasional Paper 3.

Harris, Richard L. 2008. "Latin America's Response to Neoliberalism and

Globalization." *Nueva Sociedad* 214.

Hartelius, Kristian et al. 2008. "Emerging Market Spread Compression: Is it Real or is it Liquidity?" Working Paper 08/10. Washington, D.C.: IMF.

Hattingh, Shawn. 2008. "ALBA: Creating a Regional Alternative to Neoliberalism?" Venezuelanalysis, 13 February. www.venezuelanalysis.com.

Helleiner, Eric. 2000. "The Politics of Global Financial Reregulation: Lessons from the Fight against Money Laundering." CEPA Working Paper Series III. Working Paper 15.

Henisz, Witold. J., Bennet Zelner and Mauro F. Guillén. 2005. "The Worldwide Diffusion of Market-Oriented Infrastructure Reform, 1977-1999." *American Sociological Review* 70 (6): 871-97.

Henry, James. 2003. *The Blood Bankers: Tales from the Global Underground Economy.* New York, N.Y.: Four Walls Eight Windows.

Hill, Lawrence. 1947. *Brazil.* Berkeley, Calif.: University of California Press and London, U.K.: Cambridge University Press.

Hirschman, Albert O. 1958. *The Strategy of Economic Development.* New Haven, Conn.: Yale University Press.

Hoare, Quintin, and Geoffrey Nowell-Smith. 1971. *Selections from the Prison Notebooks of Antonio Gramsci.* New York, N.Y.: International Publishers.

Hobsbawm, Eric. 1983. "Introduction." In Eric Hobsbawm and Terence Ranger, *The Invention of Tradition.* Cambridge, Mass.: Cambridge University Press.

Hollingworth, Joseph Rogers, Philippe Schmitter and Wolfgang Streeck, eds. 1994. *Governing Capitalist Economies: Performance and Control of Economic Sectors.* Oxford, U.K.: Oxford University Press.

Hornbeck, John F. 2005. "A Free Trade Area of the Americas: Major Policy Issues and Status of Negotiations." CRS Report for Congress RS 20864. Washington, D.C.: Congressional Research Service.

Howell, Jude, and Jenny Pearce. 2001. *Civil Society and Development: A Critical Exploration.* Boulder, Colo.: Lynne Rienner Publishers.

Huber, Evelyne, ed. 2002. *Models of Capitalism: Lessons from Latin America.* University Park: Pennsylvania University Press.

Huber, Evelyne et al. 2006. "Politics and Inequality in Latin America and the Caribbean." *American Sociological Review* 71 (6):943-63.

Hülsse, Rainer and Dieter Kerwer. 2007. "Global Standards in Action: Insights from Anti-Money Laundering Regulation." Organization 14: 625-42.

Hurrell, Andrew. 2005. "Hegemony and Regional Governance in the Americas." In Louise Fawcett and Mónica Serrano, eds., *Regionalism and Governance in the Americas: Continental Drift.* London, U.K.: Palgrave Macmillan, 185-208.

Ianni, Octavio. 1971. *Estado e planejamento no Brasil (1930-64).* Rio de Janeiro, Brazil: Civilização Brasileira.

IBGE. *Contas nacionais trimestrais.* www.ipeadata.gov.br.

——. 2006. *Pesquisa Nacional por Amostra de Domicílios (PNAD).*

——. 2007. *Pesquisa Nacional por Amostra de Domicílios (PNAD)*

——. 2008. *Indicadores sociais, 2008.* www.ibge.gov.br.

——. 2010. *Resultados do 1° Trimestre de 2010—Indicadores de volume e valores correntes.*

http://www.ibge.gov.br/home/estatistica/indicadores/pib/defaulttabelas.shtm

"IDB Aims to Stay Relevant." 2008. *The Banker* 1 July.

"IDB President Calls for Heritage Preservation to Spur Economic and Social Development." 2000. Press Release, World Bank Headquarters 29 March.

IDB. 2006. *The Politics of Policies.* Washington, D.C.: IDB.

———. 2009. "Our History." Washington, D.C.: Inter-American Development Bank.

IEA. 2003. *World Energy Investment Outlook: 2003 Insights.* Paris, France: Organization for Economic Cooperation and Development/International Energy Agency.

———. 2009. *Oil Market Report*, 14 May.

ILO. 2009. "Brazil Extends Bolsa Familia During the Economic Crisis," ILO News, 20 March.

IMF. 2004. *Global Finance Stability Report.* Washington, D.C.: IMF.

———. 2009. "IMF Managing Director Dominique Strauss-Kahn Welcomes Brazil's Intention to Invest Up To US$10 Billion in Notes Issued by the IMF." 10 June.

INEP. 2006. http://www.inep.gov.br/superior/enade/default.asp.

Instituto Patricia Galvão. 2004. *Pesquisa Ibope: O que a sociedade pensa sobre a violência contra as mulheres.* Rio de Janeiro, Brazil.

International Development Bank. *Monumenta—Executive Summary.* http://idbdocs.iadb.org/wsdocs/getdocument.aspx?docnum=437363.

———. *Projects at the International Development Bank.* http://www.bid.org.uy/projects/project.cfm?id= BR0261&lang=en.

Investment Properties Mexico. www.goarticles.com/cgi.

IPEA. *PIB (preços 2009).* www.ipea.data.gov.br.

———. 2006. *Relatório de avaliação da Bolsa Família,* Brasília, Brazil.

———. 2008a. *Mercado de trabalho, trabalho infantil e previdência: primeiras análises.* Brasília, Brasil.

———. 2008b. *PNAD 2007: primeiras análises.* October.

———. *Taxa de câmbio comercial.* www.ipea.data.gov.br.

Itaú-Unibanco Banco Múltiplo S.A. 2009. "Approval of the Merger between Itaú and Unibanco." Press Release, 20 February.

Jackson, Gregory and Richard Deeg. 2006. "How Many Varieties of Capitalism? Comparing the Comparative Institutional Analyses of Capitalist Diversity." MPIfG Discussion Papers, 06/2.

James, Ian. 2006. "Chavez Boost Heating Oil Program for U.S. Poor; Goes After Bush Again." *The Washington Post,* 21 September.

Jardim, María C. 2009. "Domesticação e/ou moralização do capitalismo no governo Lula: inclusão social via mercado e via fundos de pensão." *Revista de Ciências Sociais* 52: 123-59.

Jelin, Elizabeth. 1998. "Toward a Culture of Participation and Citizenship: Challenges for a More Equitable World." In Sonia E. Alvarez; Evelina Dagnino and Arturo Escobar, eds., *Cultures of Politics, Politics of Cultures: Revisioning Latin American Movements.* Boulder, Colo.: Westview Press.

Jochem, Sven and Nico A. Siegel, eds. 2003. *Konzertierung, Verhandlungsdemokratie und Reformpolitik im Wohlfahrtsstaad.* Oplanden: Leske/Budrich.

Jornadas pelo Aborto Legal e Seguro. 2005.

Jornal Mulherio. May/July 1983.

Jornal Opinião. 1973. no 19.

Katzenstein, Peter J. 2005. *A World of Regions: Asia and Europe in the American Imperium.* Ithaca, N.Y.: Cornell University Press.

Kearney, Christine A. 2001. "The Comparative Influence of Neoliberal Ideas: Economic Culture and Stabilization in Brazil." Ph.D. Diss. Brown University.

Keck, Margaret E. 1992. *Workers' Party and Democratization in Brazil.* New Haven, Conn.: Yale University Press.

Kellogg, Paul. 2007. "Regional Integration in Latin America: Dawn of an Alternative to Neoliberalism?" *New Political Science* 29 (2): 187-209.

Kennedy, Paul M. 1988. *The Rise and Fall of the Great Powers.* London, U.K.: Fontana Press.

Kindleberger, Charles P. 1987. *The World in Depression, 1929-1939.* Middlesex, U.K.: Penguin Books.

Kitschelt, Herbert, et al. 1999. *Continuity and Change in Contemporary Capitalism.* Cambridge, Mass.: Cambridge University Press.

Kiyosaki, Kim. 2006. *Rich Woman: A Book on Investing for Women.* Rich Publishing, LLC.

Kiyosaki, Robert T. and Sharon L. Lechter. 2000. *Rich Dad, Poor Dad: What the Rich Teach their Kids Abou Money—That the Poor and Middle Class do Not!* Warner Business Books.

Klein, Cristian. 2007. *O desafio da reforma política: conseqüências dos sistemas eleitorais de listas aberta e fechadas.* Rio de Janeiro, Brazil: Mauad.

Knight, Jack. 2001. "Explaining the Rise of Neoliberalism: Mechanisms of Institutional Change." In John L. Campbell and Ove K. Pedersen, eds., *The Rise of Neoliberalism and Institutional Analysis.* Princeton, N.J.: Princeton University Press.

Knox, John. 1969. "Contest Between Legal-Tender Note and National Bank Note, 1862-1878," In *A History of Banking in the United States, Reprints of Economic Classics.* New York, N.Y.: August M. Kelley Publishers.

Knudsen, Laura M. 2006. *Reproductive Rights in a Global Context.* Nashville, Tenn.: Vanderbilt University Press.

Kohli, Atul. 2004. *State Directed Development: Political Power and Industrialization in the Global Periphery.* Cambridge, Mass.: Cambridge University Press.

Kottak, Conrad. 2009. *Prime-Time Society: An Anthropological Analysis of Television and Culture.* Walnut Creek, Calif.: Left Coast Press.

Kuczinsky, Pedro-Pablo and John Williamson. 2004. *Depois do Consenso de Washington: retomando o crescimento e a reforma na América Latina.* São Paulo: Editora Saraiva.

Kudrle, Robert T. 2008. "Did Blacklisting Hurt the Tax Havens?" Paolo Baffi Centre Research Paper Series 23. http://papers.ssrn.com/sol3/papers.cfm?abstract_id=1243695.

Kurtz, Marcus. 2001. "State Developmentalism without a Developmentalist State: The Public Foundations of the 'Free-Market Miracle' in Chile." *Latin American Politics and Society* 43 (2): 1-25.

Lacerda, João. 1938. *O Estado Novo: democracia e corporatismo, a posição do Brasil.* Rio de Janeiro, Brazil: Editora Nacional.

Lafer, Celso. 1970. *O sistema político brasileiro.* São Paulo, Brazil: Perspectiva.

——. 2009. "Brazil and the World." In Ignacy Sachs et al., eds., *Brazil: A Century of Change.* Chapel Hill, N.C.: University of North Carolina Press, 101-19.

Lamounier, Bolivar and Raquel Meneguello. 1986. *Partidos políticos e consolidação democrática.* São Paulo, Brazil: Brasiliense.

Lange, Matthew and Dietrich Rueschemeyer, eds. 2005. *States and Development: Historical Antecedents of Stagnation and Advance.* New York, N.Y.: Palgrave MacMillan.

Lavalle, Adrián G., Peter P. Houtzager, and Graziela Castello. 2006. "Democracia, pluralização da representação e sociedade civil." *Lua Nova*, 67: 49-103.

Leff, Nathaniel. 1977. *Política econômica e desenvolvimento no Brasil (1947-64).* São Paulo, Brazil: Perspectiva.

Lei Maria da Penha, Lei n° 11.340, de 7 de Agosto de 2006. http://www.planalto.gov.br/ccivil_03/_Ato2004-2006/2006/Lei/L11340.htm.

LeVine, Steve. 2009. "Free Trade in the Slow Lane." *Business Week*, 21 September: 59.

Levy, María B. 1967. *História dos bancos comerciais no Brasil.* Rio de Janeiro, Brazil: IBMEC.

Lindblom, Charles E. and Edward J. Woodhouse. 1993. *The Policy Making Process.* New Jersey: Prentice Hall.

Lins, Alvaro. 1962. *Rio-Branco.* São Paulo, Brazil: Cia. Editora Nacional.

Loureiro, Maria Rita. 1997. *Os economistas no governo: gestão econômica e democracia.* Rio de Janeiro, Brazil: Editora FGV.

Loureiro, Maria Rita, and Fernando Abrucio. 1999. "Política e burocracia no presidencialismo brasileiro: o papel do Ministério da Fazenda no primeiro governo Fernando Henrique Cardoso." *Revista Braileira de Ciências Sociais* 14(41): 69-89.

Löwy, Michael. 1999. "Pontos de referência para uma história do Marxismo na América Latina." In Michael Löwy, ed., *O Marxismo na América Latina: uma antologia de 1909 aos dias atuais.* São Paulo, Brazil: Editora Fundação Perseu Abramo, 9-64.

"Lula Wants to Fight; Invigorated by the Crisis, Brazil's President says He's Praying for Obama." 2009. *Newsweek*, 30 March: 43.

Lustig, Nora. 2009. "Poverty, Inequality, and the New Left in Latin America," Presentation given at Woodrow Wilson International Center for Scholars, Wasghinton, D.C., July 21.

MacCannell, Dean. 1999. *The Tourist: A New Theory of the Leisure Class.* Berkeley: University of California Press.

MacDonald, Austin. 1954. *Latin American Politics and Government.* New York, N.Y.: Thomas Y. Crowell Company.

Mace, Gordon and Jean-Philippe Thérien. 2007. "Inter-American Governance: a Sysyphean Endeavor?" In G. Mace, J.P. Thérien, and P. Haslam, eds., *Governing the Americas: Assessing Multilateral Institutions.* Boulder, Colo.: Lynne Rienner, 45-67.

Machado, Lia Zanotta. 1998. "Matar e morrer no masculino e no feminino." In

Ricardo Lima, Djaci Oliveira, and Elen Geraldes, eds., *A primavera já partiu.* Petrópolis, Brazil: Editora Vozes e M.N.D.H.

——. 2001. *Eficácia e desafios das delegacias especializadas no atendimento às mulheres: o futuro dos direitos à não violência.* Brasília, Brazil: Conselho Nacional dos Direitos da Mulher.

——. 2002. "Atender vítimas, criminalizar violências: dilemas das delegacias da mulher." *Série Antropologia* 319. Brasília: UnB Press.

——. 2004. "Masculinidades e violências: o mal-estar da contemporaneidade." In Mônica Schpun, ed., *Masculinidades.* São Paulo, Brazil: Boitempo.

——. 2008. "Os novos contextos e os novos têrmos do debate contemporâneo sobre o aborto: a questão de gênero e o impacto social das novas narrativas biológicas, jurídicas e religiosas." *Série Antropologia* 419. Brasília, Brazil: UnB Press.

Machado, Maíra Rocha. 2008. "Financial Regulation and International Criminal Policy: The Anti-Money Laundering System in Brazil and Argentina." Paper presented at the 2006 Law and Society Meeting, Baltimore, Maryland.

Machado, Sérgio. 1998. *Reforma político partidária: relatório final.* Brasília, Brazil: Senado Federal.

Machinea, José Luis and Narcís Serra, eds. 2007. *Visiones del desarrollo en América Latina.* Santiago, Chile: CEPAL.

Magalhães, Aloisio. 1997. *E triunfo? a questão dos bens culturais no Brasil.* Rio de Janeiro, Brazil: Nova Fronteira.

Mahoney, James. 2000. "Path Dependence in Historical Sociology." *Theory and Society* 29 (4).

Mainwaring, Scott. 1993. "Presidentialism, multipartism and democracy: the difficult combination." *Comparative Political Studies* 26(2):198-228.

Mainwaring, Scott and Timothy R. Scully, eds. 1995. *Building Democratic Institutions—Party Systems in Latin America.* Palo Alto, Calif.: Stanford University Press.

Malamud, Andrés. 2005. "Mercosur Turns 15: Between Rising Rhetoric and Declining Achievement." *Cambridge Review of International Affairs* 18 (3): 421-36.

Mancuso, Wagner P. 2004. "O lobby da indústria no congresso nacional: empresariado e política no Brasil contemporâneo." *Dados* 47 (3): 505-47.

——. 2007. "O empresariado como ator político no Brasil: balanço da literatura e agenda de pesquisa." *Revista de Sociologia e Política* 28: 131-46.

Margolis, Mac. 2008. "Cutting Things Down to Size; As Brazil Becomes a More Powerful Player, its Neighbors are Becoming Increasingly Aggressive." *Newsweek,* 24 November: 52-53.

Marques, Myriam Silva. 1999. *Não é o certo, mas foi o certo prá mim: um estudo sobre aborto provocado entre adolescentes.* M.A. Diss. Bahia/Minas Gerais, Brazil: Grupo Ânima.

Marques Pereira, Jaime and Bruno Théret. 2009. "Mediations Institutionnelles de la Regulation Sociale et Dynamiques Macro-economiques." *Ponto de Vista* 9.

Marquetti, Adalmir. 2007. "Experiências de orçamento participativo no Brasil: uma proposta de classificação." In Evelina Dagnino and Luciana Tatagiba, eds., *Democracia, sociedade civil e participação.* Chapecó, Brazil: Argos, 77-95.

Martin, Randy. 2002. *Financialization of Daily Life.* Philadelphia, Penn.: Temple

University Press.

Martínez, Juan and Javier Santiso. 2003. "Financial Markets and Politics. The Confidence Game in Latin American Emerging Economies." *International Political Science Review* 24 (3): 363-95.

Martins, Andréa. Personal Interview. August 10, 2008.

Martins, Carlos E. 1974. *Tecnocracia e capitalismo.* São Paulo, Brazil: Brasiliense/ CEBRAP.

Martins, Luciano. 1985. *Estado capitalista e burocracia no Brasil pós-64.* Rio de Janeiro, Brazil: Paz e Terra.

Martins dos Santos, Francisco. 1941. *O fato moral e o fato social da década getuliana.* Rio de Janeiro, Brazil: Z. Valverde.

Mattar, Eliana. 2003. "Dos arquivos em defesa do Estado ao Estado em defesa dos arquivos." In Eliana Mattar, ed., *Acesso à informação e política de arquivos.* Rio de Janeiro, Brazil: Arquivo Nacional.

Mattos, Paul and Diogo Coutinho. 2008. "Law and the New Developmental State: Pilot Project on Brazil," unpublished project document.

Maxwell, Kenneth. 1999. "The Two Brazils." *The Wilson Quarterly* 23.

McCann, Bryan. 2004. *Hello, Hello Brazil: Popular Music in the Making of Modern Brazil.* Durham, N.C.: Duke University Press.

McGee, Micki 2005. *Self-Help, Inc.: Makeover Culture in American Life.* London, U.K.: Oxford University Press.

McGillivray, Warren. 2001. "Contribution Evasion: Implications for Social Security Pension Schemes." *International Social Security Association Review* 54 (2): 3-22.

McKinsey & Company, Inc. 2004. *Eliminando as barreiras ao crescimento econômico e a economia formal no Brasil.* São Paulo, Brazil: McKinsey & Company.

Médici, André Cezar and Marco Maciel. 1996. "A dinâmica do gasto social nas três esferas de governo: 1980-92," *Decentralização e políticas sociais.* São Paulo, Brazil: *FUNDAP.*

Medeiros, Rogério de Souza. 2007. "Crítica e resignação nas atuais relações entre as ONGs e o Estado no Brasil." In Evelina Dagnino and Luciana Tatagiba, eds., *Democracia, sociedade civil e participação.* Chapecó: Argos, 167-202.

Meira, Ana Lúcia. 2004. *O passado no futuro da cidade: políticas públicas e participação dos cidadãos na preservação do patrimônio cultural de Porto Alegre.* Porto Alegre, Brazil: Editora da Universidade Federal do Rio Grande do Sul.

Meirelles, Henrique de Campos. 2010. "Estabilidade macroeconomica e crescimento." Presentation on Central Bank of Brazil website. http://www.bcb.gov.br/?RED1-APRESPRONUNC.

Melo, Carlos Ranuflo. 2004. *Retirando as cadeiras do lugar: migração partidária na Câmara dos Deputados (1985-2002).* Belo Horizonte, Brazil: Editora da UFMG.

——. 2006. "Sistema partidário, presidencialismo e reforma política no Brasil." In Gláucio Soares, and Lúcio Rennó, *Reforma política: lições da história contemporânea.* Rio de Janeiro, Brazil: Editora da FGV, 157-75.

Melo, Marcus André. "Institutional Choice and the Diffusion of Policy Paradigms: Brazil and the Second Wave of Pension Reform." *International Political Science Review* 25 (3): 320-41.

Meneguello, Rachel. 1998. *Partidos e governos no Brasil contemporâneo (1985-1997).* São Paulo, Brazil: Paz e Terra.

Menz, Georg. 2003. "Re-regulating the Single Market: National Varieties of Capitalism and their Responses to Europeanization." *Journal of European Public Policy* 10 (4): 532-55.

Mesa-Lago, Carmelo. 2000. "Comentarios a la reforma de la seguridad social en Venezuela." Caracas: ILDIS-GTZ.

——. 2002. "The Politics Pension Reform in Latin America." *Journal of Latin America Studies* 34 (3): 687-715.

——. 2004. "Las reformas de pensiones en América Latina y su impacto en los principios de la seguridad social", *Financiamiento del desarrollo* 144, Santiago de Chile, Comisión Económica para América Latina (CEPAL).

Meynaud, Jean. 1964. *La Technocracie: Mythe ou Realite.* Paris, France: Payot

Miliband, Ralph. 1983. *Class Power and State Power.* London, U.K.: Verso.

Ministerio da Cultura. 1980. *Proteção e revitilização do patrimônio cultural no Brasil: uma trajetória.* Brasília, Brazil: SPHAN/Pro-Memória.

Ministério da Fazenda. 2008. *Relatório de atividades da COAF.* Brasília, Brazil: Ministério da Fazenda.

Ministério da Previdência e Assistência Social. 1999. *Informe da previdência* 11 (11).

——. 2004. *Informe da previdência* 16 (1).

——. 2004. *Resultado do regime geral de previdência social.* Nota Técnica n° 003/04.

Ministério da Previdência Social. 2008. *Overview of Brazilian Social Welfare*, Brasília, Brazil.

Ministério do Planejamento, Orçamento e Gestão. 2003a. *Boletim estatístico de pessoal* 92. Brasília, Brasil: MP.

——. 2003b. *Projeções do orçamento para 2004.* Brasília, Brazil: MP.

——. 2008. *Boletim estatístico de pessoal* 152. Brasília, Brazil: MP.

"More Bounty." 2008. *The Economist*, 19 April: 82.

Moreira, Ajax et al. 2008. "O papel dos fundamentos domésticos na vulnerabilidade econômica dos emergentes." Texto para Discussão 1358. Rio de Janeiro, Brazil: IPEA.

Moreira, Mauricio Mesquita. 2009. "Trade Policy: Old and New Issues." In Lael Brainard and Leonardo Martinez-Diaz, eds., *Brazil as an Economic Superpower? Understanding Brazil's Changing Role in the Global Economy.* Washington, D.C.: Brookings Institution Press.

Moreira, Vicente Deocleciano. 2007. "Vivaldo e o Maciel." In Jeferson Bacelar and Claudio Pereira, eds., *Vivaldo da Costa Lima: intérprete do Afro-Brasil.* Salvador, Brazil: EDUFBA.

Moreno, Luis Alberto. 2008. "Enhancing Competitiveness in Latin America: the Role of Infrastructure." Speech given at Canning House Conference, London, 21 January.

Morley, Samuel and David Coady. 2003. *From Social Assistance to Social Development: A Review of Targeted Education Subsidies in Developing Countries.* International Food Policy Research Institute, Washington, D.C., February.

Motta Veiga, Pedro da. 2009. "Brazil's Trade Policy: Moving Away from Old Paradigms." In Lael Brainard and Leonardo Martinez-Diaz, eds., *Brazil as an Economic Superpower? Understanding Brazil's Changing Role in the Global Economy.* Washington, D.C.: Brookings Institution Press, 113-136.

Mueller, Charles C. 2009. "Agricultural, Agrarian, and Environmental Policy

Formation under Lula: The Role of Policy Networks." In Joseph L. Love and Werner Baer, eds., *Brazil Under Lula: Economy, Politics, and Society under the Worker-President.* New York, N.Y.: Palgrave-MacMillan, 136-50.

Müller. Lucia. 2006. *Mercado exemplar: estudo antropológico sobre a bolsa de valores.* Porto Alegre, Brazil: Zouk.

Murro, Ernesto. 2001. "As tendências na América Latina e a reforma Uruguaiana da previdência social." Paper presented at the Conference, "Previdência Social e Pública—desafios para sua preservação," Brasília, Brazil, October.

Najjar, Jorge and Rosana Najjar. 2007. "Reflections on the Relationship between Education and Archaeology: An Analysis of IPHAN's Role as Collective Educator" *Archaeologies* 3: 169-78.

Nakahodo, Sidney Nakao, and José Roberto Ferreira Savoia. 2008. "Reforma da previdência no Brasil: Estudo Comparativo dos Governos Fernando Henrique Cardoso e Lula." *Revista Brasileira de Ciências Sociais* 23: 45-58.

Nau, Henry R. 1990. *The Myth of America's Decline: Leading the World Economy into the 1990's.* New York, N.Y.: Oxford University Press.

Neri, Marcelo. 2001. "Recursos existem, falta qualidade." *Conjuntura Economica* 55(11) Nov.: 78-79.

——. 2002. "Decent Work and the Informal Sector." *Ensaios Economicos EPGE* 461.

Neuhaus, Paulo 1975. *História Monetária do Brasil 1900 -1945.* Rio de Janeiro, Brazil: IBMEC.

"New Horizons: Petrobrás." 2009. *The Banker*, 10 March.

Nicolau, Jairo. 2004. "Receita para reduzir escândalos." *O Globo*, 4 March: 7.

——. 2006a. "Lista aberta-lista fechada." In Leonardo Arvitzer, and Fátima Anastásia, eds., *Reforma política no Brasil.* Belo Horizonte, Brazil: Editora da UFMG, 133-36.

——. 2006b. "Voto personalizado e reforma eleitoral no Brasil." In Gláucio Soares, and Lúcio Rennó, eds., *Reforma política: lições da história contemporânea.* Rio de Janeiro, Brazil: Editora da FGV, 23-33.

——. 2007. "Cinco opções, uma escolha: o debate sobre a reforma do sistema eleitoral no Brasil" Plenarium [Câmara dos Deputados] 4: 70-79.

Nóbrega, Maílson da. 2005. *O futuro chegou: instituições e desenvolvimento no Brasil.* São Paulo: Editora Globo.

Nogueira, Antonio Gilberto Ramos. 2005. *Por um inventario dos sentidos: Mario de Andrade e a concepçâo de patrimonio e inventario.* São Paulo, Brazil: Editora Hucitec.

Novaro, Marcos. 2000. *Representación y liderazgo en las democracias contemporaneâs.* Rosario, Argentina: HomoSapiens Ediciones.

Nonneman, Gerd, ed. 1996. *Political and Economic Liberalization: Dynamics and Linkages in Comparative Perspective.* Boulder, Colo.: Lynne Rienner Publishers.

North, Douglas. 1990. *Institutions, Institutional Change and Economic Performance.* Cambridge, Mass.: Cambridge University Press.

——. 1998. "Economic Performance Through Time." In M. C. Brinton and V. Nee. *The New Institutionalism in Sociology.* Stanford, CA: Stanford University Press.

——. 2005. *Understanding the Process of Economic Change.* Princeton, N.J.: Princeton

University Press.

Northcote, Stafford H. and Charles E. Trevelyan. 1854. *Report on the Organization of the Permanent Civil Service, 1853*. London, House of Commons: Her Majesty's Stationery Office.

"Número de investidores de varejo na BM&F Bovespa bate recorde em outubro." 2009. *Infomoney*, 6 November.

Nunes, Edson. 1997. *A gramática política do Brasil: clientelismo e insulamento burocrático*. Rio de Janeiro, Brazil: Zahar.

Nylen, William. 2003. *Participatory Democracy Versus Elitist Democracy: Lessons from Brazil*. London, U.K.: Palgrave Macmillan.

O'Donnell, Guillermo. 1975. "Sobre o corporativismo e a questão do Estado." *Cadernos DCP*, Belo Horizonte, Brazil.

OECD. 2002. Social Expenditure Database 1980-1998. November. www.oecd.org.

——. 2009. Brazil: OECD Economic Survey. Paris: OECD Development Center, July.

"Oil price history and analysis." WTRG Economics. www.wtrg.com.

OLADE. 2007. *Energy Economic Information System: Energy Statistics*. Quito, Ecuador: Latin American Energy Association.

Oliveira, Francisco, Kaizô Beltrão, and Mônica Ferreira. 1997. "Reforma da previdência." Texto para discussão n° 508. Rio de Janeiro, Brazil: IPEA.

Olivieri, Cecília. 2007. "Política, burocracia e redes sociais: as nomeaçõ es para lo alto escalão do Banco Central do Brazil." *Revista de Sociologia Política* 29.

——. 2010a. *A lógica política do controle interno: o monitoramento das políticas públicas no presidencialismo brasileiro*. São Paulo, Brazil: Annablume.

——. 2010b. *Política e burocracia no Brasil: o controle sobre a execução das políticas públicas*. Tese de Doutorado, EAESP/FGV, São Paulo.

Olson, Mancur. 2000. *Power and Prosperity. Outgrowing Communist and Capitalist Dictatorships*. New York, N.Y.: Basic Books.

Onody, Oliver. 1960. *A inflação brasileira, 1820-1958*. Rio de Janeiro, Brazil: [s.n.]

Orçamento Participativo. 2008. *Regimento interno—critérios gerais, técnicos e regionais—2008/2009*. Porto Alegre, Brazil: Prefeitura Municipal de Porto Alegre.

Organización Latinoamerica de Solidariedad. 1967. "Declaración General de La Primera Conferencia Latinoamericana de Solidaridad." In Michael Löwy, ed., *O Marxismo na América Latina: uma antologia de 1909 aos dias atuais*. São Paulo, Brazil: Editoria Perseu Abramo, 303-14.

Packeman, Robert. 1994. *The Politics of Economic Liberalization: Argentina and Brazil in Comparative Perspective*. Ft. Wayne, Ind.: University of Notre Dame/Kellogg Institute, April.

Palermo, Vicente. 2000. "Como se governa o Brasil? O debate sobre instituições políticas e gestão do governo". *Dados* 43(3): 521-558.

Palier, Bruno and Yves Surel. 2005. "Les 'Trois I' et l'Analyse de l'Etat en Action." *Revue Française de Science Politique* 55 (1): 7-32.

Panizza, Francisco. 2006. "'Brazil needs to change': Change as iteration and the iteration of change in Brazil's 2002 presidential election." *Cuadernos del CLAFH* 1, Special ed.

Paoli, Maria Célia and Vera da Silva Telles. 1998. "Social Rights: Conflicts and Negotiations in Contemporary Brazil." In Sonia E. Alvarez; Evelina Dagnino and Arturo Escobar, eds., *Cultures of Politics. Politics of Cultures: Revisioning Latin American Movements*. Boulder, Colo.: Westview Press.

Parra, Sebastián Neto and Javier Santiso. 2008. "Wall Street and Elections in Latin American Emerging Democracies." *Latin American Economic Outlook*. Working Paper 272.

Parra-Bernal, Guillermo and Lester Pimentel. 2008. "Brazil Became Net Creditor for First Time in January (Update 4)." *Bloomberg LP* 21 February. www.bloomberg.com.

Partido dos Trabalhores. 1990. "Resolução do 7 encontro nacional do PT." In Michael Löwy, ed., *O Marxismo na América Latina: uma antologia de 1909 aos dias atuais*. São Paulo: Editora Fundacão Perseu Abramo, 496-503.

Paula, Ana Paula Paes de and Thomaz Wood Jr. 2002. "Pop-management: contos de paixão, lucro e poder." *Encontro de Estudos Organizacionais* 9 (24): 39-51.

Pearce, Jenny. 2004. "Collective Action or Public Administration?: Civil Society and the Public Sphere in Post-Transition Latin America." In Marlies Glasius, David Lewis and Hakan Seckinelgin, eds., *Exploring Civil Society: Political and Cultural Contexts*. New York, N.Y.: Routledge, 61-70.

Pedersen, Jorgen D. 2008. *Globalization, Development and the State the Performance of India and Brazil since 1990*. London, U.K.: Palgrave Macmillan.

Peixoto, João Paulo M. (Org). 2008. *Governando o governo: modernização da administração pública no Brasil*. São Paulo, Brazil: Atlas.

Perusso, Mari, et al. 2008. "The Practice. The Initial Experience of Implementation in the 17 Regions of Porto Alegre." In Jandira Feijó and Augusto de Franco, eds., *Views on the the Local Solidary Governance in Porto Alegre*. Porto Alegre, Brazil: EDIPUCRS, 63-92.

Phillips, Tom. 2009. "Brazil pledges deep emission cuts in 'political gesture' to rich nations." *The Guardian*, 10 November.

Pierson, Paul. 1998. "Irresistible forces, immovable objects: post-industrial welfare states confront permanent austerity." *Journal of European Public Policy* 5 (4): 539-60.

———. 2004. *Politics in Time, History, Institutions and Social Analysis*. Princeton, N.J.: Princeton University Press.

Pinto, Céli Regina Jardim. 2003. *Uma história do feminismo no Brasil*. São Paulo, Brazil: Editora Fundação Perseu Abramo.

Polanyi, Karl. 1944. *The Great Transformation*. Boston, Mass.: Beacon Press.

Power, Timothy J. 1997. *A Social Democracia no Brasil e no Mundo*. Porto Alegre, Brazil: Instituto Teotônio Vilela/Fundação Pedroso Horta.

Prebisch, Raúl. 1949. *The Economic Development of Latin America and Some of its Problems*. Santiago, Chile: Economic Commission for Latin America.

Preda, Alex. 2001. "The Rise of Popular Investor: Financial Knowledge and Investing in England and France, 1840-1880." *The Sociological Quartely* 42: 205-32.

Przeworksi, Adam. 1985. *Capitalism and Social Democracy*. Cambridge, Mass. and New York, N.Y.: Cambridge University Press.

Przeworski, Adam and Carolina Curvale. 2007. "Instituciones políticas y desarrollo económico en las Américas: el largo plazo." In José Luis Machinea and Narcís Serra, eds., *Visiones del desarrollo en América Latina.* Santiago, Chile: CEPAL.

Przeworski, Adam, Susan Stokes, and Bernard Manin, eds. 1999. *Democracy, Accountability and Representation.* Cambridge: Cambridge University Press.

Públicas. 2005. Brasília, Brazil: CEPAL and SPM.

Pujol, Júlio. 2008. Personal Interview. 13 May.

Putnam, Robert. 1993. *Making Democracy Work: Civil Traditions in Modern Italy.* Princeton, N.J.: Princeton University Press.

Queiroz, Jose Eduardo and Marina de Carvalho Anselmo. 2005. "The New Brazilian Bankruptcy Law." *International Finance Law Review* 01 Mar.

Radler, Marilyn. 2009. "Oil, gas reserves rise as oil output declines." *Oil and Gas Journal*, 21 Dec.: 18.

Ramos, Lauro. 2007. "O desempenho recente do mercado de trabalho brasileiro: tendências, fatos estilizados e padrões espaciais." Texto para discussão n° 1255. Rio de Janeiro, Brazil: IPEA.

Ratton Jr., Amorin and José Luiz. 1996. *Violência e crime no Brasil contemporâneo.* Brasília, Brazil: Cidade Gráfica Editora.

Razavi, Hossein. 1996. *Financing energy projects in emerging economies.* Tulsa, Okla.: PennWell Publishing.

Rego, Antonio Carlos Pojo and João Paulo M. Peixoto. 1998. *A Política das reformas econômicas no Brasil.* Rio de Janeiro, Brazil: Expressão e Cultura.

Reinert, Erik. 2007. *How Rich Countries Got Rich...and Why Poor Countries Stay Poor.* London, U.K.: Constable.

Reis, Bruno. 2007. "O presidencialismo de coalizão sob pressão: da formação de maiorias democráticas à formação democrática de maiorias." Plenarium [Câmara dos Deputados] 4: 80-103.

Relativo ao Estatuto Jurídico da Igreja Católica no Brasil, 2008. Website. http://www.camara.gov.br/sileg/integras/637903.pdf

Renault, Sérgio, and Pierpaulo Bottini. 2005. *Reforma do judiciário.* São Paulo, Brazil: Saraiva.

Rennó, Lúcio, ed. 2007. *Reforma política em questão.* Brasília, Brazil: Editora da UnB.

Ribeiro, Benedito and Mário M. Guimarães. 1967. *História dos bancos e do desenvolvimento financeiro do Brasil.* São Paulo, Brazil: Editora Pro-Service.

Ribeiro, Renato Janine. 2003. "Sobre o voto obrigatório." In Maria Victória Benevides, Paulo Vannuchi, and Fábio Kerche, eds., *Reforma política e cidadania.* São Paulo, Brazil: Fundação Perseu Abramo. 182-91.

Ribeiro, Sandra Bernardes. 2005. *Brasília: memória, cidadania e gestão do patrimônio cultural.* São Paulo, Brazil: Editora Annablume.

Roberts, Kenneth. 1998. *Deepening Democracy? The Modern Left and Social Movements in Peru and Chile.* Stanford, Calif.: Stanford University Press.

Rocha, Roberto and Marcelo Caetano. 2008. "O sistema previdenciário brasileiro: uma perspectiva comparada." Texto para discussão no. 1331. Rio de Janeiro, Brazil: IPEA.

Rodrik, Dani. 2004. "Rethinking Growth Policies in the Developing World" Luca d'Agliano Lecture in Development Economics, Torino, Italy. October.

——. 2007. *One Economics, Many Recipes: Globalization, Institutions, and Economic*

Growth. Princeton, N. J.: Princeton University Press.

Romero, Simon. 2010. "Sealing Shift, Chávez Gives Contracts to Western Oil Companies." *New York Times*, 12 February.

Rosado Nunes, Maria José and Regina Kurjewicz. 1999. "Aborto: un tema en discusión en la Iglesia Católica.: El Surgimiento de las Católicas por el derecho de decidir." In Lucila Scavone, ed., *Género y salud reproductiva en América Latina*. Cartago, Costa Rica: LUR.

Rostow, Walt W. 1960. *The Stages of Economic Growth: A Non-Communist Manifesto*. Cambridge, Mass.: Cambridge University Press.

Rubim, Antônio Albino Canelas. 2007. "Políticas culturais no Brasil: tristes tradições, enormes desafios." In Antônio Albino Canelas Rubim and Alexandre Barbalho, eds., *Políticas culturais no Brasil*. Salvador, Brazil: EDUFBA, 1-37.

Rueschemeyer, Dietrich, Evelyne Huber Stephens and John Stephens. 1992. *Capitalist Development and Democracy*. Cambridge, Mass.: Polity Press.

Rumsey, John. 2008. "Latin America: Energy Rich, Cash Poor." *The Banker*, 2 June.

Sá, Graciano. 2003. "A revolução cultural no mercado acionário." *Revista de Administração da USP* 38: 112-125.

Sadek, Maria Tereza. 2002. *Reforma do judiciário*. Rio de Janeiro: Konrad Adenauer Stiftung.

——. 2004. "Poder judiciário: perspectivas de reforma." *Opinião Pública* [Campinas] 10 (1): 01-62.

Sallum Brasílio. 1996. *Laberintos: dos generais à Nova República*. São Paulo: Editora Hucitec.

"The Samba Beat, with Missteps." 2008. *The Economist*, 20 December: 57.

Sandbrook, Richard, Marc Edelman, Patrick Heller, and Judith Teichman. 2007. *Social Democracy in the Global Periphery: Origins, Challenges, Prospects*. Cambridge, Mass. and New York, N.Y.: Cambridge University Press.

Santana, Carlos Henrique V. Forthcoming. "Conjuntura crítica, legados institucionais e comunidades epistêmicas: limites e possibilidades de uma agenda de desenvolvimento no Brasil." In Renato Boschi, ed., *Variedades de capitalismo, política e desenvolvimento na América Latina*. Belo Horizonte, Brazil: Ed.UFMG/IUPERJ.

Santos, André Marenco. 2006a. "Regras eleitorais importam? Modelos de listas eleitorais e seus efeitos sobre a competição partidária e o desempenho institucional." *Dados* 49 (4): 721-49.

——. 2006b. "Regras eleitorais, deputados e fidelidade partidária." In Gláucio Soares, and Lúcio Rennó, eds., *Reforma política: lições da história contemporânea*. Rio de Janeiro, Brazil: Editora da FGV, 176-92.

Santos, Eurico Cursino. 2004a. "Comentários ao PL 2.679/2003, da Comissão da Reforma Política da Câmara dos Deputados." *Revista de Informação Legislativa* 161: 15-22.

——. 2004b. "Da obrigatoriedade do voto." *Revista de Informação Legislativa* 161: 101-06.

Santos, Fabiano. 2006. "Governos de coalizão no sistema presidencial: o caso do Brasil sob a égide da Constituição de 1988." In Leonadro Avritzer, and Fátima Anastásia, eds., *Reforma política no Brasil*. Belo Horizonte, Brazil:

Editora da UFMG, 223-36.

Santos, Wanderley Guilherme dos. 2004. "A reforma política convoca impolutos." *Valor*, 4 March: A-9.

Santos Filho, Raimundo, and Vinícius Miguel. 2008. "Coligações proporcionais no sistema eleitoral brasileiro." In João Paulo Viana, and Gilmar Nascimento, eds., *O sistema político brasileiro: continuidade ou reforma?* Porto Velho, Brazil: Edufro, 199-211.

São Paulo em Perspectiva. 2006. 20 (3) Jul-Sept.

Sardenberg, Carlos Alberto. 1987. *Aventura e agonia: nos bastidores do Plano Cruzado*. São Paulo, Brazil: Companhia das Letras.

Savóia, José Roberto Ferreira. 2006. "A urgência na inserção da educação financeira no Brasil." *Valor Econômico*, 12 September.

——. 2007. "Reforma previsional en Brasil: el desafio de la inclusión laboral." *Estudios de la Seguridad Social* 100: 65-90.

Savóia, José Roberto Ferreira, André Taue Saito, and Flávia de Angelis Santana. 2007. "Paradigmas da educação financeira no Brasil." *Revista de Administração Pública* 41 (6).

Schamis, Hector E. 2002. *Re-Forming the State: The Politics of Privatization in Latin America and Europe*. Ann Arbor: The University of Michigan Press.

Schirm, Stefan A. 2009. "Brazil's Rise as an Emerging Power: Implications for the U.S. and Europe," paper presented at the conference "Brazil's Rise: A U.S.-European Assessment," Center for Transatlantic Relations, SAIS, Johns Hopkins University, Washington, D.C., June 1-2.

Schmidt-Hebbel, Klaus. 1997. "Pension Systems: From Crisis to Reform." EDI Conference volume.

Schmitter, Philippe. 1971. *Interest conflict and political change in Brazil*. Stanford, Conn.: Stanford University Press.

Schneider, Ben. 1994. *Burocracia pública e política industrial no Brasil*. São Paulo, Brazil: Editora Sumaré.

——. 1995. "El abrazo esquivo: sinergia entre el sector privado y el Estado en los países de industrialización reciente." *Política y Gobierno* 2 (1).

——. 2004. *Business Politics and the State in Twentieth Century Latin America*. Cambridge, Mass.: Cambridge University Press.

——. 2008. "Comparing Capitalisms: Liberal, Coordinated, Network, and Hierarchical Varieties." Mimeo.

Schneider, Ben R. and Sylvia Maxfield, eds. 1997. *Business and the State in Developing Countries*. Ithaca, N.Y./London, U.K.: Cornell University Press.

Schumpeter, Joseph A. 1982. *The Theory of Economic Development: An Inquiry into Profits, Capital, Credit, Interest, and the Business Cycle*. Edison, N.J.: Transaction Publishers.

Schwartz, Rosalie. 1999. *Pleasure Island: Tourism and Temptation in Cuba*. Lincoln, NE: University of Nebraska Press.

Schwarz, Roberto. 1992. *Misplaced Ideas: Essays on Brazilian Culture*. Trans. John Gledson. New York, N.Y.: Verso.

Schwartzman, Simon 2001. *Um espaço para a Ciência: a formação da comunidade científica no Brasil*. Brasília, Brazil: Ministério da Ciência e Tecnologia/CNpq and Centro de Estudos Estratégicos.

SENASP. 2001. *Diagnóstico da criminalidade no Brasil*. Brasília, Brazil: Ministério da

Justiça. http://www.mj.gov.br/services.

Seixas, Sigmaringa, and Edgar Proença. 2005. "Reformas necessárias ao Estado brasileiro." Plenarium [Câmara dos Deputados] 2: 216-42.

Senghaas, Dieter. 1985. *The European Experience: A Historical Critique of Development Theory*. Leamington Spa: Berg Publishers.

Sharman, Jason C. 2006. "The Global Anti-Money Laundering Regime and Developing Countries: Damned if they Do, Damned if they Don't?" Paper presented at the Annual ISA Convention, March 22-25, San Diego, California.

Sheahan, John. 1987. *Patterns of Development in Latin America: Poverty, Depression and Economic Strategy*. Princeton, N.J.: Princeton University Press.

Shonfield, Andrew. 1965. *Modern Capitalism*. Oxford, U.K.: Oxford University Press.

Sicsú, João, Luiz Fernando de Paula and Michel Renaut, eds. 2005. *Novo-desenvolvimentismo: um projeto nacional de crescimento com equidade social*. São Paulo, Brazil: Manole, Konrad Adenauer Stiftung.

Siegel, Nico A. 2005. "Social Pacts Revisited: 'Competite Concertation' and Complex Causality in Negotiated Welfare State Reforms." *European Journal of Industrial Relations* 11: 107.

Silva, Kelly. 2001. *As DEAMs, as corporações policiais e a violência contra as mulheres: representações, dilemas e desafios*. Brasília, Brazil: Conselho Nacional dos Direitos da Mulher.

Silva, Mônica Corrêa da. 2002. *Voto eletrônico: é mais seguro votar assim?* Florianópolis, Brazil: Editora Insular.

Simmel, George. 1990. *The Philosophy of Money*. New York, N.Y.: Routledge.

Simmons, Beth. 2000. "International Efforts against Money Laundering." In Dinah Shelton, ed., *Commitment and Compliance: The Role of Non-binding Norms in the International Legal System*. New York, NY: Oxford University Press.

Singer, Paul. 1974. *Desenvolvimento e crise*. São Paulo, Brazil: DIFEL.

Sinoti, Marta Litwinczik. 2005. *Quem me quer, nao me quer: Brasília, metropole-patrimônio*. São Paulo, Brazil: Editora Annablume.

Skidmore, Thomas E. 1967. *Politics in Brazil, 1930-1964: An Experiment in Democracy*. Oxford, U.K. and New York, N.Y.: Oxford University Press.

——. 1971. *Brasil: de Castelo a Tancredo*. São Paulo, Brazil: Paz e Terra.

——. 2006. Amanhã 217, January/February.

SMCPGL. 2005. *Governança Solidária Local*. Documento-de-referência. Porto Alegre, Brazil: Prefeitura Municipal de Porto Alegre.

——. 2008. "Definition: Local Solidarity Governance." In Jandira Feijó and Augusto de Franco, eds., *Views on the Local Solidarity Governance in Porto Alegre*. Porto Alegre, Brazil: EDIPUCRS.

Smith, Joseph. 2002. *History of Brazil 1500-2000*. London, U.K.: Pearson Education Limited.

Smith, William, Carlos H. Acuña and Eduardo A. Gamarra, eds. 1994. *Latin American Political Economy in the Age of Neoliberal Reform, Theoretical and Comparative Perspectives for the 1990s*. New Brunswick/London: Transaction Publishers.

Snow, Nick. 2009. "Clinton: Energy Security a Major US Foreign Policy Element." *Oil and Gas Journal*, 2 February: 28.

Soares de Lima, Maria Regina and Mônica Hirst. 2006. "Brazil as an Intermediate State and Regional Power: Action, Choice and Responsibilities." *International Affairs* 82 (1): 21-40.

Soares, Gláucio, and Lúcio Rennó, eds. 2006. *Reforma política: lições da história contemporânea.* Rio de Janeiro, Brazil: Editora da FGV.

Soares, Luiz, ed. 1996. *Violência e política no Rio de Janeiro.* Rio de Janeiro, Brazil: ISER/Relume Dumará.

Soares, Paulo Henrique. 2004a. "Vantagens e desvantagens do voto facultativo." *Revista de Informação Legislativa* 161: 107-16.

——. 2004b. "Reeleição e estado democrático de direito." *Revista de Informação Legislativa* 161: 117-20.

Soares, Sérgio et al. 2007. "Conditional Cash Transfers in Brazil, Chile, and Mexico: Impacts Upon Inequality." Working Paper 35, International Poverty Centre.

Södersten, Bo. 1970. *International Economics.* London, U.K.: Harper & Row Publishers.

Sola, Lourdes. 1998. *Idéias econômicas e decisões políticas.* São Paulo, Brazil: Edusp/ FAPESP.

Sorj, Bila and Paula Montero. 1985. "SOS-Mulher e a luta contra a violência." In Bruna Franchetto, Maria Laura Cavalcanti and Maria Luiza Heilborn, eds., *Perspectivas antropológicas da mulher: sobre mulher e violência.* Rio de Janeiro, Brazil: Zahar Editores.

Soskice, David. 1999. "Divergent Production Regimes: Coordinated and Uncoordinated Market Economies in the 1980's and 1990's." In H. Kitschelt et al, eds., *Continuity and Change in Contemporary Capitalism.* Cambridge, Mass.: Cambridge University Press.

Sotelino, Fernando. 1997. "O mundo mudou, e osbancos?" *Gazeta Mercantil*, 25 September.

——. 2008. "Brazil, Failing to Turn the Corner," Working Paper Series. New York: Columbia University Press.

Souza, Ednilsa Ramos de and Maria Luiza Carvalho de Lima. 2006. "Panorama da violência urbana e suas capitais." *Ciências da Saúde Coletiva* 11: 1211-22.

Souza, Robson Sávio Reis. 2003. *Homicídios Brasil: comparativo de fonte de dados.* SENASP and CRISP.

SPM. 2005a. Portaria n° 4, de 6 de Abril. Brasília, Brazil.

——. 2005b. *Relatório final dos trabalhos da Comissão de Revisão da Legislação Punitiva*, 1 August, Brasília.

——. 2008. *II Plano nacional de políticas para as mulheres.* Brasília, Brazil: Secretaria Especial de Políticas para as Mulheres.

Stallings, Barbara and Rogerio Studart. 2006. *Finance for Development: Latin America in Comparative Perspective.* Washington D.C.: Brookings Institution Press.

Stiglitz, Joseph E. 2003. *The Roaring Nineties: a New History of the World's Most Prosperous Decade.* New York, NY.: W. W. Norton & Co.

Stokes, Susan. 2001. *Mandates and Democracy: Neoliberalism by Surprise in Latin America.* Cambridge, Mass.: Cambridge University Press.

Studart, Rogerio. 2000. "Financial Opening and Deregulation in Brazil in the 1990's." *The Quarterly Review of Economics and Finance* 40 (1).

Suárez, Mirey and Lourdes Bandeira. 1999. "Introdução." In Mireya Suárez and

Lourdes Bandeira, eds., *Violência, gênero e crime no Distrito Federal.* Brasília, Brazil: Editora Universidade de Brasília.

Sullivan, Mark P., Rebecca G. Rush and Clare Ribando Seelke. 2008. "Latin America: Energy Supply, Political Developments, and U.S. Policy Approaches." CRS Report for Congress (RL 33693). Washington, DC: Congressional Research Service.

SVS. Tabela de Estimativas Vitais. Website. http://tabnet.datasus.gov.br/cgi/deftohtm.exe?sim/cnv/matuf.def.

——. 2006. *Redução de homicídios no Brasil.* Brasília, Brazil: Ministério de Saúde.

Tatagiba, Luciana. 2006. "Os desafios da articulação entre sociedade civil e sociedade política sob o marco da democracia gerencial: o caso do projeto Rede Criança em Vitória/Es." In Evelina Dagnino, Alberto J. Olvera and Aldo Panfichi, eds., *A disputa pela construção democrática na América Latina.* São Paulo, Brazil: Editora Paz e Terra, 137-78.

Tavares Filho, Newton. 2005. "Emenda Constitucional No. 45 e a reforma do Poder Judiciário: algumas observações." Plenarium [Câmara dos Deputados] 2: 202-15.

Taylor, Matthew. 2006. "Veto and voice in the courts: Policy implications of institutional design in the Brazilian Judiciary." *Comparative Politics* 38 (3): 337-55.

——. 2007. "O Judiciário e as políticas públicas no Brasil." *Dados* 50 (2): 229-57.

——. 2008. *Judging Policy: Courts and Policy Reform in Brazil.* Stanford, Calif.: Stanford University Press.

Taylor, Matthew and Luciano da Ros. 2008. "Partidos de dentro e de fora do poder: a judicialização como resultado contingente da estratégia política." *Dados* 51 (3): 438-69.

Teixeira, Letícia Miranda. 2005. "A política contra a lavagem de dinheiro no Brasil: o processo de absorção de um regime internacional." MA Diss. Universidade de Brasília.

Teixeira, Rodolfo. 2009. "Reforma política: dilemas brasileiros e experiências estrangeiras." Ph.D. Diss. Universidade de Brasília.

Telles, Mário de Pragmacio Ferreira. 2009a. "Attractive upside on high growth profile." *Credit Suisse Equity Research*, 10 December.

Telles, Mário de Pragmacio Ferreira. 2009b. "Entre a lei e as salchichas: analise dos antecedents do Decreto-Lei 25/37." Paper presented at the 5th meeting of Estudos Multidisciplinares em Cultura, Federal University of Bahia, Salvador, Brazil.

Thelen, Kathleen. 2004. *How Institutions Evolve: The Political Economy of Skills in Germany, Britain, the United States and Japan.* Cambridge, Mass.: Cambridge University Press.

Thomson, David, ed. 1982. *Political Ideas.* London, U.K.: Penguin Books.

Thrift, Nigel J. 2008. "The New Economy and a New Market Culture." In Ismail Erturk, Julie Froud, Sukhdev Johal, Adam Leaver, and Karel Williams, eds., *Financialization at Work: Key Texts and Commentary.* New York, N.Y.: Routledge.

Tockman, Jason. 2009. "Multipolar Machinations: Chávez Endeavors to "Sow the Oil" with Russia and China." *NACLA*, 15 October.

Toledo, Roberto Pompeu de. 1994. *História do Unibanco, 1924-1994.* São Paulo, Brazil: Instituto Moreira Salles.

Topik, Steven. 1989. "The Old Republic." In Michael L.Conniff and Frank McCann eds., *Modern Brazil: Elites and Masses in Historical Perspective*. Lincoln, NE: University of Nebraska Press.

Torre, Augusto, Juan Carlos Gozzi and Sergio L. Schmukler. 2007. "El desarrollo económico en América Latina." In José Luis Machinea and Narcís Serra, eds., *Visiones del desarrollo en América Latina*. Santiago, Chile: CEPAL.

Triffin, Robert. 1960. *Gold and the Dollar Crisis: The Future of Convertibility*. New Haven, Conn.: Yale University Press

Trigueiros, Florisvaldo dos Santos. 1958. *Museu e educação*. Rio de Janeiro, Brazil: Irmãos Pongetti.

Trubek, David M. 2008. "Developmental States and the Legal Order: Toward a New Political Economy of Development and Law," Paper presented at the Conference "Social Science in the Age of Globalization. National Institute for Advanced Study on Social Science," Shanghai, China, December.

Tschoegl, Adrian E. 2006. "Foreign Ownership in Mexican Banking: A Self Correcting Phenomenon," Philadelphia, Pa.: The Wharton School of the University of Pennsylvania.

Ulyssea, Gabriel. 2005. "Informalidade no mercado de trabalho brasileiro: uma resenha da literatura." Texto para discussão n° 1070. Rio de Janeiro, Brazil: IPEA.

UNCTAD. 2009. *Trade and Development Report, 2009*. New York and Geneva: United Nations Publication.

UNESCO. *Intangible Heritage*. Web.

——. 2008. *World Heritage Information Kit*. Paris, France: UNESCO.

United Press International. 2010. "Ambitious UNASUR seeks to make impact without conflict." Jun. 16. http://www.upi.com/Top_News/Special/2010/06/16/Ambitious-UNASUR-seeks-to-make-impact-without-conflict/UPI-62331276717712/.

"Update 2 - Venezuela Gives Brazil's Odebrecht $282 mln Tax Bill." 2008. *Reuters*, 4 November.

Urbinati, Nadia. 2006. *Representative Democracy, Principles and Genealogy*. Chicago, Ill.: The University of Chicago Press.

U.S. Energy Information Administration. 2009a. "World Proved Crude Oil Reserves, 1 January 1980 - 1 January 2009, Estimates."

——. 2009b. "Country Analysis Briefs: Brazil."

——. 2010. "Renewable Energy Consumption and Electricity Preliminary 2006 Statistics."

Vargas, Getulio. 1938. *A nova política do Brasil*. Rio de Janeiro, Brazil: José Olympio.

Vásquez, Ian. 1996. "The Brady Plan and Market-Based Solutions to Debt Crises." *Cato Journal* 16 (2).

Vaticano. 2008. Acordo entre a República Federativa do Brasil e a Santa Sé Relativo ao Estatuto Jurídico da Igreja Católica no Brasil. http://www.camara.gov.br/sileg/integras/637903.pdf

Veiga, Luiz H. Cavalcante and Joaquim P. Andrade. 2006. "Money Laundering, Corruption, and Growth. An Empirical Rational for a Global Convergence on Anti-Money Laundering Regulation." Berkeley Program in Law and Economics, Paper 32. Berkeley: University of California Press.

"Venezuela's Hope of Greater Sway Dims as Riches Dip." 2009. *New York Times*, 20 May: A8.

Venzin, Markus. 2009. *Building an International Financial Services Firm*. Oxford, U.K.: Oxford University Press.

Viana, João Paulo, and Flávia Coelho. 2008. "Democracia ou partidocracia? Pontos e contrapontos da lista fechada no Brasil." In João Paulo Viana, and Gilmar Nascimento, eds., *O sistema político: continuidade ou reforma?* Porto Velho: Edufro.

Viana, João Paulo, and Gilmar Nascimento, eds. 2008. *O sistema político brasileiro: continuidade ou reforma?* Porto Velho, Brazil: Edufro.

Vianna, Luiz Werneck. 1999. *Judicialização da política e das relações sociais*. Rio de Janeiro, Brazil: Editora Revan.

——. 2002. *Democracia e os três poderes no Brasil.* Belo Horizonte, Brazil: Editora da UFMG.

Vianna, Luiz Werneck, Marcelo Baumann, and Paula Martins Salles. 2007. "Dezessete anos de judicialização da política." *Tempo Social* 19 (2): 39-85.

Viotti Da Costa, Emilia. 2000. *The Brazilian Empire: Myths and Histories*. Chapel Hill: The University of North Carolina Press.

Wallerstein, Immanuel et al. 2003. *Uma nova fase do capitalismo?* São Paulo, Brazil: Xamã.

Watkins, Eric. 2008. "Mixing Oil and Politics." *Oil and Gas Journal*, 28 July: 27.

——. 2009. "Brazil Considering OPEC's Renewed Membership Invitation." *Oil and Gas Journal*, 6 April: 30.

Weber, Max. 1984. *A Bolsa*. Lisbon, Portugal: Relógio d'água.

Weffort, Francisco. 2000. *A cultura e as revoluções da modernização*. Rio de Janeiro, Brazil: Edições Fundo Nacional de Cultura.

Weinstein, Barbara. 1997. *For Social Peace in Brazil: Industrialists and the Remaking of the Working Class in Sao Paulo, 1920-1964*. Chapel Hill: University of North Carolina Press.

Weisbrot, Mark. 2009. "More of the Same in Latin America." *International Herald Tribune*, 12 August: 6.

Weiss, Linda, ed. 2004. *States in the Global Economy: Bringing Domestic Institutions Back In*. Cambridge, Mass. and New York, N.Y.: Cambridge University Press.

Weiss, Linda. 2010. "The State in the Economy: Neoliberal or Neoactivist?" In Glenn Morgan et al, eds., *Oxford Handbook of Comparative Institutional Analysis*. Oxford, U.K.: Oxford University Press.

Werneck Vianna, Maria Lúcia Teixeira. 1987. *A administração do "milagre" o Conselho Mentário Nacional, 1964-1974*. Petrópolis: Vozes.

Wertheim, Peter Howard. 2004. "Rodriguez Reaffirms PDVSA's Energy Integration Plans." *Oil and Gas Journal*, 18 October.: 32.

Weyland, Kurt. 1996. *Democracy without Equity: Failures of Reform in Brazil*. Pittsburgh, Pa.: University of Pittsburgh Press.

Wheatley, Jonathan. 2009. "Brazil Urged to Lead at Climate Summit." *The Financial Times* (London), 5 October.

"Whose Side is Brazil On?" 2009. *The Economist*, 15 August: 10.

Williams, Daniel and Maher Chmaytelli. 2007. "Chavez Tells OPEC to Use Politics, Curb 'Imperialism.'" *Bloomberg LP*, 19 November.

Williams, Daryle. 2001. *Culture Wars in Brazil: The First Vargas Regime, 1930-1945.* Durham, N.C.: Duke University Press.

Williams, Raymond. 1977. *Marxism and Literature.* New York, N.Y.: Oxford University Press.

Williamson, John, ed. 1990. *The Progress of Policy Reform in Latin America in Latin American Adjustment: How Much Has Happened?* Washington, D.C.: Institute of International Economics.

Wirth, John Davis. 1970. *The Politics of Brazilian Development (1930-45).* Stanford, Conn.: Stanford University Press.

Wolfe, Joel. 1993. *Working Women, Working Men: São Paulo and the Rise of Brazil's Industrial Working Class, 1900-1955.* Durham, N.C.: Duke University Press.

Wood, B. Dan, and Richard W. Waterman. 1994. *Bureaucratic Dynamics—The Role of Bureaucracy in a Democracy.* Boulder, Colo.: Westview Press.

Wilson, Woodrow. 1887. "The Study of Administration," *Political Science Quarterly,* June.

World Bank. 2009. "World Development Indicators Online." Washington, D.C.: World Bank. http://data.worldbank.org/indicator/PA.NUS.FCRF.

World Energy Council. 2008. *Regional Energy Integration in Latin America and the Caribbean.* London, U.K.: World Energy Council.

WTO. 2007. *World Trade Report 2007.* Geneva, Switzerland.

——. 2008. *WTO Statistics 2008.* Geneva, Switzerland.

——. 2009. *WTO Statistics 2009.* Geneva, Switzerland.

Wu, Kang. 1995. *Energy in Latin America: Production, Consumption, and Future Growth.* Westport, Conn.: Praeger.

Yúdice, George. 2004. *The Expediency of Culture: Uses of Culture in the Global Era.* Durham, N.C.: Duke University Press.

Zakaria, Fareed. 2008. *The Post American World.* New York, N.Y.: W.W. Norton & Co.

Zalewski, Plínio. 1999. "O governo do PT." *Democracia: Cadernos de Reflexão Política* 3: 89-91.

Zelizer, Viviana. 1994. *The Social Meaning of Money.* New York, N.Y.: Princeton University Press.

Zibechi, Raúl. 2009. "Is Brazil Creating Its Own Backyard?" Americas Policy Program, 3 February. www.americas.irc-online.org.

Zovatto, Daniel G. and José Henriquez, eds. 2008. *Reforma política y electoral en América Latina.* México: UNAM e IDEA.

Zylbersztajn, Hélio, André Souza, Anderson Stancioli, and Marcelo Milan. 2003. "Aposentadoria e Eqüidade." *Folha de São Paulo*, 6 August: A3.

INDEX

About the Contributors

Monica Arruda de Almeida is Adjunct Professor in Latin American Studies at the Edmund A. Walsh School of Foreign Service at Georgetown University.

Glauco Arbix is Professor of Sociology at the University of São Paulo (USP).

Leslie Elliott Armijo is Visiting Scholar at the Mark O. Hatfield School of Government at Portland State University.

Renato Boschi is Full Professor at the Instituto de Estudos Sociais, Políticos e Econômicos (IESP) at the Rio de Janeiro State University.

John F. Collins is Associate Professor of Anthropology at Queens College and The Graduate Center of City University of New York.

David Fleischer is Professor Emeritus of Political Science at the University of Brasília.

Mauricio A. Font is Professor of Sociology at The Graduate Center of the City University of New York, and director of the Bildner Center for Western Hemisphere Studies.

Christine A. Gustafson is Associate Professor in the Politics Department at Saint Anselm College.

Elaine da Silveira Leite is a Ph.D. candidate in Sociology at the Federal University of São Carlos (UFSCar).

Maria Rita Loureiro is Full Professor at the Fundação Getulio Vargas and at the University of São Paulo (USP).

Lia Zanotta Machado is Visiting Professor at Columbia University (2009-2010) and Full Professor of Anthropology at the University of Brasília.

Ana Cristina Braga Martes is Professor of Sociology at the Fundação Getulio Vargas (FGV-EAESP).

Scott B. Martin is Part-Time Faculty at the Graduate School of International Affairs at The New School and Adjunct Assistant Professor at the School of International and Public Affairs at Columbia University.

Cecília Olivieri is Professor of Graduate Studies at the School of Arts, Sciences and Humanities at University of São Paulo (USP).

João Paulo M. Peixoto is Professor of Government at the University of Brasília.

Laura Randall is Professor Emerita of Economics at Hunter College of the City University of New York.

Janaina Saad is Research Associate at the Bildner Center for Western Hemisphere Studies.

Eiiti Sato is Professor of International Relations at the University of Brasília.

José Roberto Ferreira Savoia is Professor of Finance at the University of São Paulo (FEA-USP).

Fernando B. Sotelino is Adjunct Professor at the School of International and Public Affairs (SIPA) at Columbia University.

J. Ricardo Tranjan is a Ph.D. candidate in Global Governance at the Balsillie School of International Affairs at the University of Waterloo.

Thomas J. Trebat is the Executive Director of the Institute of Latin American Studies and the Center for Brazilian Studies at Columbia University.

www.ingramcontent.com/pod-product-compliance
Ingram Content Group UK Ltd.
Pitfield, Milton Keynes, MK11 3LW, UK
UKHW021035150926
475561UK00003B/116

9 780739 186268